PUGIN
A Gothic Passion

PUGIN

A GOTHIC PASSION

edited by

PAUL ATTERBURY &
CLIVE WAINWRIGHT

YALE UNIVERSITY PRESS · NEW HAVEN AND LONDON
in association with
THE VICTORIA & ALBERT MUSEUM

Published to coincide with the exhibition
Pugin: A Gothic Passion
held at The Victoria & Albert Museum, London
15 June to 11 September 1994

Exhibition sponsored by

·PEARSON·

Specially commissioned photography by Graham Miller

Designed by Sally Salvesen
Set in Ehrhardt by Best-set Typesetter, Hong Kong
Printed in Italy by Amilcare Pizzi SpA, Milan

Library of Congress Cataloging-in-Publication Data

Pugin, Augustus Welby Northmore, 1812–1852.
Pugin : a Gothic passion / edited by Paul Atterbury. Clive Wainwright.
p.   cm.
'Published to coincide with the exhibition . . . held at the
Victoria & Albert Museum, London, 15 June to 11 September 1994'—T.p. verso.
Includes bibliographical references and index.
ISBN 0-300-06012-2 (cloth).—ISBN 0-300-06014-9 (pbk.)
1. Pugin, Augustus Welby Northmore, 1812-1852—Exhibitions.
2. Gothic revival (Architecture)—England—Exhibition.   3. Design—
England—History—19th century.   I. Atterbury, Paul.
II. Wainwright, Clive.   III. Victoria and Albert Museum.   IV. Title.
NA997.P9A4   1994
720'.92—dc20   94-15209
                                       CIP

FRONTISPIECE: The Drawing Room, Eastnor Castle, Herefordshire, showing decoration by Pugin and Crace of
Smirke's vaulted ceiling, with Pugin's chandelier, *c.* 1849.

ENDPAPERS: Tiles from St Augustine's, Ramsgate,
bearing Pugin's monogram and device

An illustration marked † indicates
an object included in the exhibition

IN MEMORIAM
DOM BEDE MILLARD O.S.B.
1949–1993

CONTENTS

The ceiling of the chapel at Alton Towers, the fittings of
which were designed by Pugin, has recently been restored.
Alton Towers, part of the Tussauds Group, is owned by
Pearson plc.

SPONSOR'S PREFACE

This book is published in conjunction with the exhibition devoted to the work of A.W.N. Pugin held at the Victoria & Albert Museum between June and September 1994 and sponsored by Pearson plc. Although Pugin was one of the most talented and prolific designers of the nineteenth century this has never before been demonstrated in a major exhibition. He designed not only a wide range of both secular and ecclesiastical buildings but also their furnishings. Working closely with manufacturers, he played a major role in the production of textiles, wallpaper, metalwork, furniture and books. His designs for the whole of the interior of the Palace of Westminster and work shown at the Great Exhibition of 1851 had a profound effect both on other designers and public taste.

Among the objects on display in the Mediæval Court of the Great Exhibition were a stove, clad in majolica tiles made by Minton, and a superb brass chandelier, which was to hang in the hall at Alton Towers. Minton is part of Royal Doulton, now an independent public company, but which for twenty-one years, until 1993, was a subsidiary of Pearson. Alton Towers is part of the Tussauds Group, Pearson's visitor attraction business. These links make Pearson all the more proud to be associated both with the exhibition and this book, which will broaden the public knowledge of and, I hope, admiration for a great man.

As sponsor of the exhibition, Pearson has worked closely with the Victoria & Albert Museum and Yale University Press to ensure that this book discusses and illustrates as wide a range of Pugin's work as possible. We have commissioned photography of many of Pugin's buildings and their furnishings and some of these superb new photographs are published here for the first time, with yet more shown in the exhibition itself.

Though the Gothic Revival style in which Pugin worked may seem a far cry from the design world of the late twentieth century, his principles of structural honesty and truth to materials are still very much a live issue among architects and designers of today.

Michael Blakenham
CHAIRMAN, PEARSON PLC

ACKNOWLEDGEMENTS

During the preparation of this book, and the accompanying exhibition, *Pugin: A Gothic Passion*, held at the Victoria & Albert Museum, we have been able to benefit greatly from the knowledge and enthusiasm so willingly shared by so many people. The Roman Catholic faith was central to Pugin's life and work, and it is therefore eminently suitable that the Roman Catholic church today should have been so generous in its support for both book and exhibition. We are particularly indebted to the Most Reverend Maurice Couve de Murville, Archbishop of Birmingham, whose diocese is exceptionally rich in its Pugin associations; also to the Most Reverend Desmond Connell, Archbishop of Dublin; the Most Reverend Brendan Comiskey, Bishop of Ferns; to Monsignor Richard Atherton, President, Ushaw College; to Monsignor Patrick McKinney, Rector, Oscott College, the Right Reverend C. Bernard Waldron, Abbot of St Augustine's Abbey, Ramsgate; and to Sister Malachy, the Convent of Mercy, Handsworth, all of whom have been generous with their time and the help they have offered. Many priests have gone out of their way to facilitate access to the Pugin buildings and objects in their care, and special thanks are due to Father Matthias Glynn, Tagoat, County Wexford; Father Philip Jebb, Downside Abbey; Father Raymund Jones, Brewood; Father Geoffrey Scott, Douai Abbey; Father Bede Walsh, Cheadle and, above all, to the late Father Bede Millard, St Augustine's, Ramsgate, who, until his death in December 1993, was a constant inspiration to every modern Pugin enthusiast.

Our research in the various institutions associated with Pugin has been greatly helped by Richard Barton at Oscott College; Dr Jan Rhodes and Peter Seed at Ushaw College; Valerie Seymour at St Patrick's College, Maynooth; D. J. McEwen, Headmaster, St Edmund's College, Ware, and Quentin Edwards, Headmaster, Bilton Grange School. Thanks are also due to the many people who have willingly offered help that was far beyond the normal course of duty, notably Neil Birdsall, Norwich Diocesan architect; Stephen Croad and Ian Leith of RCHME; Major (Rtd) Peter Eller, Stanford Army Field Training Centre; the Venerable Anthony Foottit, Archdeacon of Lynn; Ian Gow, Historic Scotland; Richard Griffin, Irish Architectural Archive; Malcolm Hay and Graham Goode, Palace of Westminster; Mr & Mrs Hervey-Bathurst, Eastnor Castle; Andrew Hollingsworth, Alton Towers; Michael Penrudduck, Estate Manager, Lismore; Brian Precious, Albury Park; and Ken Jackson and Richard Davis of the V&A Photography Section.

Unstinting in their enthusiasm and their support have been the many members of the now extended Pugin family, and we are grateful to all those who gave so willingly their time and their knowledge, notably Mr & Mrs Franklin, Mrs Houle, Mrs Howkins, Dr & Mrs Mackey, Mr & Mrs Meldon, Mrs Mulhearn, Mrs Nunes, Mr & Mrs Purcell; also Sir John and Lady Johnson, Timothy McCann, Hugh Myers, Humphrey Osmond and Mrs Spencer-Silver.

The onerous task of editing this book and preparing the exhibition has been constantly lightened by the many Pugin scholars and enthusiasts, and their help has been invaluable. We should like to thank in particular Brian Andrews, Dr Megan Aldrich, Major & Mrs Barran, Peter Binnington, Denis Evinson, Patrick and Nikkie Gordon Bowe, Father Anthony Couchman, Richard Dennis, Jonathan Glancey, Roderick Gradidge, Peter Howell, Rosemary Hill, Donald Insall, James Joll, Joan Jones, Martin Levy, Julian Litten, Squire de Lisle, David Meara, Professor J. Mordaunt Crook, Peter Rose & Albert Gallichan, Stanley Shepherd, Anthony Symondson, Professor Will Vaughan, Mr & Dr West, Christopher Wilk, Michael Whiteway and, last but not least, that indefatigable and passionate Victorian, John Scott.

From the inspiration of this project and at all stages of the preparation we have enjoyed and been greatly assisted by the help and interest shown by Pearson plc, the sponsor of the exhibition.

We are grateful to B&I Ferries, for assistance with a research visit to Ireland.

Many other people have also, by their help and enthusiasm, made specific contributions, which are acknowledged elsewhere in this book, in footnotes and in photographic credits.

Finally, we should like to offer personal thanks to four people whose constant support and enduring patience have made the preparation of this book, and the exhibition, a considerable pleasure: John Nicoll and Sally Salvesen of Yale University Press, Graham Miller, photographer, and Juliette Foy, of the V&A Exhibitions Department.

Paul Atterbury & Clive Wainwright
13 April 1994

Chronology

ALEXANDRA WEDGWOOD

1812   Born March 1st at 39 Keppel Street, Russell Square, London, to Augustus Charles Pugin (c.1769–1832) and Catherine Welby (?–1833). Educated partly at Christ's Hospital; went on expeditions with the pupils in his father's school of architectural draughtsmanship. His family made several visits to France.

1827   designed Gothic furniture for Windsor Castle and was employed by Rundell & Bridge, the royal goldsmiths.

1829   was employed at the English Opera House as a super flyman, and subsequently at Covent Garden as a stage carpenter. Introduced to James Gillespie Graham (1776–1855), a Scottish architect, and began to help him with his commissions.

1829–31   had his own business, designing and making furniture and decorative details, which ultimately failed.

1830–31   designed stage scenery including two scenes for the ballet *Kenilworth* (March 1831). Had his own sailing-boat.

1832   his first wife, Anne Garnet (1814–1832) died one week after the birth of a daughter, Anne; his father also died; started drawing his series of ideal schemes. He concentrated on training himself as an architect, principally by making intensive study tours of medieval buildings.

1833   married Louisa Burton (c.1813–1844) and his mother died; went to live in Ramsgate; completed the second volume of his father's book, *Examples of Gothic Architecture*.

1834   collaborated with antique dealers, including Edward Hull (d.1844); from this date almost always made an annual sketching holiday on the continent. This year he went to Nuremberg for the first time.

1835   moved to a house he had himself designed, St Marie's Grange, near Salisbury. Met Charles Barry (1795–1860) and began to design interiors for him at the King Edward VI Grammar School, Birmingham. His first book of designs, *Gothic Furniture*, published. He became a Roman Catholic. He drew the entries for the competition for the new Houses of Parliament for both Charles Barry and Gillespie Graham.

1836	continued to help Charles Barry after he had won the competition for the new Houses of Parliament with the drawings needed for the preparation Hof the estimate. He published his controversial book, *Contrasts*, and brought out two further books of his designs.

1836   continued to help Charles Barry after he had won the competition for the new Houses of Parliament with the drawings needed for the preparation Hof the estimate. He published his controversial book, *Contrasts*, and brought out two further books of his designs.

1837   completed his work for Barry and began his career as an independent architect at Scarisbrick Hall, Lancashire. He was introduced to St Mary's College, Oscott, the school and seminary which became a centre for his influence in the Roman Catholic church. He met John Hardman (1811–67), a Birmingham manufacturer who became his closest friend and colleague, John, 16th Earl of Shrewsbury (1791–1852) who became his chief patron, and Ambrose de Lisle Phillipps (1809–78), a Convert to Catholicism and another important patron. He designed his first churches. By the end of the year he had abandoned St Marie's Grange and taken lodgings in Chelsea.

1838   continued to design a number of Roman Catholic churches, including St Marie's Derby; made his first visit to Ireland where he had a number of commissions. He made a long summer visit through Germany and Switzerland. George Myers (1804–75) became his principal builder and Hardman began to manufacture metalwork, particularly church plate, to his designs.

1839   began several large commissions such as the Roman Catholic Cathedral of St Chad, Birmingham, the Roman Catholic Cathedral of St George, Southwark, St John's Hospital, Alton, and the Roman Catholic church of St Wilfrid, Hulme.

1840   continued many commissions for Roman Catholic buildings; new designs included the church of St Giles, Cheadle, the Bishop's House, Birmingham, the monastery of Mount St Bernard, and the chapel at the College of St Cuthbert, Ushaw. In contact with Herbert Minton (1795–1858), the pottery manufacturer. Made friends with several of the Tractarians at Oxford.

1841   published a second edition of *Contrasts*, and *The True Principles of Pointed or Christian Architecture*. Newcastle and Nottingham Roman Catholic cathedrals were begun and Birmingham Cathedral opened.

1842   wrote articles for *The Dublin Review*. Continued an immense volume of work, principally Roman Catholic churches, including the Cathedral at Killarney. Visited Ireland once and Scotland twice.

1843   designs for Balliol College, Oxford, were rejected; published *An Apology for the Revival of Christian Architecture in England*. He started to build his own house, the Grange, at Ramsgate.

1844   his association with J.G. Crace (1809–89), the interior decorator, is closely documented from the beginning of this year. Published *The Glossary of Ecclesiastical Ornament and Costume*. His second wife died. Following the request of Charles Barry he returned to work on the interior designs of the Houses of Parliament, which remained a major occupation until his death. At Westminster he was able to use his colleagues Hardman, Minton and Crace, who understood his requirements.

1845	commissioned by the Government to rebuild the Roman Catholic College of St Patrick, Maynooth and visited Ireland three times. Began the Roman Catholic church of St Augustine, next to his own house at Ramsgate. John Hardman began to manufacture stained glass to his designs.
1846	an unhappy year for Pugin, particularly in his domestic life and his unsuccessful search for a wife. His beloved church of St Giles, Cheadle, was consecrated. His major work was at the Houses of Parliament and in Ireland but commissions for new Roman Catholic churches dropped off sharply.
1847	The House of Lords, one of Pugin's greatest works, was opened in April and much admired, though his role in its design was not widely known. He made his longest continental tour, leaving England at the end of March, travelling to Italy and returning home in the middle of June. Also made three subsequent brief trips across the Channel. He hoped to marry Selina Helen (b.1814), daughter of Edwin Sandys Lumsdaine, the rector of Upper Hardes with Stelling. She appeared willing to become a Catholic. He was doing much decorative work with J.G. Crace including designs for wallpapers, textiles and furniture.
1848	the affair with Helen Lumsdaine ended disastrously at the end of March. However, shortly after this blow, he met Jane Knill (1827–1909) and married her in August. The Roman Catholic cathedral of St George, Southwark, was opened but he experienced much criticism, particularly on the subject of rood screens, from Roman Catholics. He designed major additions at Alton Towers and Alton Castle was under construction.
1849	spent more time at home, much of it devoted to his church of St Augustine. He published *Floriated Ornament* and designed much stained glass, metalwork, internal decorations and ceramics, mostly tiles.
1850	continued his decorative work and together with Myers, Hardman, Minton and Crace began to plan their participation in the Great Exhibition. His eldest daughter, Anne (1832–97), married John Hardman Powell (1827–95), Hardman's nephew who had been working at the Grange as Pugin's pupil. Published a pamphlet in answer to recent criticism.
1851	the exhibit of Pugin and his colleagues at the Great Exhibition which was called the Medieval Court, was generally acclaimed. Published *A Treatise on Chancel Screens and Rood Lofts*. Designs for the interiors of the Houses of Parliament continued to be a major concern.
1852	by the end of February when the House of Commons was finally opened, his health had broken down. From then he had only short intervals of lucidity before his death at Ramsgate on 14 September.

1.† The only surviving photograph of Pugin, probably copied after his death from a Daguerreotype taken in the early 1840s.

CHAPTER ONE

'Not a Style but a Principle' Pugin & His Influence

CLIVE WAINWRIGHT

Pugin grew up amid the glamour, chaos, excitement and the rapidly accelerating change of late Georgian London. Many ancient buildings survived, but were being demolished to be replaced by the gimcrack stucco of Nash and even less scrupulous developers. Pugin was himself always an outsider and this was to be strengthened by his conversion to Catholicism at the age of twenty-two. His father Augustus Charles (plate 3) was an outsider too, an engaging Frenchman with architectural and artistic talents. In the aftermath of the French Revolution England was benefitting from one of those periodic injections of continental talent which have done so much to improve our insular culture.

The elder Pugin, like so many ex-patriots somewhat embroidered his past; for a while he became de Pugin, even hinting that he was actually a Count – his son was to continue the de Pugin fiction on his bookplate (plate 2). He gained a coat of arms including the 'temple haunting martlet' which was to be oddly appropriate for his hyperactive son, who used it constantly on everything from his chairs and wallpaper to his candlesticks (plate 349). A.C. Pugin let drop that he had known David the painter well, had met Napoleon and had been in Paris during the revolution. Around 1800 in London, if one was a French fugitive from the revolutionary terror, it was naturally assumed that one had, at the very least, aristocratic sympathies. The truth as recent research has established is rather less dramatic. It seems that he was established in Paris before 1789 as an artist and designer and came of his own volition to London to further his career. In this respect he was quite successful, for he carried out some architectural works and may have worked at Carlton House for the Prince Regent and at Eaton Hall for the Duke of Westminster. As an artist in collaboration with Rudolph Ackermann the pioneering publisher – another foreigner – he was closely involved in a number of publishing projects, including *The Microcosm of London*. He also worked with that interesting auto-didact, antiquary and publisher John Britton.

He was fortunate to marry a very intelligent and practical woman. Ferrey described her thus:

> Catherine Welby, the daughter of a distinguished barrister, and a relative of Sir William Welby Bart., of Denton Hall, Lincolnshire . . . she was possessed of no ordinary charms, and known as the 'Belle of Islington'. Islington be it remembered, was at that day the headquarters of the Royalist emigration.

At first they lived at the Angel, then they moved into a newly built house in Keppel Street – a continuation of Store Street – in Bloomsbury. It was here that in 1812 Augustus, their only child, was born. Two charming portraits of him as a child survive (plates 4 and 5), one probably painted by his father.

The Pugins later moved a short distance to Great Russell Street, where they all lived until the death of the elder Pugin in 1832 and Catherine in 1833. The house, which was on the corner of Gower Street, has been replaced in a singular coincidence by the Kenilworth Hotel. Pugin was to design the stage sets for a production of Scott's *Kenilworth*.

2. Pugin's bookplate.

3.† Augustus Charles Pugin, artist unknown (Private Collection).

4.† Pugin aged seven, by A.J. Oliver (Private Collection).

It was in this house, along with the other pupils of his father, that Pugin grew up. The elder Pugin was not an entirely practical man and his wife gave order to the household against considerable odds. Money was often short due to the episodic nature of her husband's design and publishing ventures. Even in his last illness he was trying unsuccessfully to provide for his wife and son. Pugin had little formal education, though his mother is likely to have taught him to some extent. Ferrey says that he was a day boy at Christ's Hospital School in the city, but he was never officially registered there. The school rules were very liberal at this time and it was possible to attend some classes as a visitor but how often Pugin went is unknown. He was probably more attracted by their drawing classes, which had been famous since the mid-eighteenth century. He certainly grew up speaking excellent French, but his Latin seems to have been shaky and in later life he betrays all the signs of lacking a disciplined education.

He learned to draw quickly and well and to paint in watercolours, but this was mainly from his work with his father and his pupils. We know very little about the circles in which he and his family moved, but they lived in the thick of London's artistic and literary community. Literary figures like John Britton, Carlyle and Henry Crabb Robinson lived close by, while Flaxman and a number of other artists formed a colony in Charlotte Street. Many collectors lived in Bloomsbury: Francis Douce for instance was in Gower Street

and Aders (see p. 94) in Euston Square. Covent Garden was nearby, with a plethora of bookshops and print shops, and the theatres which were to play such a key role in Pugin's early career (chapter 2). The shops of the antiquities brokers, which were to become so important to him (chapter 6), were a short walk away in Soho. Indeed that of Edward Baldock, the most celebrated dealer of the 1820s, was in Hanway Street, five minutes walk away.

The British Museum was fifty yards from the Pugin front door. Pugin obviously used the whole museum but his use of the Print Room was of particular significance for his career. Pugin recorded in his autobiography that on 31 May 1831 'I was introduced into the Reading Room of the British Museum by my friend J.T. Smith Esq Keeper of the Prints and Drawings.' It is likely that Smith was a friend of A.C. Pugin and his breadth of knowledge of London and his picturesque character would have delighted the young Pugin. He had been born in a Hackney carriage and was a pupil of the sculptor Nollekens, who he portrayed in his engaging book *Nollekens and His Times*. Few people knew the topography of London better and Smith published widely on this, including the posthumous *Cries of London* with his own etched plates.

What did Augustus Welby Northmore Pugin (1812–52) look like, how did he dress, what im-

John Hardman Powell, his son-in-law (plate 22), in his memoir 'Pugin at Home' described him in his early thirties as:

> . . . only just middle height but very strong, broad chest, large hands, massive forehead, nose and chin, well curved flexible mouth, and restless grey eyes, the expression of which turned inwards when in deep thought. His hair was darkest brown, thick, not crisp, and he shaved clean like a sailor. All his movements were rapid, full of mental and bodily energy, showing a nervous and choleric temperament . . . He was passionate, but believed his anger was always another's fault, honest rages with no malice in them, blowing over without leaving resentment.

The only surviving photograph (plate 1) shows him at this age.

His restless energy was noticed by all who met him. The obituary in *The Ecclesiologist* noted 'His energy was boundless, his powers of application almost unrivalled and the versatility of his powers inexhaustible'. It was however his clothes on which most people remarked: apparently he never cared about them, for his mother wrote in a letter, when he was a small and very talented boy, 'if he only knew how to dress I would consider him a universal genius'. As Amherst noted, in his twenties Pugin cared little about his appearance, and this trend continued as Ferrey tells us:

> His slovenliness in dress at this time amounted to eccentricity. He was in the habit of wearing a sailor's jacket, loose pilot trousers, jack boots, and a wide awake hat. In such a costume landing on one occasion from the Calais boat, he entered, as was his custom a first-class railway carriage, and was accosted with a 'Halloa, my man, you have mistaken, I think your carriage'. 'By Jove' was his reply, 'I think you are right: I thought that I was in the company of gentlemen'. This cutting repartee at once called forth an apology. The remainder of the journey was passed in examining his portfolio filled with sketches just taken in Normandy.

Powell described his clothes in more detail:

> At home for many years he always wore his pilot suits, and liked the old one best. Occasional patching used to shock fastidious lady friends, but he was ignorant of being unusual and when cut by acquaintances insisted on knowing and walking with them. He was never at any time in his life, what is called 'dressed in fashion', but

pression did he make on those who met him, what was his character? Even by early nineteenth-century standards he was quite short; to judge from his coffin, which was recently examined when the family vault was opened, he was about five feet four tall. Bishop Amherst, who knew Pugin while a student at Oscott when Pugin was Professor of Ecclesiastical Antiquities there, described him thus:

> We used to hear Pugin's loud voice (avast!) as he gave directions, sounding through the corridor, or his rising laugh when he was struck by some ridiculous idea. He was then quite a young man not more than two or three and twenty, beardless, with long thick straight hair, an eye which took in everything and with genius and enthusiasm in every line of his face and play of his features. He was rather below ordinary stature, and of a thick-set figure, and the style of his dress inclined to that of the dissenting minister of those days, combined with a touch of a sailor. A wide-skirted black dress-coat, loose trousers, shapeless shoes tied anyhow, and a black silk handkerchief thrown negligently round his neck were his usual attire. To say that he was eccentric is to say what may be predicated of most men of genius, but he certainly presented features which were not ordinary, and most persons seeing him for the first time would be sure to ask *Who is THAT?*

6.   Pugin's tomb chest, St Augustine's, Ramsgate, by E.W. Pugin, 1852.

rather on what he called 'true principles' plenty of room for toes spreading in shoes, coat tails long enough to keep his legs dry, 'Rig outs' for all weathers, sketching coat with inside pockets roomy enough for biggest sketch books and apparatus, black silk knee-breeches and silver buckled shoes for Sundays and Feasts an ample black velvet gown for professional wear.

He is seen wearing his velvet gown; his tomb effigy at Ramsgate (plate 6) also shows him wearing it, as does the figure of him on the Albert Memorial (plate 7).

His pragmatism in dress allowed him to move quickly during his ceaseless travels in this country and abroad, as he wrote to Lord Shrewsbury from Basle in 1840:

> I never saw heavier rain, and those who had any luggage got soaked; thanks to my large pockets and mackintosh I escaped dry. It is quite delightful to travel without Incumbrances. I care not for customs houses and baggage offices. I have everything about me, and cannot leave anything, it is the only way to travel with comfort. I met two Oscott students with six large packages, out for only three weeks tour!!!

Amherst who met him on one of his Continental trips describes how:

> One of his fancies was to have the hook of his umbrella at the point instead of the usual position . . . he had a cloak constructed with numerous and capacious pockets for the storing away of goods and chattels . . . taking only one shirt with him when he went upon an artistic tour, and one on his back. Once at Cologne I asked him how he managed with such a limited stock of linen. 'Oh my dear fellow' he replied, 'I buy a new one when I want one, and there are plenty of poor fellows who would be glad of this one when I have done with it'; pointing at the same time to a not very clean specimen of linen.

Such garments, though unusual today, were more widely used in the past, Dr Johnson always had his overcoats made with inside 'quarto pockets'. The purpose of his back-to-front umbrella is unknown. Michael Whiteway suggests that it was so that he could hang it up, sit underneath, and sketch in the rain.

These practical traits he also displayed indoors, for Powell tells us that at Ramsgate:

Pugin was a sailor, not only in appearance, but in habit of life 'A place for everything and everything in its place' (was a household rule with him). Books, papers, hats and telescopes, he kept all things 'shipshape' every drawing put away each night, books levelled on shelves, candles uprighted – a rare thing for a genius to be orderly.

Unfortunately for us his tidiness caused him to burn all the letters he received as soon as he had replied to them and of those he sent he kept no copies. As he had no clerk or secretary he had to be economical about his paperwork.

His daily life at Ramsgate was rigorously planned; he rose to pray at 6am, then worked in his library until family prayers at 8, seven minutes for breakfast, worked until 1pm when he had a fifteen-minute lunch. He worked or received visitors until compline in the chapel at 8, had supper at 9, then went bed at 10. He did not smoke or drink and ate plain food such as bread, cheese, celery, rice pudding, beef and ham.

Despite all these practical habits of his daily life he was less rational mentally. Powell tells us 'There was nothing speculative in his mind, all was practical', yet he had 'a curious want of the sense of proportion of things; he would bear with patient resignation real troubles and griefs, but a mere trifle would make him angry and unhappy'. Also added to this 'was the absence of discernment of character "except old friends". He trusted everybody he met, and all they said, until "found out".' These traits led to disputes and disagreements in his professional life and there are many accounts of them.

He was frightened of haunted rooms and the dark. He wrote to Lord Shrewsbury, describing a stay at Hornby Castle, 'I passed the night I cannot say slept in a curious room where the moment I entered with my candle I saw myself reflected in the glasses on all sides it was an awful room – horribly indistinct in the firelight.'

He was however as Powell tells us:

What is called 'good company', a capital mimic and told anecdotes to the life, so with his endless knowledge of Ecclesiology, Liturgy, History, Memoirs, Antiquarian lore, his original thought and imagination, wit and quaint humour, he was always a welcome guest. His spirit never flagged, people might get tired of keeping pace but not of himself.

There is perhaps a hint of Pugin having one of those manic personalities which drove him always

7. Pugin as represented on the frieze of the Albert Memorial, London.

to be the life and soul of any party. It is not altogether a surprise when Powell adds 'generally others remained silent when he was present'.

Pugin was also very attractive to women. Besides being married three times, he was near to marriage three times during the four years between the death of his second wife and his marriage to the third. Powell remarks that 'those who never knew him may smile at his being able to fall in love again and again but it is the truth, he was always young through pure vitality and would be happy or miserable like a boy.' He married the seventeen-year-old Anne Garnet in 1831 when he was aged nineteen and she died in 1832 (plate 8), following the birth of Anne, his first child (plates 11, 21). In 1833 he married the twenty-year-old Louisa Burton (plate 9), who, despite constant ill-health, bore him Edward, Cuthbert, Agnes, Katherine and Mary and died in 1844. Then in 1848 he married the twenty-one-year-old Jane Knill (plates 10, 12, 15), who outlived him by fifty-seven years, dying only in 1909. She bore him Peter Paul and Margaret. He wrote to a friend on the day of his wedding to Jane 'I am married, I have got a first-rate Gothic woman at last, who perfectly understands and delights in spires, chancels, screens, stained glass, brasses vestments etc.'

Pugin's appearance was certainly eccentric for a serious professional Victorian architect. Seen however in the context of the literary, artistic and theatrical world of the 1820s and early 1830s, with the romantic movement at its full flood, it would not have been unusual. The long hair with a black

8. Memorial brass, designed by Pugin for his first wife, Anne (Christchurch Priory, Hampshire).

9.† Louisa Pugin aged thirty-one, drawing and frame by Pugin (Private Collection).

silk handkerchief around the neck is surely a Byronic affectation common in the 1820s. Artists often dressed as working men so why not a sailor! Add to this his frequent visits to Paris where he must have come into contact or at least been aware of the romantics of the Hugo and Gautier circle, who had gained such notoriety at the first night of Hugo's play *Hernani* in February 1830. Indeed, on 19 May 1831 Pugin recorded in his Autobiography, 'after a week of the greatest exertion completed the theatre. The play performed was Hernani'. This was a private theatre created for Lord Leveson Gower who had just translated the play into English.

Here perhaps is a clue to the better understanding of Pugin; though he was already twenty-five when Victoria came to the throne, he is usually considered the very embodiment of Victorian Gothic Revival. This attitude was strengthened in 1932 by Trappes Lomax in the title of his influential biography *Pugin A Mediaeval Victorian*. However, his character and attitudes were fully formed by the early 1830s and he is a child of the Romantic Movement in art and literature. Certainly his love of all things medieval is not an intellectual one, but it has the passionate character of the Romantics. It is closer to the ethos of Keats's 'St Agnes Eve' and Scott's *Ivanhoe*, than Carlyle's *Past and Present*.

In architectural terms, despite his protestations in *True Principles*, many of his buildings and his use of ornament look back to the Picturesque Movement, rather than forward to the spareness of High Victorian Gothic. One only has to compare his interiors at the New Palace of Westminster with those at Street's Law Courts to see this amply demonstrated. Westminster, though solidly constructed following Pugin's principles, is in the ornamental tradition of Fonthill and Ashridge. Even so the high seriousness of the ecclesiological architects like Butterfield, Street and Carpenter,

who were well established before Pugin died, is somehow so different from Pugin's approach.

The Victorian professional architects usually had large offices in central London like those of Scott or Street with his supporting assistants, Shaw and Webb. Pugin had no office, nor indeed any architectural training – he was the lone romantic genius working himself to death in his Gothic house on the cliffs at Ramsgate, in an attempt to change the world of architecture and design. He belonged more to the world of Bonington, Haydon or Shelley than Leighton, Landseer and Browning.

With this academically undisciplined background it was perhaps unlikely that Pugin would develop into a major scholar in medieval history and antiquities as Burges was to do in the next generation. His most scholarly book is the *Glossary*, where the ecclesiologist Bernard Smith

10. Jane Pugin and her children, detail of Pugin's tomb (plate 6).

11.† Anne Hardman Powell, Pugin's eldest daughter, pencil (Private Collection).

12. Card celebrating the wedding in 1848 of Pugin and Jane Knill, bearing the arms of both families.

helped a great deal with the text and the Latin translations. He was a doer rather than a thinker, and he seems not to have read large amounts of architectural theory (chapter 6). A close examination of the contents of his library shows that he had few theoretical treatises, either religious or architectural. There were few modern architectural books, though he did have Blore's *Monumental Remains* and Warton, Bentham and Grose's *Essays on Gothic Architecture*. He also had Bardwell's *Temples* in which he wrote caustic comments.

He had very little literature, ancient or modern: there was a copy of Gower's *De Confessione Amantis* but no Malory, Shakespeare or Chaucer. There was no Scott, yet he designed the sets for Kenilworth, no Keats, Byron, not even Pope. There were numerous topographical books – both English and continental – which would have been of great practical use in planning his journeys. The books on architecture and antiquities tend to be those with useful illustrations such as Dugdale's *St Paul's* and the *Monasticon*. For the continent Mabillon's *Musaeum Italicum*, Montfaucon's *Monumens* and Pommeraye's *Histoire de l'eglise*

Cathédral de Rouen are packed with useful illustrations; likewise his several early emblem books, including Junius's *Emblemata*. His lack of book learning did not stop him holding strong opinions on almost every subject, not least religion.

His contemporaries frequently mention his remarkable memory and he obviously readily absorbed information from all sources, but reading was perhaps not a particularly important one. He was so busy travelling and designing during his short life that he had little time for quiet study; conversations with his friends and contemporaries are a more likely source. As for architecture and antiquities, he learned about them by travelling to see them and drawing them, his hundreds of surviving drawings are testimony to this.

These remarks also apply to his religious knowledge, for his library was not packed with books new or old on the theory of religion. Again it was often the illustrations which caught his attention, as in his book on the treatment of heretics (chapter 6). He specifically mentions the woman pressed to death, a graphic illustration, *not* a description buried deep in the Latin text.

After his conversion to Catholicism in 1835 with characteristic gusto he immediately involved himself in the latest controversies. The next year his publication of *Contrasts* raised a storm of protest. As in every other field he soon held strong views on religion. For the rest of his life he was involved in religious debate, eventually falling out

13. *The Priory Church and the ruined Castellan's House, Christchurch, Hampshire, from Ferrey, Recollections of A.W.N. Pugin . . . , 1861.*

14.† One of a set of six candlesticks presented by Pugin to the chapel at Oscott in 1838 to give thanks for his survival during a storm at sea (St Mary's College, Oscott).

with many in his own church. He rarely seems to have taken up an intellectually sound position and his impetuosity and lack of tact, combined with his less than subtle grasp of the *realpolitik* of the position of the Catholic establishment could only lead to conflict.

Most of Pugin's knowledge was picked up here and there in conversation rather than by reading Catholic tracts. He certainly knew all the leading Catholic figures including Montalembert, Newman, Wiseman, the fourteenth Duke of Norfolk and Lord Shrewsbury. Many of them visited him at Ramsgate. He even had an audience with the Pope while in Rome in 1847, when he pressed a specially bound copy of *Contrasts* upon him (plate 289). The Pope gave him a gold medal, though whether this made up for the shock of classical Rome is a moot point. Pugin wrote home:

> The modern churches here are frightful; St Peters is far more ugly than I expected, and vilely constructed – a mass of imposition – bad taste of every kind seems to have run riot in this place; one good effect however results from these abortions; I feel grateful for living in a country where the real glories of Catholic art are being revived and appreciated.

The need to make a living as an architect left little time even for his religion for, as Powell notes at Ramsgate, 'At eight [pm] the Chapel bell rang for Compline, which was solemnly recited by Pugin in Cassock and Surplice, followed by De Profundis, but too rapidly for a stranger to respond readily'. He also says that Pugin 'accepted the great mysteries of his Faith like a man of the Middle ages, and with the same childlike awe of the Supernatural'.

The brief but excellent *Lord Shrewsbury, Pugin and the Catholic Revival* written by Denis Gwynn in 1946, reveals much about Pugin's relationship with his major Catholic patron and Margaret Pawley's *Faith and Family. The Life and Circle of Ambrose Phillipps de Lisle* (1993) elucidates his association with his other important patron. Pugin's Catholic friends and clients are discussed in chapters 4 and 5.

An aspect of Pugin's life that has nothing to do with his architecture and design, but one that meant a great deal to him, was sailing and the sea. He once said 'There is nothing worth living for but christian architecture and a boat'. When this enthusiasm first emerged is unclear – there was nothing particularly nautical about Bloomsbury, though the Pool of London was of course alive with shipping at this date. He would however have crossed the channel on his trips with his parents to France; his first visit to Paris, for instance, was in 1819, when he was seven years old. Surviving sketches by him of boats at Hastings date from 1824. His love affair with the sea probably began during a long stay at the seaside at Christchurch in Hampshire in 1825, while convalescing from an illness. A sketch done by Pugin at this time and illustrated by Ferrey (plate 13) has a distinctly nautical flavour.

Late in the 1820s he bought his first boat as Ferrey describes:

> Regardless of the eminent position which laid within his reach, he made up his mind to go to sea. First, owner of a small boat which he kept for his own pleasure, he successively commanded a smack and afterwards a schooner in which amongst other merchandise he generally managed to bring over many interesting carvings and other antiquities purchased in the old stores of Holland and Flanders.

Ferrey, who is usually right in general but shaky on the detail, gets some of the types of boat wrong. This is not altogether surprising, as by 1861, when he published his book, he was remembering events of thirty years earlier. He remembered that Pugin's father was less than pleased with his son's new career move which:

> . . . was as may be imagined, a source of pain and anguish to his parents and friends, more especially to the refined tastes of his father, who on meeting a friend, exclaimed with much grief 'God bless my soul, it was but this morning I met my boy Auguste in the disguise of a common sailor, carrying on his shoulder a tub of water'.

Surely here we can see the young romantic hero in Pugin, for the urge to run away to sea is a well known one. We are in the very same decade as Byron and Shelley and their devotion to sailing. Indeed Shelley's fate almost befell Pugin, for Ferrey describes how:

> During one of these voyages he was wrecked on the Scotch coast, some distance below Leith where he and his men all but perished . . . Having lost everything, he arrived in Edinburgh in destitute condition. Knowing Mr Graham by fame he applied to him and was received with the greatest kindness . . . Mr Graham gave him his own pocket compasses.

Pugin met the architect Gillespie Graham in September 1829 and the compasses are engraved 1830 so Ferrey must have made a mistake. Another version of the wreck story is given by Powell: 'Pugin had been shipwrecked in early life and getting to shore crawled some miles to a cottage. The housewife fed him, left him to sleep and dried his clothes'. Pugin told Powell 'Only the ignorant despise the dangers of the sea.'

The two accounts do not actually conflict, for the logical date for the wreck was 1830, so if we suppose that the cottage was near Leith, even with dry clothes Pugin would have still been destitute and could well have made his way to nearby Edinburgh, where, if he *already* knew Graham, it would have been logical to ask him for help. The compasses certainly still exist and they are in Pugin's hand in the celebrated portrait of him by his friend Herbert (plate 16). Ferrey was close to Pugin at this date and the story is probably essentially true; indeed if we remove the phrase 'by fame' in his account it makes sense as it stands.

In 1838 when the chapel at Oscott was consecrated Pugin presented six candlesticks for the high altar (plate 14). They are a votive offering following his escape from a violent storm. Engraved on them are storm clouds and a flash of lightning with the inscription 'Beatae Mariae Virgini sospes ex turbidine et diris fulminibus Augustus Welby Pugin, An: Sal: MDCCCXXXVIII Ex Voto'. The storm in question is, I suggest, that which wrecked his ship some years before.

The actual chronology of his ownership of boats is unclear through the 1830s and early '40s; he certainly had periods without one. It is reasonable to assume that, as Ferrey said, when he had one he used it to travel to the continent and bring

15.† Jane Pugin, by G.A. Freezor, 1859 (Royal Institute of British Architects, on loan to the Palace of Westminster).

16.† A.W.N. Pugin, by J.R. Herbert, 1845 (Palace of Westminster). Both frames are to Pugin's design.

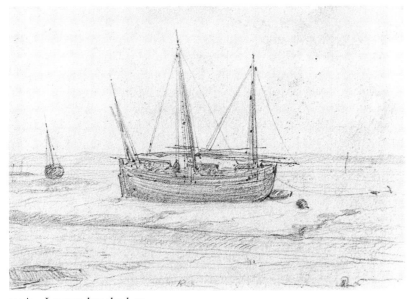

17.† Lugger beached at Honfleur, by Pugin, 1836 (Private Collection).

18.† Lugger beached at Brighton, engraving after a drawing by E.W. Cooke, 1830.

back antiquities (chapter 6). It is tempting to believe that the boat (plate 17) drawn by Pugin at Honfleur in Normandy in 1836 was his own. David Cordingly, who has given me a great deal of advice concerning boats, suggests that the drawing is of an English south coast lugger. Where Pugin moored his early boat is unclear, but presumably somewhere in London, possibly Westminster, for in his diary for May 1831 he records 'Started from Westminster Bridge in my own boat, Elizabeth, for an excursion.' Then later that month: 'Left Gravesend 6 am . . . reached Westminster at 6 o'clock pm.'

As soon as he took his cottage in Ramsgate in 1833 he could have kept a boat in the harbour and the obvious one to have was a Deal or Ramsgate Lugger. They were especially suitable for launching quickly from a shingle beach as can be clearly seen (plate 18). This excellent illustration of just such a lugger is by E.W. Cooke, Pugin's friend and fellow pupil of A.C. Pugin, who became a celebrated marine painter and probably went sailing with Pugin.

His most serious boat came much later and he noted in his diary on 21 February 1849: 'Bought the lugger Caroline with Mr Lucke for £70'. Luck was his friend Alfred Luck, who was to rent the Grange at Ramsgate after Pugin's death. As David Meara has pointed out he wrote excitedly to Hardman: 'I have got a boat fit for any work. She is just 6 inches longer than my studio 40 feet six inches & will carry 36 tons – I shall have a red cross painted on the foresail . . . & she can carry out anchors for an Indiaman'. The sketch proudly included in the letter (plate 19) is entitled 'The Caroline under full sail'. The cross of St George is

clearly visible on the foresail. This was clearly not a pleasure boat as is obvious from the letter Pugin wrote to Lord Shrewsbury at about this time:

I have just purchased a large Lugger for assisting vessels and wrecking – we have made two trips to the wreck of the 'Floridian' which your Lordship has seen in the *Times*. – We have got a great deal of cargo out, and I have every expectation she will pay . . . 30 tons – and a splendid model – I have got a capital crew – she can carry a three ton anchor out, and a chain cable. I bought her cheap and fitted her out with every requisite – from chains for heaving up anchors, tools for breaking up wrecks – and instruments for raising sunk cargoes.

His diary of 5 March records 'The Caroline sailed for the wreck at 1/2 9 pm'. This must have been the one mentioned in his letter; *The Times* of 5 March describes the wreck of the 500 ton barque Floridian from Antwerp on the Goodwin sands:

The most frightful catastrophe that probably ever occurred on this part of the English coast. viz, the total loss of a large emigrant ship, on the long sands with nearly 200 souls on board . . . upwards of 200 vessels started on saturday morning for the spot where the wreck lies, with a view of picking up what portion of her cargo might be floating about. Several Revenue Cutters also proceeded to the scene to protect it from the ravages of the wreckers.

Wrecking must be a dangerous business at the best of times, particularly at night, was this the occasion Powell describes? 'One stormy night one of his crew a stalwart fellow not quite recovered

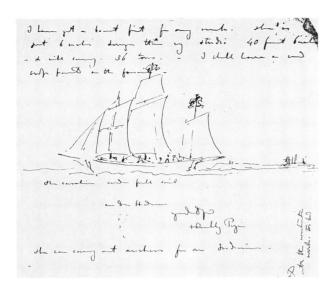

from fever, would join his comrades and died of exposure, to Pugin's sorrow'. Soon afterwards on 22 March Pugin wrote to Crace:

> On Sunday night a large galliot from Amsterdam for Bilbao with a very valuable cargo stuck on the Goodwin sands the crew and captain were about to abandon her when my Lugger hove in sight & succeeded in getting a boat through then breakers to them – carried out two anchors & got the complete ship off & into Ramsgate harbour the job will almost pay me all the cost of the boat back and a large share for every man besides.

He also wrote to Hardman that the cargo was: 'tobacco & gin . . . it is the best thing that has turned up. There were four in the gales ashore altogether'. Salvage money would have been paid to Pugin and his crew by the ship's grateful owners, but had the galliot's crew been drowned it would have been a free-for-all to take as much cargo as possible. There are many accounts of luggers on this coast being quickly launched from the beach and racing each other to a wreck. Pugin, from the vantage point of his tower at the highest point in Ramsgate, would have seen the wrecks before any of the other lugger captains. The Deal Luggers, specifically designed to operate in these waters, had a shallow draught and three square lug-sails which could be used in different combinations allowing them to operate in weather conditions which kept other vessels in port. The Caroline was unusually large for a lugger – twenty tons and thirty-five feet long was considered big at this date.

All the biographies stress that his boat rescued mariners. In 1845 he organized a mass at the Grange for eighty German Catholics saved from the Goodwin Sands and he had a special part of the graveyard set aside to bury foreign sailors. The whole wrecking aspect throws a more commercial light on his activities, though this was common practice in Ramsgate and, while not strictly illegal, one did have to evade the Revenue Cutters; nor was it exactly Christian. The Royal National Lifeboat Institution records show that, though there had been a lifeboat in Ramsgate until 1824, between that date and 1851 there was no lifeboat operating. This made the activities of the lugger captains both necessary and profitable, but from 1851 they and Pugin would have competed with the newly launched lifeboat. His old friend Cooke showed in the Royal Academy an appropriately named painting of an actual event: 'The Ramsgate lifeboat and a pilot boat going to the assistance of an East Indiamen foundering on the North Sand Head of the Goodwin Sands'. Cooke probably went sailing with Pugin from Ramsgate; Clarkson Stanfield certainly did.

The sea was very important to Pugin throughout his life and his enthusiasm for sailing demonstrates that he was far more a man of action than a thinker. Ferrey remarks that 'Pugin was extremely delicate as a youth, but his present mode of life [sailing] had certainly had one good effect, by giving him Herculean strength, which doubtless enabled him so effectually to carry out the work he so gloriously accomplished'.

Before the railway came to Ramsgate in 1846 the fastest way to get to London was by ship and Pugin worked whenever he could. There are several accounts of his drawing in rough seas and Powell tells us that one of his Ramsgate friends, Captain Warman commanded the 'Resolution' a large sloop, sailing between London and Ramsgate. It was on board his boat that Pugin made the design of a brass throne for the House of Peers. A steam packet with paddle wheels had operated to London from 1816, though perhaps Pugin preferred a sailing ship.

It was even more difficult to etch at sea: Ferrey describes how Pugin arrived at his publisher, Weale's, in a 'huge pilot coat' and when told that he looked bizarre said:

> I caught up the first garment in my way, getting into harbour after a stiff gale off Calais; but here are the plates for my book'; – at the same time pulling out a heap of copper-plates from under the ample folds of his coat. 'They are all ready for proving'. 'But how and where did you finish

19. Pugin's own lugger, *The Caroline*, sketched by him in a letter to Hardman, 1849.

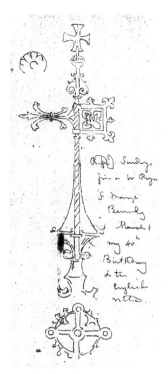

20. Design for a floriated cross for St Mary's, Beverley (Myers Family Trust); Pugin's last recorded drawing.

21.† Anne Pugin, wife of John Hardman Powell, daguerreotype.

22.† John Hardman Powell, daguerreotype.

the etchings?' 'Oh' said Pugin, 'I finished them on the boat'. 'Impossible', replied Mr Weale. 'Not a bit of it' retorted Pugin; 'The motion of the sea makes no difference to me;' and truly, many of the outlines illustrating *The Apology* [published 1843] were etched by him under these apparently impossible circumstances.

Using the contemporary railway timetables in conjunction with Pugin's diary one could fully chart his hectic journeys about England. The opening-up of the railway network throughout Britain coincided precisely with the development of Pugin's architectural career. The first reference to train travel in his diary occurs on 12 March 1836: 'From York to Manchester and Liverpool by rail'. From this moment he never looked back, relying increasingly upon the train for the demanding schedules he set himself. As with sailing, he used the train as a convenient place to write and draw. Travelling often overnight, he was able to prepare sets of sketches and drawings needed for meetings with clients or contractors the next day. Frequently he moved on, or returned home the same day, and there are a number of comments in his letters, notably to his third wife Jane, that underline this point and the relative difficulties of long-distance travel in a network of predominantly small, local and privately run railway companies: 'Today I have done an immense distance, about 200 miles continually changing lines and carriages' (26 June 1851). Other comments make clear that, although dependent upon the rail network, Pugin was no lover of the train: 'The railways are dreadful. Our train was 1 hour late, the mail broke

down, last night Crace was kept 2 hours at the station at Paddington, 5 hours altogether, Myers was 3 hours at Euston station. Travelling is miserable . . .' (18 November 1850). His remarkable ability as a draftsman remained with him even during the madness associated with his final illness. Ferrey relates how shortly before his death on 14 September 1852:

> One night he became much excited and attacked Mr. Myers, but was ultimately calmed; and the latter in order to turn his attention to a subject of interest, reproached him for keeping the scaffolding up at Beverley as they waited for drawings. 'Give me a pencil', said Pugin, and on the back of a large envelope he designed an elegant vane, clear and precise, which has since been placed on the corner pinnacle of St Mary's at Beverley.

This poignant drawing (plate 20) is his last design and jotted on it in a shaky hand the thoughts of a disordered mind ending 'my 40th birthday & the English nation'.

By the time of his death Pugin's theories and especially those published in *True Principles* were well known far beyond architectural circles. Purcell in his appendix to Ferrey quotes from an article in *The Times* on 'Pugin and the Revival of Architecture in England'. The opening sentence has a curiously modern ring:

> Of all the arts which combine the useful with the beautiful there is not one that has descended in this country to such degradation as architecture, and there is not one which now gives greater hope for the future. That very little of the architecture of the last century and the present is beautiful is not the heaviest charge that we have to bring against it, the heaviest charge is that it is utterly false, utterly inappropriate, and not durable . . . Pugin is dead. Let us remember in his honour that if now there seems to be the dawn of a better architecture, if our edifices seem more correct in taste, more genuine in material, more honest in construction, and more sure to last, it was he who first showed us that our architecture offended not only against the law of beauty but also against the laws of morality.

Pugin had no pupils other than his son-in-law, John Hardman Powell (plate 22), who helped him in his last years, and, though he went on to run the firm of Hardman, did no architectural work. Thus

there were no architects other than his young half-trained son Edward to carry on where he left off. Edward's contribution and that of his younger brothers is dealt with in chapter 20, but unlike their father they were never in the forefront of architecture. Besides his buildings, Edward designed a number of pieces of furniture of varying quality. His most successful pieces are a set of chairs which he designed for the Grange at Ramsgate in about 1864. In the late 1870s after his death these were manufactured in quantity with other furniture to his design by the London cabinet makers C. & R. Light. The chair appears at the top left in plate 24 and the table top centre was also designed for the Grange. He also designed furniture for Scarisbrick where he continued his father's work (plate 23). Though this table has tusked tenons and curved structural braces the whole design is overloaded with too much carved ornament.

In the years just before and after Pugin's death a number of architects were building churches directly influenced by him. George Gilbert Scott was perhaps the one most inspired by his example. Scott had actually met Pugin as early as 1838 and as he wrote in his *Recollections* he found:

> An excuse to write to Pugin, and to my almost tremulous delight, I was invited to call. He was tremendously jolly, and showed almost too much *bonhomie* to accord with my romantic expectations. I rarely saw him again, though I became a devoted reader of his written and visitor to his erected works . . . I was in fact a new man.

Scott's St Giles's, Camberwell of 1842–4 represents an early example of Pugin's influence and others were soon to follow. As Scott observed: 'Amongst Anglican architects, Carpenter and Butterfield were apostles of the high church school – I of the multitude. I had begun earlier than they, indeed Camberwell church dates before their commencement'. They were soon followed by Street and White and then after Pugin's death Seddon, Shaw and Burges.

With the publication in the first half of the 1850s of Ruskin's *Stones of Venice* and Street's *Brick & Marble Architecture in the Middle Ages Notes of a Tour in the North of Italy* structural polychromy rapidly superseded the plain stonework favoured by Pugin. The interior of Deane and Woodward's University Museum of the later 1850s (plate 25) amply demonstrates brick, marble and stone structural polychromy used to decorate an internal wall whereas Pugin would have had it painted and stencilled. Had Pugin lived it is likely

23. Table designed by E.W. Pugin for Scarisbrick Hall, late 1850s.

24. Furniture to E.W. Pugin's designs, manufactured by C. & R. Light of Shoreditch, *c*.1880.

25. The interior of the Oxford University Museum, by Deane and Woodward.

that he would have incorporated Italian Gothic forms into his work, for, though he hated Rome, he was excited by other architecture. In 1847, well before Street and Ruskin had published on the subject, he wrote from Florence to Lord Shrewsbury:

> Ever since I left Rome I have been delighted by Italy . . . the sacristies are full of Gothic shrines, reliquaries and chalices, &c. I am in a perfect mine of Gothic art . . . What absurdities people have talked and written about the pointed style not being adapted to Italy! Why it is full of it; there is not a little town that does not contain some fine specimens, to my astonishment.

26. Pulpit, St James the Less, Westminster, by G.E. Street, 1860.

27. Pulpit, All Saints, Margaret Street, by William Butterfield, *c*.1860.

28. The dog kennel at Gayhurst, by William Burges, *c*.1860.

29. Binding by R.N. Shaw for his *Architectural Sketches on the Continent*, 1858.

30. Binding by W.E. Nesfield for his *Specimens of Mediaeval Architecture*, 1862.

Building on Pugin's love of naturalistic stone carving Street pushed this to new levels of sophistication and quality at St James the Less, Westminster (plate 26) in 1860. In the same building however he combined it with coloured marbles as he had seen done in Italy, much as Butterfield was doing at All Saints', Margaret Street at the same time (plate 27).

Other continental architectural sources were rapidly coming into fashion, particularly an interest in chunky romanesque and early medieval forms of an earlier date than had inspired Pugin. One of Burges's works at Gayhurst, of about 1860,

is an excellent example of this new use of these robust forms (plate 28). These continental sources were made widely available in two books by Pugin's younger disciples Shaw and Nesfield. Though they never met Pugin, by singular coincidence they chose to travel to Ramsgate to sketch Pugin's house and church on the very day of his funeral and ended up attending it as mourners. In 1858 Shaw published his *Architectural Sketches from the Continent*, following a sketching trip in France, Italy and Germany. For the French part he followed in Pugin's footsteps, sketching, as he had done for his book *Details of Ancient Timber Houses*, in Amiens and Rouen. Even the binding (plate 29) is obviously inspired by Pugin's later books (plates 296–8).

In 1862 Nesfield published the results of his own continental tour in *Specimens of Mediaeval Architecture chiefly selected from examples of the 12th and 13th centuries in France & Italy*. Again he visited Amiens and Rouen, but, like Shaw, devoted a considerable amount of time to the Italian Gothic architecture popularized by Street and Ruskin. When it came to the binding, Nesfield, while like Shaw obviously inspired by Pugin's example of an architect designing bindings for his own works, came up with a very powerful and original design, far more advanced than either Pugin or Shaw (plate 30).

It is not in the transmission of precise architectural forms that Pugin's influence manifested itself, but rather it was his principles that had a widespread and long lasting impact. Pugin himself encouraged this for in *An Apology* he wrote:

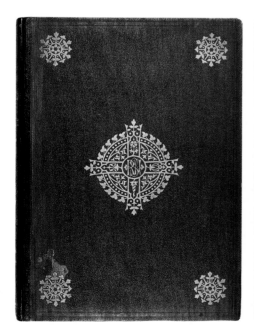

We do not wish to produce mere servile imitators of former excellence of any kind, but men imbued with the consistent spirit of the ancient architects, who would work on their principles, and carry them out as the old men would have done, had they been placed in similar circumstances, and with similar wants to ourselves.

He then took the matter even further:

We do not want to revive a facsimile of the works or style of any particular, individual, or even period; but it is the devotion, majesty, and repose of Christian [Gothic] art, for which we are contending; – it is not a style, but a principle.

His True Principles of honest and revealed construction and truth to materials were taken up throughout the world. Scott in his *Remarks on Secular & Domestic Architecture* of 1855 put this succinctly:

Pugin had he done nothing else, would have established his name for all future ages as the great reformer of architecture. His noble protest has been followed by others, and it is a proud thing to think of, that among those who follow out the Gothic revival, the principle of truthfulness is universally acknowledged as their guiding star.

By 1876 when Thomas Hardy – who had trained as an architect – wrote *The Hand of Ethelberta* he presumed that Pugin and his principles needed no introduction to his readers.

It was on a dull stagnant, noiseless afternoon of autumn that Ethelberta first crossed the thresh-

old of Enckworth Court . . . It was a house in which Pugin would have torn his hair. Those massive blocks of red-veined marble lining the hall – emulating in their surface glitter the escalier de Marbre at Versailles – were cunning imitations in paint and plaster . . . The dark green columns and pilasters corresponding were brick at the core. Nay, the external walls, apparently massive and solid free-stone, were only veneered in that material, being, like the pillars brick inside.

The specific application of his principles can be particularly well demonstrated in his influence on the applied arts. Indeed Pugin himself had certain limitations as an architect and in terms of sheer architectural genius he stands below Street, Butterfield, Burges and Shaw, but as a designer of flat pattern and in the applied arts he is second to none. Eastlake, writing in 1872 in his *A History of the Gothic Revival*, suggested that:

The carver, the cabinet maker, the silversmith who sought his assistance, or whose work he was called on to superintend, might reckon with safety on the rich fertility of his inventive power and in truth Pugin's influence on the progress of art manufacture may be described a more remarkable than his skill as an architect.

Scott wrote in *Recollections*:

Though his actual architecture was scarcely worthy of his genius, the result of his efforts in the revival of 'true principles' as well as in the recovery of all sorts of subsidiary arts, glass painting, carving, sculpture, works in iron, brass, the precious metals and jewellery, painted decoration needlework, bookbinding, woven fabrics and encaustic tiles.

Street writing in the *Ecclesiologist* in 1853 declared:

I believe it to be just as necessary that an archi-

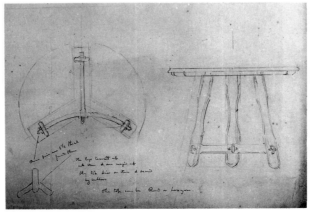

31.† Table, made by George Myers to the design of G.E. Street, for Cuddesdon College near Oxford (Trustees of the Victoria & Albert Museum).

32. Detail of a sheet of designs for three-legged tables by Pugin (Trustees of the Victoria & Albert Museum).

tect should know what the furniture of a house to be, as that his eye should superintend every decoration in colour on wall, or window, or floor of a church and does any one know anything about ordinary furniture of modern houses, and not recognize the wretched principles upon which it is generally designed? In Mr Pugin we lost an artist who in this, as in many other branches of his art, was very pre-eminent . . . all his designs in this branch of his profession were very decidedly marked by their extreme reality and truthfulness . . . with no more material consumed in their construction than was necessary for their solidity, and no sham or incongruous ornaments.

This was written in the very year that Street designed his tables for Cuddesdon College in Oxfordshire (plate 31). These massive oak tables, with their construction exposed as tusked tenons, are clearly inspired by Pugin. One wonders if Street had access to the 1849 drawing (plate 32) belonging to Crace which shows Pugin experimenting with the three-legged round table form. There is no extant Pugin table to these designs so it is difficult to assess how it would compare with Street's, which is the most remarkable table known from the 1850s. The Pugin connection extends further, for the building contractor at Cuddesdon also made the furniture and he was none other than Myers, who was not only Pugin's usual builder but made furniture for him. His remarkable understanding of wood and its structural requirements made him an essential example for later designers.

Street had imbibed Pugin's principles while in

Scott's office in the 1840s, but in 1849 he went to Cornwall to build his first church and met that other advanced Goth, William White. In that very year White was designing his dramatic pews (plate 33) for his restoration of the church at Gerrans in Cornwall with their Puginian tenons, dowels and pegs. These point the way to Street's Cuddesdon table. White continued to be inspired by Pugin and his chair (now in the V&A), designed for another Cornish building has a wholly Puginian preoccupation with structural forms.

In Street's office from 1859 to 1862 Norman Shaw was an assistant, and in 1861 he designed for his own use what I believe to be the most remarkable and exciting piece of nineteenth-century furniture. In overall form it bears no resemblance to any Pugin cabinet (plates 32) indeed the inlaid roundels are clearly inspired by Venetian or at the very least Italian prototypes. When we examine the fully expressed structural forms (plate 34) – front leg locked into place by an exposed dovetail with honestly revealed dowels securing the hidden vertical tenons of the upright timbers – the inspiration of Pugin is all too clear. The hinges and the

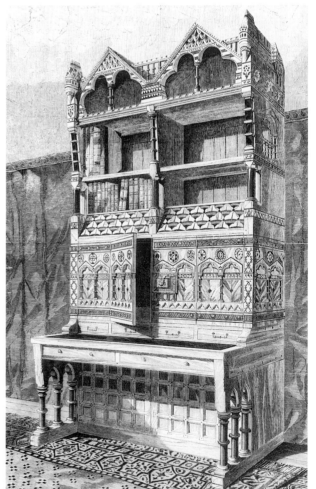

33. Pews at Gerrans, Cornwall, by William White, 1849.

34. Engraving of the cabinet by R.N. Shaw, shown at the 1862 exhibition.

lock closely follow Pugin's principles for metal-work, for as he wrote in *True Principles*:

> Hinges, locks, bolts, nails &c., which are always concealed in modern designs, were rendered in pointed architecture rich and beautiful decorations . . . ancient hinges, which extended the whole width of the door, and were bolted through in various places.

Shaw took these ideas even further than Pugin, for, if one opens the doors of the cabinet, the nuts of the bolts which secure the hinges are fully exposed on the back of the doors.

This cabinet was shown in the Mediæval Court of the International Exhibition of 1862 which was inspired by Pugin's Mediæval Court of 1851 (chapter 18). It was packed (plates 445–7) with metalwork, glass, textiles, furniture, stone and wood carvings, the majority of which could not have been created without Pugin's example. The Court was laid out by William Burges, who, rather as Street had done with Myers, used one of Pugin's firms in his early work. In 1855 Crace made a table (plate 37) for Treverbyn Vean, a house that Burges had designed in Cornwall. This table had a base taken straight from a Pugin design manufactured by Crace in the late 1840s, which was to lead to the table shown in the 1851 exhibition. The elaborate polychromatic marquetry top depicting the wheel of fortune was wholly a Burges design.

Prominent in the Mediæval Court of 1862

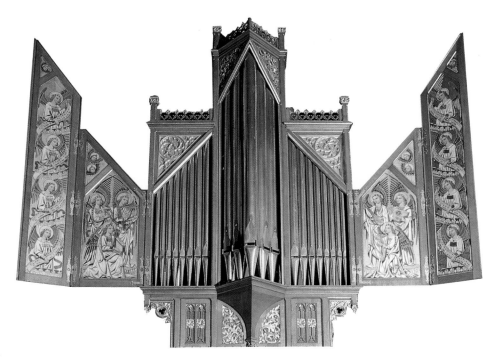

(plate 358) were several painted cabinets by William Burges, which, at first sight, seem unrelated to Pugin, who, though he knew that much medieval furniture was painted, never designed a piece himself. Pugin did however design a painted organ case for Jesus College Chapel, Cambridge (plate 35) so it is no coincidence that when Burges designed his first piece of painted furniture it was an organ case. This was for the Lille Cathedral

35. Painted organ case by Pugin (Jesus College, Cambridge).

36. Detail of the cabinet illustrated in plate 34, showing its revealed construction.

37. Wheel of Fortune Table, made by Crace to Burges's design, for Treverbyn Vean, Cornwall, 1858 (Private Collection, Birkenhead).

38.† St George Cabinet, designed by Philip Webb, painted by William Morris, and shown at the 1862 Exhibition (Trustees of the Victoria & Albert Museum).

39. Adjustable dressing mirror, designed by Philip Webb, c.1861 (Private Collection).

40. Tile alphabet designed by J.P. Seddon for Maw & Co.

competition in 1855, then a year or two later, he designed and had made his first domestic painted piece – the Yatman cabinet.

The Wines and Beers Cabinet was shown at the 1862 exhibition, where it was purchased by the South Kensington Museum. While the shape and the character of the painted decoration are all Burges's own, in two respects it is inspired by Pugin. The prominent strap hinges, the large decorative lock and the handle, like those on the Shaw cabinet, follow Pugin's principles for metal-work, even to the extent of being made of tinned iron. As several contemporary critics observed, the iconography of the painted decoration, depicting the battle of the wines and beers, is totally honest and prepares us for the fact that the cabinet was designed to contain drinks.

The painted Morris pieces like the St George Cabinet (plate 38) have decoration which in no way relates to their function. This issue would never have been raised before the publication of *True Principles*. Yet, though Morris's own painted decoration on the St George Cabinet has no Puginian connection, the curved braces which Webb designed as part of the base are directly inspired by Pugin's furniture. Webb, it should be remembered, was in Street's office when the Cuddesdon table was made and he was later joined there by the young William Morris and so they both imbibed their Pugin via Street. Webb's debt to Pugin is also obvious in a table now in the V&A which exposed dowels and cross members supporting a shelf which fits over the horizontal ones. An even more spare and elegant manifestation of the influence of Pugin's theories of revealed construction on Webb's work is the adjustable mirror (plate 34). This was probably designed and made in 1860 along with several other pieces for Webb's early patron Major Gillum.

Elsewhere in the Mediæval Court J.P. Seddon was interpreting Pugin in his typically eccentric way. He, along with other Goths like Burges, White, Street and Shaw, made the exhibition the springing point for the Reformed Gothic Style which was to transform design and which owed its very existence to Pugin. Seddon, taking a lead from Pugin's encaustic tiles and the alphabets from his *Glossary* (plate 311), designed a range of alphabet tiles (plate 40) for the firm of Maw. They were vigorously competing with Minton, who were still selling large numbers of tiles to Pugin's design (chapter 10).

Seddon's chair, with tusked tenons securing the top rail, prominent framing of the back and the curved arms, pays homage to Pugin, although Rossetti's painted decoration would excite most attention were this missing chair re-discovered today. The most spectacular Seddon piece was the King René Honeymoon Cabinet (plate 42), whose prominent hinges and exposed structural base members are indebted to Pugin. The painted decoration was by the Morris circle and six of the painted panels depict crafts which the newly established Morris & Company could undertake, Morris himself being depicted as the blacksmith. Indeed today it is Morris who is credited with the craft revival. There is no doubt, however, that Pugin was setting new standards for craftsmen and reviving lost craft techniques twenty years before Morris & Company was founded.

Eastlake, in his influential book on the applied arts *Hints on Household Taste* of 1872, published some of his own designs for furniture. The cabinet is made from one of them and displays all the familiar Pugin characteristics of structural honesty.

These examples demonstrate the wide-ranging nature of Pugin's influence upon High Victorian design. One further point ought perhaps to be made: Pugin's book *Floriated Ornament* of 1849 (plates 119 and 312) established principles for the

use of natural forms which were as influential in the world of flat pattern as his other principles were in architecture, metalwork and furniture. He pointed out the inadequate use of natural forms in the 1840s:

> The great difference between antient and modern artists in their adaptation of nature for decorative purposes, is as follows. The former disposed the leaves and flowers of which their design was composed into geometrical forms and figures, carefully arranging the stems and component parts so as to *fill up* the space the intended to enrich . . . a modern painter would endeavour to give a fictitious idea of relief, as if *bunches* of flowers were laid on.

His ideas were immediately taken up and the often-quoted attacks on the carpets decorated with cabbage roses shown in the Crystal Palace stem directly from the principles for flat pattern design laid down by Pugin. They rapidly entered the syllabus of the Government schools of design and along with his other principles underpinned Henry Cole's celebrated 'Chamber of Horrors' at Marlborough House. One of Cole's lecturers at the Schools was Christopher Dresser and it is no surprise that he should have been greatly influenced by Pugin. The binding of one of Dresser's most celebrated books *The Art of Decorative Design* of 1862 (plate 43) clearly demonstrates his debt to Pugin. It hardly needs saying that Morris's flat pattern could not have happened without the example of both Dresser and Pugin.

41. Cabinet designed and made by Ernest Barnsley for his own use, 1901 (Trustees of the Victoria & Albert Museum).

42. King René Honeymoon Cabinet, designed by J.P. Seddon for his own use, shown at the 1862 Exhibition; detail of a painted panel depicting William Morris as a blacksmith (Trustees of the Victoria & Albert Museum).

For the next fifty years both in architecture and the applied arts Pugin's principles were to underpin the whole of the Arts and Crafts Movement in Britain and America. In reviewing the exhibition of the Arts & Crafts Exhibition Society in the *RIBA Journal* in 1889 J.D. Sedding stated:

> Pugin found a very bathos of bad taste in architecture and our industries, and he did what he could . . . He went to Birmingham and preached the gospel to the heathen there, as Morris – his true lineal descendent – has recently been doing to much effect.

Pugin's principles of honest construction and truth to materials imbued the arts and crafts objects. As F.L. Griggs, the engraver, described Ernest Gimson's cottage around 1900, 'Newly cut stone and oak, bright steel and glass, and white walls reflecting the sunshine nothing but for use or comfort, and all without any sort of make-believe.' Pugin would not have approved of the white walls but all else follows his ideas. Sometimes motifs from Pugin re-emerge and are adapted to new uses as with the curved stretchers of the Gimson table. Ernest Barnsley, Gimson's collaborator in the

43. Binding designed by Christopher Dresser for *The Art of Decorative Design*, 1862 (Private Collection).

44. Headpiece designed by C.F.A. Voysey for an article about Pugin in the RIBA *Transactions*, 1918.

45. Writing cabinet, designed by C.F.A. Voysey, 1896 (Trustees of the Victoria & Albert Museum).

Cotswolds designed the massive over-structured cabinet (plate 41) just after 1900. The solid oak planks dowelled together with the tenons of the horizontal members so obviously expressed at the front makes far more of a virtue of revealed construction than Pugin ever did, but certainly pays full homage to his teaching.

The Lethaby oak dresser of 1900 reveals the construction of the arched shelf supports and the drawers, yet is more subtle than the Barnsley piece. The celebrated Voysey cabinet (plate 45) with revealed construction of the door frame and other structural characteristics uses no specific Pugin forms, but follows his principles. I was surprised when I first learned of Voysey's admiration for Pugin from John Brandon Jones, who knew Voysey and heard him speak admiringly of Pugin. Voysey in his book *Individuality* of 1915 wrote, in what could well have been the founding manifesto of the Arts and Crafts Movement, that Pugin:

> Adopted the forms most suited to the materials and requirements, and was governed by no pre-existing examples, but faithfully met, to the best of his knowledge and ability, all those requirements and conditions which were presented to his mind, classifying them and anointing them with his devout spirit . . . the mode adapted by Pugin was one born and bred in Britain alone thoroughly germane to the climate, and national in character.

Later in the same book Voysey follows Pugin's dislike of exotic woods and his preference for simple materials of the sort that were available in medieval Britain:

> The material native to a country is more harmonious with that country than any importation.

Unpolished oak, stone, brick or slate agree with our climate, light and national character far more than, polished wood, marble and mosaic.

It therefore comes as no surprise that Voysey should design an iconographically complex headpiece for a biographical sketch of Pugin's life published in the RIBA *Transactions* in 1918 (plate 43). Here Voysey demonstrates that, not only has he thoroughly absorbed all of Pugin's 'True Principles', but he goes further and when he incorporates them into the symbols at the bottom of his design he adds love and literature for good measure.

A shrewd appreciation of the importance of Pugin's influence on the designers who followed him from the 1850s onwards was made by Hermann Muthesius in 1904 in *Das englische Haus*:

> Looking back today at the achievement of the Gothicists in the field of artistic handicrafts, one can have no doubt that Pugin's work stands supreme. Not only did he create the whole repertoire in which the next generation worked but also put into it the best of anything that was ever done. His flat patterns remained the order of the day, nothing could surpass his glass and metal, his furniture was either imitated or replaced by other, inferior furniture. The whole Gothicist tradition that was available in the nineteenth century had been evolved and established by him throughout the whole range.

Perhaps the last word should be given to Shaw, who was still alive and in practice when Muthesius was writing. He was one of Pugin's earliest followers and though his architecture had become increasingly neo-classical in style as he grew older he continued to admire Pugin. When appropriate he still worked in the Gothic style, but gave it an unique Arts and Crafts flavour. In 1892, while working on All Saints', Richard's Castle, he visited Ramsgate and wrote to Mrs Foster, his Shropshire patron:

> There is a charming little church here (Roman Catholic), built by the great Pugin, some forty five years ago, for himself. He designed and paid for the whole thing, and it is full of interest all through . . . a most delightful and interesting work, and done *so* long ago. I am afraid we have not advanced much. Such work makes one feel small, *very* small.

This short essay attempts to describe Pugin's character, his friends and the circles in which he moved, dwelling upon aspects of his life not covered in the following chapters. The chronology (pp. XI–XIII) lays out very clearly the key facts and dates. Several biographies exist, which all owe a great debt to *Recollections of A.W.N. Pugin and his father Augustus Pugin*, written by Benjamin Ferrey. It was published in 1861 and I edited a new edition in 1978. Ferrey (1810–80) was a close friend and contemporary of Pugin and a fellow pupil in A.C. Pugin's *atelier*. Many of the facts about Pugin's life are known only from this source. These are supplemented by three important modern publications: two catalogues of Pugin's drawings, both compiled by Alexandra Wedgwood, and Margaret Belcher's Pugin bibliography.

Research on Pugin continues apace: *Pugin's Builder: The Life and Work of George Myers* by Myers's descendent, Patricia Spencer-Silver, was published in 1993. This makes a major contribution not only to the study of Pugin, but to our knowledge of the nineteenth-century building industry. Hilary Davidson's book, *Sir John Sutton, a Study in True Principles*, on one of Pugin's important patrons and his mentor for the design of his church organs, also appeared in 1993. Margaret Belcher is hard at work on an edition of Pugin's letters, which, when taken with the transcripts of his diaries published by Wedgwood in her catalogue of the V&A drawings, will underpin all future Pugin studies. Almost every aspect of Pugin's life can be documented and from the diaries his day-by-day movements can be traced. Rosemary Hill is writing what promises to be the best biography since Ferrey and has through her research already contributed a great deal to my understanding of Pugin. It is even possible that the massive biography which Phoebe Stanton has been working on for forty-five years might eventually appear. All these sources and many others are cited in the footnotes in the following chapters.

A design for a Church a pugin 1821

46. 'A Design for a
Church', drawn by the
nine-year-old Pugin in
1821. Reproduced from
Ferrey, *Recollections of
A.W.N. Pugin . . .* , 1861.

CHAPTER TWO

The Early Years

ALEXANDRA WEDGWOOD

Pugin was the precocious and much admired only child of older parents (plate 4). He achieved a spectacular debut at the age of fifteen with one or probably two royal commissions, but an uneasy period of adolescence followed, in which he had some glamorous successes designing for the stage, some failures with his own interior decoration business, but no clear direction. At the same time he was struggling to resolve his understanding of his faith, which led inexorably to his conversion to Catholicism. Then, in quick sequence, all his closest relations and his wife died. For a few years more he tried a number of possibilities, as a scholar, an author, a designer, an assistant to other architects, that all depended on his ability as a superb draughtsman. By the age of twenty-five he had found his vocation as an architect, designer and propagandist for the close combination of the Gothic style and the Catholic Church.

Little is known of the French background of Pugin's father, Augustus Charles, though it seems likely that he came of an artistic family with claims to nobility. One of his two sisters married the history painter Louis Lafitte and when he was young he knew Jacques-Louis David and Jean-Baptiste Isabey,[1] both court painters to Napoleon. He came to England during the French Revolution, though the exact circumstances and date are not known. He was in London by March 1792[2] and he was soon working as a draughtsman to the architect John Nash in Wales. About 1796 Nash returned to London with Pugin, who was by then established as his expert in Gothic detail and as one of the best architectural draughtsmen of the day. Gradually Augustus Charles became independent of Nash and began to form connections with publishers and topographical writers, first

Rudolph Ackermann, and then John Britton and E.W. Brayley.

In 1802 he married Catherine, the daughter of William Welby, a barrister. She was known as the 'Belle of Islington' and the marriage did not greatly please her family.[3] She was clearly a woman of strong character and determination, in contrast to her husband's easy-going nature. Ten years later their only child, Augustus Welby Northmore, was born. From his mother he inherited the ability to express verbally[4] and from his father skill with pencil, pen and ink.

The young Pugin's first memories were of the great medieval buildings in Yorkshire and Lincolnshire which the family visited in the autumn of 1818.[5] It was on this visit that E.J. Willson, a Roman Catholic architect in Lincoln, approached Augustus Charles with the idea of producing a book where a builder could find measured drawings of details of Gothic architecture. As a result the two volumes of *Specimens of Gothic Architecture*, 1821 and 1823, appeared with a text by E.J. Willson. In order to do this work, Pugin took on pupils and he had soon established a flourishing school of architectural drawing based in his house. The office routine was varied with long sketching expeditions to medieval sites in Britain and also in northern France. Augustus Charles certainly retained many contacts in France besides his own relations, including several scholars and antiquarians, such as E.H. Langlois, A. de Caumont and N.X. Willemin. All the family made frequent visits there from 1819.

As well as Gothic buildings the young Pugin therefore must have been surrounded by drawings and the apparatus of drawing from his earliest days. All accounts emphasise his precocious gifts: 'He had an almost intuitive talent for drawing, and

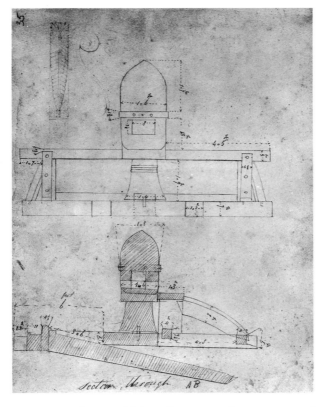

47.   Drawing of capstans from a sketchbook of views at Hastings, 1824 (Trustees of the Victoria & Albert Museum).

as soon as he could handle a pencil commenced sketching.'[6] In his own words he said: 'I began to learn drawing and perspective regularly and made a drawing of the Corinthian capital in perspective. I was very fond of perspective and made a good proficiency in it, began to design buildings etc.'[7] His formal education at Christ's Hospital, by contrast, seems to have been haphazard and incomplete;[8] it was not what interested him. From the evidence of a delightful sketchbook of buildings in Hastings made in 1824,[9] it seems likely that at this date he was being taught by J.D. Harding, the painter and engraver who later did the lithographs for A.C. Pugin's book, *Gothic Ornaments*. There might have been some thought that the young boy would have become a landscape painter, but even in the sketchbook there is a fascination with structure rather than pretty views as is shown in the *Plan, elevation and Longitudinal/section of one of the Capstons* (plate 47). By 1825 he was helping his father produce plates for his books: 'Assisted my father in his work of Normandy by making several sketches. I worked very hard all the time and measured a great deal . . . We returned by the route of Havre, Honfleur and so to Calais and returned to England after an absence of about three months.'[10] It seems clear, however, that he was always treated differently from his father's other pupils,[11] several of whom were close to him in age. They included T.T. Bury, who became a

life-long friend, F.T. Dollman, and Benjamin Ferrey, who was to write his biography. His energy and his formidable knowledge of medieval sources combined with his skill as a draughtsman and his originality as a designer contributed to a growing reputation which kept him apart from the more humdrum activities of his father's office.

Augustus Charles had considerable knowledge not only of Gothic architecture, but also of the decorative arts, and he both collected medieval artifacts and designed new ones. Several of his furniture designs were published in Ackermann's *Repository of Arts*, and from these it can be seen[12] that he was among those who fitted up Eaton Hall for Earl Grosvenor. Twenty-seven plates, all of which had been printed originally in the *Repository of Arts* between June 1825 and September 1827, were gathered together into a book which was published with the title *Pugin's Gothic Furniture*. This interest must also have been reciprocated by his son and led in 1827 to a prestigious commission for the younger Pugin. The task of furnishing the new apartments at Windsor Castle had been given the previous year to the firm of Morel & Seddon.

> Mr Morel . . . applied to the elder Pugin to aid them in the execution of their commission. This was just the opportunity calculated to draw forth the abilities of his son, to whom his father immediately transferred the business.'[13] The young boy also documented the work: 'June 26 went to design and make working drawings for the gothic furniture of Windsor Castle at £1.1s. per day for the following rooms: the long gallery, the coffee room, the vestibule anti-room, halls, grand staircase, octagon room in the Brunswick Tower, and Great Dining Room. I likewise superintended the execution of them at Mr Seddon's manufactory, Aldergate Street in the city. The cast iron candelabras for the gallery were executed by Summers of Bond Street.[14]

All these statements can be proved to be accurate.[15]

The most complete set of furnishings by Pugin was for the Great Dining Room (now the State Dining Room) for which he designed the dining-table and chairs, a great sideboard, two small sideboards, two cellarets and two side tables, all *en suite* in rosewood, with gilding and gilt bronze enrichments. All these survive except the great sideboard, which was destroyed by fire in November 1992. Pugin's distinctive drawing for this sideboard, however, exists (plate 48). It was executed

closely following this design, including the glass at the back with its Gothic arcaded frame and the central projecting canopy surmounted by the royal arms with angelic supporters. The superstructure was, however, removed at an early date.[16] With its simple clear lines and rich colours this grand suite is very close to his father's work. More original were his designs for oak stools, benches and occasional tables and candelabra (plates 49). The tables in particular have an aggressive quirkiness which seems to fit the young Pugin's character.

The work at Windsor probably occupied Pugin on and off for about a year; the King took up residence in his new apartments in December 1828. At the same time, and slightly predating his connection with Morel and Seddon, Pugin had met the royal goldsmiths, Rundell and Bridge. Again there was a special quality in his work that stood out when a member of the firm discovered him in the Print Room of the British Museum copying the prints of Dürer. This account is given by Ferrey[17] who states that his services were immediately secured and much beautiful plate was executed by the firm to his designs. This story can be substantiated by two important examples, one attributed and one definite. The attributed example is the silver gilt standing cup set with diamonds and precious stones, later misleadingly

called the Coronation Cup (plate 328), in the Royal Collection.[18] This item appears in Rundell's invoice dated 27 September 1827 and has a fundamentally different character from the three other standing cups made by them at this period for George IV. The main motifs of the Coronation Cup are angels bearing armorial shields and an

48.† Design for a sideboard for the Great Dining Room, Windsor Castle, watercolour (Trustees of the Victoria & Albert Museum).

49.† Oak occasional table made for Windsor Castle, c.1827 (The Royal Collection, H.M. Queen Elizabeth II).

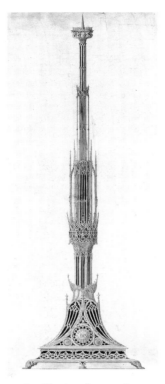

50.† Design for an altar candlestick, watercolour, 1827 (Trustees of the Victoria & Albert Museum). Probably intended to be part of a set of altar plate to be made by Rundell, Bridge & Rundell for St George's Chapel, Windsor, but never executed.

51. Design for chalice, watercolour, 1827 (Trustees of the Victoria & Albert Museum). Part of the same set as plate 50.

52. Letter from Pugin to W. Grieve, c.1831 (Metropolitan Museum of Art, New York).

the truth about her attitude, Pugin soon had several theatrical friends who got him back-stage, apparently starting with George Dayes whom he had met in Morel and Seddon's workshop. Between the middle of 1829 and early 1832 the theatre was one of his major preoccupations. He started as a 'super flyman' and then served a season as a stage carpenter which clearly gave him considerable and lasting practical insights into the nature of wood construction. But his special gift of draughtsmanship and his knowledge of medieval sources led to stage design and work and friendship with the Grieve brothers and Clarkson Stanfield, who at that time was also a scenery painter. W. Grieve was stage designer at the King's Theatre from 1829 until his death in 1844. He was responsible for a revolution in the scenery department, with his moonlight scenes being particularly notable.[22] One of the highlights for Pugin of this period was the scenery of the ballet *Kenilworth* which was performed at the King's Theatre in March 1831, where he painted two of the scenes and gave advice on the costumes and other scenery (plate 71). With choreography by A.J.J. Deshayes and music by Costa, it was considered to be a great success. Pugin clearly felt great respect and affection for W. Grieve (plate 52) and made a note in his diary the day he died.

The theatre, however, did not occupy all his time. On 19 September 1829 Pugin wrote: 'Was introduced to Mr. Gillespie Graham, architect of Edinburgh, and began to design for him.'[23] Gillespie was almost as old as Pugin's father, an established architect with an extensive practice in

ogee-headed arcade ornamented with crockets and finials on the bowl of the cup. The base of the bowl is modelled as a fan vault with a central pendant supported by pierced brackets. All these elements derive from medieval architecture. They have strong similarities with a magnificent set of five drawings for altar plate (plates 50, 51). These are all signed *A Pugin Junr. Invent et fecit 1827* and countersigned *verso* by John Gawler Bridge. It seems most probable that the King ordered the cup to place on his new Gothic sideboard and at one time planned a new set of plate for St George's Chapel, Windsor.

After this glamorous introduction to the world of work it is not surprising that Pugin found it difficult to settle down to the self-effacing drawing done in his father's office; he was attracted by the spectacle and excitement of the stage.[19] From the beginning of 1822 Pugin had been making notes about theatrical productions, principally those at Covent Garden, Drury Lane and the King's Theatre, and how they were received.[20] Again he probably inherited his love for the theatre from his father, who was a friend of Charles Matthews, the actor, whom he had met in Wales.[21] In this context it is odd that Ferrey states that Pugin never entered a theatre until 1827 because of his mother's strict principles. There is, however, an unexpected blank in his notes for the year 1828 when perhaps she attempted a prohibition. Whatever

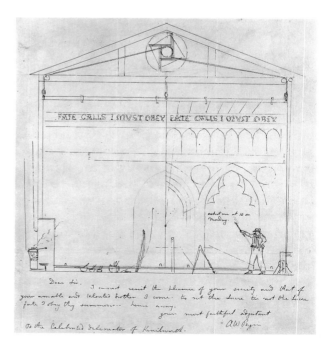

Scotland. He specialised in Gothic churches and castellated country houses and, though it is not known who effected the introduction, the meeting is yet another sign of Pugin's reputation for unusual skill as a draughtsman and a designer. Gillespie Graham asked Pugin to help him with the designs for Murthly New Castle near Dunkeld, Perthshire, an ambitious project to be built in a Jacobean style for Sir John Stewart. Pugin immediately went off to Hatfield House to get examples of this style and later recorded all the interior decorations that he designed for this house: 'They consisted of the great hall, chapel, entrance hall and staircase, anti-room, Library and Drawing room, all with the exception of the last in the style of James I, the drawing room in the style of Louis 14th.'[24] All these rooms are marked on the existing plan of the principal floor but work on the house was halted in 1832, and it remained a shell until demolished in the middle of the twentieth century.[25] Pugin was supplying fittings from 10 October 1829 until the end of 1831.[26] Most of these fittings appear to have been kept, because following a fire in the old castle in 1850 they were used to fit up the surviving great hall and French drawing room[27] (plate 53), which therefore constitute Pugin's earliest known interiors.

Pugin's collaboration with Gillespie Graham was to last until the 1840s,[28] long after he became an independent architect. Though the dramatic account of a shipwreck off the coast of Scotland, from which he was rescued by Gillespie Graham,[29] cannot be an account of their introduction, some such event, and the firm advice of Gillespie Graham that he should become an architect, may explain the deep sense of obligation that Pugin seems to have felt towards him. The pocket compasses which Pugin used thoughout his life were apparently engraved James Gillespie Graham, architect, Edinburgh, 1830.[30]

Pugin soon started to help Gillespie Graham on architectural matters, but his work at Murthly was principally for fittings. Perhaps this gave him ideas: just two months after the beginning of this commission he recorded: 'began business for myself in the carving and joinering line at 12, Hart Street, Covent Garden.'[31] A number of designs for furniture and metalwork survive from this period (plates 54, 244, 245), and their aggressively exaggerated and bulbous features appear in the oak fittings of the great hall at Murthly old castle. There is also a sudden change in his draughtsmanship at this period, with the predominant characteristics becoming a hard outline usually heavily drawn in blue ink. His style favoured strong curv-

53. The Great Hall, Murthly Old Castle, photograph c.1875.

54. Design for six stools, possibly intended as a catalogue for Pugin's Hart Street business, blue pen, c.1831 (RIBA Drawings Collection).

55.† Communion table, made and presented to Christchurch Priory by Pugin, 1831.

56. Detail from designs for furniture for Mrs Gough, Perry Hall, Birmingham, pencil, 1831 (Trustees of the Victoria & Albert Museum).

57. Page from a sketchbook showing designs for 'Contrasted Domestic Architecture', pen and ink, 1832 (Trustees of the Victoria & Albert Museum).

58.† Page from *Le Chasteau*, pen and ink, 1833 (Trustees of the Victoria & Albert Museum), one of the first examples of Pugin's use of a bird's-eye-view to illustrate a large and complicated building.

ing shapes, based on sixteenth-century Flemish or Jacobean examples. Many of the designs appear too extravagant and impractical to execute, but it is probably significant that in the case of the altar for Christchurch Priory, where both the design and the finished work are known (plates 55), considerable simplification has taken place in execution. There is no doubt that the young Pugin experienced many difficulties in his first business venture. They are documented in a series of letters and designs for furniture which Pugin sent to Mrs Gough at Perry Hall, Birmingham, between 17 June 1830 and 1 September 1831[32] (plate 56). By October 1830 he was short of money, in March he was having legal wrangles with a workman and was in considerable financial difficulties, and eventually the business failed. In his final letter to Mrs Gough he wrote:

In every endeavour to render my designs as handsome as possible I have never spared any money in their execution, and as in most cases my prime cost has far exceeded my estimate and in no work in which I have been hitherto engaged in have I ever been able to clear any remuneration for my exertions, I have at length determined to relinquish the execution of work myself, and to confine myself entirely to my original profession of an architect and designer.

The opportunities to practise architecture, however, were not there and Talbot Bury, then his best friend, wrote[33] that following the failure of his business venture he took to sailing, which accommodated his 'adventurous spirit and active energy'. Certainly he had a boat at this period.[34] It seems also that he was being troubled in another way: he was trying to resolve his religious beliefs. Benjamin Ferrey was a full-time resident in the Pugin household between 1826 and 1832[35] and he tells the story of how on Sundays Pugin used to accompany his mother to hear the then immensely popular and fashionable Edward Irving preach at the Caledonian chapel in Hatton Garden.[36] Ferrey was convinced that it was these tedious services in unattractive surroundings which were responsible for making Pugin turn to Catholicism. Whatever the initial stimuli, and they must have been chiefly visual ones, from 1831 Pugin's drawings for church plate[37] begin to reveal a deep fascination with Catholic ritual and the setting of the Mass. An important sketchbook[38] contains a number of drawings dated 1831 and 1832 which are titled *Design for a Catholic Chapel*. They show an extremely ornate building (plate 59) in the Decorated style in plans, elevations and details. In the same sketchbook is the first representation of another theme which was occupying him closely at this date, that of contrasting the plain and dreary architecture of his own day with the richness and beauty of that of the late Middle Ages (plate 57). These thoughts led eventually to the publication of *Contrasts* in 1836, in which he placed the blame for the 'decay of taste' on the Reformation and the introduction of 'Paganism' into architecture. It is interesting to see therefore in his first *Contrasted Domestic Architecture* that he includes an elaborate

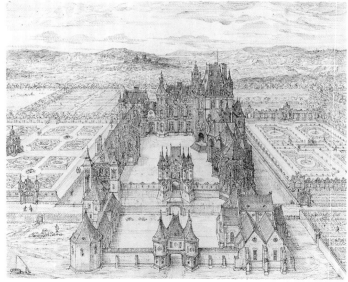

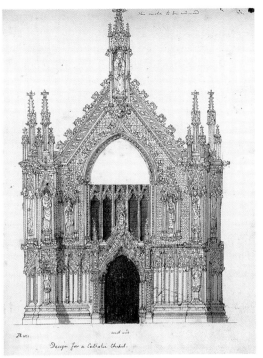

SIDE OF THE SHRINE

house of 1532 in a Flemish early Renaissance style.

Following this sketchbook comes a series of beautiful little manuscript books, each illustrating an imaginary scheme. All but one has a religious theme and it appears that Pugin was exploring the Catholic faith in intensely visual terms for his own pleasure and instruction. The first of these is probably *The Chest* of 1832,[39] where a handsome panelled fifteenth-century chest is shown to contain an astonishing range of church plate, plus a few secular items. There is an element of theatricality about the ancient chest which contains these treasures, but this aspect is balanced by the extraordinary knowledge of medieval plate which is revealed by the objects. Pugin's sources would have been cathedral treasuries, Dürer's prints and perhaps fifteenth-century paintings or illuminated manuscripts which show a priest celebrating Mass at an altar. There is nothing pedantic or antiquarian about Pugin's approach; it shows youthful confidence in working out new and elaborate designs (plate 61) for ecclesiastical plate not then in use in the Anglican Church and indeed little used by Catholics. His next scheme, also of 1832, is called *The Shrine*,[40] and gives an imaginary reconstruction of the thirteenth-century shrine of St Edmund, Archbishop of Canterbury, at Fontenay in France, and some of the reliquaries belonging to it. St Edmund's shrine exists, in fact, at Pontigny and Pugin has clearly not made a scholarly study of his subject but has recreated in some splendid drawings (plate 60) the glamour of the great medieval pilgrimage centres.

From 1833 come five more such schemes, which were perhaps executed in the following order: The *Parish Church*,[41] which is the longest with seventy-four drawings, *The Hospital of Saynt John*,[42] *The Deanery*,[43] *Le Chasteau*,[44] the only one with a secular subject, and *St. Margaret's Chapel*.[45] The series ends the following year with *St Marie's College*,[46] another major scheme with sixty-four drawings. In all of these there is more emphasis on architecture, with plans, elevations and perspectives given, but *The Parish Church* still has a vestry full of plate, altar cloths and vestments, and such things are also shown as belonging to *St Margaret's Chapel*. The interior of this chapel has a most complicated vault with flying transverse ribs. The perspective demonstrates Pugin's love of framing the spaces within his buildings in a way that recalls the proscenium arch; it gives a strong impression of a stage set for a sacred drama. Rich and beautiful medieval settings were no doubt what Pugin felt to be essential for Catholic worship. *The Hospital of Saynt John* and *The Deanery* are slightly more believable early Tudor style buildings. *Le Chasteau* is again an immensely grand and complicated building of about 1525, which contains a mixture of late Gothic and early Renaissance detail (plate 58). All the inscriptions are given in archaic French, and it may be interesting to speculate why. It seems likely that at this period Pugin was often in France and may have been designing scenery for the Parisian theatre. Throughout this series Pugin's draughtsmanship was developing; the hard blue outlines of his early schemes dis-

59.† Page from a sketchbook showing a 'Design for a Catholic Chapel', pen and wash, 1831 (Trustees of the Victoria & Albert Museum). This appears to be based on the Slipper Chapel, Houghton St Giles, Norfolk.

60.† Page from *The Shrine*, pen and ink, 1832 (Trustees of the Victoria & Albert Museum).

61. Detail of a page from *The Chest*, pen and ink, 1832 (Trustees of the Victoria & Albert Museum). This design for a monstrance is indicative of Pugin's early interest in Catholic ritual.

appear from his work for ever and are replaced by his familiar light but sure touch. The culmination of this process are his drawings for *St Marie's College*, where in the frontispiece (plate 308) he shows himself as a medieval illuminator and scholar. His ability to organise very complicated drawings without losing clarity is always evident as is the extraordinarily delicate penmanship of which he is now capable. In this final book Pugin again includes church plate, which is here much more closely based on fifteenth-century proto-types and therefore much more practical. The design for a monstrance he reused two years later in his book, *Designs for Gold and Silversmiths*, and it became an established pattern that he regularly drew and made for the rest of his life.

Complementary with the Gothic settings of the Catholic faith in these ideal schemes, Pugin continued to explore his theme contrasting contemporary architecture of different types of buildings with their medieval counterparts. He made a collection of fourteen such 'Contrasts' in 1833.[47] They show generalised examples of a range of buildings and fittings, such as 'Ecclesiastical Architecture', 'Street Architecture', 'Wells', 'Sepulchral Slabs', 'Gate-piers' and 'Altars'. In his published book of three years later he used specific buildings.

While he was evoking the elaborate Gothic and Catholic dream world of his imaginary schemes, real life was much more prosaic. After the failure of his own decorating business and the lessening of his work for the theatre, his principal activity was helping his father with his publications. The attractive relationship between father and son is well illustrated in a letter written by Pugin senior to his wife in Salisbury on 29 August 1832:[48]

My dear Catherine, I send you everything you ordered and have added 25 sheets of tracing paper for Augustus, whom I am very happy to hear is much better for health and very successful over his profession as well as connection – the patronage of a Dean is a great thing, and I trust in the end will prove profitable. My present intention is to leave London to go to Bath and Wells on Wednesday next this day week. . . . Meanwhile yourself and Augustus could set off from Salisbury, there is a coach going to Wells which passes though Salisbury, whenever Augustus has done all that he has to do. Arrived at Wells, Augustus may begin what he may consider proper for my work,[49] and direct Dollman in what he has to do, and by so doing, it will much forward my object. Please

explain to Augustus that it is my full wish and intention to pay him so much per day for all the time he may be employed for me, and whatsoever price he will fix I shall be happy to comply – half of the money I shall pay him directly, the other half in diminutions of our former account.

A.C. Pugin had only a few months to live when he wrote this letter and he died in London on 19 December 1832. A.W. Pugin honoured his father's achievement in the splendid frontispiece to the second volume of *Examples of Gothic Architecture*, which was published in 1836. The elder Pugin had made it possible for the Gothic Revival to become historically accurate and provided his son with the foundation that he needed to build his different career.

This was the second death in his family that year. In 1831 Pugin had married Anne Garnet, whom he had met through his theatrical connections, but she died in childbirth in May 1832.[50] The following year his mother died and he married Louisa Burton. There are hints that neither of his first two wives were considered by his family to be his social equals.[51] After his mother died he moved to Ramsgate, no doubt to be near to his aunt Selina Welby who was very kind to him. Her death came suddenly and unexpectedly on 4 September 1834[52] and completed the tragic sequence of losses. It did, however, result in Pugin inheriting some money, and hence a certain independence while he worked out what to do with his life. His first thoughts after his father died were to continue his architectural books. He wrote to E.J. Willson on 26 February 1833:[53] 'after mature consideration and consulting my best friends I have resolved to give up my theatrical connection altogether and to devote *myself entirely* to the pursuit of Gothic architecture and particularly to the prosecution and compleation of the works commenced or intended by my late father.' A year later, on 31 March 1834, he again emphasised his scholarly work:[54] 'And as I have determined to devote my entire time to the study and delineation of our venerable architecture I trust the result of my Labour will prove worthy [of] the attention of all patrons professors and students of that grand and sublime style termed Gothic.' He did publish the second volume of his father's *Examples of Gothic Architecture*, with some difficulty as E.J. Willson was extremely slow to deliver the text, and drew the first part of volume three.

Much of his time was therefore taken up with visiting and studying great medieval buildings and, as discussed above, trying to resolve his religious feelings. He wrote in January 1834 to his friend William Osmond, a sculptor in Salisbury:[55] 'I can assure you after a most close and impartial investigation I feel perfectly convinced the roman Catholick church is the only true one and the only one in which the grand and sublime style of church architecture can ever be restored . . . A very good chapel is now building in the North and when compleat I certainly think I shall recant.' Pugin realised that his change of faith would be attributed to architecture alone. He wrote to E.J. Willson, who played a considerable part in his conversion:[56] 'I trust no man will attribute my motives *solely* to my love for antient architecture for al[t]hough I will allow the change has been brought about in me owing to *my studies of antient art* yet I have still higher reasons which I can satisfactorily account for if required for my belief.' He was finally received into the Catholic church on Whitsun Eve, 6 June 1835, in Salisbury.

In the summer of 1834 he made a long continental tour of northern Europe, going to Nuremberg and Flanders for the first time,[57] which provided him with a whole new range of mental stimuli. The urge to create, however, was always stronger than the urge to study. Pugin was an excellent and serious scholar, but he used this discipline chiefly as an aid to design. He constantly studied interesting buildings and artifacts and went on at least one Continental sketching tour each year from this time onwards. His immense knowledge of medieval forms gave him the ability to design new buildings and objects entirely in the spirit of the old without pedantic copying.

Apart from his help with Gillespie Graham's schemes, Pugin still did not have any scope for architectural work, and it must have seemed more probable to him that he would find work through his designs for furniture where he had already had some success. In 1834 he made a set of such drawings[58] for Edward Hull, who was a well known antique dealer in Wardour Street. Hull and his fellow dealers John Webb and John Swaby, who catered to the growing interest in the collection of British medieval artifacts and frequently made up pieces of furniture from old fragments, would no doubt all have been familiar with Pugin's skills. Swaby supplied oak carvings for Murthly.[59] Pugin's designs for Hull were for elaborate pieces of furniture (plate 63) and it is interesting to contrast them with a much simpler and more practical scheme for furnishing three rooms of a house,[60] which he made for the architect Charles Barry probably in 1834 or early 1835. Finally he was also preparing the drawings[61] for his own book

Gothic Furniture of the 15th Cent. designed and etched by A.W.N. Pugin, which was published by Ackermann & Co. on 1 April 1835. This book represents Pugin's first wholly independent work to be published. It has no text. It is frequently confused with his father's book, *Pugin's Gothic Furniture*, which was also published by Ackermann. By contrast with the earlier plates, which showed furniture that was often spindly with simple and repetitive decorative motifs, these ones are now based on a much more scholarly interpretation of actual fifteenth-century examples, perhaps with several being taken from illuminated manuscripts. Two of Pugin's major innovations as a furniture designer appear in this book. These are the new form of the x-frame chair with the x placed sideways, and his use of revealed construction as shown in the illustration of stools (plate 240).

It was, however, his scheme for Charles Barry that proved to be a turning-point from which his architectural career would develop. Pugin noted in his diary[62] that he dined with Barry on 18 April 1835 and ten days later he wrote 'Began Mr. Barry's drawings.' These designs, which marked the beginning of their fruitful collaboration, were for the interiors of the King Edward VI Grammar School, New Street, Birmingham. In July 1832 Barry had won the competition to rebuild the school with an impressive Perpendicular design. The contract working drawings[63] were executed in 1833 and provided for the main two rooms on the upper floor, with the library on the street façade

63.† Design for a State Bed for Edward Hull, pen and ink, 1834 (Trustees of the Victoria & Albert Museum).

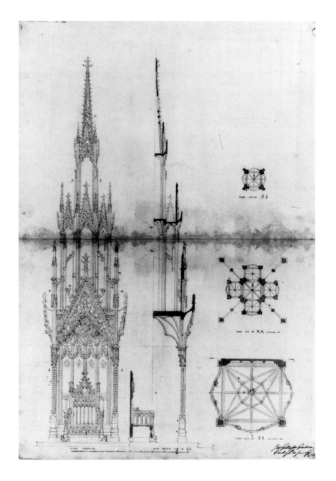

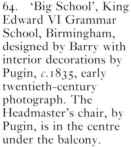

64. 'Big School', King Edward VI Grammar School, Birmingham, designed by Barry with interior decorations by Pugin, c.1835, early twentieth-century photograph. The Headmaster's chair, by Pugin, is in the centre under the balcony.

65. Design for the throne of the Moderator of the General Assembly, Holyrood Abbey, Edinburgh, pen and ink, 1836 (Scottish Record Office). This drawing shows strong similarities with Pugin's contemporary work in the Palace of Westminster.

and the schoolroom at the back, reached by a two-storey corridor. The Headmaster's house was in one of the cross-wings. A number of Pugin's drawings for architectural decorative details, furniture and woodwork survive.[64] These, some photographs taken before the building was demolished (plate 64), and the upper corridor which, with its stained glass, was reassembled on the new site as the school chapel, record the importance of Pugin's contributions. They were everywhere strong and original with a forceful individualism, as in the Headmaster's chair, known from its inscription as 'Sapientia', or the stone carvings in the chapel, which give a lively medieval character to the entire building. It is clear that Barry was impressed; he had no hesitation in asking Pugin for his help with the competition for the Houses of Parliament[65] later in the year, and neither did Gillespie Graham.

In 1835 Pugin's life began to change; he had his first experience as an architect when he started to build his own house,[66] St Marie's Grange, near Salisbury, and he was assisting both Charles Barry and Gillespie Graham. On 16 August he wrote to E.J. Willson:[67] 'I am much driven for time, having never had one quarter of the business I

have at present. Drawings and designs to be done comming (sic) in from all quarters but I manage to get through them by keeping them all going on together and leaving nothing quite neglected.' He was at the same time preparing another two pattern books for the decorative arts: *Designs for Iron and Brass Work in the style of the XV and XVI centuries* was published by Ackermann on 1 February 1836 and *Designs for Gold & Silversmiths* was also published by Ackermann on 4 April 1836. Both of these showed more glamorous and unusual objects, and the superb drawings for them survive[68] (plates 332, 333). He advertised them with the hope that 'they will prove equally interesting to the Antiquary, as useful to the Architect and Designer.'[69]

The following year the pattern was similar. He continued to work on the project for the Houses of Parliament after Barry was declared the winner at the end of January; the next step was to provide drawings from which an estimate could be produced. Gillespie Graham also had important schemes in hand, for restorations at Glasgow Cathedral and Holyrood Abbey, for which he needed Pugin's help, but which in fact were never executed. Pugin's drawings for the throne for the

Moderator of the General Assembly in Holyrood Abbey (plate 65) show him bringing together all his recent experience. His major concern, however, was his book of *Contrasts*, with its theme of comparing works of the middle ages with their early nineteenth-century counterparts (plates 193, 196), a subject which had long interested him. He wrote to E.J. Willson on 6 May 1836:[70] 'I am worked up into a fever about my contrasts. I have been indefatigable. Early & late I have worked . . . you will be delighted with the work. The letter press is very severe but not a bit much so.' The book was eventually published at his own expense in Salisbury on 4 August. His text[71] is direct and forceful. He writes from his new standpoint as a Catholic when he describes 'the feelings which produced the great edifices of the Middle Ages', and places the blame for architectural decline on the Reformation, ending with 'the wretched state of architecture at the present day.' This message is pressed home in the illustrations which contrast the beautiful medieval buildings with their mean and inappropriate modern counterparts, and imply the moral worth of the society which produced them. The book certainly established Pugin's reputation as a propagandist for the Gothic and the Catholic. It sold widely[72] and brought him to the attention of influential Catholics. Dr Daniel Rock, then the domestic chaplain to the Earl of Shrewsbury,

wrote[73] to him in August to congratulate him on his book, *Designs for Gold and Silversmiths*, and by the beginning of October he was in contact with the Earl himself,[74] who was to become his major patron.

By his twenty-fifth birthday in March 1837 Pugin was ready to launch himself as an independent architect. In this month he made his first visits to Scarisbrick Hall, Lancashire, where over the next few years he designed substantial alterations and additions (plates 82–5),[75] and to St Mary's College, Oscott, a Catholic school and seminary near Birmingham, a crucial meeting place from which his influence spread rapidly through the Catholic Church,[76] so that by the end of the year he had already designed several new churches. The first phase of his work on the rebuilding of the Houses of Parliament for Charles Barry was at an end[77] though he continued to collaborate with Gillespie Graham.[78] His practical experience with furniture, metalwork and stage sets gave him extraordinary versatility as a designer for the decorative arts. His knowledge of architectural practice had been learnt entirely from first-hand study of medieval examples. These early years provided him with his ability to draw old work and to design new, combined with a religious mission, so that he was uniquely qualified to further the cause of the Gothic Revival, and to give it a moral force.

66.†   Design for *Henry VIII* Act II, Scene iv,
a hall in Blackfriars set for the Trial of the Queen,
tempera with gold (Theatre Museum, London).

CHAPTER THREE

Pugin and the Theatre

LIONEL LAMBOURNE

'Ha! Mr Editor, I have you on the hip. Look to yourself.'[1] The voice is unmistakable – that of Augustus Welby Northmore Pugin enjoying a far from friendly disagreement with the hostile editor of the *Rambler*. Although written twenty years after his close involvement with the stage, Pugin's prose style still displays his love of the drama of the theatre. During the formative years of his youth from the ages of fifteen to twenty, he was in intimate contact with the theatre. Brief though this period was the experiences gained were of crucial importance in determining the directions taken in his later career.

His father, Augustus Charles Pugin's early publications included the famous collaboration with Thomas Rowlandson on the aquatint views in *The Microcosm of London* 1808, among which were depictions of the interiors of twelve London theatres (plate 69).

A number of talented young men studied with the elder Pugin, such as Joseph Nash (1808–78), later a well known artist; Decimus Burton (1800–81), later the architect of the Colosseum, the panoramic entertainment which vied with Pugin's own Diorama; James D'Egville (*c*.1806–post 1860) son of the ballet master at the Italian Opera; and Charles James Matthews (1803–78) the son of the elder Pugin's close friend Charles Matthews, the finest light comic actor of his time who had formed a famous collection of theatrical paintings now in the Garrick Club. To house it the elder Pugin helped Charles James Matthews to design a picture gallery for his father's cottage in Kentish Town frequented by Byron, Scott, Moore, Coleridge, Lamb, Leigh Hunt and other eminent literary figures. After his father's death in 1835 Matthews junior abandoned architecture and

also became a famous comic actor, who, with his wife Madame Vestris, renowned for her interpretation of male roles and beautiful legs, virtually invented the revue form.

At his home the young Pugin would have heard theatrical gossip on weekdays from the Matthewses and on Sundays, accompanied by his sternly evangelical mother, he visited the Hatton Garden Chapel where the great Presbyterian preacher Edward Irving devoted sermons of three hours' duration to such lofty themes as *An Argument for Judgment to Come*, published as a protest against the *Visions of Judgment* of Byron and Shelley.

Although Irving was endowed with a melodious, resonant voice, noble presence, commanding stature and handsome features, the young Pugin loathed 'the long hours of ennui pent up for hours together, in a pew like a cattle-pen when so magnificent a building as Westminster Abbey, with its beautiful and solemn services, was within reach'.[2] The experience led him later to 'always express his unmitigated disgust at the cold and sterile forms of the Scotch Church; and the moment he broke loose from the trammels imposed upon him by his mother, he rushed into the arms of a Church (whose) ceremonies (were) attractive to his imaginative mind'.[3] The oratory of both stage and pulpit were to prove potent influences on the young Pugin. These observations were made by Benjamin Ferrey, Pugin's first biographer, who on a student visit to Paris with Pugin senior sketched the Théâtre des Variétés (plate 67) and the two cylindrical drums of the Parisian panoramas. Panoramas, illusionistic 360° paintings, form with dioramas what may be described as the archaeology of the cinema. A Diorama was a large flat picture with an illusion of depth, capable of

67. *Théâtre des Variétés*, by Benjamin Ferrey, watercolour (Trustees of the Victoria & Albert Museum).

68. Ground plan of the Diorama, by A.C. Pugin (RIBA Drawings Collection, London).

69.† *Covent Garden Theatre*, by A.C. Pugin, coloured aquatint from *The Microcosm of London*

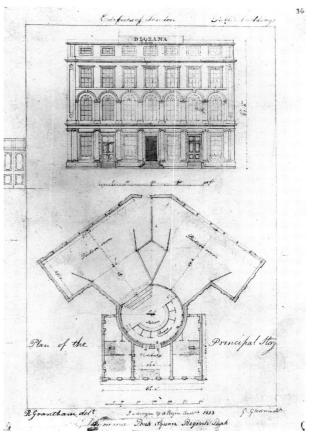

I was on Saturday at the private view of the 'Diorama' – it is a transparency, the spectator in a dark chamber – it is very pleasing & has great illusion – it is without the pale of Art because its object is deception-Claude's never was – or any other great landscape painter's. The style of the pictures is French, which is decidedly against them. Some real stones, as bits of brown paper & a bit of silver lace turned on a wheel . . . – to help. The place was filled with foreigners – & I seemed to be in a cage of magpies.

changes in lighting so dramatic as to alter its whole aspect. It was the idea of Louis Daguerre, an experienced stage designer later to achieve immortality as one of the fathers of photography. Its opening in Paris in 1822 was an immediate sensation, which led Daguerre, whose wife had English connections, the Arrowsmiths, to try and establish a similar exhibition in London. Augustus Charles, who knew the Arrowsmiths and still practised as an architect, was asked to approach his old patron and colleague John Nash, and the Diorama, Augustus Charles's most famous building (which amazingly still stands today, plate 68), was built in a Nash terrace near Regent's Park opening on 23 September, 1823. An early visitor was John Constable (whose agent was also an Arrowsmith). He wrote to his friend Archdeacon Fisher:

As sketches of the stage machinery for the building in his hand survive, it can be assumed that Augustus Welby Northmore, then aged eleven, would have been aware of the attractions staged at the Diorama, – a landscape and an architectural interior were generally shown in tandem, the auditorium bearing the audience revolving from one scene to the next. In the first few years the spectacles were: *The Valley of Sarnen* and *A Chapel in Canterbury Cathedral* 1823, *The Port of Brest* and *Interior of Chartres Cathedral* 1824, *The Ruins of Holyrood Chapel by Moonlight* (plate 70) and a reprise of Chartres Cathedral in 1825 and in 1826 *Roslyn Chapel, effect of Sun* and *The Port of Rouen*.[4]

In 1828, the Diorama's attractions were threatened by a rival establishment, the British Diorama, with paintings by two well known theatrical scene painters – David Roberts, who showed *St George's Chapel, Windsor* and *The Ruins of Tintern Abbey*, and Clarkson Stanfield, who exhibited *The Kent East Indiaman Afire* and *Lago Maggiore* and added a topical note the next year by painting *The Burning of York Minster*. Pugin met Clarkson Stanfield at about this time and they remained close friends for many years, for even in the 1840s Pugin wrote chiding Stanfield for recommending a play which turned out to be 'execrable humbug . . . who ever painted the sets for it ought to be stifled in Priming'.[5]

Given this background it is not surprising that the young Pugin was pre-occupied from boyhood with both the theatre and theatrical gossip. As early as 1822 at the age of ten he had noted precociously in his diary: 'March 23rd. Mr Hughes Ball elopes with Mademoiselle Mercandotti of the King's Theatre'. The subsequent marriage was the talk of London for several weeks, Maria Mercandotti being an accomplished Spanish dancer of great quality, and Hughes Ball one of the richest young men in London, nicknamed 'Golden Ball' and reputed to have lost £45,000 in one night gambling at Wattier's Club in Piccadilly. Throughout the diary for the next ten years Pugin continued to record such gossip, but also information of real interest to the theatrical historian. On Saturday, 26 April 1826, he noted 'TRDL (The Theatre Royal, Drury Lane) Aladdin. Opera. Not successful. The machinery wretchedly worked'. The entry demonstrates Pugin's interest in the complicated machinery used to produce the elaborate scenic effects then in vogue. This led him to experiment by turning the entire upper floor of his parent's house into a miniature theatre for which he designed 'the most exquisite scenery, with . . . every magic change of which stage mechanism is capable . . . every part was so admirably adjusted that the changes in the scenes, wings and sky-pieces were effected with marvellous rapidity, for it was provided with lines, pulleys, grooves, balance weights, machines for descent and ascent, etc.'[6] A notebook contains Pugin's vigorous drawing of a device for raising wings into the flies, the area above the stage concealed by the proscenium arch. He may have been able to solve this problem because of his knowledge of sailing, another early enthusiasm, but one which was to continue throughout his life.

In the real theatres of the Regency, theatrical effects, particularly the craze for dramatic representations of fires and storms, had their dangers. On 11 April 1827, Pugin noted: 'At 1/2 past 1 this

70. *Ruins of Holyrood Chapel, Edinburgh*, by Louis Daguerre, oil on canvas (Walker Art Gallery, Liverpool).

morning the Royalty Theatre was discovered to be on fire and in a very short time was totally destroyed. The fire is supposed to have originated in some sparks from a representation of Mount Vesuvius the previous evening lodging among the scenery. No lives lost.'

While working in the London office of the furniture-makers, Morel and Seddon, for the Wyatville additions to Windsor Castle, Pugin became friendly with a studio assistant, George Dayes, son of Edward Dayes, the famous watercolour painter who taught Turner and Girtin. George Dayes was also employed as scene-shifter at Covent Garden. 'It was through him', Pugin noted 'that I first imbibed that taste for stage machinery and scenic representation to which I afterwards applied myself so closely'.[7] This he did in July 1829 by serving in the perilous role of as a super flyman at the English Opera House in a revival of Weber's opera *Der Freischütz*. To do this job you have to be able to stand on tiny precarious platforms high over the stage and supervise the clear ascent and descent of backcloths and the fact that Pugin could do so tells us that he was both extremely brave with an excellent head for heights, and very strong. Courage of a different sort was called for on 23 November when Pugin 'Began in business for myself in the carving and joining line'.[8] It is possible that these two jobs complemented each other. Later, on 8 October 1829, Pugin summed up his progress 'I first went on the stage at Covent Garden as a stageman for the scenery department, and the Devil's Elixir was the first piece I was regularly in at this house. It was through the perseverance I had to serve as stage carpenter all the season that I acquired that practical part of the stage business which has so materially served me since'.[9]

71. Design for Kenilworth, pencil (RIBA Drawings Collection, London).

72. Zoë Beaupré as Queen Elizabeth, by Alphonse Edouard Chalon, watercolour (Trustees of the Victoria & Albert Museum).

1831 was to be a remarkable year for Pugin, then aged nineteen. In rapid succession his decorative business went bankrupt, and he narrowly escaped imprisonment for debt. He fell in love and married Anne Garnett, the niece of his friend George Dayes. Tragically she died the next year, on 27 May 1832. But while his business ventures failed, his first great chance as a stage designer arose in March 1831. Laporte, manager of the King's Theatre since 1828, had begun a policy of lavishly mounted ballet productions, which heralded the golden age of the romantic ballet starring dancers of the calibre of the famous 'pas de quatre', Taglioni, Grisi, Cerrito and Essler; the male dancer Jules Perrot, known as the Flaxman of the ballet; while the excellent choreographer, Deshayes, and the talented designer, William Grieve, transformed the art of the dance. Grieve was stage designer at the King's Theatre from 1829 until his death in 1844, and founded one of the most famous and versatile family firms of theatrical designers of the nineteenth century.

One of the finest early productions was the ballet *Kenilworth*, choreographed by Deshayes with remarkable fidelity to Sir Walter Scott's romance. 'For this ballet,' Pugin noted, 'I painted two scenes the interior of Cumnor Place and Greenwich Palace with the exception of the backcloth by Mr Grieve. I likewise furnished Documents for

costumes and other scenes of the ballet'.[10] His phrase 'furnished Documents for costume' refers to contemporary attempts to achieve historical accuracy in stage dress by careful research, a process pioneered in the 1820s by the antiquarian author of the first history of costume, James Robinson Planché, who was also Somerset Herald and the author of over fifty extremely funny pantomimes, many frequently revived today by the Players' Theatre.

Alfred Edouard Chalon's vivacious sketch of Zoë Beaupré as Queen Elizabeth in *Kenilworth* (plate 72) provides a rare glimpse of Pugin as costume designer, while his own drawings of Cumnor Place and Greenwich Palace help us to see why this scene made such a powerful impact on the ballet critics of the day (plate 71). It also had the added distinction of introducing ballet to two of the most powerful rulers of the nineteenth century, Queen Victoria, who, as the eleven-year-old Princess, saw it on 19 April, and Napoleon III, then Prince Louis Napoleon, who saw it with his mother on 31 May.

A letter, or rather an inscribed drawing to William Grieve in the Metropolitan Museum, New York (plate 52), demonstrates the enjoyment with which Pugin entered into the world behind the scenes. It shows a proscenium arch, some stage machinery and a self-portrait wearing a cap and holding a paint brush and says 'expect me at 10 on Monday'. While the mock-serious letter is addressed 'To the Celebrated delineator of Kenilworth' and reads 'Dear Sir, I cannot resist the pleasure of your society and that of your aimiable and talented brother. I come. tis not the lucre, tis not the lucre. Fate, I obey thy summons . . . hence away. Your most faithful adjutant A W Pugin'.

Pugin's theatrical activities continued. A fortnight later, on 17 March 1831, at the King's Theatre he recorded: 'L'ultimo Giorno di Pompeii. I assisted Mr W. Grieve in the bringing out of the opera for 10 days'.[11] His friendship with Grieve was to have important results. On 19 May he wrote: 'Began to work on Private Theatre for the Marquis of Stafford recommended by Mr W. Grieve'. This was probably at Stafford House, then a centre for London society. He continues: 'After a week of the greatest exertion, completed the theatre. The play performed was "Hernani" . . . Miss Fanny Kemble playing the heroine . . . the whole went off with great éclat'.[12] This was the first performance in England of Victor Hugo's drama, only a year after its sensational Parisian opening, marred by riots between classical and romantic factions in the audience.

Important though *Kenilworth* was as an event in Pugin's career, the work which was to cast the longest shadow over his later thoughts and works was the production of Shakespeare's *King Henry VIII* put on at Covent Garden on 24 October 1831 with the great stars of the day, Charles Kemble as Henry VIII, Charles Young as Wolsey and Fanny Kemble as Queen Katherine. From surviving playbills (plate 75) we can see that Pugin was one of the Grieve family team. Extensive model scenery and designs have survived which enable us to form a vivid impression of the spectacular stage effects, culminating in the great procession and coronation scene of Queen Anne Boleyn. One particularly notable effect was provided by the moving panorama of London (plate 76), based on Hollar's long *Prospect of London* of 1647. This consisted of a canvas of enormous length which unwound horizontally across the stage to a second concealed spool, while actors mimed rowing a boat out to Henry VIII's ship, the *Royal George*.

One can imagine how exciting it was for the young Pugin to assist either in that moment or to see the stage directions for Act 2 Scene 4 come to life when Queen Katherine is brought to trial in a Hall in Blackfriars, London:

Trumpets, sennet and cornets. Enter two Ver-

gers, with short silver wands; next them, two scribes in the habit of Doctors; after them, the Archbishop of Canterbury alone; after him, the Bishops of Lincoln, Ely, Rochester and Saint Asaph; next them, with some small distance, follows a Gentleman bearing the purse, with the great seal, and a Cardinal's hat; then two Priests, bearing each a silver cross, then a Gentleman Usher bareheaded, accompanied with a Sergeant at Arms bearing a silver mace; then two gentlemen bearing two great silver pillars, after them, side by side, the two Cardinals, Wolsey and Campeius, two Noblemen with the sword and mace. Then enter the King and

73.† Thrones, probably for the trial scene, *Henry VIII* (Theatre Museum, London).

74. *The Trial of Queen Katherine, Henry VIII*, Act II, Scene i, Covent Garden 1831, by Henry Andrews, oil on canvas (The RSC Collection, Royal Shakespeare Theatre).

75.† Playbill for *Henry VIII* (Theatre Museum, London).

76.† Studies for a Panorama of the city of London, based on Wenceslas Hollar's, for *Henry VIII*, 8 panels (Theatre Museum, London).

Queen with their Trains. The king takes place under the cloth of state; the two Cardinals sit under him as Judges. The Queen takes place some distance from the King. The Bishops place themselves on each side the court, in manner of a consistory; below them the Scribes etc etc. (plates 66, 73)

A painting by Henry Andrews (plate 74) gives a striking presentation of the scene, and also illustrates the scale of Covent Garden and the practice of playing right down stage among the audience even after the demise of the proscenium arch doors. The play, then as now rarely performed, presents the historical moment which led to the foundation of the Anglican church and the dispossession of abbeys, cathedrals and monasteries. Such themes were always present in Pugin's mind, who died leaving unfinished *An Apology for the Separated Church of England since the reign of Henry VIII*. It is also interesting to note his use of the theme of Henry VIII and his wives in the King's Room at Scarisbrick Hall between 1837 and 1840 (plate 85).

The ability to be adaptable is vital for a successful career in the theatre, and two months later Pugin was at work on the less congenial task of painting the scenery for the pantomime *Hop O' My Thumb And His Brothers* which opened at Covent Garden on 26 December 1831. This was to be the last English production of which documentary evidence survives of Pugin's involvement. But according to his son Edward,[13] Pugin also designed scenery for two operas produced in Paris, *Comte Ory* by Rossini 1828 and *La Juive* by Halévy 1835, although by the latter date he had completely stopped theatrical work in England and this assertion must be considered unlikely.

A sheet of designs, relating to an unspecified production, shows why the stylistic versatility so vitally important for the successful stage designer ultimately proved repugnant to Pugin, leading him to abandon the theatre. His natural bent for the Gothic style is apparent in the first design, but theatrical necessity then drove him to the strange mélange of styles in later variations of the central feature of this set, the fountain, which goes through a weird mixture of Romanesque, Baroque, and late eighteenth-century French classicism.

Why did Pugin abandon the stage? In a letter to Willson dated 26 Febuary 1833 he writes 'after mature consideration and consulting my best friends I have resolved to give up my theatrical connection altogether and to devote *myself entirely* to the pursuit of Gothic architecture.'[14]

Perhaps the greatest lesson the impetuous young man had learned from his work as a theatrical designer was the discipline necessary for achieving pragmatic solutions for the difficult design problems inherent in working to theatrical deadlines. This was invaluable training for a man who in 1844 opened three new churches (one a cathedral) within eight days.

More directly it is possible to relate the stage commissions to 'provide documents' for Kenilworth and the surviving scenic maquettes for Henry VIII to the remarkable 'ideal schemes' – a number of small illuminated books intended as devout exercises in recreating the romance of past eras which include some drawings of extreme theatricality (see chapter 2). Two of the books are entitled *Le Chasteau*, of 1832, an ideal château in the style of François I, and *The Shrine* of 1833, an imaginary edifice to St Edmund. *The Procession* from the latter work might almost be a scene from some ideal romantic theatrical peformance, like the great series of productions of Shakespeare's works staged by Charles Keane at Her Majesty's in the 1850s. Certainly both the *Bird's Eye View of the Château* (plate 58) and *The View of an Imaginary Town* bear a striking resemblance to theatrical back drops, the latter in particular possessing a strong compositional resemblance to the moving panorama for *Henry VIII*.

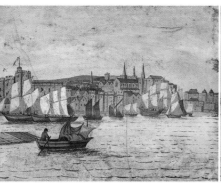

Another benefit from Pugin's training as a theatrical designer was the development of the eclectic versatility which is apparent in his best known book, his great satire, *Contrasts*, published in 1836, which parallels the architecture of the fifteenth and nineteenth centuries, and marks the start of the chief phase in Pugin's career (plates 193, 196).

On 16 October 1834, fire, which had burnt down so many Regency theatres, destroyed the old Palace of Westminster. This gave Pugin the opportunity to devise, no longer the ephemeral scenery of theatrical settings, but the romantic interiors of London's most impressive Victorian silhouette, the new Palace of Westminster. The dramatic intensity of the interiors reflects the ongoing drama of the Houses of Lords and Commons, which at the annual opening of Parliament by the Queen come together in a procession which may owe something to Pugin's theatrical gift for marshalling crowds.

But the most lasting and important result of Pugin's early exposure to the theatre was its influence on the prose style of his ten books. In 1851 (a year before he died) in his *Treatise on Chancel Screens and Rood Lofts*, he was still capable of writing an electric description of the sacking of a chancel screen by Protestant zealots that reads like the stage directions for a sensational melodrama. His love for the proscenium arch of the theatre had been exalted into a passion for the rood screen that framed the Sacred Drama. The present writer was fortunate enough to witness the celebration of mass at St Chad's in Birmingham before the removal of the Rood Screen, and the effect of the Priest and acolytes emerging and retreating from and to its shelter, was an unforgettable experience, providing the congregation with ritual of an effective and highly theatrical nature.

In his later years Pugin lost virtually all contact with the theatre, noting only one rare exception in his diary, when he visited Covent Garden on 14 May 1841, where his old family friend Charles James Matthews starred as Mr Dazzle in Dion Boucicault's *London Assurance*. Pugin dined with another old friend, William Grieve, at his home on 22 October 1844, and sadly noted his death three weeks later on 12 November.

Today, film stars and architects alike suffer from the continuing presence of their earliest mistakes and both professions are not short of candid friends ready to point out such errors. So it was in Pugin's time and an accusation of theatricality was always a convenient stick with which to beat him and his work.

'A PROTESTANT' in 1836 wondered whether Pugin's conversion to Roman Catholicism was due to '. . . an habituated fondness for STAGE *effect*? for splendid mummery?'[15] While for Richard Simpson, in 1861 Pugin's mind could never 'emancipate itself from its slavery to theatrical effect'[16] and James Fergusson in 1862 considered that 'the true bent of Pugin's mind was towards the theatre; . . . throughout life, the theatrical was the one and the only branch of his art which he perfectly understood.'[17] These remarks are pejorative in intention, but the dramatic power of Pugin's cathedrals, churches and Palace of Westminster does indeed owe something to his work for the theatre.

CHAPTER FOUR

Domestic Architecture

ALEXANDRA WEDGWOOD

Pugin is not known for his domestic architecture. It has never been studied in detail and its documentation[1] is more difficult than that of his religious architecture. Alton Towers, the house which would seem to be most obviously attached to his name, is one where he was working within earlier buildings, mostly by providing interior fittings which have been subsequently destroyed. In others major alterations were made later by E.W. Pugin, as at Scarisbrick Hall. Elsewhere there has simply been a mistaken attribution in the twentieth century, as at Albury Park.[2] All this has confused the appreciation of this section of Pugin's oeuvre. This contribution should only be considered as preliminary. It is not comprehensive, but will try to show the great originality, importance and influence of Pugin's domestic architecture.

The first building that Pugin built was in fact his own house, St Marie's Grange, Alderbury, Wiltshire. When his parents died he had moved his young family to Ramsgate to be near his aunt. Following her death in September 1834 and the inheritance of some money, his first thought seems to have been to build a house for himself. His choice of a site near Salisbury was no doubt influenced by the presence of a great medieval cathedral nearby and a number of friends in the area. On 1 January 1835 he wrote[3] from Ramsgate to his friend E.J. Willson:

> I have at length made a purchase of my land, and by the time you receive this the masons' mallets will be working large blocks of stone into doorheads, jambs, mullions etc. etc. It is a most beautiful piece of ground, close to Salisbury commanding a magnificent view of the cathedral and city with the river Avon win-

ding through the beautiful valley. Under me is Longford Castle, seat of Lord Radnor, with its turrets and chimneyshafts rising among the venerable oaks and elms. This piece of ground which is 370 ft long by 280 wide is on a declivity bounded at bottom by the river Avon, at top by the Southampton road by which passes the Southampton and Bath coaches 6 times a day.

The reconstruction of Pugin's original plan (plate 79), which has been comprehensively changed, has been worked out by the present owner,[4] an architect who has made a special study of the house. His interpretation of the building is basically that given in what follows. The site is beautiful but difficult, because the steep slope to the river meant that, in order to obtain the views that Pugin wanted, the house had to be placed very near the road. His drive, however, came in below and around the house, with the principal view of it from the south-east where the asymmetrical composition is seen at its best (plates 78 and 80). It is at once obvious that Pugin has produced a radically unusual plan and employed an unusual material, red brick, for his small Gothic country-house. Pugin's pioneering use of red brick for his houses from this date should be stressed; the Red House, Bexley Heath, was built by Philip Webb for William Morris twenty-five years later. St Marie's Grange was not based on any particular medieval building, indeed the type of house belongs to the post-medieval period, but it was also quite different from any contemporary building. He has approached the problem in a personal and new way, desiring romantic and picturesque qualities in the composition but also seriously respecting materials and functions. It also has all a young man's disregard for practicalities. His plan was an

77. The Grange, Ramsgate, view of the garden front, 1843–4. The one-storey extension on the left was added by E.W. Pugin in the 1860s.

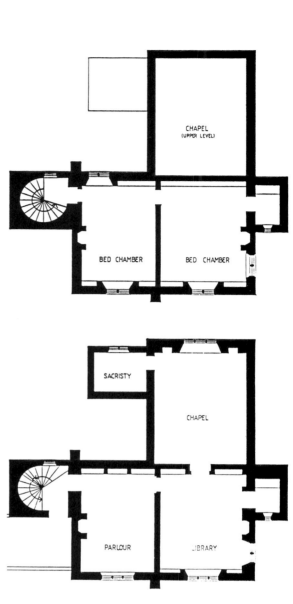

78. St Marie's Grange, Alderbury, from the south-west, watercolour, c.1835 (Private Collection).

79. St Marie's Grange, reconstruction of the plan in 1835.

80. St Marie's Grange, photograph showing the major alterations of the 1840s.

L shape with the entrance at the end of one wing, where the only stair, a spiral one, was placed. There were no corridors, and all the rooms opened out of one another. The spiral stair finishes in a square tower which rises to the top of the roof. It is balanced on the other side of the building with the garderobe turret which has strategically placed windows looking at Salisbury cathedral. The main rooms were all on the first floor to which the approach from outside was up a flight of steps[5] in the bank below the road to a drawbridge and through the spiral stair. The paraphernalia of defence in the building may have been in part a fantasy of what Pugin felt was needed in a medieval building or in part protection that Pugin felt has required for the largest room in his house, the chapel. He planned his chapel with its sacristy even before his official conversion to Catholicism, and with its stone traceried three-light east window and belfry it formed the chief feature of the principal view of the house. He also announced its presence and his authorship emphatically, even if in Latin, on a carved stone panel which was originally placed conspicuously on its south wall between two 'M's picked out in black brick which also recall its dedication to St Marie. (Pugin used this form of the name more or less consistently throughout his life.) He was not afraid to be controversial. Perhaps he thought he might need to defend himself; more likely he wanted to draw attention to himself and his architecture.

When Pugin wrote to Willson in January he was anticipating quite a slow building period during which time he would himself execute carvings in the chapel. Nothing in Pugin's life, however, happened slowly and on 17 July 1835 he wrote again to Willson when he was busy fitting up the house:[6] 'My house is now nearly compleated and is in every part a compleat building of the 15th cent. The minutest details have been attended to and the whole effect is very good . . . the great thickness of the walls . . . the approach over a drawbridge, the chapel with its little belfry, the antient letters worked in bricks in the walls, the gilt vanes on the roof, and the small windows all have astonished the people about here beyond measure.' Pugin claimed that the stone was the same as that which had been used at 'the cathedral at Sarum'. The steep slate roofs to the main wing surmounted by cresting and vanes at the apexes have a decidedly French feel to them. The sacristy and the garderobe turret had pyramidal roofs. Apart from the chapel window, which has been removed, all the windows were square headed with mullions and uncusped lights.

Internally there are some original carved stone fireplaces and doorways and splendid timbers to the ceilings. There is also a little stained glass, very similar in style to his work at King Edward VI School, Birmingham. If there was ever glass in the chapel window it has gone, and if there was any panelling it has been removed and the painted friezes shown in a watercolour (plate 81) no longer survive. It seems clear, however, that Pugin's original idea that he should himself decorate his own house disappeared as his architectural practice suddenly expanded and he needed to travel constantly in the course of his work. Salisbury was no longer a convenient place for him to be; moreover his wife found the situation unhealthy[7] and the house with only two bedrooms became too small when his third child was born in October 1836.

81.   St Marie's Grange, view from the library to the chapel, watercolour, c.1835, present whereabouts unknown, reproduced from S. Ayling, *Photographs from Sketches by A.W.N. Pugin*, 1865.

In September 1837 he took lodgings in Chelsea and St Marie's Grange was abandoned. It was eventually put up for sale but its strange character meant that there were no buyers. In April 1841 Pugin stayed in Salisbury for three days and it seems quite possible that he was arranging for additions to be made to the house.[8] The major alteration was to add an entrance staircase hall and corridors, thus turning the L plan into a rectangle and neatly removing the main inconveniences of the earlier plan. Such a staircase hall became a favourite with Pugin, as in his own second house or at Oswaldcroft, Liverpool. At St Marie's Grange great care was taken with the original features with every window and doorway being moved and reset, a concern which seems to indicate Pugin's own hand. The new circular corner turret perhaps depended on designs which Pugin made for the stables at Scarisbrick Hall, and has a northern European character. Though Pugin may have made some drawings for these alterations it does not seem probable that he carried them out. In particular the added bay windows are not like his work.

Pugin's first independent architectural commission, which became a very large one, was for Scarisbrick Hall, Lancashire. Here he was remodelling an existing building, but was able to draw together his knowledge of medieval architecture and the decorative arts and ideas from his own

82. Scarisbrick Hall, perspective drawing of the entrance façade, pencil, 1836 (RIBA Drawings Collection). This clock tower, later replaced by E.W. Pugin, is a prototype for the one at the Palace of Westminster.

83. Scarisbrick Hall, the garden front, showing the porch which Pugin added *c*.1838. The later tower can be seen in the background.

84. Scarisbrick Hall, the Great Hall, showing the two-storey screens passage at the entrance end, and one of the oriels, early 1840s. The woodwork includes many earlier carvings, mostly Flemish, fifteenth to seventeenth centuries. The metalwork balustrade of the first-floor oriel is by E.W. Pugin.

ideal schemes[9] to create some splendid and inventive architecture. Scarisbrick Hall was the old seat of the Scarisbricks, a recusant Catholic family, and may have begun as a large sixteenth-century half-timbered manor-house. At the beginning of the nineteenth century the house had probably been neglected and substantial improvements were made between 1813 and 1816 by Thomas Rickman for Thomas Scarisbrick. It seems certain[10] that Rickman refaced the house with stone, made several new windows, some in cast iron, and added lots of Gothic details. It also seems most likely that Rickman created the great hall and its unusual arrangement of bay windows. In 1833 Thomas Scarisbrick died and was succeeded by Pugin's patron, Charles (1800–60), who was eventually to become an eccentric recluse. He seems to have immediately set about building up a collection of antique objects and paintings.[11] He bought chiefly in London, where the antique dealer Edward Hull of Wardour Street was his major supplier for the interior furnishings of Scarisbrick Hall. It seems most probable therefore that Hull[12] introduced Pugin to Scarisbrick. The original commission, in 1836, was for minor work, a roofed garden seat and the fireplace in the great hall. On 14 March 1837 Pugin visited Scarisbrick for the first time. He returned there at the end of the month and on 23 April he wrote in his diary[13] 'Began Mr. Scarisbrick's house.' Pugin must have relished the opportunity to work on the ancestral home of a rich Catholic patron who was an enthusiastic collector of medieval objects, and Scarisbrick appreciated his young architect and kept many of his drawings.[14]

His first ideas for the house were clear and deci-sive and were to a large extent carried out. They are recorded in some of the finest examples of his draughtsmanship. The pencil drawing of the entrance façade (plate 82) shows that his ideal for an 'Old English Catholic mansion' was already established. It also shows the best existing view of his scheme for the clock tower, generally considered to be the prototype for that at the Houses of Parliament. This tower was destroyed in E.W. Pugin's later additions to the house, and unfortunately it is not known how close this design was to the executed work. Also it may be assumed that the handsome Decorated windows divided by buttresses which can be seen in the drawing projecting eastward from the tower were those of a chapel. Pugin must have felt that such a chapel was an essential part of his plan for this house, where a room had been used for Catholic worship throughout the seventeenth and eighteenth centuries, but he presumably could not persuade Scarisbrick to build it.

Pugin's architectural work began with adding details to enliven the exterior and major reconstructions to the eastern or service wing. A good example of the former is the garden porch which Pugin added (plate 83) to the earlier dull façade. It consists of two canted turrets either side of the door with a small oriel between them on the first floor. This feature with its bold and striking clear lines shows all the strength and simplicity of his earliest group of drawings, also seen in his design for the kitchen. The drawing shows a square kitchen, whereas the one executed was octagonal and derived more closely from the abbot's kitchen at Glastonbury and from the kitchen in Pugin's own imaginary design of 1833 for a deanery.[15] His

85.   Scarisbrick Hall, the King's Room, *c.*1838. The paintings of Henry VIII's family are probably by E.T. Parris.

wall with an open space next to the great hall (plate 84). This both provides borrowed light to the great hall and also easier access to bedrooms. At the western end of the corridor Pugin brilliantly fitted in the main staircase into a small rectangle, also lit from above. The design for it is dated 1840. As Mark Girouard has pointed out,[16] it is a highly personal version of the continuous newel staircase of the early seventeenth century.

Pugin's ability clearly tempted Scarisbrick and the commission quickly expanded to include elaborate settings for Scarisbrick's great collection in the western half of the house, which was marked 'all this part of the house unchanged' in the first plan of 1837. Though only those wood carvings which were built into the fabric now remain, a tiny part of Scarisbrick's original collection, they still produce an effect of overwhelming richness. It is therefore important to emphasise Pugin's purely architectural achievements in the house, as distinct from the extraordinary virtuosity with which he welded together the varied carvings of different dates and styles, mostly late fifteenth- to seventeenth-century Flemish pieces. It seems probable that most of the carvings were fitted into their settings in Hull's London workshop.[17] In the Oak room and the King's room (plate 85) it is often difficult to differentiate between Pugin's framework and the older carvings. The end result, as in the chimneypiece in the library (now the Red Drawing Room), does not belong to any one period. As Mark Girouard has commented,[18] 'When one tries to visualise the surviving Pugin work at Scarisbrick as the setting of a vanished collection, one ends up with something not in the least bit medieval in feeling, but more like the sumptuous *bric-à-brac* backgrounds of some of Rembrandt's paintings, or the variegated chiaroscuro and multitude of incident in Charles Scarisbrick's favourite paintings by John Martin. It was in fact an antiquary's hide-out, a glorified junkbox put together with jackdaw rather than connoisseur enthusiasm.'

The densely covered rooms in the west wing reveal as much about Scarisbrick as about Pugin and were probably their first interiors in the house. The major reconstruction of the great hall, however, does not seem to have been started until 1840 and a drawing for the louvre is dated 1845. It contains more characteristic Pugin work, both internally and externally. There are many delightful details, like the bosses, the pious texts and the shields hanging on the branches of oak trees which decorate the deep mouldings of the arches to the bay windows. Another feature in the great hall and

design for the stable court with its steeply roofed octagonal corner towers and robust gatehouse, which is sometimes attributed to E.W. Pugin, shows the strong influence of his recent visit to Nuremberg. His most inventive design, however, was his solution to the problem of lighting the two main corridors in the house, planned to run one above the other. His idea was to have a skylight in the roof and to make the floor of the first floor corridor half the width of that below so that the light would penetrate through the open wooden framework to the ground floor. In the design the corridors are shown as being only in the eastern half of the main block with the upper one placed in the centre of the space as a bridge. As executed they run the full length of the main block and the first floor corridor runs alongside the northern corridors which must be entirely his is the stunning mosaic floor with its lovely design and colours. Later he always used Minton's encaustic tiles and he made very little use of this technique, but here it is most successful.

At the outset of the commission Pugin travelled to Scarisbrick regularly, but by 1842 his visits became less frequent. A letter from Pugin to Scarisbrick,[19] written on 1 March 1844 following Pugin's visit to the house at the end of February 1844, is full of criticism of the slow and inadequate work being done on the roof by only two workmen. There are strong hints that Pugin gave Scarisbrick special terms when he started the commission as an unknown architect: 'Things are very different with me than formerly. I have a great business and my time is very valuable. I cannot look after work for the mere cost of the drawings but I would put you to as little expense as possible, but really in the way things are going on they are working badly for both sides for it is impossible to get such a great work executed as your hall without proper men and proper superintendance.' His last visit to Scarisbrick was on 13 September 1845 when he probably made his final drawing for the louvre. At this time he was working hard on the designs for the House of Lords. One wonders how he then viewed the extravagance of his earlier work, but he was clearly still proud of his design for the hall. In the letter quoted he wrote: 'I have my heart and soul in the thing and could fairly cry to see it go on so badly.'

Contemporary with the first work at Scarisbrick Hall, and showing many fascinating stylistic similarities to it, were the additions made by Gillespie Graham at Taymouth Castle in Perthshire between 1838 and 1842. The main block of this great pile was made for the first Marquess of Breadalbane by Archibald and James Elliot between 1806 and 1810, with a dramatic central staircase tower and the main rooms on the first floor. A long straggling east wing was added by William Atkinson after 1818, and between 1827 and 1828 he also gothicised and altered the west wing which had originally been built by William Adam. In 1834 the first Marquess died and in 1837 the second Marquess decided that he wanted a library, calling in Gillespie Graham to enlarge and redesign the west wing. The evidence that Pugin helped him is incontrovertible. Pugin made a list in his diary of 'Drawings sent 19th April' 1837, which are all relevant for this scheme and for which he was paid £25 4s. These drawings must have represented the first ideas. He further noted two long visits from Gillespie Graham between 30

86. Taymouth Castle, Perthshire, the Banner Hall, showing one of the screens on either side of the south window, c.1839.

September and 18 October 1837 and from 20 to 28 March 1838 when he wrote in his diary 'Mr Graham left. Paid 40£.' These visits must have been principally concerned with the re-modelling at Taymouth, although the earlier one would also have included detailed discussion about proposed work at Glasgow Cathedral.[20] They show how the two men collaborated: Gillespie Graham must have brought with him survey plans of the site; together they discussed the design and Pugin produced scaled drawings. He never visited the place during construction, but may have seen the finished work while in Scotland in August 1842.

Early in May 1838 Gillespie Graham was able to write[21] to Lord Breadalbane saying that he was about to send elevations of the west wing. He created an ingenious link building between the main block and the west wing, containing on the first floor the Grand, or Great Gothic Hall, which became known as the Banner Hall after Queen Victoria's visit of 1842. The southern end of this room has two matching richly carved woodwork screens forming splayed compartments to either side of a great Perpendicular window (plate 86). This clever design, a good example of the theatrical effects at which Gillespie Graham excelled, masks to one side the space occupied by the corner turret to the main block and to the other hides the entrance to the Gallery and the Library (plate 87). The perpendicular window is repeated at the opposite end of the room. On 12 November 1838 Gillespie Graham wrote to Sir William Drummond Stewart:[22]

87. Taymouth Castle, Perthshire, the Library, with fittings designed by Pugin c.1837 and executed by Trotters of Edinburgh, c.1839–40.

This Grand Hall will afford a splendid access to the Gallery and all the apartments in the Wing. The external appearance of this portion of the building is intended to convey the idea of the Domestic Chapel. The ends are fitted with Rich Gothic windows and each surmounted with a handsome cross . . . The Old Library is considerably enlarged and to be fitted up in the richest Gothic style and in place of the Tea Caddy appearance which this building formerly exhibited, it has now the effect of a grand Gothic Tower of past centuries. The under tier windows and all the details of the Building are taken from an old castle in Normandy.

The exterior of the Banner Hall with its two great traceried windows and octagonal turret at the rear shows characteristic work by Pugin but more distinctive and close to Scarisbrick are the elaborate interiors. Contemporaries[23] considered the gem of the castle to be the Library. It is a room where every surface is ornamented, with a blue and gold ceiling divided by oak ribs and carved panelling on every wall. As at Scarisbrick, many antique fragments, both wood carving and stained glass, were incorporated in the new work.[24] These pieces may, again as at Scarisbrick, have been provided by a London antique dealer, but no documentation for them has as yet been found. A letter including an estimate for the fitting up of the Library exists.[25] It came from George Potts, who worked for Trotters, the important Edinburgh

interior decorators. This firm seems to have been transformed under the combined influence of Gillespie Graham's enthusiasm and Pugin's drawings. In 1838 T.F. Dibdin gave an ecstatic account[26] of the oak carvings that it was producing for the chapel of Heriot's Hospital to Gillespie Graham's designs. One of Pugin's drawings, probably made in 1835, for some panelling in the chapel survives[27] in albums which originate from Trotter's workshop. In the same place is an elevation, undoubtedly by Pugin, for the fireplace of the Library and copies of his drawings for other work at Taymouth.[28] It is fascinating to see how faithfully Trotter's craftsmen have been able to interpret Pugin's design for the fireplace and its overmantel, where there are only minor differences between the drawing and the executed work. Inevitably, however, in other places Pugin's work was misunderstood or modified by subsequent designs, possibly made to suit the patron's wishes. This may explain the untypical but magnificent fireplace in the Banner Hall which is made of the local blue chlorite stone, and the somewhat awkward details of the doors to the Library. Also in the panelling in the Great Dining Room Pugin's heraldic birds have been interpreted naturalistically and do not integrate with their backgrounds in the way that Pugin would have intended. As in all their collaborations, except that at Murthly,[29] Pugin's contribution remained entirely hidden from everyone except Gillespie Graham. It is astonishing that so much of Pugin's style survived this treatment.

The Taymouth commission was a most lavish one: between 1838 and 1842 the expenditure on the alterations amounted to £13,000, and Gillespie Graham's fee for the designs and working drawings amounted to £650.[30] Also at Taymouth Castle in 1842 was J.G. Crace, redecorating the early nineteenth-century rooms in the main block and painting and furnishing Gillespie Graham's work in anticipation of the visit of Queen Victoria. His contacts with Pugin are fully documented from the beginning of 1844.[31] Crace was responsible for plaster-work, papering, painting, gilding, brass-work and upholstery, as well as the supply of tapestries and armour. The accounts[32] amount to £6671. The heraldic painting that Crace carried out in the Banner Hall is so close to Pugin's ideas that it seems inconceivable that it was not done to his design. The two men probably already knew each other in London. It is also noteworthy that in the Drawing Room at Taymouth where Crace was independent of Gillespie Graham his painting is in a quite different 'Gothic Arabesque' style. However, the plasterwork in those rooms decorated by Crace shows some understanding of Pugin's medievalism.

A new type of domestic building confronted Pugin when he started to design the Bishop's House, Birmingham in 1840 (plates 88 and 89).[33] Like the Cathedral of St Chad, which was almost opposite and which had been begun the previous year, it was built of brick with stone dressings and was in a similar Flemish or North German style. Pugin had determined from the start that his church should advertise itself by its unusual character, and the Bishop's House had obviously followed in the same style. About his first scheme of June 1837 he wrote:[34] 'I have adopted a foreign style of pointed architecture because it is both cheap and effective and likewise because it is totally different from any *protestant* erection.' Little thought had been given to residences for Catholic priests in England for many years, and Pugin turned to medieval examples which 'exhibited a solid solemn and scholastic character that bespoke them at once to be the habitations of men who were removed far beyond the ordinary pursuits of life.'[35] He produced a most sophisticated and dense plan and, by intelligent use of the falling site, he obtained a lot of accommodation for an economical outlay. The plan provided for building to be placed on three sides of a courtyard, with the entrance into a low walled passage on the fourth. All the main rooms were on the first floor. This compact plan was very suitable for its urban setting and certainly influenced William Butterfield when, from 1850, he came to design All Saints, Margaret Street, London, with its vicarage and choir school all built in brick and set around a courtyard. The structure, as with almost all Pugin's Catholic buildings, had to be economical, and the composition depended on the frank expression of the various elements of the design, the three-light traceried windows to the hall and chapel, bay windows to the important rooms, staircase tower and chimneystacks. Decoration on the exterior was minimal, with a very small amount of carved stone and the initials of Thomas Walsh, the Bishop who had commissioned the house and the cathedral, worked into the walls with vitrified bricks. In the interior (plate 236) Pugin managed to introduce some panelling, carving, furniture and painted decoration and stained glass through the generosity of benefactors. The Bishop's House must have been both an attractive and efficient building. Its destruction for road widening in the early 1960s was a grievous loss.

From the time of the Bishop's House, project-

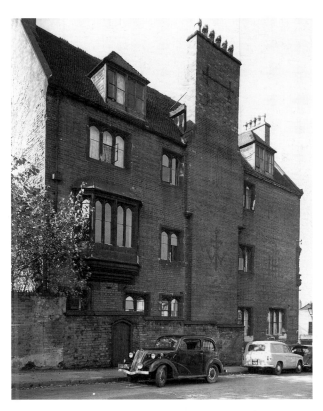

88. The Bishop's House, Birmingham, side elevation, 1840 (demolished 1960s).

89. The Bishop's House, Birmingham, plan and entrance façade engraved in *The Present State of Ecclesiastical Architecture in England*, 1843.

ing chimneystacks are nearly always a major feature of Pugin's domestic architecture. He recommended them specifically, in connection with collegiate buildings, in the main exposition of his architectural theory, *The True Principles of Pointed or Christian Architecture*, which was published in 1841. He stated the practical reasons of the gain

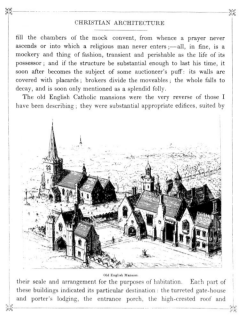

fill the chambers of the mock convent, from whence a prayer never ascends or into which a religious man never enters;—all, in fine, is a mockery and thing of fashion, transient and perishable as the life of its possessor; and if the structure be substantial enough to last his time, it soon after becomes the subject of some auctioneer's puff: its walls are covered with placards; brokers divide the moveables; the whole falls to decay, and is soon only mentioned as a splendid folly.

The old English Catholic mansions were the very reverse of those I have been describing; they were substantial appropriate edifices, suited by

Old English Mansion

their scale and arrangement for the purposes of habitation. Each part of these buildings indicated its particular destination: the turreted gate-house and porter's lodging, the entrance porch, the high-crested roof and

90. 'Old English Mansion', engraved in *The True Principles of Pointed or Christian architecture*, 1841.

91. Detail from 'The Consistent Principles of Old Domestick Architecture applied to Modern Street Buildings', in *An Apology for the Revival of Christian Architecture*, 1843.

92. The Gate House, Oxenford Farm, Surrey, 1842.

G. EDWARDS, GROCER AND TEA DEALER.

of space, added stability, and avoidance of fires in roofs and then added an aesthetic reason: 'A great variety of light and shadow, and a succession of bold features are gained in the building.'[36] In the engraving that he gave of an 'Old English Mansion'[37] (plate 90), he showed these chimneystacks in very prominent positions. As with churches, Pugin felt that all parts of a house should express their function: 'not masked or concealed under one monotonous front, but by their variety in form and outline increasing the effect of the building.'[38] This message was as influential as it was with churches. Butterfield's design for the vicarage at Coalpit Heath, Gloucestershire, in 1844 has been called an architectural land-mark,[39] but all its elements, the simple projecting porch, the tall battered chimney stack, the ample gabled roof and bay windows followed directly from Pugin's examples. It also led on to the domestic work of G.E. Street and Philip Webb.

In his next book, *An Apology for the Revival of Christian Architecture*, which was written two years later, Pugin gave more advice on how to adapt Gothic to the nineteenth century. He was anxious to show that the style could be practical: 'Any modern invention which conduces to comfort, cleanliness, or durability, should be adopted by the consistent architect.'[40] He advocated the use of brick in towns. 'There is no reason in the world why noble cities, combining all possible convenience of drainage, water-courses and conveyance of gas, may not be erected in the most consistent and yet Christian character. *Every building that is*

treated naturally, without disguise or concealment, cannot fail to look well.'[41] The accompanying illustration (plate 91) showed very effective elevations for urban architecture, and makes one wish that Pugin had had more opportunities of this kind. Unfortunately it is not known if he gothicised the street façade of 42 Cheyne Walk, London, where he lived between 1841 and 1844. The charming front elevation that he created for 10 Cheyne Walk was, however, recorded before its demolition.[42]

In the same book, Pugin pursued his ideas with reference to vernacular architecture: '*In matters of ordinary use, a man must go out of his way to make a bad thing:* hence, in some of the rural districts, where workmen had not been poisoned by modern ideas, barns, sheds &s were built and framed, till very lately, on the true old principles, with braces, knees and the high pitch.'[43] Pugin did in fact at this period receive a commission for just such work when he designed a group of farm buildings at Oxenford Grange, then part of the Peper Harow estate, for Lord Midleton. The delightful results, built in the local Bargate stone and still in use for their original purpose, completely justify Pugin's theory of 'Natural Architecture'. The simple large barn is particularly splendid, and relies for its effect entirely on its proportions and materials (plates 93). A gatehouse forms part of the group (plate 92). It is Pugin's picturesque version of the lodge which, though more obviously contrived than the farm buildings, could still be explained in functional terms with some symbolical decoration. Pugin designed a number of similar gatehouses, the earlier brick ones at Oscott College and two later ones to Alton Towers, of stone. His simple

red brick school at Spetchley, Worcestershire, of 1841, belongs to the same group of designs for vernacular buildings.

Nearly all Pugin's patrons came from a very small circle connected with the Catholic aristocracy. Captain John Hubert Washington Hibbert bought the estate of Bilton Grange near Rugby when in 1839 he married Julia Mary Magdalen, the daughter of Sir Henry Tichbourne. She was the widow of Colonel Charles Talbot, and their son was the heir to the sixteenth Earl of Shrewsbury, which explains their choice of Pugin as their architect. There is surprisingly little information about this large commission in Pugin's diaries, but he visited Rugby on 12 October 1841. This date probably marked its start, but it may have got under way slowly, as Pugin wrote to Lord Shrewsbsury on 14 February 1844:[44] 'I am stopping with Captain Hibbert and arranging his proposed wing.' The balustrade of the terrace and the clock on the entrance tower are dated 1846, by which time the structure, built by George Myers, was presumably complete. The interior decoration was carried out by J.G. Crace from about 1846 until 1848, when the sum of £1300 is shown for it in their accounts.[45] Pugin exhibited a painting of the house at the Royal Academy in 1849, but its whereabouts is not now known.

The plan is odd, with a huge addition made to a low undistinguished older house. Pugin is said to have found Hibbert 'a most difficult client',[46] quarrelling with both Pugin and Myers, altering the plans and refusing to spend money. There is probably much truth in the account given in the *Illustrated London News* in 1855:[47] 'The general design of the house was Captain Hibbert's own, and the details were carried out under the personal superintendance of the late lamented Mr Pugin, who justly considered the interior one of his chefs-d'oeuvre.' The exterior is of red brick and stone dressings with Hibbert's monogram frequently picked out in black bricks. There is an impressive tall entrance tower with the gabled great hall and originally a small chapel (since rebuilt) to its right, forming one side of the entrance court. Behind the entrance there lies a large L-shaped building containing the main reception rooms, which overlook the garden. A great gallery runs the full length of the house and connects with the older building at its far end. A small office courtyard lay behind the great hall and chapel, and two sides of a vast stable yard beyond that, with Pugin's kitchen and its splendid battered chimneystack linking the two. On the garden side of the stable yard range is a long conservatory which seems also to be to Pugin's design.[48] The interiors still retain much fine woodwork (plates 94, 95), fireplaces, encaustic tiles, stained glass and painted decoration, full of references to the Hibbert and Tichbourne families and also to St Hubert, Hibbert's patron saint. When seen complete with their original wallpaper, furniture and lightings all by Pugin, they must have been magnificent. Particularly successful are the interconnecting library and drawing-room.

Pugin's contribution to the architecture of Alton Towers, the seat of his principal patron, John Talbot, sixteenth Earl of Shrewsbury, was

93. The Barn, Oxenford Farm, and a detail of the construction of the door.

94. Bilton Grange, near Rugby, part of the main staircase.

95. Bilton Grange, fireplace and overmantel in the former drawing room, executed by Crace, c.1846.

limited. His first visit there was at the end of August 1837 and by that date all the major construction had taken place. A contemporary account related how Charles, the fifteenth Earl, decided to make Alton Abbey, as it was then called, his principal seat:[49] 'he made considerable additions to the mansion, to make it fit for the accommodation of his establishment. These additions being made at different periods, and by different architects, as necessity or convenience required, and without any general design, its appearance is perhaps more picturesque than symmetrical.' John, the sixteenth Earl, succeeded his uncle in 1827: 'Finding the mansion too small for his family and retinue, he built the noble series of galleries, with the immense wing containing the state apartments, and the beautiful chapel.'[50] The chapel, had been completed in 1833 and all that Pugin did was to add the screen, a new altar and other fittings in the sanctuary.[51] The patronage that the Earl gave to Pugin was overwhelmingly in the form of financial support for the building and furnishing of new Catholic churches and institutions. At Alton Towers Pugin was limited to designing internal decorations and fittings[52] and providing glamorous medieval set-pieces like the equestrian statue of the Great Talbot[53] and the copy of his tomb.[54] From the description of the house it is easy to pick out Pugin's contributions – the large Gothic lanterns,[55] the wallpapers[56] and fireplaces.[57] It is clear that his only major work was the Dining Room between 1847 and 1849 (plate 97). This was in fact a remodelling of an existing room which already had the character of a great hall. It was lit by two windows, one above the other, which were filled with stained glass.[58] Pugin had to argue strongly to achieve even this alteration:

> This is the very first room at the Towers that I was called upon to design and it was quite natural that I should wish to produce something that would have a striking effect. . . . So far from pulling under I really must decline undertaking the alteration unless your Lordship will consent to its being made worthy of your dignity and residence. . . . I have nailed my colours to the mast: a bay window, high open roof, lantern, 2 grand fire places, a great sideboard, screen, minstrel gallery, all or none.[59]

It seems that Pugin did get things almost all his way and, even in its present depleted state, it is a noble room, with an effective exterior.

Alton Castle, separated by a deep moat from the chapel and Hospital of St John which was the Earl's first major commission to Pugin, is a differ-

96. Alton Castle, Staffordshire, *c.*1847, from the valley of the Churnet.

97. Alton Towers, Staffordshire. On the left is Pugin's Dining Hall, 1847–9; on the right the State Apartments, completed before Pugin's first visit in 1837.

ent story. Here the Earl seems to be pushing an unwilling Pugin into building on the ruins of the medieval castle. Pugin had started to design the Hospital in 1839. He intended it to consist of a chapel, school, lodgings for the warden, chaplains and poor brethren and a residence for the school-master, but the actual use seems to have been rather different. By 1843 the chapel and the school existed, both using the same building, the school-master's house was also built and probably there were some nuns of the Convent of Mercy in the range closest to the chapel. At about this date the Earl appears to have conceived the idea of rebuild-ing the castle as a home for retired priests. There are two anguished letters of June 1843 from Pugin trying to dissuade him: 'This castle at Alton has made me sick at heart. After writing a book against mock Castles, a book dedicated to your Lordship, you call on me to violate every principle and build a Castle *for Priests!!!!*'[60] and then 'Once more I implore and entreat of your Lordship to abandon that dreadful idea of building castles (I hope they will prove in the air) for ecclesiastical residences. It would be far better to build a place for the sisters and complete the hospital according to the original intention.'[61]

The idea of providing accommodation for priests was completely dropped but Shrewsbury still wanted his castle rebuilt and the project was revived about 1847. The intended occupants were never identified and this uncertainty over its use and a slow period of construction[62] no doubt af-fected its design. The long range was built to be seen rising on its wooded rock above the valley of the Churnet, like a castle on the Rhine. The other major factor affecting the composition of the castle was the Earl's determination to use the medieval foundations despite the existence of outcrops of the bedrock, resulting in a difficult L-shaped plan. The chapel is built directly above the original thir-teenth-century crypt, at the corner of the building, making it impossible to have a grand staircase near the entrance. The exterior, however, is particu-larly dramatic with its three towers and the col-oured tiles to the chapel roof (plates 96 and 98). It is clear that the Earl took great interest in the development of the design. Pugin wrote to him, probably in 1847:[63] 'I herewith send the Elevation of the gable of the Castle which I trust will meet your Lordship's approbation. I think the look-out turret will look very picturesque. . . . In the course of a day or 2 I will send another window for the

98. Alton Castle, the approach across the moat from St John's Hospital.

Chapel gable.' The long range overlooking the valley is tall and rather bleak and its design seems to have been the result of the Earl's influence. Pugin wrote to him about it on 30 July 1847:[64]

There is no comparison between this building and Linlithgow. The latter is an immense pile with a gigantic hall, towers and turrets in every direction, while the castle building, if carried up so high with dormers, will look like the beginning[?] of a row of houses. Nothing can be more dangerous than looking at prints or buildings and trying to imitate bits of them . . . If a high roof was to be added the 3rd storey could have well been dispensed with. I am very unhappy about it.

The most successful and original part of the building is the chapel. It consists of a tall ante-chapel of two bays, which has openings into it from the first-floor rooms and is lit from above. The chapel itself is narrow and high with a polygonal apse and coupled lancet windows with geometrical tracery. It has a stone rib-vault, which is unusual for Pugin, and the long vaulting shafts stand on angel corbels.

Pugin prepared two unexecuted projects for remodelling major medieval buildings, Dartington Hall for Mr Champernowne, in 1844–5, and Hornby Castle, North Riding, Yorkshire, for the Duke of Leeds, in 1847–8. Drawings for both

99. Eastnor Castle, Herefordshire, drawing room fireplace and painted genealogical tree above, designed in 1849 and executed by J.G. Crace.

100. Detail of a design for the Presbytery, Warwick Bridge, Carlisle, pen and ink, 1840, originally supplied to George Myers (Myers Family Trust).

101. The Presbytery, Warwick Bridge, Carlisle.

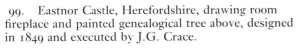

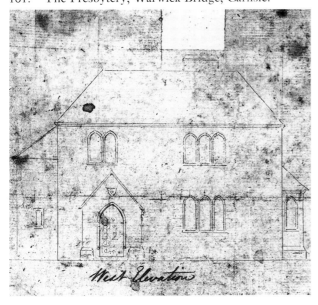

places survive.[65] He also produced drawings[66] for a dream house for his friend Ambrose Lisle March-Phillipps, and built a more practical service wing for his existing house of Grace Dieu, Leicestershire.

He also designed several important schemes for internal decorative work together with his colleague, J.G. Crace. Among these were interiors at Chirk Castle, Clwyd, for Colonel Myddelton Biddulph between 1846 and 1848, which included redecorating three eighteenth-century rooms, Burton Closes, Derbyshire, for John Allcard also between 1846 and 1848, Eastnor Castle, Herefordshire, for Earl Somers in 1846 and 1850 (plates 99) and Lismore Castle, County Waterford, for the Duke of Devonshire, mostly designed in 1850 and carried out after Pugin's death (plate 415). Two other late projects were Abney Hall, Cheshire, for James Watts, and Leighton Hall, Powys, for John Naylor, both of which seem to have come about as a result of the success of the Mediæval Court at the Great Exhibition and were executed by Crace after Pugin's death. Most of this decorative work involved wallpapers[67] and furniture.[68]

Forming an interesting group of a new type of domestic building were Pugin's presbyteries. His aim was to design simple, cheap but dignified buildings which would complement his new churches. This aim was already evident at one of his first churches, St Marie's, Derby, where a charming gabled presbytery of c.1839, now demolished, framed one side of the west end of the church, with a school to the other side. As with the churches, there was never much money for such buildings. There was a minimum of decorative details, externally and internally, but they are usually well planned and well built. The presbytery to St Peter's, Woolwich, of c.1843 had a handsome two-storey bay window to the street façade, and that to St Mary, Brewood, Staffordshire, of c.1844 is a red brick box of such startling simplicity that it appears to belong to the 1930s. Pugin's presbyteries have been frequently altered and enlarged, as in the sandstone one of 1840 at Warwick Bridge (plates 100 and 101) and the flint and red brick one at Marlow. The stock brick presbytery to the church of St Thomas of Canterbury, Fulham, of 1848, however, can still be appreciated much as it was intended (plates 103 and 104), although it has

105.† The Grange and St Augustine's, Ramsgate, watercolour exhibited at the Royal Academy in 1849 (Private Collection). The building beside the entrance gate is the Cartoon Room, where stained-glass designs were prepared. The bell chamber and spire of the church were never built, and the cloister was completed by E.W. Pugin, with some changes.

lost its original open setting. The donor, Mrs Bowden, paid for the church, school and master's house as well as the presbytery and so there was no money for frills. The plan of a neat rectangle clearly shows Pugin's ability to design a compact, efficient and appropriate house, well built and well organised but cheap. It is attractive, with good proportions but minimum decoration.

Houses for the middle classes, which were typically detached houses in both country and suburb, became important examples of domestic architecture during the Victorian period. Pugin designed three such houses: the Grange at Ramsgate, which he built for himself between 1843 and 1844, Oswaldcroft in Liverpool for Henry Sharples

between 1844 and 1847, and the Rectory at Rampisham (plate 102) from 1846 to 1847. A fourth similar house, for W. G. Ward at St Edmund's College Ware, built in 1846, has been much altered. Pugin's own house stands on the edge of a cliff with the sea beyond (plates 77, 105). The entrance courtyard has been much obscured by later additions and now presents a very cluttered appearance, but an attempt has been made here to reconstruct the original ground plan (plate 106). The exterior of drab brick and stone dressings was always simple and severe. On the entrance façade the kitchen wing projects to one side of the entrance and the window to the staircase hall, and is balanced on the other by the

106. The Grange, Ramsgate, reconstruction of the ground plan in 1843–4. The service wing projecting into the courtyard is unusual.

107.† *The Grange, Ramsgate, view into the Chapel*, watercolour, *c.*1844 (Private Collection). The chapel included an organ and the stained glass is by William Wailes.

108.† The Grange, Ramsgate, entrance staircase hall.

109.† *The Grange, Ramsgate, looking from the Library into the Drawing Room*, by P.P. Pugin, watercolour, *c.*1870 (Private Collection). E.W. Pugin altered these rooms in the 1860s.

chimneystack to the drawing room. On the garden façade all the main reception rooms overlook the sea; Pugin's library where he worked and his bedroom above are marked by bay windows and a gable; there is a staircase tower with a look-out at the top, and Pugin's little chapel (plate 107) projects at the end of the range. Internally the most remarkable space is that of the staircase entrance hall (plate 108). It is well lit and provides the circulation to the main rooms on the ground and first floor. It has moreover a most unusual and intriguing balustrade, which seems to derive ultimately from timber framing. The house still retains some original fireplaces, encaustic tiles, stained glass (plates 394, 481), panelling and painted ceilings, enough to give an impression of

its former beauty.[69] There are strong similarities between the plan for the Grange and that of Oswaldcroft and the Rampisham Rectory, both of which also have a staircase entrance hall. At Oswaldcroft, in a suburban setting, he tucked the house into another neat rectangle, and at Rampisham, in the countryside, he allowed a long service wing.

These buildings have very few direct references to medieval work and show how independent as an architect he could be. They depend for their effect principally on an efficient plan, good proportions and the harmonious grouping of the various parts. It is deeply to be regretted that Pugin was not commissioned to produce more architecture of this kind.

110.† *Evening view of St Augustine's and the Grange, Ramsgate looking west*, by P.P. Pugin, watercolour, *c*.1875 (Private Collection).

CHAPTER FIVE

Pugin as a Church Architect

RODERICK O'DONNELL

Pugin was received into the Catholic Church in Salisbury on the eve of Pentecost 1835. The laconic entry in his diary reads 'Finished alterations at Chapel received into the Holy Catholic Church'.[1] As early as January 1834 he had written to the Catholic architect E.J. Willson[2] 'after a most close and impartial investigation, I feel perfectly convinced that the Roman Catholic Church is the only true one, and the only one in which the grand and sublime style of architecture can ever be restored'.[3] For Pugin the connection between architectural and religious conviction was unshakeable. Such a conversion was an extraordinary step for a budding church-architect to take. Pugin later claimed to have had little sense of the minor scale of Catholic church building, which was adequately provided both with London-based Catholic architects such as J.J. Scoles, and one or two provincials. Catholics called their churches chapels and built them accordingly. His revolutionary programme for the building of rich and elaborately furnished churches was initially widely accepted. The influential *Dublin Review* wrote that the opening of Pugin's St Marie's, Derby (plate 112) 'will fix the point of decided transition from chapel to church architecture amongst us . . . '.[4] But others had different ideas. That most perceptive critic, the future Cardinal Newman, was to conclude that the whole Gothic Revival was a form of escapism and the building of cathedrals when the Church had not the bishops to staff them was 'Puginism'.[5] Newman's comment shows him to be one of the 'vert' or convert party and he identified Pugin as the head of Gothic or 'English' party in the Catholic Church in England.

Pugin's father was a lapsed Catholic. The religious influence of his upbringing was his moth-er's enthusiastic evangelical Protestantism, which must have been antipathetic to his precocious romantic nature. No doubt the piety of his Catholic aunts in Paris was more to his taste. But he brought his mother's enthusiasm to his pugnacious Catholicism, which he was never ashamed to demonstrate, for example crossing himself in public to the scandal of a lady railway traveller. He did not see the Catholic church in England as a branch of the English Nonconformist tradition, nor as an offshoot of contemporary continental Catholicism, but as the re-embodiment of the Catholic Church in England of the middle ages. As he explained in his apologia in *Some Remarks* (1850):

> I gained my knowledge of the ancient faith beneath the vaults of a Lincoln or a Westminster . . . The reredoses, though defaced, and the sacraria in the walls, showed the site of numerous altars for the propitiatory sacrifice of the mass . . . By the help of the histories of the devout and painful Dugdale . . . I could almost realise the venerable Hugh celebrating in the glorious choir which he had raised . . . I indulged in a sort of Catholic utopia.[6]

But his claim '. . . I had seen little or nothing of the Catholic body in England . . . I saw nothing that reminded me of the ancient religion . . . Everything seemed strange and new . . .'[7] was at variance with the 1834 statement to Willson 'a very good chapel is building in the North and when it is complete I think I shall recant',[8] implying a close investigation of contemporary Catholic church-

111. St Giles's, Cheadle; the nave and the rood screen with figures of Our Lady and St John, the Crucifix is hidden by the modern coronas. The Blessed Sacrament Chapel is on the right and the Lady Altar on the left.

or schools, and bigotry often denied them even building sites. The Catholic population of England and Wales increased by one quarter from 1830 to 1840, more than doubled between 1840 and 1850, and by another half from 1850 to 1860. The 250,000 Catholics of 1830 had become 846,000 by 1850.[9] It was this Church, seen – not only by its opponents – as an engine of an Irish invasion, to which Pope Pius IX appointed territorial bishops in 1850. For Catholics this was the 'Restoration of the Hierarchy', but for the government and *The Times* it was 'Papal aggression'. An anti-Catholic meeting was held at Ramsgate to which Pugin replied by pamphlet.[10] Although none of Pugin's churches was ever attacked by a mob, the foundations of his Cambridge church had to be protected by the Irish at night, and undergraduates provoked a riot there as late as 1863.[11]

Pugin's Catholicism seems far removed from this world, preferring the romantic and reactionary, and opposed to the world of towns, democracy and industrialisation which most Catholics inhabited. Pugin was close to the High Tory politics of the young Disraeli. *Coningsby or the New Generation* (1844) encapsulates, in the figure of Eustache Lyle, Pugin's two patrons Lord Shrewsbury and Ambrose Phillipps de Lisle. Pugin was a pious and devout convert, but one senses a distrust of the clergy as a group. His claim to the Newcastle church-building committee that 'I had always been the *friend and adviser* of my employers & those employers mostly ecclesiastics whom I serve in love and conscience . . .' does not ring true.[12] He did not understand the powerful *esprit de corps* of the clergy and the threat of a clerically dominated, proletarianisation of the Church, which began with the arrival of large numbers of destitute Irish Catholics, was not a model Pugin relished. Pugin not only disliked the Irish but clashed with conservative bishops such as Dr Baines, a noted 'old Catholic', as well as challenging the middle-class church-building committees in the towns.

For Pugin the perfect bishop was old Dr Walsh, bishop of the Midland District since 1826, who did Shrewsbury's and Pugin's bidding by moving meekly from his fine Baroque gentleman's house in Wolverhampton to the bishop's house Pugin built next to the Cathedral in Birmingham (plate 88), a highly doctrinaire recreation of a medieval hall-house, and then to the brick presbytery at Nottingham as the wave of church-building proceeded. In the last year of his life he resolutely refused to make the move to London and he is buried in St Chad's Cathedral, Birmingham, hold-

building. This for Pugin was the most pressing task, while others might have chosen to concentrate on church government, educating the clergy or building schools.

Pugin found himself to be the propagandist of a particular party within the church. He identified himself immediately with the lay Catholic leader and grand seigneur John Talbot, the sixteenth Earl of Shrewsbury, whose seat, Alton Towers in Staffordshire, acted as a sort of Catholic summer-school. These 'English Catholics' saw the Gothic Revival as an area of rapprochement with the Church of England as represented by the Oxford Movement with which Pugin made early contacts. They were opposed equally to the conservatism and liturgical minimalism of the so-called 'old Catholics', whose piety continued the habits of the secret Catholicism of the country house chapel and the town garret and to the later and specifically Continental and Counter-Reformation enthusiasm of 'vert' Anglicans, who followed Newman into the Catholic Church after 1845, that is ten years after Pugin.

The factionalism evident among Catholics was as nothing compared to the impact of poverty and the demographic explosion induced by the arrival of the Irish, fleeing the Great Famine. No state funds were available for either Catholic churches

ing the model of the new church in his hands (plate 372). Pugin's hope 'that I expected to find a Wykeham in every bishop'[13] was at least partly true of Walsh. Pugin defended Bishop Walsh against his critics as '. . . the only Bishop in England who has really advanced the dignity of religion. Dr Walsh found the churches in his district worse than Barns; he will leave them sumptuous erections.'[14]

Although Pugin claimed to know 'little or nothing of the Catholic body in England',[15] he had some understanding of the sociology of the English Catholic church. The laity, either the land-owning class or the middle class congregations in the towns, were more important politically than was the rudimentary system of church government.

England was technically a 'mission' country, but in fact the church received little more from Rome than carping criticism. Until 1850 there were no territorial dioceses or parishes and even the bishops had no strategy for church-building, trusting instead on the ambition of the priest, a rich lay patron or the congregation. The latter, represented by the 'furious committee man,'[16] Pugin accused of being content 'to worship in a room inferior to many Wesleyan meeting-houses,'[17] referring not only to a style of architecture but also to the democratic church government such committees represented. Where Pugin had the support of Shrewsbury and the clergy, as at St George's, Southwark he overcame this 'Methodism' to build large churches which effectively undermined the committee system.

Church-building for Pugin had a specific propagandist purpose, as the sale of handbills and prints, as well as the many highly didactic descriptions of his churches in the contemporary Catholic press illustrate. Articles in the *London and Dublin Orthodox Journal* described the foundation of Pugin's first church at Reading in December 1837, and the first opening, at St Augustine's Solihull, in February 1839. These reports heavily emphasised Pugin's role and status as the architect. He developed his own apologia for the church of St Mary, Uttoxeter in July 1839 into an attack in the August number on the church of St Francis Xavier, Hereford (1836–8), by the Catholic architect Charles Day, because it was in the Greek Revival style.[18] Pugin's buildings were also published in the *Dublin Review*, the various editions of the *Catholic Magazine* and the *Catholic Directory*, and the *Tablet*. Pugin himself wrote many of these, ranging from the long technical description of St Giles's, Cheadle in the *Morning Post* to letters rebutting

113. 'The Present Revival of Christian Architecture', frontispiece to the *Apology for the Revival of Christian Architecture*, 1843.

wild rumours describing a church as 'having 3 spires . . . a cathedral when I had not attempted anything but [a] large parochial church' or local reports of his own church in Kent.[19] Pugin wrote of himself in an heroic mould: 'I who have the whole weight of the revival on my shoulders'[20] and thus justified his use of only one builder – George Myers – for his churches, which were to be furnished and decorated by John Hardman and his other collaborators. His highly prescriptive views were often misunderstood, if not directly opposed and he wrote in despair, 'But the real truth is the churches I build do little or no good for want of men who know how to use them . . . I now almost despair, I do indeed . . . The church at Dudley is a compleat[sic] facsimile one of the old English parish churches, and nobody seems to know how to use it.'[21]

Pugin realised that he had to convert the mission clergy and the students in the seminaries to his views. The wider public he propagandised through his books with their captivating illustrations. The Gothic Revival was already well understood in architectural circles when Pugin published *Contrasts* in 1836, and the name Pugin was well known through his father's publications of Gothic details. For Pugin the Gothic style was not an option but an historical, moral and religious necessity, particularly for English Catholics who

114. Sacred Heart, Ackworth Grange, Yorkshire ('The Jesus Chapel near Pomfret'), demolished.

115. St Mary's, Warwick Bridge, Carlisle.

116. Sacred Heart, Ackworth Grange, the derelict Sanctuary, showing medieval forms of furnishing revived by Pugin.

117. St Mary's, Warwick Bridge, Carlisle; a small church with polychrome decoration and lavish liturgical furniture.

claimed descent from the church of the Middle Ages. Pugin was a brilliant propagandist, as his anti-Protestant broadside *Contrasts* (1836) showed; but he was equally determined to demonise the use of the neo-classical style as 'Pagan'. His point is demonstrated in a form worthy of the plates of *Contrasts* itself at Ackworth Grange, Yorkshire, where he built a neo-Decorated private chapel which dwarfs and satirises the adjacent Regency villa of Miss Anna Maria Tempest (plate 114).

The Tempests had provided mass at Ackworth since 1804. Their decision to build a church was part of the long process of self-emancipation which the Catholics were undergoing. They had gained freedom of worship in 1778 and the right to sit in Parliament in 1829. But three hundred years of religious persecution, which dulled into political and social isolation, had left English Catholics marginalised. However the religious and Romantic Revival which succeeded the French Revolu-

tion was already affecting the insularity of English Catholicism, and was to produce 'the Second Spring' of Cardinal Newman's phrase. Pugin was to be one of its leaders, and the coining by his opponents of the phrase 'Puginism' is a witness to his influence.

Pugin illustrated twenty-four of his churches (plate 113) in the frontispiece to the *Apology for the Revival of Christian Architecture* (1843) dedicated to his patron, the Earl of Shrewsbury. By this time he had been in practice as a church architect for a mere six years, and had, by Wiseman's reckoning, thirty-five churches to his credit. Pugin now considered the churches in the frontispiece to be what he called his 'glorious authorities'.[22] From about

1841 this meant the English Decorated Gothic of the fourteenth century, when he rejected his earlier use of the Norman, Early English and Perpendicular styles. In his subsequent publications he quite shamelessly suppressed information on his early churches.

Pugin made significant use of the neo-Norman style in his earlier churches. St James's, Reading (1837–40), and St Michael's, Gorey, co. Wexford (1839–42) were designed in the Norman style. In the special case of the crypt chapels at St Chad's Cathedral, Birmingham, a Norman style was used to suggest an earlier historical phase surviving under a later medieval church (plate 118). There were numerous Early English designs: St Mary's, Uttoxeter (1838–9), the first of Pugin's churches to be begun; the first chapel scheme for Ushaw (1840); St Wilfrid's, Hulme (1840–2) and the small church of St Andrew's, Cambridge (1841–3). Even large churches such as the cathedrals at Nottingham and Killarney were in the Early English or lancet style.

The Perpendicular style was used for such prominent early churches as St Marie's, Derby (1838–41), the first designs for St George's, Southwark (1838) and St Marie's, Manchester (1838), and St Alban's, Macclesfield (1839–41). In order to mask their details, Derby and Macclesfield were tidied away in the middle distance of the *Apology* frontispiece. The small brick Perpendicular church at Solihull (1839), the first of Pugin's churches to be opened, was also omitted. Instead, pride of place is given to St Giles's, Cheadle (1840–6) and to a host of proud spires, that is to 'a very fine revival of the decorated period.'[23]

Pugin had quite distinct church plan forms depending on the status of the individual mission.

The simplest churches were for newly founded missions such as Stone (1843–4) and Wandsworth (1846–7), where the bishop agreed to begin the school but not the full-scale church Pugin had designed. With the support of Ambrose Phillipps de Lisle, a simple aisled church with a school in the basement was built at Shepshed (1841–2) (plate 119). Where a mission was already established, but was still small in numbers, two-cell aisleless nave and chancel churches of the Uttoxeter type were built; whether Early English or Decorated in style they form the bulk of Pugin's early churches, as well as his most frequently altered buildings. A miraculously fully furnished and unaltered example is St Mary's, Warwick Bridge, outside Carlisle (1840–1; plate 115). Pugin suggests additional historical interest by alternating two-light traceried Decorated windows with the Early English lancets. The profusion of fittings even for such a small country mission, as well as their quality, should be noted (plate 117).

121.† The High Altar from Alton Towers Chapel. The gilt-wood reredos with enamel plaques and painted figures of the Earl and Countess of Shrewsbury is attributed to Pugin. The gilt-bronze altar is earlier. Since 1862 it has been at Bromsgrove Catholic Church.

It is surprising that the chapel at Ackworth Grange, Yorkshire (plate 114) was the only complete new private chapel attached to a Catholic seat which Pugin built. It was a two-cell plan, built in stone and richly detailed (plate 116). Pugin illustrated it in *Present State*, and under the title of the Jesus Chapel, Pomfret, made it one of the three foreground buildings in the *Apology* frontispiece. The minor brick chapel built for the Amherst family at Kenilworth (plate 120), was another.[24] However, he altered and refurnished a number of private chapels, notably Alton Towers for Lord Shrewsbury. The altar, with its distinctive metal predella and painted reredos showing the kneeling Earl and Countess of Shrewsbury (plate 121),

survives.[25] Pugin also made additions and furnishings at Grace Dieu for Ambrose Phillipps.[26]

The 'country church' as the model for Gothic Revival church-building of the 1840s and 1850s was to be Pugin's most influential contribution. Some country Catholic congregations could even afford to build without the patronage of the Catholic gentry. St Oswald's, Old Swann, outside Liverpool (1840–3), shown in the middle distance of the *Apology* plate,[26] had already been published in *Present State* and was 'a new model, almost a new building type, quite discontinuous with Georgian church architecture'.[27] It was this idealised fourteenth-century country parish church which both Pugin's Catholic followers, and the *Ecclesiologist*, the magazine of the Cambridge Camden Society, were to reproduce almost *ad infinitum*, and which Pugin expressed mostly richly at St Giles's, Cheadle.

The restrictions of the 'country church' model for towns was much debated in the 1850s, and Pugin in fact anticipated what came to be called the 'town church'. At St Mary's, Stockton (1840–1) he was already moving away from the rigidly symmetrical plan of nave and aisles with west tower seen at St Marie's, Derby and Macclesfield. Instead he evolved an asymmetrical plan of a nave with an aisle embracing a tower, which was particularly successful for small town churches. St Osmund's, Salisbury (1847–8) is a late example, with a nave and chancel balanced by a south aisle tower doubling up as a west end porch and a Lady Chapel with sacristy behind the east end (plate 122).[28]

Pugin employed two other plans for larger, well established town congregations, the clerestoried nave and aisles with apsed east end of Derby and the three-aisle plan of St George's, Southwark (1840–8; plate 123), which was repeated with modifications at Newcastle (plate 124), and on a smaller scale at St Thomas of Canterbury, Fulham. The model for Pugin's favourite 'triple roof [and] high gables'[29] elevation and three-aisle plan was that of the late medieval preaching or hall-church, in this case the London Austin Friars. Both at Southwark and Newcastle Pugin claimed to be able to seat large numbers 'on the ground as galleries are inadmissible in a Catholic church'.[30] The sanctuaries of both were somewhat cramped, and externally the distinction between nave and sanctuary was dispensed with altogether. The screens which Pugin intended at Newcastle were not erected until the middle 1850s (plate 125).[31]

Pugin defended his 'triple roof' against the Newcastle church-building committee's prefer-

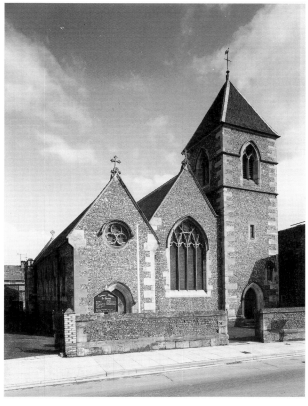

ence for a church with lean-to aisles and a clerestory since 'a clerestory . . . does not properly belong to the period I have selected.'[32] He also thought the committee's proposal too countrified: 'it is completely surrounded by lofty houses [so] that a low church would appear crushed & mere aisles without high gables would never answer'.[33] But at St Mary's, Liverpool, where he was unable to obtain any light through the outer walls, he did design a generous clerestory like those at Derby and Macclesfield as well as massive east and west windows. Like the Newcastle church, it also lacked screens, and Pugin complained to the priest 'Your church is ruined for want of screens . . . grievous[?] to see it so naked.'[34]

122. St Osmund's, Salisbury, which achieves medieval asymmetry and uses local building materials.

123.† St George's Cathedral, Southwark (Private Collection). The watercolour emphasises the complex east end; the spire was never built, and the church was destroyed in 1941.

124. St Mary's, Newcastle; Pugin's favourite triple-aisle plan; the tower and spire are by Dunn and Hansom, 1872.

125. St Mary's, Newcastle, c.1900, with the rood screen by G. Goldie, 1853, and later painting.

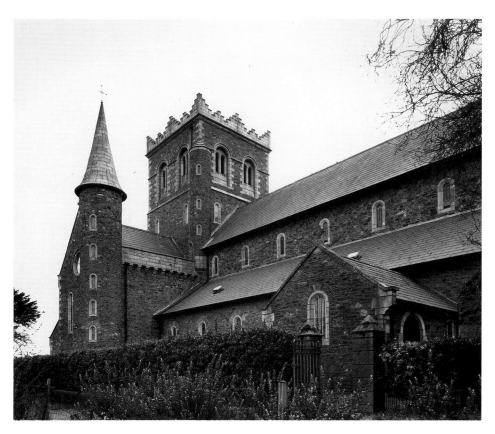

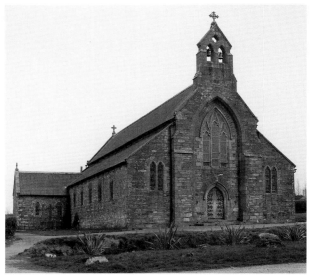

126.   St Michael's, Gorey, Wexford.

127.   St Peter's College, Wexford. The painted wood High Altar and triptych are the similar to those originally at Uttoxeter. The rose window has Shrewsbury's arms.

128.   St Mary's Cathedral, Killarney, co. Kerry, completed 1912. Pugin's Irish churches were delayed by the Great Famine and completed by others.

129.   St Alphonsus, Barntown, co. Wexford.

Ireland with its enormous Catholic population seemed to present an ideal opportunity for Pugin. He met the MP J.H. Talbot, the Countess of Shrewsbury's cousin, at Alton. Talbot was to obtain the commission for the chapel at St Peter's College, Wexford (1838–41; plate 127) and to be the intermediary for designs for a number of churches which Pugin was however not prepared to acknowledge later. Only two Irish churches appear in the *Apology* frontispiece, the earliest was the large neo-Norman church of St Michael's, Gorey (1839–42/3; plate 126) and the second was the Early English Killarney Cathedral (plate 128). His first neo-Decorated church was St Alphonsus's, Barntown, co. Wexford (1844–51; plate 129). Pugin's commissions were confined to the south of Ireland, where the few Catholic gentry and aristocrats such as the Earl of Kenmare at Killarney were unusual among the almost exclusively Protestant landowning class. The Catholic mass peasantry and a small urban middle-class were untouched by Pugin's message and his only work near Dublin was the refurnishing of a convent chapel. However Pugin built two cathedrals as well as the commission for the enormous extensions to St Patrick's College, Maynooth in 1845 (plate 157).

Pugin's impact on Ireland was further confused by the long campaigns his buildings involved: of his two cathedrals, Killarney (1842–9; plate 128) was notoriously left unusable until the middle 1850s and only completed in 1912. Both Killarney and St Aidan's Cathedral, Enniscorthy, are cruciform in plan, with central towers. Pugin was anxious for collaborators in Ireland and evidently found it difficult to supervise his churches: he worked with the Wexford builder Richard Pierce and the architect J.J. McCarthy, who made Killarney useable between 1853 and 1856, was described as a 'friend and fellow labourer' of Pugin 'his great master.'[35] Thomas Earley and Henry Powell set up a Dublin branch of Hardman's in 1853 and E.W. Pugin, who first visited Ireland in the mid-1850s, set up a Dublin partnership in 1859. Despite the many draw-backs, the Pugin style was in fact received enthusiastically in Ireland. Arguments about church-furnishing were not an issue as they were in England, perhaps because none of Pugin's churches except St Peter's College, Wexford (plate 127) was furnished according to his views.

In contrast to the tensions with Catholic clergy, Pugin had a handful of sympathetic Anglican patrons for whom some of his most attractive work was done, forming a fascinating counter-point

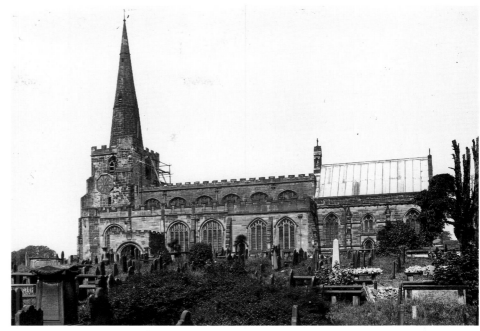

130. St Oswald's (C of E), Winwick. Pugin rebuilt and furnished the chancel in the Decorated style, in contrast to the medieval Perpendicular church.

both to his new churches and to the vexed question of church restoration. Pugin's Anglican commissions were highly agreeable to him, particularly the rebuilding and furnishing of the chancel at Winwick, Lancashire (1848–53; plate 130) with its Hardman glass and painting[36] and the long rebuilding campaign of St Mary's, Wymeswold, Leicestershire (1844–53).[37] Even more discerning patrons commissioned the jewel-like details of Pugin's Anglican chantries (plates 165, 393).

Informed patronage was the key to Pugin's Anglican work, but some patrons such as Sir John Sutton at Cambridge and West Tofts, Norfolk followed him into the Catholic Church. A 'fifth column' accusation against his patrons was always in the background, and sectarian prejudice undoubtedly lost Pugin work including the restoration of Balliol College, Oxford in 1843. The problem of acknowledging the supremacy of a 'papist' architect, as a local newspaper at Peper Harrow described Pugin, was acute. His teachings on style were therefore disseminated through the Cambridge Camden Society and its enormously influential journal the *Ecclesiologist*, but in 1846 the Camden Society broke with him by publishing the particularly vicious attack 'On the artistic merit of Mr Pugin.'[38]

Until the Pope gave the Catholic bishops in England territorial sees they did not technically require cathedrals. However in 1834 Dr Walsh, the Midland District bishop, issued an appeal for 'a cathedral worthy of the metropolis of the whole district,' that is for Birmingham.[39] Although the local architects Joseph Hansom and Thomas

131. St Chad's Cathedral, Birmingham, the east end from the canal, engraving by Alphege Pippet, c.1874.

133. Medieval statue of Our Lady, given by Pugin to St Chad's, 1840.

132. St Chad's, Birmingham, the rood screen (1841, demolished in 1967, the figures are to be rehung in 1994). The medieval pulpit and polychrome decoration survive.

Rickman were spoken of, Pugin was proposed, first for a chapel scheme and in 1839 for the cathedral, supported by Lord Shrewsbury, the Hardmans and the Bishop.

A similar pattern emerges at Southwark where Pugin took his brief literally and produced elaborate drawings for a cathedral with cloisters and chapter house, which the committee rejected. He was persuaded to join a limited competition in 1839, which he won, no doubt because Lord Shrewsbury's gift of £1000 was available for his scheme alone. He frequently threatened to resign both the Newcastle and Liverpool St Mary commissions when faced by the demands of the building committees.[40] Where he was appointed Pugin successfully shocked such committees out of what he thought of as their narrow 'congregational' habits, committing them and their clergy to the long-term planning and borrowing required to finance his churches.

To modern eyes, if not to those of the mid-Victorians, Pugin's most successful cathedral is St Chad's, Birmingham (1839–41) the work, not of the lifetime he demanded at Southwark, but two years. It is built of brick laid in English bond, with Bath stone dressings and slate roofs, of one continuous pitch over nave and aisles and elaborately

hipped at the east end which towered over the sloping canalside (plate 131). St Chad's was an early large-scale collaboration with George Myers and the unusual scale and precision of the contract drawings was not later to be characteristic of them.[41] The size, over one hundred and fifty feet long by sixty feet wide, also impressed commentators: a correspondent to the *Orthodox Journal* exclaimed 'the cathedral church of St Chad . . . being, as it deserves to be, called a "Cathedral".'[42]

St Chad's was not only 'late' in style, but continental rather than English in its sources. Internally the church is not compartmentalised, but is more like a German hall-church with its slender arcades and large windows. The floor is carried on iron girders, with a large crypt below. The attenuated proportions of its seventy-five foot high arcades are reminiscent of the 1838 Southwark cathedral scheme. In reaction against the 'late' style, Pugin was by 1840 designing furnishings in the Decorated style. There are two different designs for the Lady Altar and reredos, the first in 1839 with a gabled triptych reredos in a 'late' style, the second of 1840 as part executed was Decorated.[43] Pugin supplied antique furnishings as he did at Oscott, such as the pulpit from Louvain and German carvings reused in the stalls and rood screen.

Pugin himself gave a fifteenth-century statue of the Virgin (plate 133). The painted and gilded stone high altar and reredos (plate 134) were surmounted by a 'feretory' for the recently rediscovered relics of St Chad, all under a gilt-wood ciborium modelled on that of Robert the Wise in Sta Chiara, Naples. The most important furnishing for Pugin was the Rood Screen mentioned in a description of the foundation in November 1839 (plate 132).[44] He also designed stained glass made by Warrington, which was based on fourteenth-century windows at Tewkesbury Abbey.

Overall colour was an essential ingredient in the interior: not only the fittings but the walls and roofs were painted in diapers of rich primary colours and texts. The floors were laid in coloured encaustic tiles. The Earl of Shrewsbury gave both antique and modern vestments and the fifteenth-century brass lectern for the opening, which Pugin orchestrated with five days of ceremonies.[45] Later furniture included the tomb of Bishop Walsh executed by Myers (plate 372) and much Hardman glass.

St Barnabas's, Nottingham (1843–6) only became a cathedral in 1852, although it was obviously designed with this status in mind (plate 135). It was built of stone ashlar with a central tower and stone spire, and an elaborate and successful east end arrangement of sanctuary and side chapels. The windows are lancets and the overall style chosen is that of the mid-thirteenth century. The forms is based on the ruined Cistercian Abbey of Croxden, Staffordshire, a foundation of an ancestor of Lord Shrewsbury, the major benefactor, and its primitive rusticity sits oddly among the red-brick villas of Nottingham. As so often the interior has lost its furnishings, except for the richly painted Blessed Sacrament Chapel. The complex variations in levels at the east end should be noted. The interior as Pugin thought of it is illustrated in *Present State*.[46] Pugin also built a large house intended as the bishop's residence and presbytery.

Pugin's two most famous churches are in the Decorated style. Both St Giles's, Cheadle and St Augustine's, Ramsgate were the gift of their generous founders, Lord Shrewsbury and Pugin himself. During its building Pugin spoke of Cheadle as 'Cheadle perfect Cheadle, my consolation in all afflictions'.[47] It marked the climax of the archaeological phase of Gothic Revival church-building, 'a perfect revival of an English parish church of the time of Edward I'[48] (plate 137). Lord Shrewsbury told Pugin 'I expect when finished it will be a text book for all good people . . . (and) will im-

134. St Chad's, Birmingham, the High Altar, Reredos and Ciborium with the Reliquary of St Chad (1841).

135. St Barnabas's Cathedral, Nottingham.

136. St Giles's, Cheadle, plan, 1842, published in *Present State*, 1843. The separate liturgical spaces are clearly distinguished; as built it was even more elaborate.

137. St Giles's, Cheadle, from the east end.

138. St Giles's, Cheadle, the High Altar, painted and gilded alabaster. Pugin provided casts for the craftsmen to copy.

139. St Giles's, Cheadle, the Blessed Sacrament Chapel. The iconography refers to the Catholic belief of the Real Presence of Christ in the reserved Sacrament.

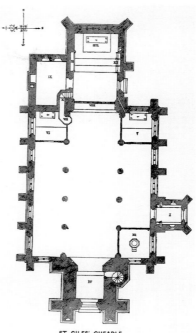

ST. GILES', CHEADLE.

I. Porch	VIII. Screen and Rood
II. Holy water stoups	IX. Sacristy
III. Font and Baptistery	X. Staircase to Rood
IV. Tower	XI. Sepulchre
V. St. Mary's Chapel	XII. Sedilia
VI. St. John's Chapel	XIII. High altar
VII. Pulpit	

prove the taste of young England', referring to the 'Young England' group associated with Disraeli.[49] For Pugin its consecration was the climax of his career as an apologist of the Catholic and the Gothic Revivals, attended by leaders in Britain and Europe, including A.N. Didron and Henri Gerente from Paris and August Reichensperger from Cologne.[50] It was praised by Newman, who was shortly to turn against Pugin,[51] and it was even privately inspected by G.G. Scott, a leading Anglican architect.

Cheadle is an elaborate building (particularly its tower and spire), while the decoration of the interior is almost baffling (plate 111). H.R. Hitchcock likened it to 'the orchestration of the great Romantic composers . . . a major monument of late Romanticism', comparable to the work of Berlioz, Turner and Delacroix.[52] Pugin was later to claim that the dense decoration was due to Lord Shrewsbury who made more funds available as the commission progressed. However Pugin's supposed

140. St Giles's, Cheadle, a: the alabaster font, with wooden cover and metal screens; b: the west doors, employing the Shrewsbury talbot on a grand scale; c: detail of the wall decoration in the Blessed Sacrament Chapel.

desire for 'a plain parochial country church'[53] does not agree either with the plan (plate 136) or the interiors published in *Present State*. It was Pugin himself who urged further ritual spaces and decoration. Fittings such as the Easter Sepulchre and the pulpit were drawn to scale in 1840, rather than being after-thoughts.[54] Pugin fought Shrewsbury's suggestion of a west gallery, and pressed for a stone vaulted south porch and separate Blessed Sacrament Chapel (plate 139).[55] The use of lead for the roofs and the dramatic heightening of the spire to over 200 feet high were settled on as more funds became available. As a result, St Giles's dominates an English market town as no other Catholic church does.

Pugin was always urging further decoration as his travels and researches broadened. He wrote from Norfolk in the spring of 1844:

I am half frantic with delight. I have seen such churches with the *painting and gilding near perfect !!!!* Such screens, exquisite painting. I shall have glorious authorities for Cheadle. I am delighted beyond measure to have seen than before we begin decoration at Cheadle.[56]

East Anglian carved woodwork therefore served as the model for the angels on the reredos of the alabaster high altar where a sculptural group of the Coronation of the Virgin occupies the usual place of a tabernacle (plate 138). A visit to the Sainte Chapelle in Paris was the inspiration for the dark tones and dense design of the stained glass.[57] From Paris he also 'purchased a great many casts of the most beautiful character which will be just the thing for the images on the spire at Cheadle & also for the reredos & chancel.'[58] Medieval manuscripts suggested iconography for wall paintings, some of them by Crace.[59] Cheadle, like the work at Alton

village, was built by the estate staff under the clerk of works John Denny, who had also built the Uttoxeter church. Roddis, who had worked at Oscott and Solihull, was the architectural sculptor; Kearns, the painter; and the stained glass, which particularly impressed G.G. Scott, was by William Wailes.[60]

The iconographic complexity of the church is overwhelming: the interior really is a 'text book' in Shrewsbury's phrase. There is Shrewsbury heraldry everywhere (plate 140b), and inscriptions in English in the floor tiles, sculpture and glass. The sanctuary and side chapels (plate 140c) have liturgical inscriptions, and appropriate iconography. There are antiquarian furnishings such as the fifteenth-century Flemish reredos in the Lady Chapel. There were chapels at the ends of both aisles and a separate baptistery with an alabaster font and wooden cover (plate 140a), and ambry for the holy oils. The rood screen divided the sanctuary, with its alabaster high altar, a sepulchre, sedilia and piscina, from the church. The sacristy and the organ loft above were both heated. Not only the plaster is painted (plate 140c), but also the stone, alabaster and woodwork. Pugin used a medley of different materials: oak and brass for the font screen; oak for the rood screen and benches; stone, alabaster, zinc and copper panels in the Sepulchre; tiles and glass, as well as the textiles and metalwork ornaments of the altars. Over the chancel arch is the Doom or Last Judgement painted on canvas by Hauser. Polychromy is also insistent in the glass and the encaustic floor and dado tiles (plates 265, 272), particularly in the Blessed Sacrament Chapel which brought Newman to his knees: '. . . a blaze of light - and I could not help saying to myself "Porta Coeli".'[61] It was colour that *The Illustrated London News* noted[62] and A.N. Didron wrote 'M.

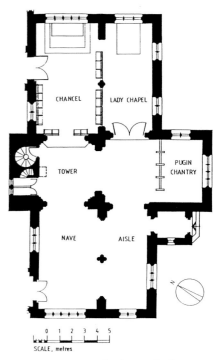

141. St Augustine's, Ramsgate, built as an ex-voto offering next to the Grange, using local flint, with stone dressings. The large south transept houses the Pugin Chantry (see plan).

Pugin a ressuscité le moyen âge entier, corps et âme . . . un effet réellement magique . . . Tout est en couleur . . . or et lumière.'[63]

By contrast with Cheadle, Pugin's church at Ramsgate (plate 141) was largely unknown at his death. Given Pugin's appetite for self-publicity, this is strange. In the famous mea culpa in *Some Remarks* Pugin wrote:

I believe, as regards architecture, few men have been as unfortunate as myself. I have passed my life in thinking of fine things, studying fine things, designing fine things, and realising very poor ones . . . had I not been permitted by the providence of the God to have raised the church at St Augustine's, I must have appeared as a man whose principles and works were strangely at variance.[64]

Rather than through his publications, it was as a workshop that Ramsgate was to be influential, for here his craftsmen, family and pupils (particularly his son Edward and his future son-in-law John Hardman Powell) were 'school'd',[65] in Pugin's phrase. From 1845, Hardman's stained glass cartoon shop was set up here. The building of the church progressed as Pugin's professional earnings allowed from 1844, to a cost of over £14,864, an astonishing act of piety.[66] As he explained to Edward Pugin, 'watch the church, there shall not be a single "true principle" broken.'[67] The plan is a Kent type: central tower and spire balancing a nave and chancel, with a large south transept projecting beyond a south aisle (plate 141).[68] Pugin

began building with a tower and sacristy used as a temporary church and school, a set of service rooms and one range of the cloisters. Pugin's bird's-eye view watercolour at the Royal Academy in 1849 is surrounded by vignettes of the interior showing the furniture and it was substantially completed by 1850. The knapped flint and fish-scale plain tile roofs, are, like the plan, local; the Whitby stone dressing arrived by sea as ballast. The central spire was not carried up above the bell stage.

Since Pugin was 'both paymaster and architect'[69] no expense was spared on the structure. The internal walls were lined in Whitby stone ashlar, and a watercolour shows the roofs were to be panelled over densely set scissor trusses which remain exposed in the nave. The nave arcade with its clustered shafts and leaf capitals was modelled on the chancel north arcade at St Mary's, Beverley, which Pugin was restoring; this Decorated form was frequently used by the young E.W. Pugin. Pugin had by now moved away from the dense, overall pattern-making of Cheadle. Ramsgate impresses by its restraint and simplicity, and in the balance between furnishing and structure (plate 142). The interior spaces are deliberately asymmetrical, and the position and scale of the nave windows deliberately random. Some furnishings were already installed before Pugin's death. Both the tabernacle and font presented by Myers were shown at the 1851 Exhibition, and their placing is clear in the 1849 Royal Academy watercolour (plate 105). In the aisle is the magnificent stone

142.† St Augustine's, Ramsgate, the Crossing and Sanctuary with the rood screen (since removed). The tabernacle and throne shown at the 1851 Exhibition are on the High Altar (both now demolished).

143.† St Augustine's, Ramsgate, south aisle with the Seven Sacrament font and cover shown at the 1851 Exhibition.

144. St Augustine's, Ramsgate, statue of Our Lady by Myers and the Pugin Chantry parclose screen with the Pugin hatchment above. Stone ashlar walls have now replaced the polychromy of Cheadle.

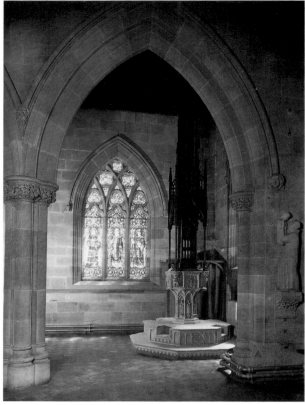

carved Seven Sacrament font, with its wooden spire cover (plate 143), and in front of the Lady Chapel the statue of the Virgin, both by Myers (plate 144). Within the inner crossing arch was the oak rood screen with its medieval *crucifixus* figure, and in the sanctuary choir stalls. The Blessed Sacrament was reserved in the massive tabernacle under a benediction throne and spire shown at the 1851 Exhibition (see plate 446). Its over-large scale in relation to the simple column and slab altar, a type Pugin used in buildings of an earlier style, suggests that the altar as an ensemble may be a posthumous hybrid.

Pugin's church was in use from 1850 and here he organised a liturgy to his taste, with plain-chant singing at Mass, and Sunday Vespers rather than Benediction. Pugin himself acted as cantor, with John Hardman Powell and Edward Pugin as servers and sacristans, the latter being charged by Hardman for a thurible and incense in 1849.[70] The church was also a family burial place and chantry, to which the south transept was given over. Tragically A.W. Pugin's was to be the first burial, in a tomb designed by the young E.W. Pugin (plate 6). Recalling his pupilship here, John Hardman Powell called St Augustine's 'Pugin's "church-tomb". There in stone, oak, iron and glass the inner spirit of his genius lives – Faith and Truth'.[71]

The commissions for the seminaries were of great tactical importance to Pugin since he realised that the training of the parish clergy would be the key to the acceptance of his stylistic and liturgical views. Unlike his more often described churches, his three major seminary chapel commissions survive largely intact. The commission for St Mary's College, Oscott began in May 1837 when Pugin arrived in the guise not of an architect but an antique dealer. Here he found almost completed the new seminary for the Midland District, under the Catholic architect Robert Potter (plate 145). It was another project of Bishop Walsh. Although Pugin did not supplant Potter until 1839, he was soon supplying eye-catching drawings of architectural details such as the roof bosses in the chapel (plate 146).[72] It was such details and particularly furniture which Pugin introduced, rather than the supposed addition of the five-sided apse to the Potter Chapel which is sometimes attributed to him.[73] Pugin's famous etching showing the antiquities he was to install was cut in June 1837. It also showed the clergy vested in the full Gothic chasubles, which were worn for the first time at the consecration.[74] At the opening Pugin was remembered 'with his dark eyes flashing and tears on his cheeks, (he) superintended the procession of the clergy and declared it the greatest day for the Church in England since the Reformation'.[75] Shrewsbury anticipated 'a new race of zealous English Missionaries; such as are now bringing up at Oscott under the good Bishop and Pugin'.[76] The enthusiasm for the Gothic Revival the seminarians learnt at Oscott was intended to transform the English Catholic Church. For Pugin, it was the show-case of his talents as architect to the whole Catholic Revival which seemed to take off with the consecration of the chapel in June 1838.

Pugin was 'Professor of Ecclesiastical Antiquities' at Oscott and the lectures he gave were later partly published as *True Principles of Pointed or Christian Architecture*. Here he established in 1838–9 the 'Museum' described as 'A school of art . . . and a very interesting ecclesiastical museum . . . to which any of the boys may have access . . . I hope great things from this as I think it will inspire a rising generation with true taste and make them appreciate the works of their Catholic ancestors.'[77] His 1838 'church ornaments' bill included 'old carvings of the museum'[78] and in 1839 Thomas Morley was paid 'To fit up Museum complete £68'.[79] The Museum was placed next to the chapel and the labelled carved Gothic details survive in their cabinets (plate 182). Pugin used scaled drawings of tracery to illustrate his lectures

145. St Mary's College, Oscott, by Joseph Potter. Pugin furnished and decorated the Chapel on the right and designed the statue of Our Lady under the niche.

146.† Design for roof bosses for the apse of St Mary's College, Oscott, signed and dated 1838 (Private Collection). The iconography draws on the Litany of Our Lady.

which also survive. His teaching method is explained in a letter to the Newcastle church committee: '. . . The drawings requisite to be syzed [sic] are contained in the large sheet which you saw at Newcastle. I set out all the mouldings etc at once on zinc templates & for carvings etc I always select ancient examples & have them cast everything essential is set out on the drawing.'[80] It was this short-hand method, first used at Oscott, which later served for Myers's craftsmen, and for the stained glass cartoon shop at Ramsgate.

The Oscott archives include one of the most important documents of Pugin's decorative career, his furnishing bill for 1838 totalling £2573.[81] Pugin acted as the middleman for the purchase, supply and fitting of antiquities such as the fifteenth-century Flemish reredos (plate 380) bought from the London dealer Edward Hull of Wardour St for £600 and the baroque stalls from Webb of Bond St for £92.[82] Pugin also installed medieval furniture in the sacristies to house vestments, sacred vessels and devotional objects. He furnished rooms for the Bishop, the President, the main guest room, the dining room and library (plates 228, 243). The whole of Oscott was in-

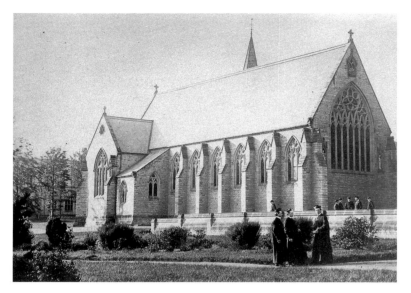

St Cuthbert's College, Ushaw, 147. The Chapel before rebuilding in 1882–4 (photo: Private Collection), 148. Pugin's High Altar and lectern reused in the later church, 149. The Lady Chapel, redecorated by J.F. Bentley (1899).

tended to be a museum, a didactic collection of antiquarian objects, not only for study, but in daily use in the chapel and halls of the seminary. Pugin's refurnishing of Oscott was certainly to the standard achieved by contemporary antiquarian collectors such as Charles Scarisbrick and his most important furnishing commission since that for Windsor Castle.[83]

Despite the central place Oscott held in Pugin's early career, he was seldom there after the mid-1840s. But he was already cultivating contacts elsewhere. One of these led to the commission for the new chapel at St Peter's College, Wexford (1838–41). In the same year Pugin began his connection with the seminary for the Northern District at Ushaw just outside Durham. Dr Charles Newsham, President from 1837 to 1863, was an important patron both for A.W. and E.W. Pugin. A complete college chapel was designed by A.W. in the Early English style in 1840, for which one of Pugin's book-form sets of sketches survives (plate 288),[84] but another scheme was produced and a Decorated church was built (1844–8). The chapel (plate 147) followed the medieval collegiate plan of a straight-ended sanctuary and stalled choir (plate 148) divided from the antechapel by a rood screen. It was replaced by a larger apsidal church by Dunn and Hansom (1882–4), who re-used Pugin's stained glass and window tracery, and other details;[96] the high altar and double piscina were reassembled in the antechapel, and the stone double jubé screen was later repainted by J.F. Bentley. Pugin's Lady Chapel was also reassembled using his altar, floor tiles and stained glass (plate 149). His seated wooden figure of St Cuthbert in a tripartite niche, with the Shrewsbury talbot, is in the antechapel. A magnificent *Liber Vitae* bound by Hardman, lists the donors, beginning with clergy, the nobility and gentry among whom John Hardman included himself: it is illustrated with charming miniatures including one of the church (plate 293).[85] Pugin's elaborate double door survives in the organ tribune cloister and in the cloisters to the north of the church are the Relic Chapel (1851) and St Joseph's or the Servants' Chapel (1851–2).[86] Pugin also rearranged the refectory and other service areas (plate 150). Although Pugin was still making designs in 1852, some were handed over to others, and the commission for the new library was given to his rivals Joseph and Charles Hansom.

The seminary for the London District, St Edmund's College, Ware, was established like Ushaw, in 1793 by refugees from the English College at Douai. Pugin's first visit to St Edmund's in November 1842 resulted in an enthusiastic address from the students to which he made a charming illuminated reply. Without strong leadership at the college Pugin's church design (1845–6) was left unfinished on Bishop Griffiths's death in 1847 and thus it remained, largely because of his successor, Cardinal Wiseman's, distraction with London business. The collection of sketch and presentation drawings at St Edmund's reflects this confused history and allows us to follow the development, beginning with a plan of a church and cloister labelled 'college chapel Dr Griffiths', an east end elevation showing the intended spire (1845), and an interior of the choir and sanctuary (1847). There are further working drawings for mouldings and colour schemes. Pugin made designs for Bishop Griffiths's tomb, and a Lady Chapel. The first drawing of the rood with an elaborate and heavily structured pierced dado is dated 1848; without its 'popish' figures it was shown at the Mediæval Court at the Great Exhibition.[87] Other rood screen drawings showing the jubé are dated 1850.[88] By contrast there are no surviving drawings for the high altar and reredos, which was paid for by 1848. Instead of Pugin's proposed sedilia, the stone panelling round the sanctuary walls was paid for by the clergy of southern England, evidence of their reaction to his liturgical views.[89]

Although the *Tablet* reported in 1851 that the church was 'finished (so) that little except the stalls are required',[90] the church was not opened until 1853. As so often with Pugin, the visual excitement of his furnishings is in strong contrast to the undernourished architecture: the chapel was built of stock brick, its tall roof supported by spindly roof trusses, in contrast to the elaborate Decorated tracery, particularly the east window filled with Hardman glass of 1847–8. The accusation of 'starving the roof tree to gild the altar' could be levelled particularly at St Edmund's.

Pugin's romantic Catholicism identified strongly with the revival of the religious orders. He had definite views on the necessity of a strict enclosure required by the rule of orders of monks and nuns founded in the middle ages. It is ironic

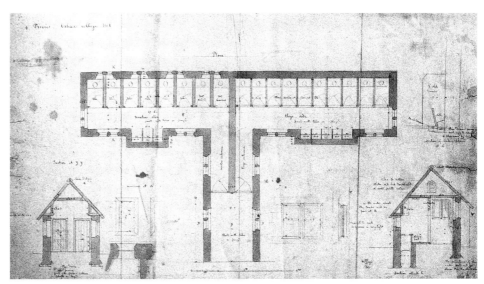

150. St Cuthbert's College, Ushaw, design for the College privies, signed and dated 1841 (Private Collection). The drawing shows Pugin's attention to details of ventilation, drainage and the separation of students from masters.

therefore that his best convents were for the distinctly 'modern' Sisters of Mercy, founded in Dublin in 1827 by Mother Catherine McAuley, who was actively opposed to any enclosure. Pugin built their first English convent at Bermondsey (1839–40), which he drew and described in the *Catholic Directory*.[91] When Mother McAuley arrived she criticised it: 'the sleeping rooms are too large, the corridors confined and not well lighted, and all the Gothic work made it expensive.'[92] It was to be followed by those at Handsworth, Birmingham (1840–1), Liverpool (1841–3) and Nottingham (1845), and one in Ireland. Handsworth (plates 151, 152) was the gift of John Hardman senior and his daughter Mary was among the first nuns.[93] Bird's-eye drawings signed by J.H. Powell in 1841 for 'Hardman's Hospital' survive. The original buildings consisted of two intersecting ranges forming an L, the refectory range with cells above for the nuns, and a small stalled chapel, with a cloister to complete the enclosure.[94] Here however Catherine McAuley was able to give clear directions on the plan required, telling Dr Walsh, 'I am not so afraid of Mr Pugin as I was, he is so fond of high walls and few windows.'[95] The later church (1846–7) had a tower embraced by one of the aisles of the double-aisle plan and could accommodate over four hundred (plate 152).[95]

Architecturally the most impressive of the series of Mercy Convents is at Nottingham. Like Handsworth it seems to have been considerably extended. It is built round three sides of a quadrangle with a large gabled chapel on an upper floor: the screen and stalls by Myers and the east window by Hardman are probably reused.

151. Convent of Mercy, Handsworth, Birmingham, the refectory with Pugin's furniture and stained glass.

152. The church added to the Convent of Mercy, Handsworth, in 1847–8 was demolished after minor bomb damage.

153. The Chapel and Priest's House, St John's Hospital, Alton.

Pugin also built small parochial convent, school or presbytery groups such as those found at Cheadle, Rugby and Spetchley in Worcestershire. But he preferred the grander scale of the late medieval 'hospital' or almshouse as the architectural type for his convent buildings.[96] He based the plan of the Handsworth convent on that of the fifteenth-century Brown's Hospital at Stamford. St John's Hospital in Alton village on the Shrewsbury estate, which Pugin designed in the autumn 1839, began in 1840 and continued until his death. It was, in Pugin's phrase, 'a perfect revival of a Catholic hospital of the old time', in contrast to the 'prisons now substituted for those convicted of poverty', that is workhouses.[97] The chapel and east range of school, priest's house and tower

(plate 153) are some of Pugin's richest buildings, built of fine local sandstone.[98] The intermittent building campaign and uncertain brief are typical of the 'will to build' which Pugin seemed to impose on the Earl of Shrewsbury and E.W. Pugin was still working here in the middle 1850s (plate 499).[99] On the seventeenth Earl's death in 1856 the unendowed buildings faced closure. The last two Catholic Earls are buried here, with brasses to other family members.

Both St John's Hospital and Mount St Bernard's Abbey occupied highly picturesque sites as they appear in the background of the *Apology* frontispiece. Both are examples of Pugin's 'sort of Catholic utopia', a neo-medieval world ruled over by Shrewsbury and Ambrose Phillipps. But the nineteenth century rudely intruded as Pugin discovered to his fury, when a fund-raising bazaar for Mount St Bernard's, presided over by the Countess of Shrewsbury and Mrs Phillipps was advertised; Pugin was even teased by an April Fools Day announcement that the monks would attend.[100]

Ambrose Phillipps had begun a Cistercian monastery on his estate in 1837 using William Railton as his architect. The appointment of Pugin resulted from the visit to the site in Charnwood Forest of the previously sceptical Earl of Shrewsbury, who:

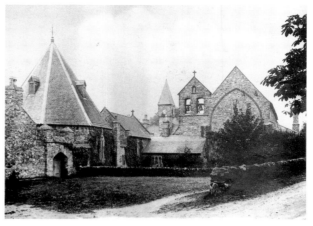

154. Mount St Bernard's Abbey, Leicestershire, engraving, *Present State*. The neo-medieval plan was repeated at other Pugin convents.

155. Mount St Bernard's Abbey, Leicestershire; the reality of the incomplete church contrasts with plate 154, and the conical-roofed chapter house is by E.W. Pugin. Ambrose Phillipps de Lisle was buried here.

156. Ratcliffe College, Leicester, east front; built of local brick, it repeats forms intended for Balliol College, Oxford.

... in the course of the evening ... offering £2000 but on the condition that the new monastery should be commenced on the very spot that had excited his imagination. Mr Pugin arrived a few weeks after this and having given a plan ... offering his services gratis.[101]

Myers agreed to charge only at prime cost.

The Picturesque garden tradition, which informed the choice of site, also influenced the position of the first public Calvary erected in England since the Reformation and fourteen Stations of the Cross on rocky outcrops in 1843; a 'Chapel of the Holy Sepulchre on the Rocks' was added in 1849. Pugin illustrated the completed church and monastery in *Present State* (plate 154)[102] and the same plates were also issued with Phillipps's appeal pamphlet '... a most solemn and picturesque monastery, which forms a perfect specimen of an old English abbey, containing cloisters, cemetery, chapter-house, refectory, lavatory, novitiate, calefactory, kitchens, guest apartments, infirmary, and library' which were built 1840–2.[103] The nave of the church followed (1842–4) complete with a stone jubé screen. Pugin later built the gate-house or guest range (plate 155).[104]

The opening of the church was reported not only in the Catholic press, but even *The Times*.[105] The buildings were much visited: 'strangers of the highest rank visit ... from all quarters ... this very summer they had the honour to receive even a royal visit',[106] and another year over fifty carriages and three hundred visitors were recorded.[107] These were as diverse as J.R. Herbert who painted the monks harvesting in the fields, Dickens who described it in *Household Words* and the young G.F. Bodley who kept a description of it at his bedside.

Mount St Bernard's was so important a model because the other great medieval order of monks in England, the Benedictines, avoided building dur-

ing this period, perhaps because of the shock of Pugin's visionary scheme of 1841 for Downside.[108] Another unexecuted scheme for the restoration of Balliol College, Oxford was re-used for the long frontage of Ratcliffe College (1843–44; plate 156) for the Rosminians, a 'new order' brought to Leicestershire by Phillipps.

Pugin's largest conventual building is St Patrick's College, Maynooth, Ireland where he built the second court (1846–53). Because of its enormous scale, Maynooth is certainly a 'factory of learning' to use Pugin's pejorative phrase.[109] Its three storey elevation, double depth plan, and endless internal cloisters have the scale if not the picturesque elements of a Gothic fantasy (plate 157) but the contract drawings are decidedly practical, including central pivot cast-iron casement windows. It is certainly markedly different from the additive planning and elevations which Pugin recommended in *True Principles* and used so successfully at Ratcliffe.[110] Three sides of the intended St Patrick's Square were built, omitting the hall and chapel, which Pugin drew in a birds-eye view in 1845.[111] The entrance gatehouse has two angle towers with conical roofs and a central oriel. Another range consists of the nine-bay refectory and screens passage giving access to the kitchen yard and an external stair tower. The eleven-bay library above is cantilevered out over

157. St Patrick's College, Maynooth, co. Kildare, St Patrick's Court (Pugin's largest building). The Chapel is by J.J. McCarthy and the tower by Robinson.

158. St Patrick's College, Maynooth, the library.

an arcade on one side, with the lean-to cloister on the other. The library has a hammerbeam roof, tracery windows and between them painted texts of Church historians, ending with the Dr Lingard who had criticised Pugin's church-furniture at Ushaw. The tables, if not the bookcases can be attributed to Pugin (plate 158). Maynooth is one of Pugin's most significant later buildings. Its hard-edged style anticipates High Victorian Gothic,

particularly in its flush tracery and two-tone polychromy of contrasted silvery limestone dressings with grey building stone and prominent roofs. Pugin employed Richard Pierce as his clerk of works, and the contract went to the Dublin builder William Beardwood.

Church furnishing was of obsessive interest to Pugin, and he was a great authority on the medieval liturgy. Pugin failed to realise that the minutiae of medieval church furniture were unfamiliar not only to the clergy but to the laity, and so he never made his teachings accessible in hand-book form. His peremptory marshalling of the clergy at the consecration of Oscott and his highly prescriptive liturgical views caused Dr Walsh to refer to him as 'Archbishop Pugens'.[112]

Pugin designed a vast amount of fixed furniture in wood and stone and as well as moveable furniture such as metalwork, textiles, painted decoration and stained glass. His insistence on rood screens and his altar designs were often the cause of clashes with the clergy's own conception of the liturgy. Many of his church furnishings were specifically condemned by the first Provincial Synod of Westminster in 1852.

The provision of rood screens in churches, dividing the sanctuary from the nave and the clergy from the laity, was a fixed principle of Pugin's church-planning. He called it the 'grand division between sacrifice and worshippers, priest and people'.[113] Screens had fallen out of favour during the Baroque period when the Catholic

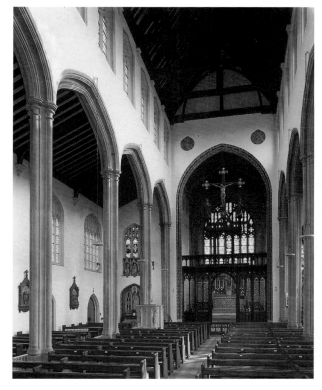

liturgy evolved a highly visual character, particularly in the Benediction service. Pugin did not design screens at Oscott, or at Uttoxeter or Derby and when he first saw the rood screen Phillipps had erected in the chapel at Grace Dieu he embraced him with the words 'Now at last I have found a Christian after my own heart!'[114] Pugin replaced it in 1842 with a more 'correct' Decorated type incorporating a medieval crucifix (plate 160). The first church with a full screen to be opened was St Alban's, Macclesfield (plate 159) in May 1841. His most famous screen, mentioned in the first descriptions of the church in 1839 and illustrated in the *Present State* articles, was that at St Chad's, Birmingham (plate 132).[115] However just before the opening of the church, Wiseman's criticism caused Pugin to exclaim to Phillipps, 'An affair has happened at Birmingham which has gone through me like a stab . . . Dr Wiseman has at last shown his real sentiments by attempting to abolish the great Rood-Screen . . .'.[116] Although Wiseman was put off and Pugin claimed that the St Chad's screen had converted its critics so that 'the effect of (the) high altar is very good and seen through the screen at benediction it is magnificent,'[117] his critics were merely biding their time.

With the St Chad's screen, Pugin not only revived a redundant medieval furnishing but he incorporated actual medieval fragments such as bas-reliefs and figures of prophets against the mullions of the tracery. Architecturally it was rela-

tively open: a low dado and wide tracery openings which allowed a good view of the altar.[118]

Pugin designed not only timber screens of open-work tracery form but also the more solid masonry jubé or double depth screen, divided into three arches supporting a vaulted platform. Within the outer arches were altars, the centre forming the entrance. Pugin built them at Mount St Bernard's, Ushaw, St George's Southwark, and St Edmund's Ware, but described a series of historic examples rather his own designs in his *Treatise on Chancel Screens and Rood Lofts* (1851) where in the frontispiece the distinction is made between the 'cathedral screen', a jubé, and the simpler 'parochial screen'.[119] The surviving jubé screens at St Edmund's (plate 161) and at Ushaw are of painted and gilded stone, with the inner tracery filled with stained glass and altars placed within the arches. The stone jubé at St George's replaced the wooden screen shown in *Present State*.[120] The opening of St George's therefore sparked off the rumbling arguments against Pugin which were now orchestrated by the *Rambler* magazine, known as the 'Rood Screen Controversy'.[121] Not only was there opposition to the visual intrusion of screens but also certain confusion as to their use. The architect Hadfield wrote to Pugin to ask how holy communion could be distributed where a screen intervened between the priest and the people. Newman and his followers attacked them; others such as Fr Doyle at St George's

159. St Alban's, Macclesfield, the interior, with rood screen.

160. Grace Dieu Manor, Leicestershire, Ambrose Phillipps de Lisle's private chapel; Pugin designed the chancel arch, rood screen and side altars, 1841 (largely destroyed 1960s).

161. St Edmund's College, Ware, the stone jubé screen and rood cross, shown without the Crucifixus figure, which was deemed 'too Popish', at the 1851 Exhibition.

162.† St Mary's (C of E), West Tofts, Norfolk, rood screen; the chancel is by E.W. Pugin; the Sutton Chantry is on the right.

defended them. Hadfield, C.F. Hansom and Wardell, and other Catholic architects under Pugin's influence, built screens without attracting the odium attached to those of Pugin in the 'Controversy'. It was certainly on the issue of screens that the most recent Oxford Movement, 'verts' such as W.G. Ward, and the Oratorians, Newman and Faber, were able to challenge the ascendency of the Pugin-Shrewsbury party. It was under their influence that the screen at St Thomas of Canterbury, Fulham was demolished the day before the opening.[122] Pugin wrote of the temporary church opened by the Oratorians in London in 1849 with its classical furniture and lack of a screen that 'no men have been more disappointing than these . . . why it is worst than the socialists'.[123] Rood screens were prominent features of Pugin's Anglican churches such as West Tofts, Norfolk (plate 162).[124]

Pugin provided sedilia or fixed wall seats within his screened chancels for the three priests required at full scale high masses, either of wood as at St Chad's, or more often stone as at Cheadle and St George's, Southwark. The St Chad's and Nottingham sets were modelled on the sedilia at Westminster Abbey, the so-called Tomb of Sebert. At Newcastle Pugin had to explain that while the sedilia themselves were Caen stone, the actual seats were made of oak.[125] The arrangement of the sedilia at Cheadle followed the rubrics of the me-

dieval Sarum rite, with the celebrant nearest the altar rather than in the middle according to the Roman rite. At St Edmund's, the sedilia Pugin proposed were not built, the money being used instead to line the sanctuary walls in stone.[126] The liturgical decrees of the First Provincial Synod of Westminster ruled that seats for the clergy must be free standing benches, not sedilia recessed into the wall. The sedilia at St Chad's were suppressed in 1854.

Pugin explained his church furniture requirements, such as the 'sacrarium' or piscina for the water and wine cruets at Mass, in the first of the *Present State* articles.[127] These were usually small stone wall niches, those at Cheadle incorporated into the sedilia in the sanctuary, and let into the plinth of the pulpit at the Lady Altar. An enormous set was provided at Ushaw. Pugin also described the much less familiar 'arched tomb to serve as the sepulchre for holy week',[128] in commemoration of Christ's entombment, which Pugin cheerfully admitted was not required in the Roman rite, but which he nevertheless recommended. The richest of these was at Cheadle, with a painting of the Man of Sorrows within the recess. As with sedilia, they were forbidden in 1852. Such sepulchres were perhaps intentionally confused with the 'founders' tombs', such as Henry Howard's at St Mary's, Warwick Bridge (plate 163), which appear frequently in Puginesque churches. Pugin used altar tomb recesses to divide the main sanctuary from the adjacent chantry chapels at Alton Hospital and at Ackworth Grange, both of which were used for burials.[129]

Although such tiny churches as Warwick Bridge had screens, sedilia and a sepulchre, such essential fittings as confessionals were underplayed by Pugin, despite the importance of private auricular confession in Catholic religious practice. Pugin certainly drew a two-seater confessional on the St Chad's contract drawings in 1839, and another confessional in the crypt at St Chad's may be an early work of his.[130] The elaborately drafted building and furnishing specifications for St Mary's, Newcastle, omitted confessionals, despite a direct request from the priest, the future Bishop Riddell.[131] Pugin claimed that none survived from earlier than the eighteenth century.[132] At Oscott a Flemish baroque confessional was brought in, perhaps more for its interest as piece of furniture, than for its use. They were omitted at St George's and had to be added as an afterthought between the buttresses. A two-door confessional behind stone arches, prominent in the watercolours of the church under construction, is let into the wall at Ramsgate.

When Pugin became a Catholic, the sacrament of Baptism was commonly administered at home. Pugin caricatured this as: 'old Bottles and jugs are but sorry substitutes for baptismal fonts'[133] and said they 'administer baptism out of an old physic phial' and 'jug or basin, such as might be used by protestants or fanatics being the . . . substitute, and these in places where silver tea services are being subscribed for the clergyman'.[134] Pugin made fonts prominent in his church plans. A complete screened baptistery with stone font and wooden cover was provided at Cheadle (plate 140)[135] and the magnificent font and open-work tracery font cover at Ramsgate were based on East Anglian fifteenth-century models (plate 142).[136] Pugin also provided wall cupboards for the holy oils.

Although prominent pulpits were important furnishings in late medieval churches, Pugin preferred the simple litany desk or *prie-dieu* type he designed at Newcastle and at Nottingham. At Warwick Bridge Pugin made a small pulpit opening through the wall from the adjacent sacristy (plate 117) The pulpit at Oscott, high up the wall by the chancel arch and elaborately decorated is attributable to Pugin. At Cheadle (plate 111) Pugin designed a stone bowl pulpit on a squat plinth. The most magnificent – the octagonal pulpit modelled on Italian Gothic examples at St George's, Southwark – was carved in Myers's

163. St Mary's, Warwick Bridge, Carlisle, the wall tomb of Henry Howard, part donor of the church, 1840–41.

workshop with relief panels on appropriate themes, its lavishness a reference no doubt to the importance attached to preaching in the new cathedral for Catholic London.

The altar was the centre of the church, for here during the mass in Catholic belief the bread and wine were transformed into the body and blood of Christ, and afterwards the consecrated host was reserved in the tabernacle. Pugin experimented with altars in every style and arrangement. In *Present State* he analysed the historical development of altars either as solid masonry plinths or columns supporting a stone slab. Reredoses or 'dossals' of painted wood or stone could be attached either to the altar or the wall.[136] Pugin showed simple altars, unadorned except during mass with two candlesticks, with linen cloths, a coloured frontal and hanging curtains, in contrast to the contemporary over-loading with 'all the nicknackery of the work-room, the toilette table, and the bazaar' which he associated with pious 'societies of ladies.'[137] Pugin described the altar at St Wilfrid's, Hulme, with columns supporting the altar slab with a reliquary beneath as a 'very early form'. Those in the crypt of St Chad's, Birmingham, and at Nottingham, with one single gradine step conform with the 'early' styles of their settings.[138] 'The altar for a country church' shown at the Mediæval Court was also of this form.[139] He made early Decorated designs with large wooden triptych reredoses for St Peter's College, Wexford, *c.*1839, and for St Mary's, Uttoxeter. The fourteenth-century Decorated type with solid plinths and attached reredoses appears at Cheadle (plate 138).[140] The Newcastle high altar under

in Birmingham or the stone feretory shown under the high altar at St Wilfrid's, Hulme. Another was shown in the Mediæval Court at the Great Exhibition. He preferred the Blessed Sacrament to be kept on a separate side altar even in small churches such as Alton Hospital. At Grace Dieu a complete Blessed Sacrament aisle was added in 1848, with a plain stone altar intended to be vested under a stone ciborium (plate 164). At Cheadle (plate 139), Newcastle and Nottingham separate Blessed Sacrament Chapels of rich iconography and contrasting materials were provided. However such side-lining of the reserved Sacrament was inimical to the clergy who wished to emphasise its centrality. Pugin therefore evolved a series of much larger altars with related panelled reredoses which incorporated tabernacles at Fulham and St Marie's, Sheffield. Moreover at Ushaw, St George's and St Edmund's open-work niches or 'thrones' rose above the tabernacle to house the monstrance at Benediction. The largest of these – over fifteen feet tall – was shown in the Mediæval Court and was later installed at Ramsgate (plate 446). Such thrones and spires were a development of the medieval 'towers' or 'sacrament houses' which Pugin noted on the continent.[146] It would seem therefore that he was responsible for the evolution of the so-called 'Benediction altar' which was to be so characteristic of Catholic High Victorian sanctuaries especially in his sons' churches.

Pugin was an important propagandist for appropriate Catholic burial rites, which were as much subject to the vagaries of clerical minimalism as other parts of the liturgy. Catholic belief emphasised the importance of prayers for the dead, as well as elaborate funeral services. Under Pugin's influence the Birmingham 'Catholic Sick and Burial Society' founded in 1795 became the 'Holy Guild of St Chad' and Catholic self-help burial clubs elsewhere were similarly transformed into neo-medieval guilds. The freehold mausoleum in the crypt of St Chad's promised to the Hardman family became the chantry of St John with its chapel, screen and altar: in Pugin's words 'the first really Catholic place of sepulture [sic] to be revived.'[147] For requiem masses Pugin designed elaborate hearses and catafalques such as that illustrated in the end paper of the *Glossary of Ecclesiastical Ornament*, his most attractive and expensive publication.[148] The furnishings for Louisa Pugin's funeral in 1844 were given by him to St Chad's.[149]

Complete chapels commemorating the death of rich or pious individuals and their families known as chantries had been important architectural and

164. Grace Dieu Manor, Leicestershire, the Blessed Sacrament aisle, with a stone altar and baldachino. The crucifix is from the rood screen to the main chapel (see plate 160).

three nodding crocketted canopies Pugin thought 'a very fine revival of the decorated'[141] and explained to the bishop that 'I have got my casts from France so the subjects for the reredos will be greatly improved'.[142] More abstract heraldic reliefs were used on the Lady Altar at Ushaw. Finally a Perpendicular style altar with both a reredos attached to the altar and repeated as a detached wall decoration was designed by Pugin and carved by Myers for M.E. Hadfield's St Marie's, Sheffield in 1849. Pugin evidently intended in this 'late' style to suggest the passage of historical time in the furnishing of the church like the fifteenth-century-style font at Ramsgate.[143] Even the most elaborately carved altars had coloured frontals for seasonal use, for example the gold and purple hanging at St Chad's, Birmingham.[144]

The Blessed Sacrament was kept in the tabernacle on the altar, which Pugin decried as decidedly modern. At Uttoxeter he designed a suspended 'pix, enclosed within a silver dove, surrounded by rays of glory' for the reserved Sacrament.[145] Rather than tabernacles, Pugin, in accordance with medieval practice, highlighted reliquaries such as the feretory for St Chad's relics

financial elements of late medieval piety. They were not necessarily places of burial but the endowments which supported their commemorative masses were a rich source of income for the clergy or church concerned. Pugin designed a complete free-standing chantry chapel for Bishop Milner in 1839 at Oscott, which was never built; that for Bishop Griffiths at St Edmund's was left incomplete, both presumably for lack of funds. At St George's £1000 was left for masses to be said daily at the miniature altar of the Petre chantry, a Perpendicular design of 1849 executed by Myers. By contrast Pugin's Anglican chantries were merely places of burial, without specific liturgical meaning. But architecturally the chantries and church restorations at Albury, Surrey for Henry Drummond (plate 165) for Lady Rolle at Bicton in Devon (plate 393) and for Sir John Sutton at West Tofts, Norfolk,[150] are among his most important works.

At Ramsgate the foundation of the south transept of the church was a simple stock brick vault, above which Pugin arranged a family chantry screened off from the church. Others were intended off the cloisters to the west of the church. The Pugin chantry itself is rich in iconography and family portraiture, mostly dating from E.W. Pugin's time (plate 10) notably his father's tomb – his son's most sincere and self-effacing tribute to his father's memory. It is here that we can join Edward's plea to John Hardman to 'Please obtain all the prayers you can for my poor father'.[151]

Although the *Builder* could describe Pugin as 'the virtual pope or chief pontiff' of the Gothic Revival,[152] his fellow Catholics found him far from infallible. Given his opposition to much in the contemporary Catholic Church, it is remarkable that he had the success he did between the opening of Oscott in 1838 and St George's, Southwark in 1848. The forces which were ranged against him from the apathy of the old school clerics to the Roman enthusiasms of Wiseman and the 'verts' conspired to frustrate Pugin's medieval vision. Although Pugin himself was obviously worsted in

the Rood Screen Controversy, he was successful in establishing the Gothic as the normative style of church building and decoration within the Catholic Church as well as outside it. His unexpected death did not lead to the banishment of the Gothic and his son Edward proved to be one of the most important Catholic High Victorian architects in the Gothic style from the middle of the century.

165. The Drummond Chantry, Albury, Surrey, 1847, painting by Thomas Earley. The intense decoration, with heraldic and religious iconography, is comparable to contemporary work in the Palace of Westminster.

166.† *Kelso Abbey*, panel, *c.*1830 (Private Collection).

CHAPTER SIX

The Antiquary and Collector

Clive Wainwright

Pugin's activities as an antiquary and a collector are not two separate aspects of his life, but rather the two sides of a coin. It was his scholarship as an antiquary that informed the creation of his collection. There are a few tantalizing clues to the nature and extent of this, but sadly neither Pugin nor any of his friends left a full account of it: there is only one illustration and no comprehensive description of how it was displayed in his several houses.

As in every other aspect of his life Pugin was precocious – in 1825, when only thirteen, he was sent to Christchurch in Hampshire after an illness. His mother wrote on 6 September:

> . . . after a particularly agreeable journey to Augustus, for whose health, pleasure and improvement, it was undertook. At Christchurch he recovered his looks surprisingly but when he returned to Salisbury he lost them again . . . he has made a great many drawings while in the country and some very extraordinary and scientific for his age, papa was surprised and delighted and grudged not to pay the carriage by waggon of two large chests full of antiquities besides a very ancient chair which cost I know not what in packing which he talked and coaxed the old lady out of with whom he lodged at Salisbury.[1]

There is no evidence of what these antiquities were nor is there a description of the chair. He may well have gone to Christchurch because Benjamin Ferrey, a fellow pupil in his father's studio, was a native of the town. Ferrey would have been able to direct Pugin to the antiquities brokers' shops in Christchurch. The town must have attracted Pugin, because he even contemplated building a house there near the sea, and in 1832 he was to bury his first wife in the Priory Church.

The objects Pugin acquired on his trip to Christchurch were crammed into the modest terrace house at 105 Great Russell Street – a hundred yards from the British Museum – where Pugin lived with his parents. It already contained his father's collection and his library and one cannot tell if A.W.'s objects were kept separately. Some knowledge of A.C. Pugin's collection can be gained from the four-day sale following his death. This started on 4 June 1833, and was accompanied by *A Catalogue of Original Drawings, Books of Prints, and an Extensive General Architectural Library with an exceedingly fine and perfectly unique collection of Basso Relievo casts from Rouen Cathedral & other Norman Ecclesiastical Edifices. . . . Auction by Mr Wheatley. . . .* There were 665 lots of books, prints and drawings and 26 lots of casts, but no antiquites. Pugin's reasons for selling his parents' collection are not known, but with his father, mother and wife dead, it is possible that he wanted to start anew and may have been short of money. Augustus Charles certainly owned some ancient pieces. It is not immediately obvious whether an illustration entitled 'Petits Meubles en Fer Ouvrages du XV Siecle Cabinet de M Pugin a Londres' (plate 167), refers to A.C. or A.W.N. as it is inscribed 'Pugin del'. It is plate 215 from one of the most important source books for A.W.N. Pugin, Nicolas Xavier Willemin's *Monuments Français Inédits pour servir à l'Histoire des Arts depuis le VI siècle jusqu'au commencement du XVII* . . . which was published in parts between 1806 and 1839. Willemin died in 1833, but the work was completed by André Pottier, the Conservateur of the Public Library in Rouen; though many of the plates are individually dateable, this one is not.[2]

There is evidence that points to these objects having belonged to Augustus Charles; the door

167. A group of objects from A.C. Pugin's collection illustrated by N.X. Willemin in *Monuments Français Inédits . . . ,* 1806–39.

168.† Oak chest, from A.C. Pugin's collection (St Mary's College, Oscott).

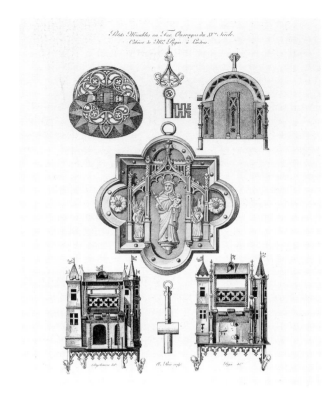

ing Blondel, Palladio, Le Pautre and Desgodetz. Many books on medieval history and architecture were included in the sale of A.W.'s library in 1853: if objects were retained from A.C.'s collection it is possible that books also were. It is easy to imagine that young Augustus could see no future use for his father's several editions of Palladio.

After the death of his parents Pugin moved out of Great Russell Street and took his collection with him to all his later houses. On 20 January 1834 he wrote to his friend, the Lincoln antiquary E.J. Willson, from Ellington Cottage, Ramsgate:

> I have a small rented house with a magnificent view of the channel well calculated for study and which I have filled with antiquities of warious [sic] sorts from William the Conquerer [sic] to henry the 8 – a collection which it would afford you as much pleasure to see as me to shew you. In my garden I have the ruins of a chapel dedicated to St Lawrence and in digging have discovered the great part of the tracery.[3]

No doubt the tracery went into Pugin's collection. Ellington Cottage still exists, but the chapel, which was indeed medieval, was demolished later in the nineteenth century.[4] By 1817 the chapel was '. . . completely unroofed and otherwise dilapidated'.[5] It is amusing to see Pugin using the cockney form 'warious' which, along with 'wery', was immortalised in the dialogue of his characters at just this time by Dickens. He lived only half a mile from the Pugin family in London and their accents may well have been similar.

The collection continued to grow quickly, for on 22 August Pugin wrote again to Willson from Ramsgate:

> I have purchased a copy of the famous (Nuremberg Chronicle) printed in 1493 and have made several additions to my collection . . . think of my collection, splendid figures, carvings in ivory, chasings in Iron and Brass, Bernard Pallisy ware of the time of Francis I, volumes of sketches you have never seen.[6]

Pugin would seem to have been intending to furnish his cottage with ancient objects, creating a series of romantic interiors, or he may even have been thinking of the house which he was already planning to build at Salisbury. On 6 November he again wrote to Willson:

> . . . glad I shall be when I can lodge you in an ancient [missing, 'room' fits best] with tapestry hangings round the walls . . . and everything en suite you will be able to fancy yourself trans-

handle was also illustrated as plate 2 in his *Examples of Gothic Architecture* (1831) along with an elaborate lock from his collection. The caption to the Willemin plate mentions that the handle had appeared in *Examples*, it also names A. Pugin, rather than A.W., suggesting that the objects in the plate are likely to have been in Augustus Charles's collection. Four medieval carved panels and an elaborate oak chest (plate 168) described as 'in the author's collection' were published in A.C. Pugin's *Gothic Ornaments from Ancient Buildings* in 1831.

A careful analysis of the 1833 sale shows that the bulk of the books were devoted to architecture and topography, mostly modern, but there were early editions of works on classical architecture includ-

ported back to the fifteenth cent and not discover your mistake till you leave the roof of your sincere friend A Welby Pugin.[7]

In 1835 Pugin, his second wife, and the collection, moved again, to the newly completed house just outside Salisbury which '... undoubtedly formed a striking contrast to the class of modern suburban houses generally erected. The place was called St Marie's Grange. Here he frequently resided, collecting old books, prints, manuscripts, pictures, &c.'[8]

The only contemporary illustration (plate 81) is a watercolour of the view from the library into the chapel. The painted inscription in the cornice over the chapel door is appropriately ecclesiastical. The altar plate must be ancient but looks distressingly Baroque rather than Gothic. The bookshelves are well filled with fat volumes, and the two chairs were made to his design by his friend Hull, the antiquities broker. The pictures are difficult to read, but they might well have been by Pugin himself. Ancient objects were mixed with those designed by Pugin, and old and new paintings hung together. At this time he was also experimenting with oil painting on panel and his view of Kelso Abbey (plate 166) would have hung in St Marie's Grange.

In 1837 they moved to London where they lived in Chelsea. The collection continued to grow, and he wrote to Willson from Salisbury on 14 October 1838:

I have purchased a most scarce book entitled Liber crudelitatum Haereticorium 1588 in which there is a plate of the death of a lady of York pressed to death for harbouring a priest whose hand is preserved now at York by the nuns do you know this book it contains a vast deal of very curious information.[9]

Soon he was on the move again and in 1843 they moved for the last time to the newly completed Grange on the clifftop at Ramsgate. At last he had a suitable home for the fast growing collection, and he acquired a boat in which he could make trips to the continent. Ferrey reports that:

He used these excursions as subservient to the object of forming a museum, which later in his life afforded him the greatest pleasure, and became one of the chief attractions of his residence at Ramsgate.[10]

Pugin was able to bring back large quantities of antiquities from the continent, and the boat also provided a quick and efficient way to transport them to Ramsgate from elsewhere in England.

This was especially true of bulky or fragile objects like stained glass. There was a considerable duty on the importation of antiquities from the continent, £1 per square foot on paintings and 1/– per pound weight on manuscripts. Pugin had organised matters so that he could, if he wished, evade this, for a tunnel – which still exists – ran from his house to a cave in the cliff face whence a rope ladder led down to his schooner. We have to rely on descriptions of the interiors and collection at Ramsgate. In 1844 John Hardman Powell, the young nephew of John Hardman of Birmingham, came to live at the Grange to help Pugin, particularly with the stained glass designs. He left a delightful account of his sojourn there. He spent much of his time in the Cartoon Room where the stained glass cartoons were produced, but which also housed part of Pugin's collection:

Finding that abroad all care for preserving old Mediaeval carvings was dead he bought up all he could and placed them in his churches, the stalls at St Chads, the Museum at Oscott, as instances, and his own Cartoon room was filled, one oak newell with a figure of B. Virgin. St Catherine and St Martin, was snatched from under a plumber's pot, and the charred parts show what a narrow escape it had.[11]

The house itself was furnished throughout with a mixture of the collection and modern objects designed by Pugin himself (plates 107–9).

The peeps into differently coloured bedrooms, with their mullioned windows, quaintly carved fireplaces and furniture, all hung with old paintings, choice impressions of etchings and engravings, Durer being prominent, was a treat for artists ... The Drawing Room ... on either side of the fireplace two large panel oil paintings by Durer which he had seen in pieces against some picture dealers wall painted on both sides for triptych purpose ... The Library ... A three light window on south side is filled with beautiful roundlets of ancient glass set in foliage and Martlets.[12]

This glass is still *in situ* (plate 169). At the top of the house under the steeply pitched roof Pugin created huge attic rooms and it was probably here that the bulk of the collection was displayed. It seems surprising that Pugin did not do any watercolours or drawings depicting the interiors of the Grange. There are however several other small pieces of evidence about his early collecting activities. Like all true collectors he was always on the look out for interesting objects and ready to exploit

169. Medieval stained glass in a window at the Grange, Ramsgate.

170. *Crucifixion*, by Mostaert, panel (Leger Galleries, London).

171. Detail of 'The Pugin Madonna', by J.H. Powell (Private Collection).

any opportunity that arose. On 6 November 1834 he wrote from Ramsgate to Willson:

A most extraordinary circumstance happened to me the other day I was selling some old silver at the refiners when in came a shabby looking man with some silver worked embroidery which I instantly discovered to be of the early part of the fifteenth century & of the most exquisite description he brought them to be burnt to sell the silver in them and by adding a few shillings more than the weight I became the happy purchaser imagine my delight in possessing these treasures. There are four in number 3 feet Long by 9 inches wide of the most beautiful embroidery & very perfect the countenances & drapery are exquisite in addition to these I have purchased a double gilt chalice of the 15th Cent which is not unlike yours in shape but about twice the size and 3 times as rich with many curious inscriptions. I shall have a most magnificent altar with embroidery for the antependium.[13]

Pugin acquired these medieval pieces of embroidery and the chalice for their rarity, but even though he did not convert to Catholicism until the next year he immediately pressed these new purchases into service as furnishings for his altar. Sadly they are not known to survive.

Pugin was very familiar with the London antiquities trade and knew a number of the key brokers who at this date mostly had their shops in Soho and especially in Wardour Street. One of the most important was Edward Hull who moved from his shop in St Martin's Lane in 1834 to 109 Wardour Street. He, in fact, took over the shop from another famous broker, John Swaby, who Pugin also knew. He also bought from another Wardour Street broker, John Coleman Isaacs, and had frequent dealings with John Webb, the celebrated Bond Street broker, who manufactured some of the most important pieces of furniture for the Palace of Westminster.[14]

Pugin also bought at auction and the collection at Ramsgate included old master paintings. On 26 April 1839 Christies auctioned the important paintings collection of Charles Aders, which consisted largely of the early German, Italian and Flemish schools. Aders, who was a German merchant, had formed his pioneering collection before 1820 and helped to introduce our artists and writers to early European art. At his house in Euston Square he entertained artists like Flaxman, Blake, Linnell and Danby, and authors like Wordsworth, Coleridge and Rogers.[15] Euston Square was a short walk from Pugin's family home, so he may well have seen the collection *in situ*, as Aders allowed interested persons to view it. Paintings of this date were not yet popular and the 1839 sale was not a great success. The diarist Henry Crabb Robinson who was also bidding remarked 'Green and Pugin the Catholic architect were real bidders'. This was not however wholly true, for, as the list of buyers' names shows, the two brokers Webb and Hull were bidding as well as the broker Horatio Rodd of Great Newport Street. Pugin was in good company, as Robinson passed several of his pictures on to William Wordsworth, '"Virgin and Child" Van der Weyden; Wordsworth takes this . . . The pictures taken by Wordsworth are presents – he made a selection of the six smallest.'[16]

Pugin bought four pictures, all on panel (lots 31, 39, 44 and 53), two of the Virgin and Child for £4 15s and £2 10s and two of the Crucifixion at £11. 0s 6d and £22. 11s 6d. In his diary for 26 April he recorded 'Bought pictures'.[17] The most expensive was lot 44, 'M. VENUSTI. THE CRUCIFIXION with MARY and ST. JOHN this picture after a Design by M. Angelo has been frequently mistaken as a work of Raffaelle.' It was 10¼ inches high and 7 inches wide and was painted on a panel,[18] and is very likely to be the 'Christ on the Cross between the Virgin and St John, on panel arched on top 10½ in by 7¼ in' attributed to Mostaert which was sold as lot 24 for £420 to the Leger Galleries on 7 December 1960[19] by Sothebys on behalf of the executors of Sebastian Pugin Powell (plate 170).

The 1960 sale also included 'Jacopo Sellaio The Madonna and Child with the infant St John . . . on panel arched on top 27 in by 17¼ in', which is likely to have been Lot 31 in the Aders sale, 'Filippo Lippi, The Virgin Child and St John a beautiful composition of this old Florentine master; full of feeling and tenderness', (panel, height 2 ft 4½ in width 1 ft 5 in). In 1960 it was sold to the Roman dealer De Castro for £1200. No photograph exists, but in 1850 John Hardman Powell painted a copy of a detail of the heads of what he called 'The Pugin Madonna' (plate 171), which might be this picture.

The 1960 sale included another nine pictures from Pugin's collection, most of similar date and type except for lot 23 bought by Agnew's[20] for £2500 – the most expensive in the sale – 'Jan Van de Velde, A Breakfast Still Life with ham on a pewter dish, nuts and bread, a glass a pipe on a wooden table covered by a black cloth' (plate 172). Then on 25 January 1961 Sothebys sold another six of his pictures, including a Steenwyck *Interior of a Cathedral*, a Wouvermans *Hunting Party* and a Domenichino *Vision of St Francis*.

The Dürer panel paintings, mentioned by

172. *Still Life*, by Jan van de Velde (Agnew's, London).

173. *Descent from the Cross*, Flemish, late fifteenth-century (Barber Institute, University of Birmingham).

Powell as in the Drawing Room at Ramsgate, fit in far better with Pugin's taste. The triptych (plate 173) belonged to Pugin and descended through the Purcell and Hardman families and it could be one of the two paintings mentioned by Powell. The relatively unfashionable early Italian and Flemish pictures which Pugin acquired give some idea of the richness of the interiors at Ramsgate. In the 1960 sale five of the pictures – none of which I have been able to trace – were bought for the not inconsiderable sum of £6450 by Julius Weitzner, which gives some indication of their quality.

There is little doubt that, as Ferrey noted, many of the best pieces were found by Pugin on the continent, certainly, thanks to the Napoleonic wars, the 1820s and 1830s were a golden age for British collectors visiting the continent.[21] On 11 May 1834 Pugin wrote to Willson: 'I am going to France & the Netherlands on an architectural expedition where I have no doubt I shall collect many rich and valuable specimens . . . I have recently added some splendid figures to my collection and expect I shall get some capital things abroad'.[22]

The sale catalogues of the two auctions which

174. Gothic Chalice, engraved by Wenceslas Hollar (Trustees of the Victoria & Albert Museum).

took place at Sothebys after Pugin's death provide some information on the collection at Ramsgate. The first sale was on 12 February 1853, and was called *Catalogue of the valuable collection of mediaeval carvings in oak and other interesting objects of art of the late eminent architect* . . . The second, on 7 April, was listed as the *Catalogue of the valuable collection of framed engravings, drawings and paintings*. . . . The latter is of prime importance for the study of Pugin's work, as it includes drawings and watercolours by him. Though there were ten early paintings, several on panel, neither the Aders pictures nor the *Crucifixion* were listed. This suggests that, as in the A.C. Pugin sale, the family had retained some of the finest objects. Among the 204 lots there were eleven Dürer prints including such celebrated subjects as *Melancholy* and *The Knight of Death*. A wide range of other prints by Goltzius, Aldegrever, Callot, de Passe and even twenty-six 'Picturesque Views of Venice', etched by Canaletto. There were no less than twenty-seven prints by Hollar, which Pugin had begun to collect in the early 1830s.[23] 'The Sacramental Chalice, adorned with figures after a drawing by Andrea Mantegna, 1640, *fine and rare*' (lot 83), has not been located, but another example is known (plate 174). The drawing from which Hollar did his engraving had come from the Earl of Arundel and was in Sir Thomas Lawrence's collection, where Pugin may well have seen it.[24] Its relevance to Pugin's metalwork designs is obvious and it is no surprise that Hardman bought it for £2 12s 6d.

The 12 February sale is informative about Pugin's collection of applied art. The 136 lots sold for £429 10s 6d. The first eighty-two were of carved wood and stone, six pieces of metalwork, eight ivories, eleven pieces of 'Stone Ware', six of 'Raffaelle Ware', thirteen of 'Majolica Ware with names inscribed on rolls' and several other assorted lots.

Fortunately the British Museum and the Museum of Ornamental Art at Marlborough House – now the Victoria & Albert Museum – bought many of the most interesting objects and most of these still survive. In a number of cases the Pugin provenance of those pieces now in the V&A had been forgotten, but it has been possible to re-establish it. Henry Cole employed John Webb to bid on behalf of the Museum of Ornamental Art at the auction, and when the objects went on display at Marlborough House they were labelled as recently purchased from Pugin's collection. After the collection moved to South Kensington in 1856 museum numbers were given to these objects. When they were published in 1863 in the first printed inventory of the South Kensington Museum the Pugin provenance had been dropped from the catalogue entries.

Among the metalwork, the most expensive object, at £24 10s, was lot 87: 'Upper part of a magnificent English Brass by the same artist as the St albans specimen, and often mentioned monumental works as in private possession, of the xivth century'. It was bought by Henry Cureton, 'Medallist & Coin Dealer, 20 River Street, Myddleton Square', for the British Museum, for whom he often acted at this date. Pugin owned this by 1847, for it was published three times in 1847 and 1848.[25] As it is Flemish it is likely that he bought it on the continent, though one of his London broker friends could also have imported it. Quite apart from its interest as a medieval object, the accurate delineation of the episcopal mitre would have attracted Pugin. He also used it as a model for his own monumental brasses (plate 361).

Cureton also bought lot 94 for £4 10s, 'An exceedingly curious Iron Chest with arched top, particularly mentioned in Mr. Willement's work'. This has nothing to do with Thomas Willement, the celebrated stained glass designer, who indeed had made glass for Pugin; it was a mistake for Willemin, for the chest (plate 175) is clearly the one illustrated by Willemin (plate 167) and had been inherited by Pugin from his father. It did not go to the British Museum, but was bought by Marlborough House in 1855.[26] It cost £2, but sadly the early records of Marlborough House (unlike the those at the British Museum) do not record the seller's name: if it was Cureton he made a considerable loss. Though the handle and several other parts are nineteenth century it consists largely of French work of the fifteenth century, as Willemin thought.

Willemin also illustrated a key, this was lot 92, 'A curious Iron Key of rare form', which Webb bought for Marlborough House for £4 15s. It is still on display in the Museum. This was certainly in A.C. Pugin's collection, for in September 1827 it appears in one of the Ackermann plates entitled 'Gothic Utensils': '. . . various utensils, such as keys, hearth broom, bell pulls &c. &c. The two keys were made in the early part of the sixteenth century and are in the writer's possession. The other articles are in imitation'.

Lot 95, 'Another Iron Chest of oblong square form, equally curious and also alluded to by Mr. Willement', does not appear to be mentioned by Willemin. It was bought by Webb for £5 for Marlborough House. Like the other coffer this has

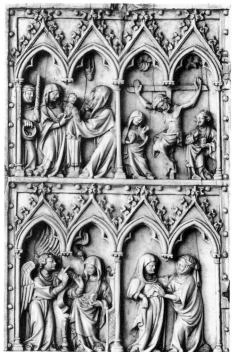

been somewhat repaired but is largely of fifteenth-century date.

Lot 85 was an 'Iron Knocker, a very elaborate and fine specimen of wrought work of the xvth century' and Webb bought it for Marlborough House for the considerable sum of £14 (plate 177). It and the key were singled out by the celebrated Professor Semper of the Government Schools of Design for special praise in his essay on metalwork in the Marlborough House Catalogue:

The cast iron knocker . . . a small but very interesting specimen of this period of transition [Gothic to Renaissance]. It is one of the earliest pieces of iron casting I know, and has a special interest from being connected with the history of this speciality. The small Gothic key, is in some respect the companion of the former work, as it shows iron forging combined with purer forms of the Gothic style.[27]

J.C. Robinson, the Curator of the Museum of Ornamental Art, also admired the new acquisition to his collection, but unlike Semper realised that it was not in fact cast iron:

Knocker in wrought iron . . . entirely executed by hand with file and chisel, and is just such a work as the famous blacksmith, Quentin Matsys, may be supposed to have produced. The small statuettes represent John the Baptist the executioner, and the daughter of Herodius with a charger.[28]

It is now thought that, though the back plate is ancient, the rest of the knocker must have been made shortly before Pugin acquired it.[29]

Pugin had certainly started buying ivories as early as 1834, and on 22 February 1839 he recorded in his diary 'Bought . . . ivory carvings'.[30] Of the eight ivories in the sale two have been traced. A report noted that 'the most precious objects were the carvings in ivory; most were bought by the Rev. Russell',[31] which is an exaggeration for Russell only bought lots 100 and 101. This was probably John Fuller Russell (1814–84), who was involved in the Society of Antiquaries and the Cambridge Camden Society, and corresponded with Pugin and Lord Shrewsbury.

Webb paid £12 for Lot 103 on behalf of Marlborough House (plate 176) (the first ivory ever acquired by the museum): 'An ivory Tablet in four Gothic compartments, representing the Salutation of the Virgin, Adoration of the Magi, and Crucifixion, beautiful gilt metal frame, of the xiv century'. The frame does not survive. This is one half of a diptych, the other half is in the Cluny Museum in Paris,[32] which may suggest that Pugin bought his half in Paris.

Cureton, acting on behalf of the British Museum, paid £4 for lot 91 (plate 178): 'An Ivory Draughtsman of the xvth century representing a walking figure, preceded by a ram, deeply cut . . . of great rarity, contained in a case thus inscribed: – "The Gift of Richard Earle Welby, Esq., 1825".' Richard Earle Welby (1779–1834)

175.† Iron coffer, French, fifteenth-century (Trustees of the Victoria & Albert Museum).

176.† Ivory tablet, French, fourteenth-century (Trustees of the Victoria & Albert Museum).

177.† Wrought-iron knocker, German, fifteenth-century (Trustees of the Victoria & Albert Museum).

178. Ivory draughts-piece, possibly English (Trustees of the British Museum).

179. Carved oak figures, English, fourteenth-century (Trustees of the Victoria & Albert Museum).

180. Stone memorial slab, French, sixteenth-century (British Museum).

was Pugin's cousin, and it is impossible to know whether this unusual object was a present to the thirteen-year-old Pugin or his father. As Welby came from an ancient Lincolnshire family this piece may have had an English provenance. The scrambled iconography would have amused Pugin, for the Ram is the sign for Aries, but here it is combined with a man carrying a faggot of wood, probably representing January[33] and thus would have formed part of a set of draughtsmen representing the months.

Two objects in lot 68 have a very interesting provenance, they were bought by Cureton for £12 15s for the British Museum (plate 180): 'Two Slabs of XVIth century, with canopy work, filled with saints and rich diaper work, perfect examples incised with great talent, They were being laid down on a bridge for pavement, when Mr. Pugin rescued them from the workmen'. The British Museum acquisitions book notes 'Supposed to have come from St Germain'. They are now thought to be late fourteenth-century and to have

been made perhaps in Flanders, then imported into France; one has the marks at the bottom where contrasting stone was inlaid into it.

It is so easy to visualise Pugin walking in Paris and suddenly coming on these slabs, about to be laid with the carved face turned towards the earth, and purchasing them from the amazed workmen, who were no doubt delighted to make a few extra francs. The abbey of Saint-Germain-des-Près was largely demolished during the Revolution and one would expect the fragments to have been used reasonably quickly, so these might have been an early addition to Pugin's collection. His first visit to Paris was in 1819; then he was there in 1823, '24, '25, '27 and '28 and many times thereafter. They were very bulky objects and, if bought on one of his later visits, would have been likely candidates for transport on his own ship.

Neither the British Museum nor Marlborough House bought any of the extensive collection of stone or wood carvings. Lot 36, 'Six figures of the Saviour, Blessed Virgin, and Apostles, seated upon thrones, and holding emblems, beautifully carved, English work of the XIVth century' was bought by the dealer Zimmerman and is likely to be the group acquired by the South Kensington Museum in 1889 from the Maskell collection (plate 179).[34]

The objects so far discussed were medieval, but curiously most of the ceramics were not, the fine pieces of majolica and the Palissy ware were wholly Renaissance: 'Large prices were given for the Raffaelle and Majolica ware of which there were many fine specimens.'[35] Although Pugin owned Palissy pieces by 1834, there were only two in the sale. Lot 134, a typical piece with a lizard and frogs, sold to the broker Gale, but lot 111 was much plainer and went at £4 4s to Webb for Marlborough House. Only one piece of Majolica was bought by the British Museum,[36] but nine pieces of majolica and Raffaelle ware were bought for Marlborough House (plate 181), making them some of the founding examples in what was to

become a major collection when the Bernal and Soulages pieces were acquired later in the 1850s.

As well as Webb, Pugin's friends, including Hardman, Hull – George, son of Edward who died in 1844 – Crace and Myers, turn up among the buyers, though the majority were London brokers including Hertz, Zimmerman, Chaffers, Davis and Durlacher. There was one other interesting private buyer, the young Charles Drury Fortnum – the celebrated Renaissance scholar and collector. He bought some woodcarvings, lot 17 'Two supports, partly figure and partly ornament'.

There is plenty of evidence that this sale only included a part of the collection, though how big a part cannot at present be established. There are certainly objects from Pugin's collection in the Museum at Oscott, though whether they were given by Pugin himself or by one of his sons is unknown. There are several carved panels, including a rather curious one from a house in Salisbury (plate 182), presumably acquired during his Salisbury days in the 1830s. Two of the panels and the splendid chest (plate 168) had once belonged to his father, for they are illustrated in the plate in *Gothic Ornaments*.[37]

The most remarkable piece at Oscott (plate 184) is however the object shown in Willemin's illustration. Willemin also tells us that this object was in his own collection before it was acquired by one or other of the Pugins. He describes it as a *Rechaud* – a brazier. It is about a foot square and is an accurate representation of a Gothic castle with a working drawbridge. It is still thought to be medieval and is the only example of this type that I can discover. It may in fact be a type of censer or perfume burner and should perhaps be compared to the twelfth-century lamp or perfume burner in

181.† Maiolica plate, Italian, sixteenth-century (Trustees of the Victoria & Albert Museum).

182.† Carved oak panel from a house in Salisbury, sixteenth-century (St Mary's College, Oscott).

183.† Carved stone boss from Utrecht (Trustees of the Victoria & Albert Museum).

184.† Iron perfume burner, French, thirteenth-century (St Mary's College, Oscott).

the shape of a Byzantine building, now in the Treasury of St Marco in Venice, though probably made in Constantinople.[38]

A considerable number of objects certainly remained in the Pugin family. In July 1945, Leigh Ashton, the Director of the V&A, went to 'The Crosslets', a house in Worcestershire where Sebastian Pugin Powell, Pugin's grandson, lived. 'He reported that he "saw a number of rather important fragments of mediaeval wooden sculpture" and he expressed the hope that they might find their way into the Museum's collection'.[39]

Instead, later that year Sebastian Pugin gave the Museum four carved and polychromed stone roof bosses of the evangelists, said to have come from Jumièges (plate 183). These have recently been convincingly shown to have originally come from Utrecht. Whether Pugin bought them on one of

185. *The Alton Towers Triptych*, bronze-gilt, gems and enamel (Trustees of the Victoria & Albert Museum).

186. Carved oak newell post, Flemish, fifteenth-century (Sotheby's, London).

187. Lectern formerly at St Mary's College, Oscott, Flemish, fifteenth-century.

his trips to the Low Countries or in London is not known.

Some at least of the objects seen in 1945 remained in Sebastian Pugin's collection and after his death were sold in 1960 as twenty lots.[40] The most important was lot 53, 'A Limoges champlevé enamel processional cross', twenty-one inches high sold to the dealer Baer for £720. Most of the lots were woodcarvings, presumably those seen by Ashton in 1945. Lot 61 (plate 186) was 'An unusual triple group in oak, perhaps a newell post, with figures of the Virgin and Child, a Bishop Saint and a female Saint . . .'. It is possible that this was the 'oak newell with a figure of B. Virgin. St Catherine and St Martin . . . snatched from under a plumber's pot', which Powell saw in the Cartoon Room at Ramsgate. It was bought for £450 by C. Norris. On 17 May 1961 Sothebys[41] sold another important Pugin object from the same collection, lot 33, 'A Gilt Bronze Angel . . . 5¾in, French, first half of the 14th Century'. It was bought by Landau for £1850 and I have been unable to trace its whereabouts or that of any of these objects.

Scattered pieces of evidence point to Pugin's involvement in the antique trade; his old friend Talbot Bury '. . . chaffed him about "smuggling over antiquities for sale".'[42] This suggests that Pugin may have imported objects in his ship for his broker friends to sell. He may then have recommended the clients for whom he was building houses or churches to go to those same London brokers to buy objects and fittings for their houses, thus potentially profiting from both sides of the transaction. Charles Scarisbrick certainly bought panelling and carving from Hull for Pugin to incorporate into his house.[43]

One of the most important medieval objects associated with Pugin is the Oscott Lectern (plate 187), which at some time between 1834 and 1836 'was brought from Brussels, and is now in possession of Mr Hull of Wardour Street'.[44] It came from St Peter's Church, Louvain in Belgium,[45] and it is not known if Hull found it, bought it and shipped it over from the Low Countries, or if Pugin, who was in Brussels in either 1834 or 1835, did. Though the lectern had been sold from the church in 1798 it presumably remained in the area until the 1830s. Lord Shrewsbury, who first met Pugin in Hull's shop in 1834 or 1835, bought it and presented it to Pugin's new cathedral of St Chad's. In 1855 it found its way to Oscott and sadly was sold from there in 1967 to the Metropolitan Museum in New York.

The remarkable fifteenth-century pulpit now at St Chad's was originally at Oscott: 'A pulpit procured through him [Pugin] and now in use at St Chads Cathedral, once stood near the Communion rails, opposite the sacristy door.'[46] This came from St Gertrude's church in Louvain and strengthens the possibility that Pugin might have done a little more shopping for or in conjunction with Hull while in the Low Countries.

It also seems likely that his immense knowledge of medieval art and the antiquities trade here and on the continent was tapped by collectors like Lord Shrewsbury for the benefit of their own collections. Pugin discusses the Alton Towers Triptych (plate 185) in the *Glossary* and it would be wholly in character if he had advised Shrewsbury on its acquisition. There is also evidence that it was restored or re-made, either just before or while owned by Shrewsbury, when the small Gothic bolt to keep it closed was probably added. It might well be that Pugin was involved with the restoration, the whole matter of restoring and improving ancient objects before re-sale was then, as now, conducted in secrecy. Both Hull and Webb had workshops which made new furniture – what else they were used for is a matter of speculation. Parts of the Oscott lectern are early nineteenth-century and were either cast for Hull while it was in his shop or by Hardman when it went to St Chad's. Pugin certainly involved them in furnishing the chapel at Oscott, where Webb supplied the stalls and Hull the altar and reredos in 1837.[47]

The reredos (plate 380) '. . . was like most of the

furniture in the chapel, by A.W. Pugin, and made up from materials gathered together by him on the Continent.'[48] The wings were modern and painted by Pugin's friend J.R. Herbert, but below them are ten Limoges enamel plaques (plate 188). These are sixteenth-century in date and are thus a singular addition to a Gothic Revival altar.

The Museum which Pugin created at Oscott probably received objects from his collection after his death, but some objects were acquired by him for the College and yet others he gave from his own collection, for example the catalogue of the collection published in 1880 reproduces 'A collection of tesselated tiles from the "Ducal Palace" Caen in Normandy. Given by A.W. Pugin, Esq.'[49] (plate 189) He probably also acquired the fifteenth-century parcel-gilt silver Pax at Oscott and he certainly illustrated it in his *Glossary*. It should also be remembered that, in his role as Professor of Ecclesiastical Antiquities at Oscott, Pugin acquired the objects particularly to illustrate his lectures.

A few years later he was acquiring several thousand plaster casts of medieval details, stone and wood carvings for similarly didactic purposes to instruct the craftsmen working on the New Palace of Westminster (plate 424). In 1863, after his death and when the works at Westminster were largely complete, these were given by the Board of Works to the South Kensington Museum and included ninety-six wood carvings.[50] Many of the wood

188. Sixteenth-century French enamel plaques, detail of the reredos in plate 380, St Mary's College, Oscott.

189.† Encaustic tiles, French, fifteenth-century (St Mary's College, Oscott).

190. Carved oak cabinet door, French, fifteenth-century (Trustees of the Victoria & Albert Museum).

191. Carved oak panel, French, fifteenth-century (Trustees of the Victoria & Albert Museum).

192. Bonfire of ancient woodwork from *Details of Antient Timber Houses*, 1837.

carvings still survive (plates 190, 191), like the newel post, they were probably saved from the demolishers' bonfire (plate 192).

Pugin also searched out and purchased medieval objects to use as patterns and examples for those craftsmen executing his designs (cf. chapters 5 and 17). Two examples demonstrate the close relationship of his collecting activities with the design and execution of objects by his trusted manufacturers. He wrote to Hardman:

I have purchased 2 objects of great interest. 1. the head of a silver monstrance which you have only to look at to appreciate it knocks our piercing to nothing it will serve 1st as a pattern and then fit up with a foot price £10. – a piece of stained glass *perfectly beautiful* in tone & colour matching these colours is possible & let it be put in a strong frame & hung up to educate the men price £3.3 you must credit me £13.3.0.[51]

These were presumably bought by Hardman and it would seem that the monstrance was re-sold when the foot had been added.

In September 1849 Pugin wrote to Crace: 'I have got a great many fine things abroad this time in various ways & a few very grand tracery panels for you for models to work by . . . they will be very useful for no drawing can give these things'.[52] It is clear that Pugin saw that a close examination of the actual ancient objects was essential to any real understanding of the principles of medieval craftsmanship.

The extent to which Pugin actually lifted designs straight from medieval sources, or transmuted everything into a unique design, is a matter for debate. The source material available to him in the form of the ancient and modern books in his remarkable library must have been influential. The books themselves, many of which were rare and interesting, also represent an important aspect of his collecting activities. The library was sold by Sothebys on 27 January 1853 in 645 lots and fortunately the catalogue has recently been republished.[53] His talents as both a collector and designer were further developed by visiting continental private collections, museums, antiquaries and scholars.[54] On his travels he produced hun-dreds of sketches of buildings and the artifacts with which they were furnished (plates 351, 382). The journeys can be fully and accurately charted from his surviving drawings, letters and diaries.

Pugin was not rich enough to create a major collection of medieval objects like that of Sir Samuel Rush Meyrick.[55] It was not even as extensive as that of his contemporary, the Gothic Revival architect L.N. Cottingham.[56] Even so, it did contain examples of art and design of importance in their own right, but much more important perhaps for the light they throw on the sources of Pugin's creative genius. These objects furnished the Grange at Ramsgate, displayed among the fittings designed by Pugin; the panel paintings, for instance, hung against polychromatic wallpaper under elaborately stencilled ceilings – the effect must have been rich indeed.

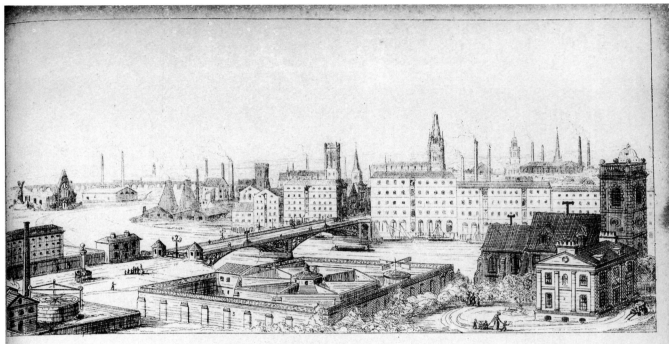

THE SAME TOWN IN 1840

1. St Michaels Tower; rebuilt in 1750. 2. New Parsonage House & Pleasure Grounds. 3. The New Jail. 4. Gas Works. 5. Lunatic Asylum. 6 Iron Works & Ruins of St Maries Abbey. 7. Mr Evans Chapel. 8. Baptist Chapel. 9. Unitarian Chapel. 10. New Church. 11 New Town Hall & Concert Room. 12 Wesleyan Centenary Chapel. 13. New Christian Society. 14 Quakers Meeting. 15. Socialist Hall of Science.

Catholic town in 1440.

1. St Michaels on the Hill. 2. Queens Cross. 3. St Thomas's Chapel. 4. St Maries Abbey. 5. All Saints. 6. St Johns. 7. St Peters. 8. St Alkmunds. 9. St Maries. 10. St Eamunds. 11. Grey Friars. 12. St Cuthberts. 13. Guild hall. 14. Trinity. 15. St Olaves. 16. St Botolphs.

CHAPTER SEVEN

Pugin Writing

Margaret Belcher

*C*ontrasts is A.W.N. Pugin's most important book.[1] He wrote it at the beginning of his career but nothing that he subsequently issued – books, pamphlets, lectures, articles in periodicals, letters to editors, broadsheets: the output is astonishing – supersedes it.[2] Typical of him in its methods, of production and distribution besides the arrangement of material, it contains the essence of his thought, representing a departure from the ways of the past and opening a new perspective for the future. *Contrasts* was an original book.

Contrasts: or, a parallel between the noble edifices of the fourteenth and fifteenth centuries, and similar buildings of the present day; shewing the present decay of taste was published in August 1836, before any building to Pugin's design had been erected, except his own house near Salisbury. For neither the first nor the last time, he was his own publisher. Success came quickly: according to a letter to E.J. Willson, an architect of Lincoln who had written the text for his father's *Examples of Gothic Architecture*, by mid-October all but one of the copies of *Contrasts* in Salisbury had been sold. Later, in June 1838, he informed Nicholas Wiseman, rector of the English College in Rome and later cardinal, that 'the work has had a most unexpected sale . . . and the coppers have been *almost worn out* in supplying the demand. . . . I never calculated on a sale of more than 400 but it has been nearly doubled – and I have thought right to supply a great part of the Clergy with copies free of charge so that in fact nearly 1000 whill have been struck off'.[3]

It was characteristic of Pugin to make a gift of copies of his publications, for he did not count the cost if he believed he could advance his cause; but what ensured the wide circulation of *Contrasts* was not so much his assiduous distribution of it as the substance he had given it in the first place. With its exclusive appropriation of excellence to the Catholicism and Gothic architecture of the Middle Ages, *Contrasts* was a contentious book and brought its author local notoriety and national attention. 'I am a marked man here at Salisbury', he told Willson in September, even before the outbreak in the county newspapers of an unedifying dispute started by a Wiltshire clergyman.[4] There was less of sectarian polemics and strident hysteria in the metropolitan notices of *Contrasts*. Pugin's biased reading of history, his partiality in architectural judgement and his incompetence in logic were recurrent points of criticism but the most conspicuous feature of the reviews was the variety of their opinions. Where one critic relished the 'boldness and freedom' of Pugin's pronouncements, another condemned him as 'an insolent reviler'.[5] According to some, his text was 'masterly', full of 'pungency and wit, . . . and just remark', but for another it proceeded from a 'fearfully diseased state of mind', guilty of 'Jesuitically distorting facts'. Pugin, some claimed, was 'childish' and 'palpably absurd', even 'a very great blockhead'; the book, maintained others, showed 'great knowledge' and was 'undoubtedly the production of a clever man'. While one reviewer was delighted by the 'spirited manner' of the etchings, another dismissed the plates as 'rude and almost shapeless scratchings'. In the eyes of one, Pugin displayed 'perfect taste' whereas for another his satire was 'coarse and burlesque'. At times the verdicts were specifically opposed. For the *Athenæum*, *Contrasts* seemed 'to contain the outpourings of disappointment' and the reviewer rebuked Pugin for the 'splenetic animosity' of one illustration; the *Gentleman's magazine*, on the

193. The most eloquent statement of his social ideal in all Pugin's publications: the plate of contrasted towns from *Contrasts*.

other hand, was pleased that Pugin's 'strictures on the modern productions are not tinctured by spleen or soured by disappointment'. The *Athenæum* wished that Pugin had remained content with architecture 'rather than thus seek for a doubtful reputation as a caricaturist'; the *Gentleman's magazine* was sure that this new work would 'increase his previous reputation'.

Making allowance for the subjectivity of response and for differences of readership, this divergence among contemporary estimates is still illuminating. Not only did the reviewers fail to agree about the quality of the book, they were not in accord about its nature. Some took it as architectural history, others as ecclesiastical; and neither group was satisfied. *Contrasts* did not fit into any generic category that its critics knew; it was different from conventional architectural history as that was written by leading scholars like Thomas Rickman and Robert Willis, whose accounts of medieval Gothic were factual, direct and informative, the verbal equivalents of A.C. Pugin's documentary pictorial records. A preference for Gothic or neo-classical or modern will not explain the diversity of reaction; nor will denominational affiliation account for it: there is no unanimity among Protestant assessments. Taken as a whole, the critical reception is confused. The anonymous architect who published a pamphlet in reply to Pugin's volume confessed that he found *Contrasts* a 'strange and novel book'; the *Athenæum* began its report with the candid admission: 'We hardly know how to treat this work'. The perplexity of contemporary criticism is a main index of the originality of Pugin's book.

Had the reviewers been able to rid themselves of expectations to which experience predisposed them, it would have been easier for them to recognize the nature of Pugin's work. Many of their objections are, on their own terms, well founded. Pugin promises in his subtitle to draw a 'parallel' and to deal with 'noble edifices' yet the modern structures he represents are usually mean and ugly, not 'similar buildings' at all. Some of the modern specimens were not erected for the purpose to which they have since been turned; some of the old examples no longer exist, some are not shown as they survive: how can reliable architectural conclusions be reached in such conditions? Pugin moreover diverts attention by the introduction of human figures. The complaint that 'there exists hardly any connexion between the plates and the letterpress' seems just, once it is found that, except for a passing allusion to the buildings of Christ Church, Oxford, in the text and the representation of its main gateway among the drawings, not one subject of the illustrations is referred to in the written part of the work.

Seen from a different angle, however, many of these alleged shortcomings assume another aspect and cease, indeed, to look like faults at all. There is a case to be made for regarding *Contrasts* as an imaginative production: not one relying on facts, not one proceeding by rational analysis, not one to be read literally. The aim is to persuade, not to inform; and for this purpose the tactics are aptly chosen. Subjects of equal beauty in each half of a contrasted plate will not make the beholder instantly take sides; splendour juxtaposed with shoddiness at least may. To exhibit the screen of Durham cathedral with its ancient glory restored, instead of in its present state of shabby neglect, is greatly to increase its appeal. The human figures in the plates are another device to attract the viewer to one scene and repel him from the other. The same strategies are at work in the text: the passage denounced by one critic as 'mere strut and swagger', a description of Buckingham Palace and other prominent buildings, is in fact a rhetorical question which Pugin can never have intended to be taken at its face-value; here as elsewhere, he is writing to make the reader share his point of view. The diction is selected for the same effect of engaging sympathy or breeding distaste: the connotations of virtue and value are ranged on the side of the old, those of unworthiness and inferiority on that of the new. What links the text and the etchings is the spirit of Pugin's meaning, the same in both media. Westminster abbey, for example, may be discussed without being depicted but the plates make comprehensively clear the 'majesty' and 'sanctity', the 'venerable' and 'solemn' character, of the ancient structures on which the text insists. Likewise, after a general description of monuments which are 'incongruous and detestable', 'vile masses of marble', 'most inappropriate and tasteless', the Rev. John Clutterbuck's tomb is a sufficient illustration. When *Contrasts* is approached in this way, as an exercise in persuasion, an essay in rhetoric, what contemporary critics stigmatized as invalidating weaknesses become triumphant strengths.

To suggest that *Contrasts* be so regarded is to move Pugin's volume out of the domain of architectural history and criticism and into that of literature; and there are other reasons for making such a transfer. When Pugin came to revise his text for the second edition, issued in London by a commercial publisher in 1841, he made alterations to his historical material by redefining the bound-

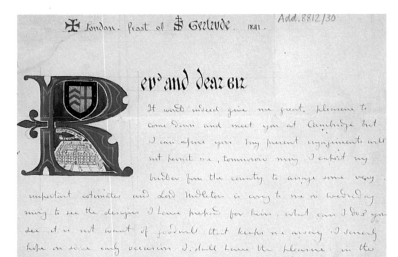

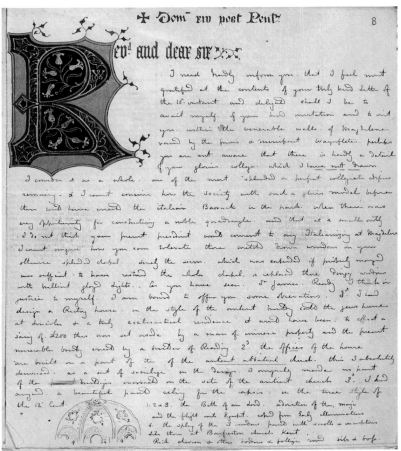

aries of the period of Gothic excellence; whereas in 1836 the reader had been invited to admire the chapel of King's College, Cambridge, for instance, he now found himself expected to follow his author in condemning it. Pugin gave a different interpretation of the cause of the suspension of the Gothic style, too. Insofar as he was correcting errors of which advanced scholarship had made him aware, he can only be respected; but changes of ground as radical as these place his credibility as a historian in grave jeopardy if they do not deliver it a mortal blow. On the other hand, if Pugin is seen as a writer dealing in the intangibles of the imagination, the precise chronological location becomes irrelevant; the taunt of the *British critic*, that he had fixed the period of perfection at the time of the Wars of the Roses, is by the way.

For Pugin in *Contrasts* is a creative artist, working not with plans and designs but with words and pictures, in the combination most typical of him as an author both of books and of letters (plates 194, 195). To claim his work for literature is not to deny his learning. As a young man he built up a valuable library and his correspondence discloses that in later life he longed to add to it but felt unable to justify the expense. Nevertheless, his collection was enviable – Pugin reported to his great friend John Hardman that one visitor to St Augustine's, 'a most learned man & a great bookworm, . . . groaned over some of my fine copies of old English & French authors'.[6] His reading stood Pugin in good stead in one part of *Contrasts*: it provided him with documentation for the ravages wrought during the Refor-mation. What is revealing, however, is that he offers no evidence for his account of the medieval period. The explanation of the absence is not far to seek: factual proof did not exist. One cannot authenticate a fiction. Pugin's picture of the Middle Ages is a vision, stimulated by his reading and by his religion, but essentially born of his imagination. It is a new construction rather than a reconstruction of the old, the representation of an ideal. An ideal cuts loose from time and ac-tuality; as an imaginative artifact, the vision mediated by *Contrasts* is ubiquitously and perennially accessible.

The most succinct expression of Pugin's ideal, together with the most unambiguous indication of the nature of his work, is to be found in one of the plates he added to the second edition of *Contrasts*. Employing as before the technique which was the

194. Illuminated letter (Magdalen College, Oxford). The virtual commencement of a correspondence with J.R. Bloxam, fellow of Magdalen College, Oxford, who from late 1840 onwards was Pugin's chief link with the Oxford Movement.

195. Illuminated letter (Cambridge University Library). Other correspondence places it almost beyond question that this letter was addressed to J.F. Russell, member of the Cambridge Camden Society.

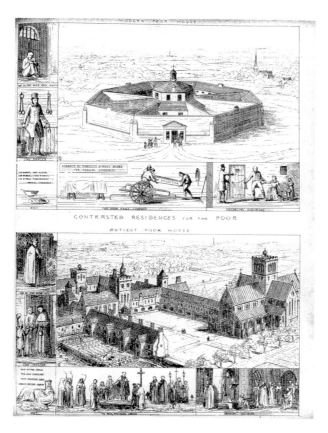

organizing principle of his text and his etchings as well as the source of his title, he set forth two views of a town, a 'Catholic town in 1440' and 'The same town in 1840' (plate 193); with characteristic attention to detail, Pugin makes even the legends below these scenes serve his purpose by contrasting the lettering he uses. Buildings form the main substance of each picture but Pugin is not interested in them for their own sake. Rather, he is concerned with what they reveal of the society which erected them and lives in them. In the medieval town, fourteen of the named buildings are churches; trees grow along the banks of the river and the bridge allows free passage. The significance of these features is defined by the opposing modern view. Where the consistent practice of the Gothic style in the old town betokens a single religious creed and humanity's contentment in both, the structures of the new town are uniform only in their harsh, monotonous ugliness. Of the original churches, two 'remain', one rebuilt, the other in ruins; the rest have gone and in their place stand four chapels belonging to different denominations, one church, one meeting-house, premises for the '*New Christian Society*' and a '*Socialist Hall of Science*'. Gasworks and ironworks have been erected and a lunatic asylum and, most conspicu-

ous of all, a vast jail, which occupies what used to be open land available for the enjoyment of all. The peaceful old churchyard has been enclosed and converted into '*Pleasure Grounds*' reserved for the family at the new parsonage. The river-banks have been turned into wharfs, the trees felled; trading vessels replace the happy sculler of the old world; the bridge is closed by a toll-gate requiring payment of a fee. Like the signs of nature, the marks of a free and generous community have disappeared; the evidence here is for social exclusiveness, a competing proliferation of sects, mechanized, dirty and noisy industry, the pursuit of money, the advent of madness and crime. In this plate, uniquely, Pugin does not divide the page into equal halves. The greater height of the 'Catholic town' provides free space into which the numerous spires can soar, reflecting humanity's aspirations and Heaven-directed life. In 1840, the horizontal is stressed; warehouses dwarf and obscure the churches which dominated the medieval scene. Contemporary man is earthbound and materialistic and his society is characterized by separation and division; it is not a society in the true sense of the word at all, not a fellowship: walls, barriers and railings abound.

The other significant illustration that Pugin drew for the edition of 1841 displays an even more overtly human interest. With a precise topicality in a decade of agitation about the Poor Law, Pugin exhibits 'Contrasted residences for the poor' (plate 196). He sets a magnificent suite of Gothic buildings, huge chapel, master's house, dining hall and other accommodation, surrounded by spacious lawns, walks, gardens and open fields, against one of the most cheerless and uncharitable structures ever conceived, a bare, angular, windowless hybrid of fortress and jail, surmounted not by a cross but by a weather-vane; Pugin took his cue from the Panopticon, the Utilitarian philosopher Jeremy Bentham's suggestion for a model prison. Bordering the bird's-eye view of each institution, Pugin sketches vignettes of episodes in the lives of the inhabitants. The medieval poor man is warmly dressed, plentifully fed, cared for by an affectionate master, and mourned by his fellows at death. The fate of the modern pauper is the exact opposite: his diet is scarcely sufficient to sustain life, he has nowhere to sit but on the floor, where he huddles solitary and shivering in his thin clothes; his master carries a whip and fetters in lieu of an open money-bag; discipline is enforced by bludgeons, locks and keys, handcuffs and chains; elsewhere, a mother is torn violently from her children; and when he dies, the modern pauper receives not a decent burial from his sorrowing brethren but a final humiliation, the sale of his corpse for dissection. The last unity, literal, corporeal unity, has gone: division hounds modern man even unto death and beyond.

Unity is the hallmark of Pugin's vision in *Contrasts*; his ideal world acknowledges one God, joins in one faith, builds in one style, and lives at one in society. There is no friction, no separation, no discord; it is a vision of perfection upon earth. Exploiting the device of contrast again for this fundamental purpose, Pugin uses this ideal as a criterion by which to identify the failings of his own time and as a standard to which it can aspire in their redress. As he interprets the quality of society from its architectural behaviour, so his work takes on the dimension of social comment: the human figures in the plates are not an intrusive diversion but an additional agent of analysis. *Contrasts* is a work of social criticism, satirizing the increasing secularization and materialism of the incipient Victorian period and endeavouring to counter those tendencies by a recall to the values imputed to the past.

If such a reading of architecture took by surprise those of his readers who had an interest in that art, those of a literary bent would not have been prepared for Pugin's vision either, it seems. There are no antecedents for his version of medieval life in such earlier literary works as his biography suggests he might have known. According to J.H. Newman, it was Walter Scott above all who 'turned men's minds in the direction of the middle ages'; and with adaptations at any rate of three of Scott's novels Pugin was familiar before he published *Contrasts* (with a fourth, *The betrothed*, the evidence of his acquaintance is not provided until 1848 when he quotes a fragment of verse from it as an epigraph to his account of his courtship of Helen Lumsdaine).[7] Performances in London of dramatized versions of *Peveril of the peak*, *Woodstock* and *Kenilworth* are mentioned in Pugin's 'Autobiography' and the last of them he must have known well since he painted sets for the production; but *Peveril of the peak* and *Woodstock* are set too late to have affected Pugin's view of the Middle Ages and it was certainly not from *Kenilworth* that he learnt to call Elizabeth I 'that female demon'.

Scott's popularity in the 1820s and 1830s was huge and it is quite possible that Pugin read more of his novels than those which his enthusiasm for the theatre brought to his notice. While none of Scott's other novels is set in England in the period which Pugin singles out as pre-eminent, *Ivanhoe* depicts England at the time of the Crusades and the *Fair maid of Perth* displays the fourteenth century in Scotland. *Ivanhoe* refers to 'merry England' in its first sentence but there any resemblance to Pugin's attitude ends, for Scott unfolds a narrative compounded of ignorance, fanaticism, greed, treachery, lust – the catalogue of barbarity and vice is long and the narrrator makes no secret of his contempt for the earlier age. There are touches of heroism and devotion but the predominant impression is of disorder, tumult and horror. The case is the same with the Scottish novel; the male protagonist maintains at one point that the people are readier to burn a church than to build one. The author's disdain for the period is patent; Scott sees the past as primitive, his own time as enlightened. Pugin found no hints here for his exalted vision of peace, reverence, loyalty, learning and solicitude.

It was another of Scott's works, *Quentin Durward*, that Victor Hugo intended to outdo with his *Notre-Dame de Paris 1482*. *Notre-Dame* made Hugo's name in England, where two translations were issued in 1833, though Pugin, being fluent in French, would not have needed to wait for those had he, knowing Paris and perhaps aware of Hugo's interest in architecture, wished to read that ambitious publication. Hugo was a member of the official Comité historique des arts et monumens and it was to this body that A.N. Didron, the French ecclesiologist who was its secretary, read the letter describing his current work which Pugin sent him in 1843 and which was published in the *Bulletin archéologique*. Pugin came to know Didron but whether he ever met Hugo or read his novel there is no proof. Had he done so, he would have discovered an attitude towards Gothic totally at variance with his own. Hugo is happy to 'read' – the metaphor is his – architecture as a symbol in the same way as Pugin does but Gothic for him is no more than one chapter in the great book of humanity, one stage in its march towards the freedom and democracy that he applauds: Hugo's political sympathies are diametrically opposed to Pugin's. For the rest, his novel, whatever its vitality and strength, depicts a world of anarchy, deceit and violence, quite the reverse of Pugin's image of dedication and harmony and joy; despite the centrality of the great cathedral of the title, there is no sense of the spiritual at all.

If these successful works are taken as representative of the current view of the Middle Ages, there is evidently nothing in them which could have encouraged Pugin directly in the formation of his ideal. Examination of them indicates, how-

197. Plate 49, 'A floriated Cross', one among several patterns of 'Crosses' in the *Glossary of ecclesiastical ornament and costume* of 1844, Pugin's most splendid publication and a masterpiece of chromolithography.

ever, from yet another angle, that Pugin was presenting his readers with something new; like comparison with previous architectural discourse, like the reactions of critics, they serve as a measure of the originality of his 'strange and novel book'.[8]

If precedents for Pugin's vision are hard to find, it is not difficult to detect works of a similar spirit in the literature that followed *Contrasts*. Two years after the second edition appeared, Thomas Carlyle, essayist and historian, published his greatest work of social criticism, *Past and present*. It is tempting to think that Carlyle was aware of Pugin's volume, for the two men were near neighbours in Chelsea and the issue of *Fraser's magazine* that reviewed *Contrasts* also carried a story by Carlyle. The title of *Past and present* already declares Carlyle's *modus operandi*. Prompted by a contemporary chronicle of a twelfth-century monastery, he recounts the life of that community, selecting and developing details from his source into a recreation of his own and infusing his animated image with distinctive values derived from his own beliefs. Fully as fictional as Pugin's ideal world, Carlyle's is marked by the same supreme spirituality as Pugin's, which gives rise to unselfconscious devotion in the individual being and to harmonious cohesion in the group. This perfect microcosm is set in opposition to Carlyle's portrait of his own day, a time compounded of shallow indifference and selfish greed, lacking both internal authority and common purpose, when instead of forming part of a huge fellowship under the governance of God the human being is a mere 'Hapless Fraction'.[9]

John Ruskin followed Carlyle, William Morris followed Ruskin. Collectively these authors compose a distinct continuum in Victorian literature, to which other writers – like Benjamin Disraeli in *Sybil* – make a homogeneous if smaller contribution. Despite their divergences, they are alike in having recourse to an idealized Gothic past in a bid to reform the unhappy present. In reaction against the atomistic, competitive condition of humanity postulated by the pervasive philosophy of Utilitarianism, their ideal worlds share the paramount virtue of a sense of mutuality and fellowship. Their works constitute the strain of literary medievalism in the Victorian period, with its affinities with the analogous Pre-Raphaelitism in art, Gothic revivalism in architecture and Tractarianism in religion. A tradition of social criticism was established; and *Contrasts* stands at the head of it.

'We rejoice in Mr. Pugin's return to his career of usefulness', announced the *Athenæum* with re-

lief as well as approbation when Pugin's next book after *Contrasts* appeared; but *Details of antient timber houses* was to be his last production in the manner of documentary record that he had learnt from his father.[10] He continued to publish for the rest of his life: always, however, in his own, new way. He issued two pamphlets in 1837 in answer to critical commentary: *An apology for a work entitled 'Contrasts'* (he uses the word 'apology' in its accepted nineteenth-century sense of 'defence') and *A reply to observations which appeared in 'Fraser's magazine'*; but between the editions of *Contrasts* he made no changes in deference to reviewers' objections, unless the dropping of the plate mocking Sir John Soane is attributable to critical reprimand rather than increased maturity. Pugin never compromised the integrity of his vision. Everything that he went on to write can be seen to serve the ideal that informs *Contrasts*. In *The true principles of Pointed or Christian Architecture* of 1841, an influential work among architects and architectural historians because of its enunciation of the two principles from which it takes its name, more is at stake than architecture. Pugin is again writing social criticism when he describes, for instance, the charitable hospitality he imagines dispensed in the Middle Ages and contrasts it with the ways of the present:

The ancient gentry . . . did not confine their guests . . . to a few fashionables who condescend to pass away a few days occasionally in a

country house; but under the oaken rafters of their capacious halls the lords of the manor used to assemble all their friends and tenants at those successive periods when the church bids all her children rejoice, while humbler guests partook of their share of bounty dealt to them by the hand of the almoner beneath the groined entrance of the gate-house. Catholic England was merry England.[11]

The writings may be didactic, hortatory, protective, but every item, however small its scale, however oblique its reference, radiates from the one centre. Be it a volume as erudite and sumptuous as his *Glossary of ecclesiastical ornament and costume*, running swiftly to a second edition in spite of its price (plate 197), or a collection of exquisite designs like those of *Floriated ornament* in 1849, for which his eventual son-in-law J.H. Powell helped him prepare the illustrations (plates 198 and 199); be it a communication to the *Tablet* repudiating responsibility for communion rails intruded into his church at Fulham or articles and letters describing the medieval style of memorial brasses or

chasubles, contradicting an august antiquarian's views on spires, giving his opinion on the School of Design, pleading for subscriptions to complete his cathedral at Killarney: permanent and widely sought or fugitive and hardly noticed, all the publications spring from Pugin's need and determination to maintain, disseminate and advance the vision he had first given public expression in *Contrasts*.[12]

In the winter of 1850–1 Pugin was busy with his usual activities. Charles Barry needed a supply of designs for the decoration and fitting of the Houses of Parliament and was asking for help with other commissions besides. Hardman had to be sent instructions and drawings; so did Pugin's other collaborators, J.G. Crace, George Myers and Herbert Minton. 'I am almost dead beat to night in finishing off the tiles for westminster but I have got done at last', Pugin wrote to Hardman in January; everybody, even his children, had 'worked at filling in – it is a very fine job'. Other architects sought Pugin's aid. Construction of his church of

200. The opening of an article Pugin wrote for the *Orthodox journal*, the first of a series of nine which he believed would be 'the means of disseminating principles of good taste among the midling & Lower classes of Catholic and . . . a capital medium for attacking the protestant'.

St Augustine and its presbytery had to continue. Besides the supervision of tradesmen and assist-ants who helped in the studio, the services of the church had to be kept up and a school maintained. In addition to this professional business and do-mestic responsibility, which was for him routine, Pugin was engaged on the extra task of co-ordinating the preparation of the Mediæval Court at the Great Exhibition (see chapter 18) and that multifarious enterprise was onerous, frustrating, exciting – and immense.

Few people in the face of such demands would have chosen to assume the additional strain of au-thorship but throughout these months Pugin con-tinued writing. At the beginning of October 1850 he dashed off a witty pamphlet satirizing the style of service conducted by the Oratorians and plead-ing for the use of Gregorian chant; *An earnest appeal for the revival of the ancient plain song* was not his first attempt to counter the opinions ex-pressed in the *Rambler*, a new liberal journal and virtual organ of Oratorianism. He wrote to his friend A.L. Phillipps, a prominent Catholic and another advocate of early music, about it:

> . . . there is an article in the Rambler . . . in which it is gravely proposed to *abolish vespers* & to introduced English Hymns in place of the Kyrie Gloria Credo sanctus &c!!!!!!!!! This is the time to . . . expose the dangers of such[?] inno-vations & to urge a return to the *true music* of *the church*. I sat up a good part of Last night & have completed an article. . . . I will beg your accept-ance of a Doz. copies to distribute. . . . God Grant it may move our clergy to a sense of the present degradation of church music – it is in-tolerable & while it Lasts pointed churches & Catholic architecture are useless.[13]

At all times Pugin kept his eye on the periodi-cals and before the year was out he felt impelled to exonerate the Earl of Shrewsbury from an imputa-tion of disloyalty to the faith, published in an Irish newspaper; a letter to the *Freeman's journal* in Dublin was printed in December and copied in the London dailies, and Lord Shrewsbury, Pugin re-lated to Hardman, sent 'a thousand thanks My Dear Pugin for your defence of me'. In March it was Wiseman's turn to be protected when the *Globe* misconstrued some of Pugin's remarks into an aspersion on the cardinal and Pugin wrote to the editor to deny the application.

Pugin had more pressing business as an author than reacting to passing slights, though, however deeply he respected the leaders of his society. For years he had meditated a book on screens; among

THE LONDON AND DUBLIN

ORTHODOX JOURNAL

Of Useful Knowledge.

Careful to preserve the Unity of the Spirit in the bond of Peace. Eph. iv. 3.

VOL. VI. SATURDAY, FEBRUARY 17, 1838. No. 138.—2d.

WEST FRONT OF ROUEN CATHEDRAL.

THE western end of Rouen Ca-thedral presents one of the grandest façades of pointed architecture ex-isting. Notwithstanding the severe injuries this noble building has sus-tained during many successive cen-turies by the combined influence of tempests, conflagrations, heretical ravages and revolutionary violence, such is the solidity of its construc-tion and majesty of its proportions, that, although only half its original beauties remain, it still overwhelms the beholder with astonishment and admiration. At the extreme ends of a mass of building 270 feet in

his contributions to the *Orthodox journal* in the late 1830s (plate 200) was a piece describing and illus-trating a screen in Rouen no longer in existence; in September 1848 he had a long letter printed in the *Tablet* as part of the controversy about screens that arose, initiated and sustained by the *Rambler*, after the opening of St George's, the church and eventual cathedral he designed in London; there and elsewhere, Pugin always incorporated a screen in his designs. Then in 1850 he found time to travel to Germany and make sketches of the screens he knew were there. *A treatise on chancel screens and rood lofts, Their Antiquity, Use, and Symbolic Signification* was published in the new year, with a text setting out Pugin's argument for the retention of the screen, on the principal ground that it guaranteed the sanctity of the chancel, and lithographs which he had to entrust to another hand. It was a satisfaction to have stated his case at last and he invited Hardman to share his elation: 'rejoice with exceedinly joy. I have I may say completed my screen book. . . . I have suc-ceeded in putting the whole question in a short compass & as forcibly as possible. . . . I have over-come Every difficulty. . . . I wrote the whole thing off in this one day. it seemed to flow into my mind like a stream'. The printed text runs to 124 pages; even allowing for the 'work of mere Labour & reference' that Pugin said was all that was left to be done before dispatch to the publisher, and remembering that he had contemplated the subject for years, composition at such speed is an astonishing feat; and the satirical portrait of the 'modern amboneclast', the destroyer of screens, with its covert allusion to Newman, the real though unseen force behind the *Rambler*, through the introduction of the word 'development', is brilliant.[14]

Long-standing intentions had to take their place beside demands of the moment in these months of Pugin's life. When the Roman Catholic hierarchy was formally restored in England at the end of September 1850 after a lapse of centuries, a hue and cry broke out all over the country in protest at this act of 'papal aggression' and Ramsgate was not exempt from the uproar. Pugin reported to Hardman that 'the whole town' was 'covered with Placards denouncing us & Popery in the fiercest manner'; the house occupied by Powell was 'pelted with mud & filth – every sort of petty persecution is carried on'; at St Augustine's his 'walls school &c' were chalked with 'vile inscriptions'. After a local meeting called to attest fidelity to the Church of England and to the Crown and thence implicitly to oppose Catholicism, since it yielded spiritual allegiance to the Pope and not to the monarch, Pugin issued a pamphlet in November, *An address to the inhabitants of Ramsgate*, appealing for tolerance. He believed it had been effective: 'My adress has done *immense* good in Ramsgate among all the respectable people – I get Letters on every side & Dr Lenny who is a high churchman but I should say a slow coach has been loud in his praises'. Before Christmas he made another attempt, in a less conciliatory tone, to secure his right to religious liberty by drawing up a broadsheet answering one of the 'placards'; this too, he considered, had 'done a deal of good' and he was grateful for the testimony conveyed by 'very kind letters' from some of 'the best protestants' of the town. Also before Christmas, because he had known nothing about an address presented to Wiseman by leading Catholics and so had not signed it, Pugin sent a letter to the *Catholic standard* explaining the omission and stressing his regret.[15]

The undertaking which confronted him with the most strenuous intellectual challenge in this period of excitement was the composition of a tract directly generated by the ecclesiastical event which provoked such fury. Taking up a question which had exercised his mind from before the time of *Contrasts*, he wrote *An earnest address, on the establishment of the hierarchy*, an exposition of the causes of the change from Catholicism to Protestantism at the time of the Reformation. His great fear was that the Catholic Church would be drawn into a dependence on the State and so lose its newly won religious freedom; it was by such a process, according to his thesis, that the medieval Church had been destroyed. Pugin applied himself to composition with such intensity that his physical health suffered but completing the manuscript was only part of his task. Wide circulation was important and Hardman was to become his ally as well as his confidant:

> . . . & now my dear Hardman you must help in the distributing of this address. it will do as much good among protestants as catholics. I am going to expend £20 *in postage*. every member of Parliament shall have one. now do you work away in Birmingham among men like that man who lectures & the dissenting fellows – & all the people who have the worst idea of us. merchants. all sorts of people. . . . let it go even among mechanicks. everybody.

Many copies were needed: Pugin informed Phillipps, whose desire for the reunion of the Catholic Church and the Church of England was at least as strong as Pugin's, that he was having 10,000 printed; later he told a friend in Belgium that 6000 copies had been distributed in three days. He insisted to Hardman that 'it is no use doing things by halves & I have fine paper copies for the Ministers big wigs Bishops Lord Chancellor &c – what a grand engine of Catholicism the penny post'. (Years before, in 1839, he had circulated his pamphlet opposing the Martyrs' Memorial in Oxford in exactly such a hopeful way, calling in person on 'the bigwigs at the colleges' to present them with copies.) Signs of approval reached him: he received 'a most kind letter from Mr Gladstone . . . really a most Satisfactory Letter'; Lord Shrewsbury sent high praise, declaring the address 'admirably written & calculated for its object'; 'some famous letters' came from Oxford and 'others quite enthusiastic from Priests also'. There were rumblings of discontent, however. Hardman reported that some priests were 'frightened' and others failed to understand; undaunted, Pugin replied: 'with all due respect I think the majority of our ecclesiasticks must be very thick if they cannot see the drift of that address'. Others complained directly to the author: some communications 'from our clergy' were 'quite abusive' and 'one friar' asserted that any schoolboy was 'a better judge of catholic history' than Pugin (the same accusation had been levelled apropos of *Contrasts* fifteen years before) while from 'the *oratorian party*' came 'vile letters. . . . they are cut to the heart – & nash the teeth – like the old Pagans'. Some readers were not convinced of the pamphlet's orthodoxy since, in his desire to encourage Tractarianism and so improve the prospect of reuniting the separated Churches, he had used expressions deemed too lenient towards the Anglican position; formal charges of heresy were a possibility. Pugin was adamant that there was 'not one word' that 'a good orthodox man would take out' and triumphant as the likelihood of denunciation receded: 'I have heard no more from the Cardinal so I suppose they cannot extract any heretical propositions. at any rate they are a Long time finding them out'. He dismissed the matter: 'as for attacking my address as too favourable to the anglicans I can only say this. if there is a litt[l]e sugar there is a strong dose of rubarb with it – & if they can swallow that it must do them good'. His mind was made up: 'it is quite time someone spoke out. it is no use building Pointed work without the revival of the true spirit'.

After he had written his *Earnest address* Pugin set about developing a concept that was related to it in its endeavour to keep the Catholic communion free from political patronage and the secular power. He elaborated a scheme for the maintenance of the hierarchy by voluntary subscription. Deprived of material resources as the Church had been by centuries of proscription, he had been fearful of a lack of support from the outset: 'It appears to me that this is a grand elevation without anything to back it up', he explained to Hardman, employing characteristic imagery to express his meaning, 'like a peice of scenery. it is all gold & glitter in front & but dirty deal & canvass behind . . . like carr[y]ing top Gallant sails without a ton of ballast in the hold'. His letter outlining the system appeared first in the *Catholic standard* in February, then in the *Tablet* in March, and as a separate leaflet too.[16] Again thousands of copies were required and Hardman was pressed into service. Pugin sought permission to distribute the address in all the churches as he hoped to animate the whole Catholic body. Apathy disgusted him: 'we thanked God for the Hierarchy. shall we let the bishops starve. Humbugs. this is a plan that I think will really do goo[d]'; it was 'worth any Labour'.

In March reactions to the *Earnest address* were being carried by the newspapers; Pugin sent a reply to one of them to both the *Tablet* and the *Catholic standard* in the middle of the month and had it too printed as a separate leaflet.[17] A fortnight later he dispatched another long letter to the *Catholic standard* in response to a further attack published there.[18] He notified Hardman of his reply: 'I suppose you read the letters in the Tablet & Standard – I am a Gallican a follower of Courayer a man who would *sell* the church for *an arch* or *the cut of a* Cope isolated & discontented with the ordinances of the Roman church – &c &c &c. . . . look *out for the next standard.* . . . there will be a letter there. a rouser. . . . I was at it all day yesterday between the services & it *will do*'. In both communications Pugin declared again his loyal, orthodox Catholicism and the supremacy of Gothic architecture and, beyond these, the need to reach and change the spirit of the people: 'I am a builder-up of men's minds and ideas, as well as of material edifices; and there is an immense work and a moral foundation yet required'.[19]

Pugin might have written even more at this time and was inclined to think that he ought to do so. He agreed with Hardman that an article in the *Dublin review* was 'very dangerous & full of fallacies but one cannot be always writing. it is too costly – & Laborious'. He had received letters about an article in the *Rambler* too, 'urging me to reply – but I dont know what to do for it takes such a time & such expense to be constantly printing. my expenses since Xmass are £150 at the least. it is almost impossible for one man to be doing everything but I see nobody who has either the know[l]edge or spirit or courage to support the movement & it is left to me. . . . I might do nothing else but write'. The date for the opening of the Great Exhibition was approaching fast, however, and it was imperative that he turn his attention elsewhere. Nevertheless, for the moment, he had taken his stand: 'I have *nailed* my Colours not to the mast but the *cross* – & no surrender'.

Pugin's *Earnest address* contains a passage that is at first sight a startling utterance to proceed from the author of *Contrasts*. By some people, he states,

All, anterior to the Reformation, is regarded and described as a sort of Utopia: – pleasant meadows, happy peasants, merry England . . . bread cheap, and beef for nothing, all holy monks, all holy priests, – holy everybody. Such charity, and such hospitality, and such unity, when every man was a Catholic. I once believed in this Utopia myself, but when tested by stern facts and history it all melts away like a dream.[20]

Without doubt there were periods when Pugin felt discouraged. He poured out his dejection to Hardman:

> . . . all that you & I have built on is so much <u>Sand</u>. . . . my eyes are open. I see it all – & the utter hopelessness – of the whole movement. . . . I go on the same as ever but not with hope. my hope is gone. I enjoy nothing. it is all hollow. hollow as a drum, Catholic shells built over sepulchres of indifference & vile ideas. . . . there are no appreciators of true things no support no union[?] – nothing. it is of the past & I fear *Gone*. a bright vision of revival Melted into air.

Such a bout of disillusion might be thought to have inspired the extract from the *Earnest address* but in fact the self-contradiction is only apparent. Pugin has not relinquished his vision. As he redefined its chronological limits between the editions of *Contrasts*, so here he simply shifts its basis again, dismissing the secular areas of experience and founding it instead solely upon the religious. There, in the ecclesiastical world of the past, his mind's eye can still show him the 'reverend array of bishops and abbots and dignitaries, in orphreyed copes and jewelled mitres', who led 'noble . . . lives' in the 'olden and better days' and were responsible for 'noble foundations and works of charity and piety', who constructed 'most glorious monuments and most sacred shrines', who with 'unalloyed zeal and devotion' upheld the 'ancient dignity of religion' and saw to the 'instruction of the people'.[21] The change of ground has done no more damage to the ideal in this case than it did in that of *Contrasts*. All its hallmarks remain: the dedication, the solicitude, the splendour – and the evidence that Pugin's overriding concern is with the quality of life.

Although he could insist in his misery that 'all the fine visions we had formed of catholic life reinfused into the antient forms are gone', Pugin's declared intentions belie his dispirited assertions of finality, quite apart from his unflagging artistic productivity. Even while he was writing the *Earnest address* in that hectic winter of 1850–1 he conceived a further work on a related topic, *A new view of an old subject; or, the English schism impartially considered*, advertised in the published pamphlet. He did not live to finish it but he carried out research and began writing. It was one of several projects that did not reach completion. The idea of an autobiography attracted him in his youth and he made notes for it then but temperament probably precluded its later continuation. One scheme was no more than a transitory joke, though his talent for satire and his command of the contemporary scene can almost induce a wish that he had given it permanence. 'have you ever read Vanity Fair by Thackeray', he asked Hardman.

> . . . it is the most profound awful book I ever read – better than all the moral sermons put together. . . . it is wonderful. Thackeray must be a very profound thinking man. a dreadful view of human nature but true true as possible. *truth itself*. I know them all – but he has not taken in all the classes of rascals – architectural ones for instance. I must write a book myself – & bring them all in & make you the real good fellow – as a standard to make the humbugs more odious.

There was nothing of the jest about another plan, his wish to publish an account of Gothic work in Italy. On his visit there he had been surprised and delighted by the quantity he found; he was in 'a perfect mine of mediæval art', he reported to Lord Shrewsbury.[22] If time forbad the fulfilment of this hope, it was choice that ruled out another possibility. When Henry Cole wrote with a suggestion about 'preparing some articles on the Exibition' of 1851, Pugin replied that he 'was quite past all that sort of thing', so he told Hardman, and gave poor health as the reason for his refusal. Nevertheless, it was not true that he was 'past all that sort of thing'. Pugin was always ready to make another attempt to advance his vision, a further statement of his ideal; the direction was always 'en avant'.

Of course actuality invariably fell short of the dream. 'I have passed my life in thinking of fine things, studying fine things, designing fine things, and realising very poor ones', he observed in 1850.[23] It was in the nature of the case that he should think so: ideals are elusive. Pugin remained to the last incapable of ridding himself of the need to fix the period of perfection in the past and so endow it with the authenticity of fact, since to admit that it was illusory would have been to undermine all that he strove to achieve, yet the ideal had its own reality, the reality of imaginative truth; and he was constant in his struggle to embody it. His life's work can be seen as an unremitting endeavour to impart to his vision material form; his own community at St Augustine's is the best demonstration of that: even at his most disconsolate he conceded that it was 'a very green spot in the desert' (see plate 105). Countless other 'fine things' were realized; but if an object – a church, a chair, a chalice – could do some good, a publication, in that it affected more people, could do more: 'while I have a pen left, and a hand to wield it, I will write, and exhort, and denounce', he declared in the *Catholic standard*; 'Building, without teaching and explaining, is useless'.[24]

'My writings much more than what I have been able to <u>do</u> have revolusionised the Taste of England', Pugin concluded to Hardman.[25] The intense application displayed in the biography and correspondence of that winter towards the end of his life and the energetic and generous measures taken for the dissemination of his views are representative of Pugin in all his undertakings. With dedica-

tion, with ceaseless effort, with learning, with wit and humour and fitting rhetoric, Pugin wrote in order to recommend and diffuse his vision to as extensive an audience as possible.

Typically Victorian in their earnest desire for social and spiritual amelioration, his publications are passionate, polemical propaganda, provocative and tendentious; they may be naive, illogical or prejudiced upon occasion but they purvey the finest thing of all that Pugin thought of, a timeless and compelling ideal. Among them, *Contrasts*, that 'strange and novel book', stands pre-eminent, the earliest mediation of the vision that inspired his life: the vision that made him 'a marked man' at the beginning of his career and the vision that enabled him to leave his enduring mark.

201.† The Royal Throne in the House of Lords, made by John Webb, 1847 (Palace of Westminster).

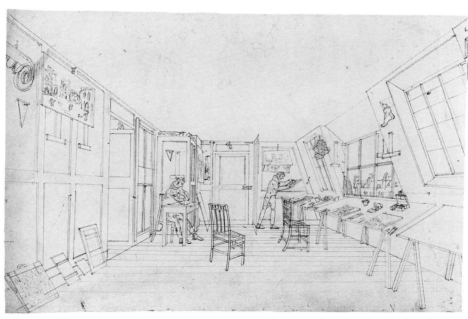

202.†   Drawing by A.C. Pugin, inscribed 'The office at Store Street, A. Pugin, 1821', showing the drawing office and studio at the top of the house in Bloomsbury, London, in which the Pugin family had moved in 1819 (Private Collection).

CHAPTER EIGHT

Wallpaper

Joanna Banham

Comparatively little attention has been paid to Pugin's wallpapers. Given the general paucity of research within this field, this neglect is not, perhaps, altogether surprising and it would be wrong to exaggerate their significance within his work as a whole. Nevertheless, in terms of sheer numbers, his output far exceeded that of William Morris whose patterns are now seen as virtually synonymous with Victorian wallpaper design, and for many of his contemporaries Pugin's wallpapers were both influential and important. Charles Locke Eastlake, for instance, author of the popular manual *Hints on Household Taste* (1867), attributed much of 'the very great improvement that we have seen of late in this branch of manufacture'[1] to his example, while later writers such as A.V. Sugden and J.L. Edmondson, whose authoritative *History of English Wallpaper* appeared in 1926, praised his work as 'an important step towards freeing his generation from the over-elaborated eccentricities of expression that piled one style on another in a meaningless medley of ornamention'.[2] Today, he is remembered chiefly as the champion of Gothic ornament and as the initiator of much-needed reforms within the sphere of nineteenth-century wallpaper design.

To understand the full significance of Pugin's role, both as a designer and as a reformer of public taste, it is first necessary to provide a context for his ideas and to review the state of wallpaper manufacture during the period in which he was working. The mid-nineteenth century was a time of enormous expansion for the industry when improvements in the printing process combined with rapid market growth to create an unprecedented increase in production and demand. The period also, however, witnessed a growing crisis of confidence in the quality of design and to many observ-

203.   Wallpaper for Captain Washington Hibbert used at Bilton Grange, Warwickshire, 1848 (Trustees of the Victoria & Albert Museum).

ers the introduction of machine printing, from
1839, simply served to hasten the industry's widespread and demoralising decline. Artifical realism
and meretricious ornament were the order of the
day, and manufacturers, bent on policies of vigorous commercialism, appeared to spare no pains to
satisfy a public who preferred 'the vulgar, the
gaudy, and the ugly even, to the beautiful and
perfect'.[3] Chief among those patterns that the critics despised were what Richard Redgrave, one of
the most respected and articulate of contemporary
spokesmen on design, described as 'the florid and
gaudy compositions, consisting of architectural
ornament in relief, with imitative flowers and foliage . . . rendered with the full force of their natural colours and light and shade'[4] (plate 204). His
remarks allude to a style of decoration that became
increasingly popular in the 1840s and which incorporated brightly-coloured, full-blown cabbage rose
motifs combined with ornate, three-dimensional
rococo scrolls. Even more objectionable, as far as
critics were concerned, were those designs that
relied upon *trompe l'œil* effects to simulate a mural
or pictorial scene. Pugin strongly disapproved of
both these styles but it was this latter group of
wallpapers, in particular, that provoked the full
force of his wrath.

The earliest exposition of his views appeared in
The True Principles of Pointed Architecture (1841)
which included a scathing critique of the abuses of
sham Gothic decoration and ornament. One of
his most spirited attacks was reserved for 'what
are termed Gothic-pattern papers . . . where a
wretched caricature of a pointed building is repeated from the skirting to the cornice in glorious

confusion, – door over pinnacle and pinnacle over
door'[5] (plate 205). Bizarre though they might
sound today, these papers had a long and quite
distinguished pedigree. As early as 1754 Horace
Walpole had hung the walls of the hall and staircase of his house at Strawberry Hill – which Pugin
knew and of course greatly disliked – with patterns
'painted in perspective to represent Gothic fret-
work', and in 1761, the poet, Thomas Gray, mentioned seeing Gothic papers printed 'to look like
stucco' at the showrooms of the London paper-
stainer Thomas Bromwich.[6] By the mid-nineteenth century, however, they had become less
exclusive and their design fell into two distinct
categories. The first comprised imitations of
Gothic screens, and the second represented
perspectival views of medieval buildings, pierced
at intervals by windows and niches. Pugin described these papers as 'a great favourite with hotel
and tavern-keepers',[7] but the fact that at least
twenty-two different examples appear in the log-
books of the high-class manufacturer Jeffrey & Co.
between the years 1837 and 1844, suggests that
they were not only quite popular, but also that
they were used for domestic as well as commercial
purposes.[8]

Pugin's dislike of these patterns was based upon
two considerations: firstly their absurd and inappropriate use of Gothic imagery, and secondly
their illegitimate use of shading, perspective and
pictorial forms. Both features were objectionable
in his eyes, but the second was reprehensible on
moral as well as aesthetic grounds. Just as in architecture he argued that it was dishonest for ornament to conceal the function or construction of a

unlike the pieces normally associated with Pugin that others may survive unrecognised.

As the 1830s progressed he became more and more involved with architecture but did not abandon furniture design. A considerable number of his pieces are inspired by Renaissance prototypes rather than just medieval ones as might be expected. Indeed he was constantly searching for medieval and Renaissance prototypes for his furniture and this continued right up to his death.

In 1834 he chose a group of Tudor pieces as the subject of an engraving (plate 226) entitled 'Ancient Furniture', indeed a portrait of Henry VIII hangs on the tapestry in a frame decorated with the royal arms and a Tudor rose. The text which is not by Pugin states:

> The subject of the annexed engraving is calculated to please from its novelty . . . Furniture of this early period is abundant; but with the almost solitary exception of Hardwick Hall in Derbyshire, the magnificent interiors of the Tudor period have never been made the painter's study.[5]

Turned ebony chairs of the type Pugin shows were at this date still considered to be Tudor and associated with Cardinal Wolsey.[6] As Pugin would have known, there were examples at Strawberry Hill, Abbotsford and Fonthill Abbey. Pugin did not design chairs closely based on this form, but he did use the barley sugar twist form of leg, taken with the square padded back and seat from another early chair type (plate 227). He probably thought

that these were Tudor, though they are actually seventeenth-century. The dining chairs which he designed for himself in about 1834 for St Marie's Grange, and those for the Pransorium at Oscott a year or two later are both closely based upon this prototype (plate 228). He retained his attachment to this form and when in the late 1840s he came to design the standard chairs for the House of Commons and the House of Lords (plate 230) he merely Gothicised the legs but kept the same overall shape. Medieval chairs did not have the padded backs or seats demanded by Pugin's patrons and, although he published in 1835 a solid wood Gothic version of this form (plate 229), no made-up example is known.

In the mid-1830s Pugin also evolved a simple arm-chair type, the first examples of which Hull made for St Marie's Grange (plate 81) and again some very similar ones were supplied – possibly also by Hull – for the Pransorium at Oscott (plate 228). The source for these is also Renaissance and is to be found in leather seated and backed Spanish or Flemish chairs of the seventeenth century. Pugin's version, when given the octagonal legs of plate 230b, evolved into the arm-chair form (plate 230c) that he used throughout the Palace of Westminster.

The x-framed chairs with a suspended leather seat designed in 1847 for the Prince's Chamber at Westminster (plate 231) are again Renaissance in form. They are close to a design published in Amsterdam in 1642 by Crispin de Passe II,[7] even down to the lions head finials. Pugin added his

229. Designs for chairs from *Gothic Furniture*, 1835.

230.† a: The standard House of Commons chair b: the standard House of Lords chair c: a House of Lords arm-chair, all designed about 1850 (Palace of Westminster).

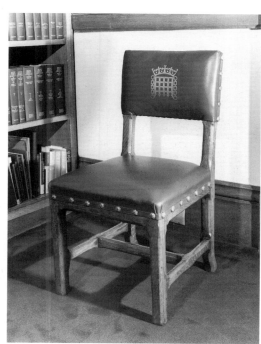

251.† A desk made for the House of Lords Library, c.1850 (Palace of Westminster).

252. Cabinet made for a room in the House of Commons, c.1851 (Palace of Westminster).

253.† Inlaid walnut writing table made by Crace for Eastnor Castle, Herefordshire, 1849.

unwell indeed and dread the idea of dying in debt'. His financial position as he supported his growing family and the construction of his church at Ramsgate was a continual worry. The letters show the battle between Crace's amoral commercial sense that the public wanted an elaborate veneered version of Gothic (plates 253, 254), and did not care a toss whether it was honestly constructed, and Pugin standing out for his 'True Principles', or the 'True Thing' as he usually called it. He wrote in December 1850 about the construction Crace was suggesting for a sideboard:

> I am astonished how a man like you can be led away by the fears of others from the true thing. It is the old mahogany dodge done in gothic. I see the same mitering of mouldings, everything that was done at Windsor when I was at Morells, I have delivered you from your horri-

206. *The Scarisbrick* wallpaper, 1847 (Trustees of the Victoria & Albert Museum). This pattern, used in the Red Drawing Room at Scarisbrick Hall, was copied from a fifteenth-century Venetian textile that Pugin copied in Italy in 1847.

207. Design for a wallpaper, pencil and coloured wash, 1851 (Trustees of the Victoria & Albert Museum). This idea came from a stencilled decoration seen in a fifteenth-century house in Salisbury and was intended for general use, as well as at the Palace of Westminster.

building, so with wallpaper he believed that any attempt to mask or disguise the solid appearance of the wall was little short of sinful. 'A wall', he wrote, 'may be enriched and decorated at pleasure, but it must always be treated in a consistent manner',[9] and, in place of *trompe l'œil* and three-dimensional effects which produced a disturbing and unlawful illusion of depth, he advocated flat treatments and conventionalised designs that would enhance, not contradict, the two-dimensional nature of its surface.

To a great extent these views were shared by other mid-century reformers, such as Redgrave, Henry Cole and Owen Jones, who argued much the same points regarding wallpaper design. What distinguished Pugin's work, however, from that of his contemporaries was his reliance upon historical sources. His passionate admiration for Gothic art led him to recommend the use of authentic Gothic ornament and his patterns almost always employed heraldic emblems or the stylised fruit and foliate forms to be found in medieval textiles and manuscripts. Wherever possible he liked to borrow directly from medieval originals and, in a letter of October 1851, he described himself as 'always on the look out'[10] for old designs that might be adapted for contemporary use. Historic textiles provided a specially rich stock of ideas and many of his patterns, such as *The Scarisbrick* (plate 206), relate closely to fifteenth-century Venetian

velvet brocades. Others, like the *Bird and Fleur de Lys* design of 1851 (plate 207), were adapted from fifteenth-century stencilled work, but in every case, irrespective of the source, his wall-papers demonstrate a thorough understanding of the principles underlying the application of Gothic ornament to flat surfaces and reveal his unswerving commitment to conventionalisation and two-dimensionality.

The first recorded mention of his wallpapers occurs in a letter to John Gregory Crace of March 1844 where Pugin discusses patterns that he was preparing for Alton Towers in Staffordshire.[11] Crace's role in the production of Pugin's wall-papers was quite important. The two had met late in 1843 and by the following year Crace was entrusted with the execution of all his designs, a task that involved not only organising their production and installation, but also developing his working drawings. Alexandra Wedgwood has pointed out that Pugin's drawings were always made at great speed and often included little precise detail.[12] In the case of his wallpapers, most were drawn out full-size or with the repeat laid out to scale, but on several occasions the design was little more than a small sketch. It was therefore important that Pugin had complete confidence in Crace's ability to interpret and elaborate his ideas and he was also, at times, asked to select the colours and to furnish details of the heraldic emblems.

The patterns themselves were printed by hand – block-printing continued alongside machine-printed work until the end of the century and for more prestigious goods this technique was always preferred – and the work was contracted out by Crace, initially at least, to Samuel Scott & Co. Pugin had little direct contact with this firm. No mention of their name appears in his diaries or correspondence and it is unlikely that he would have approved of their early work which, ironically, included several examples of sham Gothic patterns as well as naturalistic floral designs.[13] Nevertheless, to Crace, Scott's must have seemed an uncontentious choice of manufacturer. Based at 49 Lower Belgrave Place, they were a firm of some standing within the wallpaper industry. Scott himself was described as an 'excellent' designer[14] and his name appears as the proprietor of numerous patterns in the register of designs at the London Patent Office from 1839.[15] In 1846 he was joined by Thomas Cuthbertson and shortly afterwards, from 1847, the firm was listed as Scott, Cuthbertson & Co. Around 1860, the company took over the historic printing works at Whitelands House, Chelsea, which had previously been occupied first by Thomas Eckhardt and then by Hinchliff & Co., and in 1862 a Government Commission reported 104 men working for the firm, all employed in block-printing.[16] The question remains, however, as to whether Scott's were the only printers of Pugin's designs. Certainly the two were linked in contemporaries' minds and reviews of Pugin's work in the 1860s and later confidently state that his wallpapers were manufactured by Scott, Cuthbertson & Co.[17] Yet the Crace pattern-books for the decoration of the Palace of Westminster include the initials 'W.W. & Co.' and 'J.W. & Co.' beside samples of the patterns that were used. One possible explanation for this phenomenon is that the initials refer to other manufacturers – namely William Woollams and John Woollams & Co., both of whom were highly-respected London paper-stainers specialising in block-printed work. William Woollams were actually based in Wigmore Street, close to Crace's showrooms, from 1828 and were also printing some of Crace's private patterns during this time. It may be, therefore, that Crace was contracting out the work to the cheapest and/or most convenient workshop at different periods but until more information comes to light we can only speculate as to the meaning of these marks.

In general terms Pugin's wallpapers fall into three categories. The first represents those private commissions carried out for large country houses, such as Burton Closes, Oswaldcroft, Lee Castle (plates 208, 209) and Bilton Grange (plate 203), that Pugin was working on with Crace during the second half of the 1840s. The bold colours and large formats of these papers reflect the influence of Pugin's work at the Houses of Parliament but their designs were highly individual and were customised to include the clients' mottoes, monograms and armorial bearings. Indeed, these details often provided the starting point for his ideas and when he came to decorate Lismore Castle (plate 210) for the Duke of Devonshire he wrote to Crace urgently appealing for more information about the

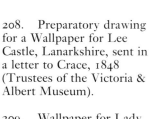

208. Preparatory drawing for a Wallpaper for Lee Castle, Lanarkshire, sent in a letter to Crace, 1848 (Trustees of the Victoria & Albert Museum).

209. Wallpaper for Lady Macdonald Lockhart, used at Lee Castle, Lanarkshire, c.1848 (Trustees of the Victoria & Albert Museum). The pattern contains the Lockhart monogram, motto and the rebus of a heart and lock.

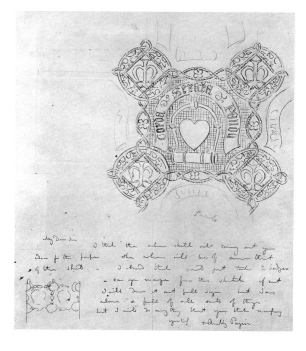

owner's ancestry and crests. A letter of 16 April 1850 records:

> I will do the best I can for Lismore but it is very difficult for me to work without some data for armorial bearings, devices or badges which would give some character to the work . . . I wish I knew something about the family and your advice about colours . . . I assure you I have no idea what sort of paper to make . . . I feel quite in the dark about it. I am not in possession of any data.[18]

The second and largest group consists of those wallpapers designed for the Palace of Westminster which date from the autumn of 1847. Pugin was the only designer involved in this area of work – in itself a task of almost Herculean proportions – and over 100 patterns in different colourways appear in the printer's log-book now kept at the Islington factory of John Perry Wallpapers where Pugin's wallpapers are still printed today (plate 211). They illustrate the enormous versatility of his work and utilise a rich vocabulary of Gothic and conventionalised natural forms. Many were also extremely imposing in terms of the size and scale of their design. The paper in the Queen's Robing Room (plate 212), for example, has a repeat of 84 cm and employs an interlacing ogee pattern derived from a fifteenth-century Italian textile. Others, like the *Rose and Portcullis* (plate 213) were produced in

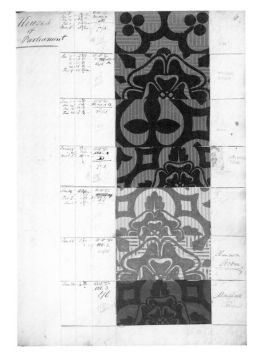

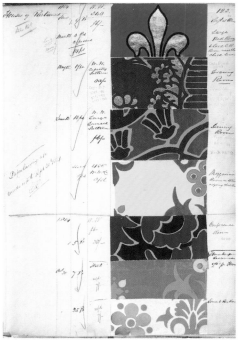

213. Wallpaper Sample Book for the Palace of Westminster, Crace & Co., 1851–4, p.14, (Trustees of the Victoria & Albert Museum).

214. This page from the Sample Book (plate 213) illustrates the contrast between wallpapers for the drawing room of the Sargeant at Arms and those for the servants' bedrooms.

215. Design for a wallpaper, c.1851 (Trustees of the Victoria & Albert Museum). One of several designs meant to carry out 'Mr. Barry's idea of introducing badges connected with the history of Westminster Palace'.

216. *Fleur de Lys and Pomegranate* wallpaper, c.1848 (Trustees of the Victoria & Albert Museum), extensively used in the Conference and Committee Rooms of the Palace of Westminster.

several sizes and finishes to suit the proportions and functions of different rooms. The Palace of Westminster was a vast complex of public and private suites and included domestic residences and servants' rooms as well as Government offices and state apartments. Pugin had a keen sense of what each setting implied and he designed his wallpapers accordingly. Thus, state and public rooms like the Royal Gallery and Conference Room (now part of the Members' Dining Room) (plate 216) were provided with large formal patterns utilising rich materials such as flock and gold leaf while less important areas like the housekeepers' residences were hung with smaller, more domestic designs. Today, the simple floral patterns that were originally used in the servants' bedrooms (plate 214) represent some of the most appealing and accessible examples of Pugin's work and, printed in light distemper colours on pale grounds, they recall the informal powdered and diaper arrangements that were illustrated in his *Floriated Ornament* of 1849.[19]

The third and final group of wallpapers represents those patterns destined for more general use. The exact size and nature of this group is hard to ascertain. Several unidentified designs for papers in the Victoria & Albert Museum may have been intended for general sale and certain patterns created for the Houses of Parliament were also used elsewhere (plate 217). Nevertheless, the notion that Pugin was producing wallpapers for wider circulation raises interesting points about the pro-

posed market for his work. Crace's clients came from the wealthiest sections of society and the private patterns were clearly extremely limited in terms of their audience and use. However, there is much evidence to suggest that Pugin wished to reach a broader market and that, in his role as propagandist for the Gothic Revival, he envisaged the sale of wallpapers and other furnishings on a more commercial basis. As early as 1844 he proposed using his house at Ramsgate, which was hung with numerous papers of his design, as a kind of 'showroom' for domestic Gothic decora-

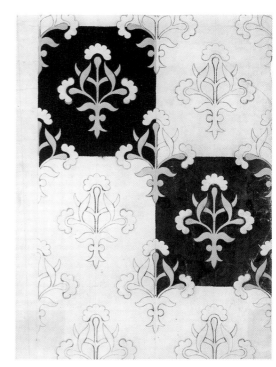

tion and in a letter of May of that year he urged Crace to send him 'his things' so that he could show them off to visitors.[20] Several years later, in 1847, he wrote to Crace that he had 'drawn out 1/2 a dozen patterns for cheap papers',[21] and in November he declared: 'I am very anxious to get lots of good patterns for papers. I am sure they will answer your purposes but when you get a stock you should make this known.'[22] Yet just how widespread the market for his patterns might have been is open to debate. The hand-printing process used in the production of his designs was labour-intensive and slow and, compared to mass-produced machine-prints, block-printed patterns were quite expensive, costing on average between 5s and 14s a yard. The flock and multi-coloured papers would therefore have been beyond the means of most middle-class consumers. Furthermore, the highly idiosyncratic nature of Pugin's designs which even sympathetic observers described as 'too ecclesiatical and traditional in character'[23] for most tastes would have made them unsuitable for general use and it was only the simple one- and two-colour prints that would have been appropriate for more ordinary homes. Notwithstanding this, in what appears to have been a concerted attempt to appeal to this market, Pugin encouraged Crace to advertise his papers in *The Builder* of 1851,[24] but his death in the following year put an end to his efforts to revolutionise public taste. Crace returned to his wealthier clients and the project to

provide Gothic wallpapers on a commercial basis was curtailed.

What, then, was the overall significance of Pugin's work? In purely visual terms his wallpapers were quite unique and there was nothing in contemporary work to compare with the appearance of their designs. He pioneered the use of authentic historical ornament long before this became general practice and at a time when the most popular patterns were little more than pastiches of French naturalism or a jumble of undigested revivalist styles. Moreover, his insistence upon two-dimensional treatments stood out sharply beside the illusionism and pictorialism of much machine- and block-printed work. Yet the legacy of his work is somewhat harder to assess. His wallpapers attracted high praise from design reformers, firstly in the *Journal of Design* where an example of a pattern used in the Houses of Parliament (plate 219) was featured in 1849, and later at the 1851 Mediæval Court where Redgrave described his work as exemplifying 'a perfect flatness and subdued harmony of colour'.[25] They also exerted some influence upon manufacturers and by 1862 several companies, including Scott's, William Woollams and Hinchliff & Co., were producing patterns in the severe medieval style that bore a close resemblance to Pugin's designs.[26] However, unlike Morris, Pugin did not spawn a generation of imitators and his work had comparatively little effect within the commercial sphere. The vogue for medieval patterns was quite shortlived and by the end of the 1850s they had been superseded by a taste for geometric forms and conventionalised floral designs.[27] By this time, too, wallpaper was increasingly viewed as a background to the objects and furnishings in a room rather than a decoration in its own right. Redgrave, in particular, recommended subdued colours and quiet, unobtrusive patterns that were retiring in effect and within this context the bold colours, scale and formality of Pugin's work were too pronounced for public taste. It was therefore as a theorist and critic of contemporary work that his influence was most strongly felt and in this capacity he did much to alter prevailing attitudes to design. His ideas on the propriety of ornament closely informed the teachings of the South Kensington School while his practical involvement with wallpaper encouraged the next generation of artist and architect-designers to turn their attention to this area of design. Even more significantly, his criticisms of pictorial and excessively naturalistic effects helped to hasten their departure from progressive work and, by the third quarter of the century, his principles of flatness and conventionalisation had become widely accepted as those upon which wallpaper design should be based.

CHAPTER NINE

Furniture

CLIVE WAINWRIGHT

Pugin is one of the most talented and original furniture designers that England has produced. Fortunately we can form a very clear idea of the range and quality of his *œuvre* as several hundred documented pieces survive. When taken with his many drawings and engraved designs for furniture there is far more material than for any other furniture designer. This sheer quantity of material might equally have proved the limited range of his work and shown clear evidence of that auto-plagiarism which often bedevils prolific designers. Yet originality accompanies his every effort at furniture design.[1] Although he was designing furniture for about twenty-five years, within just eight years of starting he had evolved most of the radical forms which were to make him so celebrated. From this time on he refined these forms and created fascinating variations of them.

Like those other major furniture designers, Kent, Adam, Wyatt, Hope, Bullock, Webb, Burges, Godwin, Waterhouse, Voysey and Mackintosh, Pugin conceived his pieces as just one part of a total scheme of interior design. It should be stressed that apart from domestic interiors he was also designing furnishings for churches, nunneries and monasteries with their special needs. One should imagine the Pugin silver and ceramics standing on the Pugin table which in turn stood beneath a Pugin ceiling on a Pugin carpet. It is this ability to articulate mass, colour, texture, flat pattern and utility and apply these to the architecture of an interior and the furnishings which it contains that demonstrates the genius of those architects listed above. It also places them above manufacturers like Vile & Cobb, Chippendale, Morel & Seddon, Gillow or Holland and plagiarising authors like Sheraton and George Smith.

The actual cabinet-makers who manufactured

220.† Pugin's own dining room cabinet, probably made by Myers, *c*.1845 (Private Collection, Birkenhead).

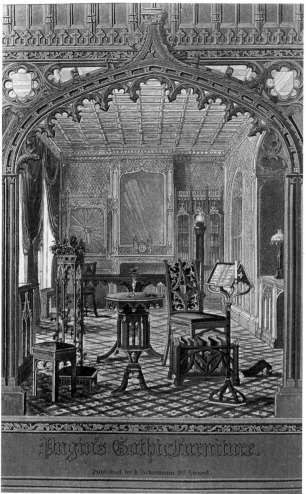

Pugin's furniture are for most of his pieces of no more than factual importance. For he, like his contemporaries, had access to a furniture industry more professional, better organised and technically superior to its eighteenth-century predecessor. Thus providing that Pugin supplied appropriately accurate drawings or other instructions and checked the finished pieces there were a number of firms who could reach his high standards. By the late 1840s, Webb, Crace, Myers, Gillow and Holland were all manufacturing to his designs. Thus, if the quality of the workmanship can be assumed, we can concentrate on the quality of the design. This was not the case with his metalwork, stained glass and ceramics. After much encouragement from Pugin, the only manufacturers able to reach the standards of craftsmanship he required were Hardman for the glass and metalwork and Minton for the ceramics.

As with every aspect of his life, Pugin was precocious as a furniture designer and he is likely to have been involved in producing designs for publication by 1825. From 1 June 1825 until October 1827 designs for Gothic furniture were published in *The Repository of Arts*, the pioneering periodical which Rudolph Ackermann had been publishing since 1809. In the October 1827 number a plate in the form of a title-page appeared bearing the legend 'Pugin's Gothic Furniture' (plate 221). Shortly afterwards these plates were published in book form with the same title. Whether both father and son were involved or whether they were only the work of the father has never been established.

The text which accompanies the plates establishes that the motifs incorporated into several of the designs come from French medieval sources: '. . . Among the few remaining specimens which can convey any idea of the ancient splendour of the interior of rooms is that of the abbess at the abbey of St Amand at Rouen'. Other sources mentioned are the Palais de Justice and the Château of Fontaine Henri – both in Normandy. In August 1825 A.C. Pugin, accompanied by his pupils, including Benjamin Ferrey and the thirteen-year-old A.W.N., '. . . set out for Normandy and crossing from Brighton to Dieppe proceeded to Rouen . . . The Palais de Justice, the convent of St Amand, the Hotel Bourgtheroulde and other buildings furnished excellent details, all of which were measured . . .'[2]

The purpose of this trip was to carry out the measured drawings which were engraved and published by A.C. Pugin in 1827 as *Specimens of the Antiquities of Normandy*. All the buildings mentioned in Ackermann, including the wonderful, flamboyant Gothic château of Fontaine Henri near Caen, appear in this book. The re-use of details from the Ackermann illustrations was in tune with the increasingly archaeological approach to the application of Gothic ornament which A.C. Pugin was himself pioneering with his publications of measured drawings of medieval buildings. It seems likely that, in just the way he was involving his young son in the Normandy publication or his *Paris & its Environs*, he would also have encouraged him to try his hand at furniture design. For when in 1826 he went to work at Windsor as a furniture designer (see chapter 2) he must have had some preparation at least for this major commission.

It is also possible that A.C. Pugin actually designed furniture for specific buildings rather than just for publication by Ackermann. If this were the case his young son would have been able to see the whole process from drawing board to the finished object. At least some of the furnishings for Eaton Hall, the Duke of Westminster's vast and elaborate Gothic Revival country house, may have been to A.C. Pugin's design. A 'Gothic lantern intended for the hall of a nobleman' published by Ackermann in August 1825 bears the Grosvenor crest and coronet. The chair from Eaton Hall (plate 223) is usually attributed on circumstantial grounds to William Porden, the architect of part of Eaton. It is far more similar in character to the Ackermann plate; it and other furnishings might well have been designed by A.C. Pugin. If this were the case and the Pugins had a track record for the design of actual furniture, it makes the awarding of the Windsor commission to the fifteen-year-old Pugin more understandable. Whatever is finally established concerning the authorship of the Ackermann plates, the stylistic characteristics of the work of the two Pugins are indistinguishable in 1827, as a comparison of the Ackermann and the Windsor designs immediately demonstrates.

Horrific though the totally gilded or parcel gilt rosewood furniture at Windsor is when compared to Pugin's mature work, it is rather better than anything being designed by anyone else in the 1820s. One only has to look at a commercial pattern book like George Smith's *Cabinet Maker and Upholsterer's Guide* of 1826 to appreciate this. Pugin himself quite properly later rejected it, describing his well known illustration of 1841 in *True Principles* (plate 222) thus:

> Upholsterers seem to think that nothing can be Gothic unless it is found in some church. Hence your modern man designs a sofa or occasional table from details culled out of Britton's Cathedrals and all the ordinary articles of furniture, which require to be simple and convenient, are made not only very expensive but very uneasy . . . A man who remains any length of time in a modern Gothic room, and escapes without being wounded by some of its minutiae, may consider himself extremely fortunate . . . I have perpetrated many of these enormities in furniture I designed some years ago for Windsor Castle.[3]

In 1829 and 1830, in a complete change of direction typical of his early life, Pugin started to design and manufacture furniture which was massive and brutal compared with the flashy perpendicular Gothic of the Windsor work. In November 1829 he set up in business in an upper loft at 12 Hart Street – now Floral Street – the same street as Covent Garden Theatre.

In those days great difficulty was felt in finding artificers and carvers capable of doing justice to the execution of designs in the medieval

Illustration of the extravagant style of Modern Gothic Furniture and Decoration.

style . . . As young Pugin now proposed not only to undertake the delineation of working drawings, but also to superintend the execution of the work which he designed . . . having secured the assistance of one or two clever carvers whom he had himself already taught, he made it known generally amongst his friends that he would undertake to supply all ornamental portions of buildings which could by possibility be executed apart from the structure and be fixed afterwards. At first his success was considerable and he obtained extensive commissions in Scotland and Ireland.[4]

Pugin also manufactured furniture and his designs of this date (plate 54) are mainly in the chunky Tudor or Jacobean versions of classicism rather than the perpendicular Gothic of the Windsor pieces. A few of the designs provide a Gothic alternative, as with the sideboards and the chairs (225). There was as yet no attempt to use the

222. Plate from *True Principles*, 1841.

223.† Arm-chair probably designed by A.C. Pugin for Eaton Hall (Trustees of the Victoria & Albert Museum).

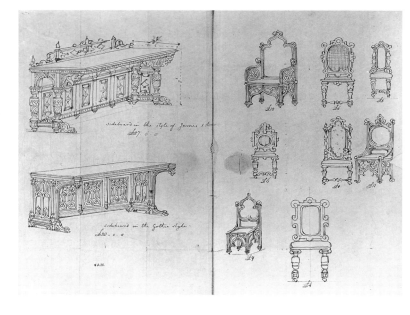

224.† An oak Tudor-style table stamped 'A. PUGIN', and made by his firm, c.1830 (Trustees of the Victoria & Albert Museum).

225. Design for furniture in the Jacobean style to be made by Pugin's firm, 1830 (Trustees of the Victoria & Albert Museum).

226. 'Ancient furniture', engraving after a drawing by Pugin, published 1834.

227. A turned chair, probably Flemish, sixteenth-century (Trustees of the Victoria & Albert Museum).

228.† Arm-chair and turned chair, made for the Pransorium at Oscott, c.1838 (St Mary's College, Oscott).

earlier medieval forms he was to so admire later in his career. His firm furnished several houses including Weston Hall in Warwickshire and Perry Hall at Handsworth near Birmingham. Though none of this furniture is known to survive, designs relating to Perry Hall are in the V&A (plate 56). The high standards of craftsmanship Pugin insisted on ate into his profits and late in 1831 he went bankrupt and he never again went into business on his own account.

The experience he gained in the practical aspects of carving and cabinet-making was of crucial importance to his future career, giving him an unusually close rapport with the craftsmen who worked on his buildings and their furnishings. It is obvious from his letters that, while designing the Windsor pieces, even before he started his own business, he spent time in the cabinet makers' workshops observing the constructional methods. These skills were further re-enforced by the practical experience of working in the theatre (chapter 3).

Only one piece of furniture made by the firm has been discovered (plate 224); it is stamped in large letters 'A.PUGIN' and, though the motifs are Tudor, it is a wholly original design. No actual Tudor table of this form ever existed, but this piece and those in the surviving designs are so

building, so with wallpaper he believed that any attempt to mask or disguise the solid appearance of the wall was little short of sinful. 'A wall', he wrote, 'may be enriched and decorated at pleasure, but it must always be treated in a consistent manner',[9] and, in place of *trompe l'œil* and three-dimensional effects which produced a disturbing and unlawful illusion of depth, he advocated flat treatments and conventionalised designs that would enhance, not contradict, the two-dimensional nature of its surface.

To a great extent these views were shared by other mid-century reformers, such as Redgrave, Henry Cole and Owen Jones, who argued much the same points regarding wallpaper design. What distinguished Pugin's work, however, from that of his contemporaries was his reliance upon historical sources. His passionate admiration for Gothic art led him to recommend the use of authentic Gothic ornament and his patterns almost always employed heraldic emblems or the stylised fruit and foliate forms to be found in medieval textiles and manuscripts. Wherever possible he liked to borrow directly from medieval originals and, in a letter of October 1851, he described himself as 'always on the look out'[10] for old designs that might be adapted for contemporary use. Historic textiles provided a specially rich stock of ideas and many of his patterns, such as *The Scarisbrick* (plate 206), relate closely to fifteenth-century Venetian

velvet brocades. Others, like the *Bird and Fleur de Lys* design of 1851 (plate 207), were adapted from fifteenth-century stencilled work, but in every case, irrespective of the source, his wall-papers demonstrate a thorough understanding of the principles underlying the application of Gothic ornament to flat surfaces and reveal his unswerving commitment to conventionalisation and two-dimensionality.

The first recorded mention of his wallpapers occurs in a letter to John Gregory Crace of March 1844 where Pugin discusses patterns that he was preparing for Alton Towers in Staffordshire.[11] Crace's role in the production of Pugin's wall-papers was quite important. The two had met late in 1843 and by the following year Crace was entrusted with the execution of all his designs, a task that involved not only organising their production and installation, but also developing his working drawings. Alexandra Wedgwood has pointed out that Pugin's drawings were always made at great speed and often included little precise detail.[12] In the case of his wallpapers, most were drawn out full-size or with the repeat laid out to scale, but on several occasions the design was little more than a small sketch. It was therefore important that Pugin had complete confidence in Crace's ability to interpret and elaborate his ideas and he was also, at times, asked to select the colours and to furnish details of the heraldic emblems.

The patterns themselves were printed by hand – block-printing continued alongside machine-printed work until the end of the century and for more prestigious goods this technique was always preferred – and the work was contracted out by Crace, initially at least, to Samuel Scott & Co. Pugin had little direct contact with this firm. No mention of their name appears in his diaries or correspondence and it is unlikely that he would have approved of their early work which, ironically, included several examples of sham Gothic patterns as well as naturalistic floral designs.[13] Nevertheless, to Crace, Scott's must have seemed an uncontentious choice of manufacturer. Based at 49 Lower Belgrave Place, they were a firm of some standing within the wallpaper industry. Scott himself was described as an 'excellent' designer[14] and his name appears as the proprietor of numerous patterns in the register of designs at the London Patent Office from 1839.[15] In 1846 he was joined by Thomas Cuthbertson and shortly afterwards, from 1847, the firm was listed as Scott, Cuthbertson & Co. Around 1860, the company took over the historic printing works at Whitelands House, Chelsea, which had previously been occupied first by Thomas Eckhardt and then by Hinchliff & Co., and in 1862 a Government Commission reported 104 men working for the firm, all employed in block-printing.[16] The question remains, however, as to whether Scott's were the only printers of Pugin's designs. Certainly the two were linked in contemporaries' minds and reviews of Pugin's work in the 1860s and later confidently state that his wallpapers were manufactured

by Scott, Cuthbertson & Co.[17] Yet the Crace pattern-books for the decoration of the Palace of Westminster include the initials 'W.W. & Co.' and 'J.W. & Co.' beside samples of the patterns that were used. One possible explanation for this phenomenon is that the initials refer to other manufacturers – namely William Woollams and John Woollams & Co., both of whom were highly-respected London paper-stainers specialising in block-printed work. William Woollams were actually based in Wigmore Street, close to Crace's showrooms, from 1828 and were also printing some of Crace's private patterns during this time. It may be, therefore, that Crace was contracting out the work to the cheapest and/or most convenient workshop at different periods but until more information comes to light we can only speculate as to the meaning of these marks.

In general terms Pugin's wallpapers fall into three categories. The first represents those private commissions carried out for large country houses, such as Burton Closes, Oswaldcroft, Lee Castle (plates 208, 209) and Bilton Grange (plate 203), that Pugin was working on with Crace during the second half of the 1840s. The bold colours and large formats of these papers reflect the influence of Pugin's work at the Houses of Parliament but their designs were highly individual and were customised to include the clients' mottoes, monograms and armorial bearings. Indeed, these details often provided the starting point for his ideas and when he came to decorate Lismore Castle (plate 210) for the Duke of Devonshire he wrote to Crace urgently appealing for more information about the

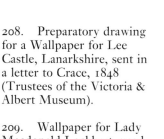

208. Preparatory drawing for a Wallpaper for Lee Castle, Lanarkshire, sent in a letter to Crace, 1848 (Trustees of the Victoria & Albert Museum).

209. Wallpaper for Lady Macdonald Lockhart, used at Lee Castle, Lanarkshire, c.1848 (Trustees of the Victoria & Albert Museum). The pattern contains the Lockhart monogram, motto and the rebus of a heart and lock.

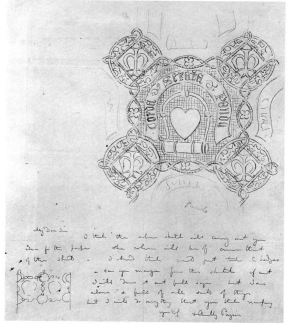

ble bondage and you would go back to your vomit & return to bestialities long exploded.

He illustrates his letter with a glue pot labelled 'The modern joint' and a tusked tenon labelled 'The old joint' (plate 255). In April 1850 he advised Crace on the design of a dining table: 'it can hardly be too plain as long as the framing is strong and well constructed. Nobody can see a dining table without a cloth, at least it is not a *desirable* sight. The great thing is good framing to keep up the beef & resist the cutting down of the slices . . .' At just the time they were producing the elaborate Eastnor pieces Pugin was trying to convince Crace that there was a market for simple honestly constructed pieces. He wrote in 1849, 'I do not think we make enough plain furniture. I shall send a lot of designs for plain things & furniture for bedrooms which would come moderate and suit gothic houses. I am sure that these things are very much wanted and will take well.' The design dated 1849 (plate 256) is likely to be one of these. The Y form of the ends is clearly inspired by medieval timber-framed house construction (plate 237). Pugin in fact had a strong practical streak:

. . . the great sale will be in articles that are within reach of the middling class, clergyman furnishing parsonage houses etc. I should advise you to let them out piece work to your men. You ought to frame a dozen of each to make them pay & keep them all ready seasoned for putting together at a days notice, keeping one of a sort

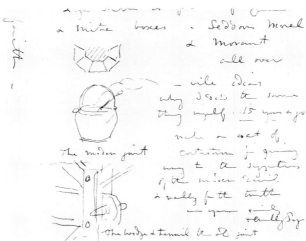

254.† A table made by Crace for Eastnor Castle, c.1849.

255. The principles of ancient and modern joints illustrated in a letter from Pugin to Crace, 1850 (RIBA Drawings Collection).

256. Detail from a sheet of designs for simple structural tables, 1849 (Trustees of the Victoria & Albert Museum).

257.† Table made for Horstead Place by John Webb in 1853 shown partly assembled (Private Collection).

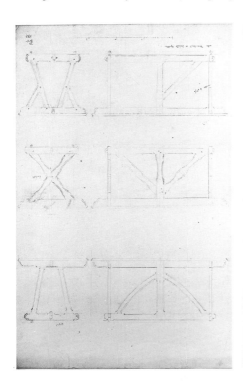

258. The lych gate, Our Lady and St Alphonsus's, Hanley Swan Blackmore Park, Worcestershire, c. 1846.

259.† Bier at Wymeswold, c.1849.

ticularly applicable to the structural tables of the Oscott type, indeed they could have been sold in 'flat packs' as much cheap furniture is today. To assemble them all that is needed is to insert the pegs to lock the stretcher in place and turn the cleverly designed L-shape blocks screwed under the table top into the slots in the table frame to secure the top. A table of this type half assembled is shown in plate 257.

There is no evidence that this plain furniture was shown at the Crystal Palace, though Crace presumably displayed it in his showroom in Wigmore Street. The whole matter of the display in the Mediæval Court at the 1851 exhibition is dealt with in chapter 18. Whether Pugin was right about the sales potential is impossible to determine, for Crace had little interest in marketing them; not only did he prefer the more elaborate pieces, but the profit margin would have been far higher on these than the simple pieces. He did not share Pugin's zeal to transform the taste of the 'middling class'.

As soon as Pugin died, Crace dropped this simple range altogether, concentrating on the elaborate marquetry pieces like the octagonal table he supplied to Abney Hall.[23] John Webb, Pugin's old friend, who made some of the most important pieces for Westminster (plates 250–52) did however supply a number of simple structural pieces in 1853 to Horsted Place in Sussex (plate 257). Others were supplied throughout the 1850s and 1860s to Westminster to his designs by firms like Holland and Gillow, and both these firms made considerable numbers of pieces to his design for domestic clients well into the 1870s. Had Pugin lived the impact of this plain and honest furniture would have been far wider.

His furniture should be seen in the context of the structural carpentry of his buildings. This includes open timber roofs, screens, ceilings, staircases and doors which all display his principles of honest construction and are clearly inspired by medieval prototypes. His designs for these constantly refer back to the continental timber forms he had studied so closely in the 1820s and 1830s and published in *Details of Antient Timber Houses* and *True Principles* (plate 237). Pugin's creative use of the motifs and techniques of medieval carpentry is demonstrated by his lych gates (plate 258) which immediately prepare one for what to expect on entering the church. Indeed those buried in a Pugin church can expect to be carried on a Pugin bier (plate 259).

always on show . . . I am also an old furniture man and have shown ladies round a ware room before now . . .

This radical concept of displaying an example of each type was one that no furniture designer or maker had ever before come up with. It was par-

CHAPTER TEN

Ceramics

PAUL ATTERBURY

260.† Bread Plate, decorated with inlaid coloured clays in the incaustic technique, made by Minton, *c.*1849 (Trustees of the Victoria & Albert Museum).

Pugin's designs for ceramics are perhaps the most familiar of all his industrial and decorative works, thanks in part to the revival of interest in tiles and Victorian pottery generally. It is, therefore, surprising to find that this area of activity is so inadequately documented. Until his first meeting with Herbert Minton, the owner of a pottery business then clearly rising rapidly towards the position of dominance it was to attain in the 1850s, Pugin seems to have had little interest in ceramic design and manufacture. There appears to be no mention of ceramics of any kind in his diaries until 1839. His own antiquarian enthusiasms had led him to collect Italian maiolica and medieval floor tiles, the latter largely rescued from sites in Britain and northern France, but his introduction to Minton, probably in 1840, came about through his need to find a suitable manufacturer for a new generation of medieval-style encaustic, or inlaid, floor tiles. As it turned out, Pugin made the right choice, for Minton quickly became an indispensible member of that small group of practical, efficient and highly skilled industrialists upon whom he depended for the successful realisation of his designs.

Born in 1793, as a young man Herbert Minton had joined the pottery business founded by his father the same year, and from the early 1820s his influence was increasingly dominant. Under his ambitious leadership the company flourished, its expanded range of products making the Minton name well known among retailers in Britain, Europe and North America. In sole control following his father's death, Herbert was quick to reveal his management skills, his enterprising approach to design and, above all else, his fascination with new technology.

It was this passion for technical improvement

261.† Tiles from the Old English series made by Minton from 1842 (Private Collection, Birkenhead).

262.† Set of encaustic tiles decorated with Evangelist symbols, c.1845. (Trustees of the Victoria & Albert Museum).

that, linked with an overriding concern for quality, was at the basis of the relationship between Minton and Pugin. Particularly important were the technical developments that made possible the production of the kind of tiles that Pugin required. The first of these was a process for making inlaid floor tiles patented by Samuel Wright of Shelton in 1830, and then perfected by Minton during five years of costly experimentation, after he had taken an interest in the patent. Wright's process, which involved forming medieval-style two-colour tiles by pouring liquid clay, or slip, into moulded indented patterns on the base tile, was in successful production at the Minton factory by 1840 (plate 261). A description of the medieval technique, with a chromolithographic illustration of modern Minton tiles, was published in *The Treasury of Ornamental Art* in 1857.[1] At the same time, Wright also leased his patent to Walter Chamberlain, a partner in the Worcester Porcelain Company, who was equally keen to re-introduce medieval floor tiling and began production from 1836. It is likely that Chamberlain, content to produce coarser tiles in the traditional colours of brown and buff, was first in the market, while Minton took more time to perfect his production methods and to introduce more colours, notably blue. During this early period Pugin may have purchased tiles from Chamberlain's standard range. Both manufacturers were clearly inspired by the new enthusiasm for Gothic engendered by antiquaries and by the inclusion of coloured illustrations of actual medieval tiles in books such as Parker's *Glossary of Architecture* (third edition, 1840). Minton's first major contract was for the flooring of the Temple Church, off Fleet Street in London, and this early commission was followed by many others, as their finely finished, multicolour tiles began to dominate the market. Another important development was Richard Prosser's technique of manufacturing

tiles and other objects such as buttons from powdered clay, and once again Minton bought a share in Prosser's dust-pressing patent. This revolutionised the production of wall tiles, but could not be used for encaustic floor tiles until 1854. Thanks to his financial interest in the Wright and Prosser patents, and his own determination to succeed in a new and challenging field, initially almost regardless of cost, Minton was very receptive to the encouragement offered to him by Pugin.

The first generation of encaustic tiles did little more than recreate known medieval patterns, and Pugin may well have shown Minton his own collection. The interest in colour and pattern that was to make floor tiling so important a part of Victorian interior design did not really emerge until the late 1840s, by which time the Minton-Pugin relationship was well established. Pugin's first recorded visit to Minton's factory was in 1842, and the same year Minton floor tiles were first used by Pugin, at Shepshed in Leicestershire. Minton's earliest tile catalogue, entitled *Early English Tile Patterns*, was also issued in 1842. This contains designs drawn primarily from medieval models, and it is not known for certain whether Pugin played any part in the selection. In any case Minton, like many other successful and fashion-conscious manufacturers of the period, had a well established interest in the Gothic style that dated back to the 1820s. Factory pattern books contain shapes that echo the decorative Gothic of the time, inspired often by the spiky ornamentation of contemporary Paris porcelain. Other wares include the extensive range of stoneware jugs with embossed decoration made from the 1830s. Minton may not have produced that famous design celebrating the Eglington tournament, but they had equivalents, often inspired by sources such as Walter Scott. From 1846 a number of these were also issued in the new Parian porcelain, a material developed initially for the reproduction of sculpture. Stoneware and Parian were also used for the range of portable fonts in the Gothic style, first produced in the 1830s. By the mid-1840s there were several models in production, most scaled-down replicas of actual Gothic fonts, but one at least designed by Pugin. It is important to remember, however, that Pugin was not the only architect to work with Minton, who are known to have produced designs between the 1840s and the 1860s by Lewis Cottingham, Matthew Digby Wyatt, George Gilbert Scott, Alfred Waterhouse, Sir Charles Barry and John Thomas.[2]

It is unfortunate that none of the many letters and drawings sent by Pugin to Herbert Minton seem to have survived, and so it is hard to document their relationship precisely. What does survive in the Minton Archive at the Minton Museum in Stoke-on-Trent, is an extensive range of watercolour designs for tiles, tablewares, and other products, many signed and dated by Pugin. Factory pattern books of this period also contain a number of shapes to which Pugin's name is firmly attached (plate 263). Pugin frequently travelled to Stoke in connection with his work for the Earl of Shrewsbury at Cheadle and Alton and, according to Dr Jewitt,[3] he spent the long hours in the night train from London designing tiles and other wares for Minton.

By all accounts Pugin and Minton enjoyed a close friendship which went far beyond their initial relationship of client and supplier. It certainly survived until Pugin's death, but was probably always underlined by a sound business association. Pugin played a major role in firing Herbert Minton's ambition to improve constantly the quality of his products, and he was happy to express his high opinion of the tiles. There is a much quoted passage from a letter sent to Minton in January 1852, first recorded by Ferrey.[4] 'I declare your St Christopher tiles the finest done in the tile way; vastly superior to any ancient work; in fact, they are the best tiles in the world, and I think my patterns and your workmanship go ahead of anything.' Ferrey also includes a detailed account of the exchange of letters between the two during Pugin's final illness, letters that demonstrate a brief falling out over a financial misunderstanding, and the efforts made on both sides to restore the friendship to its former firm footing. On 14 February 1852, Pugin wrote as follows:[5]

My Dear, Ever Dear Minton,

Your capital letter to my wife has just arrived, thus leaving nothing, my dear friend, but a perfect reconciliation between us. You must attribute a great deal to the dreadful irritation of nerves left by this terrible fever under which I suffered; but nothing would contribute so much to the final re-establishment of my improved health, as a real and hearty reconciliation with you. It is ridiculous, and a delight to the many, to see two such men as you and I quarrelling. We cannot afford it long, let us cut the row and embrace. I will endeavour when sufficiently restored to settle it over a leg of mutton at Huntfield; and if you will come and see me I will give you a better reception at St Augustine than the Emperor; for all my things are in the true style, which is more than you can say for the fancy patterns. I have written to Mr Barry by

this post that we are quite reconciled: it would be too affecting to see us really embracing over a happy combination of four tiles, so it must pass in imagination, though not less real.

Your devoted old friend,
A.W. Pugin.

263.† Pattern book used at the Minton factory to record encaustic tile designs *c.*1850 (Minton Museum, Royal Doulton Ltd).

264. Side Chapel, St John's Hospital, Alton, showing encaustic tiles decorated with Shrewsbury emblems.

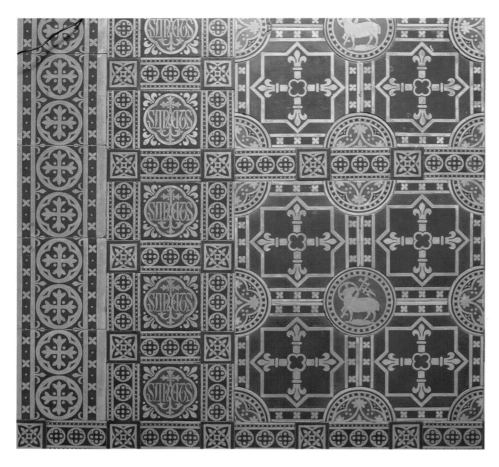

in the Crystal Palace where a wide range of well-received wares did much to consolidate his company's international reputation.

Pugin designs, or versions of them, remained in use at various Minton factories long after the death of Herbert Minton in 1858, a factor that inevitably complicates the positive identification of Pugin's original work. The known or recorded designs cover a wide range of wares. First are the encaustic floor tiles, identified as Pugin designs either from signed watercolour sketches, pattern books and other factory records, or by association. Major Pugin buildings such as the Palace of Westminster, St Giles's, Cheadle, or St Augustine's, Ramsgate were floored by Minton with specially designed tiles (plates 265–7), and many other Pugin structures featured a mixture of what might be called standard Pugin tiles combined with one-off designs (plates 264, 268). Notable among the latter are those incorporating the initials, rebus or coats-of-arms of the client, with typical examples being the letter T tiles made for the Tempest family at Ackworth, or the barrel device used for Sir John Sutton at West Tofts (plate 269). Some tiles are complete in themselves, such as the regularly-occurring crowned M design used in many Lady Chapels, while others are part of a complex design spread over four, eight or even more tiles. The standard was the basic six-inch square tile, but also made were smaller and larger squares, rectangles, diamonds, circles and semi-circles. Colours ranged from the basic two up to six. A floor would be composed of repeating and individual units, with patterns contrasted by colour changes, and relieved by areas or borders of

265. Section of encaustic floor made by Minton for St Giles's, Cheadle, *c*.1846.

266. Section of encaustic floor made by Minton for St Augustine's, Ramsgate, decorated with Pugin's monogram and the martlet emblem, *c*.1852.

267. Section of encaustic floor made by Minton for the Palace of Westminster, *c*.1850 (Trustees of the Victoria & Albert Museum).

Another factor underlining the friendship was their involvement in the Great Exhibition. Herbert Minton was one of the exhibition's original sponsors, putting up a guarantee of £10,000 at a time when the venture's success was far from certain and enjoying, as a result, a primary location

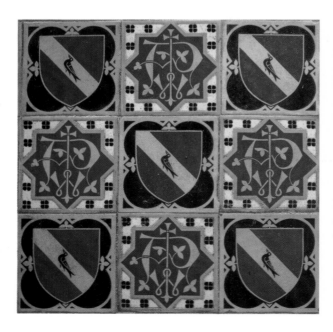

plain quarries in red or black. Most designs were based on conventional Gothic or foliate forms, but there are plenty of others inspired by heraldry, or featuring various Pugin alphabets. It is likely that many of the complex patterns covering large areas of floor were planned with the help of factory artists. However, detailed scale plans by Pugin for some tiling schemes do survive (plate 271), for example for the church of St Marie, or Our Lady of the Sea, Greenwich, with clear identification of the tiles by catalogue or type number and the quantity required.[6] It should also not be forgotten that at the same time Minton were producing many classically inspired encaustic tiles, designs such as those used at Osborne House that cannot have filled Pugin with great enthusiasm. In some of the largest commissions, for example for St George's Hall, Liverpool or for the Senate House, Melbourne, the tiled floor reveals a predictable mixture of Victorian styles, with Gothic, Classical, Renaissance and Naturalist elements side by side. It is not practical to list, or illustrate, all known Pugin floor tile designs, but a large number can be identified with certainty.

It is unlikely that Pugin ever designed tiles for the rival Chamberlain factory at Worcester, even though its products were, in the early days, closer to the medieval sources. Relatively successful through the 1840s, the Chamberlain tile works was bought by Maw & Company in 1850 and subsequently moved to Shropshire and greatly expanded. A catalogue of The Worcester Encaustic Tile Works, dating from the 1840s is in The Victoria and Albert Museum.[7] Other Minton rivals established during the 1850s include Godwins of

Lugwardine, Herefordshire, and the Architectural Pottery Company of Poole, Dorset, but clearly these have no direct Pugin association. However, there was a massive proliferation of Gothic-style floor tiles after Pugin's death, with many companies producing designs based freely on source

268. Section of encaustic floor made by Minton for Our Lady and St Adolphus's, Hanley Swan, Blackmore Park, Worcestershire

269. Section of encaustic floor made by Minton for St Mary's, West Tofts, decorated with Sutton emblems, c.1849.

270. Section of encaustic floor made by Minton for the Mausoleum, Bicton, decorated with Rolle initials and emblems, c.1850.

278.† Range of dinner and tea ware printed with the Pugin Gothic design, made by Minton and in production from about 1844 to the 1920s (Private Collection).

279.† Tureen and stand, Minton 1856 (Private Collection).

280.† Watercolour design for a colour-printed plate, 1850 (Minton Museum, Royal Doulton Ltd).

281.† Plate shown in the Great Exhibition, 1851 (Victoria & Albert Museum).

and Reynolds process, for drawings for a number of these exist in the Minton Archive bearing Pugin's signature or initials and the dates 1850 and 1851 (plates 280 and 283). It is clear from these how much Pugin enjoyed the facility for complex flat pattern decoration that this new process allowed. A number show decorative borders and centres, generally applied to plates. An unusual variant is the boat-shaped footed tazza, an untypical Minton shape that may have been designed by Pugin himself. Best known are those designs that incorporate texts or mottos within the foliate Gothic decoration. These include the service Pugin designed for his own use, with its repeating border inscription UBI AMOR IBI FIDES (plate 283), another, shown at the Great Exhibition, with a central panel of intersecting text SOUVEIGNE VOUS DE MOY, and a design with a complex border pattern incorporating the text QUI DELIGIT SUAM UXOREM SEIPSUM DELIGIT. Moralising proverbs in Gothic script are also a feature of another popular tableware range, known in the Minton records as the Motto Dinner Service, but unfortunately not supported by any Pugin drawings. The range of proverbs is considerable, and includes the following, among others:

It is a good tongue that says no ill
and a better heart that thinks none.

That thou mayst injure no man dove like be
and serpent like that none may injure thee

Wine reasonably drunk and in season
brings gladness of the heart
and cheerfulness of the mind

To invite a person to be our guest
is to undertake his happiness
whilst under our roof

College. Whatever its origins, it was undoubtedly very successful, and was still being produced at least as late as 1928.

Better documented is the range of tableware printed with multicoloured designs by the Collins

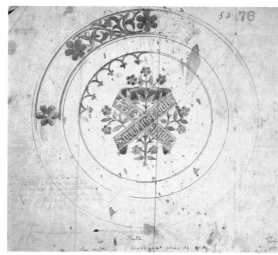

Who deceives me once
shame on him
if he deceives me twice
shame on me

The Pugin attribution for this pattern cannot be proven, even though the spirit and the style both point to him. Unfortunately, most of the pieces known today carry factory date stamps of the mid- and late-1850s. Certainly Minton treated their Pugin designs with predictable freedom. As was common practice at the time design material acquired from any source was simply added to the design library, to be used in any way that factory artists thought fit. This library was catalogued in 1871 and the Pugin material was collected together and filed under the Gothic heading, with the prefix numbers s1–s28. An indication of the way the library was used is illustrated by a simple two-colour trefoil border pattern design by Pugin in 1850. By 1855 this pattern had acquired the name Medieval and had been expanded by nine new colourways in up to four colours. In this Puginesque form it remained in production at least until 1868.[10] As a result, there are a number of Pugin-style Collins and Reynolds printed table-ware patterns made at Minton between the 1850s and the 1870s that may have had little to do directly with Pugin himself. Like all Pugin tableware designs, these appear to have been used only on earthenware.

The final group of Pugin-designed Minton wares is a diverse range of ornamental pieces. Best-known, and now widely accepted as an icon of Victorian Gothic design, is the famous bread plate, with its WASTE NOT WANT NOT motto (plate 260). Designed in 1849 and shown in the Birmingham exhibition of that year, this was the most important of a small group of domestic wares that featured the inlaid encaustic tile process. It is known in three versions, the basic and most common three-colour model, a superior six-colour encaustic variant and, most surprisingly, an earthenware version with majolica glazes. Despite the status enjoyed by the Pugin bread plate today, some critics at the time were not so enthusiastic: 'The bread plate is made on the encaustic tile principle, very dark and massive in colouring, and disagreeably associating with the bread. The design might do well for a pavement, but is rude and coarse, and unfit for an object immediately close to the eye on the table.'

The same critic was even more dismissive of a dessert plate, an octagonal lobed shape with grapes moulded in relief, a rare Pugin design for bone china dating from 1849 (plate 282).

> . . . a dessert plate, in which every principle appropriate to the treatment of china is violated in the attempt to be mediaeval. Smoothness and flatness are essential to cleanliness; but here Mr Pugin actually makes his ornament *raised*, whereby the chances are ten to one against the plate ever being clean. China is so beautiful in its texture and semi-transparecny, that no more colour should be used than conduces to heighten these charms; but Mr Pugin overlooks this most natural attribute, and covers the surface of the plate with heavy colour, thus annihilating all the white surface.[11]

Illustrated in the Minton shape and pattern books are a number of other items that carry Pugin's name. These include a garden seat (plate 285), finished in various majolica colour schemes, a jardinière and stand printed with coloured Collins and Reynolds patterns (plate 284), a large luncheon

282.† Octagonal plate with grape design moulded in relief made by Minton c.1849 (Trustees of the Victoria & Albert Museum).

283.† Watercolour design for a colour-printed plate used by Pugin at the Grange, Ramsgate, c.1850 (Minton Museum, Royal Doulton Ltd).

284.† Jardinière and stand from a series with colour printed designs made by Minton c.1850 (Private Collection).

285.† Garden seat made by Minton and decorated in majolica colours *c*.1850 (Private Collection).

286.† Watercolour designs for door plates, *c*.1850. These were probably not put into production (Minton Museum, Royal Doulton Ltd).

287. Selection of colour-printed table wares made by Minton, showing Pugin and Puginesque decoration, *c*.1850–70 (Private Collection).

tray made in a number of colours and finishes, including encaustic, and designed to be used both as a tray and mounted as a lazy susan, porcelain pedestals with blue and gilt decoration for Parian figures of St Joseph and the Madonna shown at the Birmingham Exhibition of 1849, a jug and basin set printed with a simple Collins and Reynolds foliate band in light green, a covered flagon and matching stand, richly decorated with embossed Christian motifs and clearly modelled on metal shapes, an altar vase and, perhaps most surprising of all, a range of six finger and door plates with colourful Collins and Reynolds decoration. One has a crowned VA motif and so they may have been designed for the Palace of Westminster. However, none survive, and it is not even certain they were actually produced.

The great variety of wares designed by Pugin and made by Minton underlines the close personal and business relationship that existed between the two. Success in commercial terms was confirmed by the designs, and their derivatives, that remained in production long after the deaths of both men (plate 287). Indeed, Minton maintained the relationship into the next generation, producing tiles, along with other manufacturers, designed by E.W. Pugin. An example is the tiling designed by E.W. Pugin for Chirk Castle, Clwyd, carrying on the alterations commissioned from his father by Robert Myddelton Biddulph. Still at Chirk are designs for two block-printed tiles by E.W. Pugin, with indications that these were made in 1858 by Minton. Less certain is the possibility that Pugin also designed for other pottery manufacturers. Wares are known that hint at this; but there is little evidence to confirm any such association. Apart from the Chamberlain encaustic tiles described earlier, there are a number of possible candidates from the late 1840s, including tiles made by Copeland, and altar vases from the Bloor Derby factory.[12] However, for the time being such wares must remain Puginesque, along with the flood of Pugin-style Gothic tiles that poured from the kilns of Stoke-on-Trent and the Severn Valley during the last decades of the nineteenth century.

CHAPTER ELEVEN

Book Design and Production

CLIVE WAINWRIGHT

The content of the books that Pugin wrote has been touched upon in several chapters and thorough bibliographical descriptions have already been published.[1] There has also been some analysis of the printed and manuscript sources Pugin used for his texts and illustrations,[2] but much remains to be done and the catalogue of his own library is a vital source (chapter 6). However, as his diaries, letters and many surviving sketches show, the ancient buildings and works of fine and applied art that Pugin saw in this country and in Europe provided his most significant inspiration. This can be seen in his last book, *A Treatise on Chancel Screens*, where the illustrations include screens from St Peter's in Rome, Siena, Venice, Florence, Lübeck, Münster, Hildesheim, Marburg, Metz, Antwerp, Toulouse, Toledo, Sens, Urnes near Bergen in Norway and several churches in Brittany.

That useful word *Gesamtkunstwerk* – or total work of art – could well have been coined for Pugin's books, for, not only did he write the text, but he also designed the bindings, drew and in some cases etched the illustrations, and, in at least one case, acted as publisher as well. He was not the first architect to do this, but it is the breadth and number of his publications and the manner in which he geared his works to the mass market that single him out, setting the pattern for others to follow.

In the 1760s Robert Adam and James Stuart had both designed elaborate tooled-leather bindings for presentation copies of their works,[3] but the rest were bound either in plain leather or to the taste of their owners. For his presentation volumes Pugin followed in this tradition; thus a standard copy of *Contrasts* was adorned for presentation to the Pope with an illuminated dedication and a special

288.† *Liber Vitae* for Ushaw College, bound in brass-mounted velvet (Trustees of Ushaw College).

binding (plates 289, 290). The gilded brass corners and bosses applied to boards covered in silk velvet closely followed medieval precedents. He designed such a binding for the missal at Cheadle in 1845, copying all the mounts from a German medieval example.[4] On his drawing of the original,[5] made earlier the same year in the cathedral at Mainz, he noted 'Bindings of the old choral books kept in the inner sacristies'. Similar presentation bindings survive on the founder's book at Ushaw (plate 288) and on the album of designs Pugin did for alterations to the buildings of Balliol, Oxford,[6] and other examples probably survive

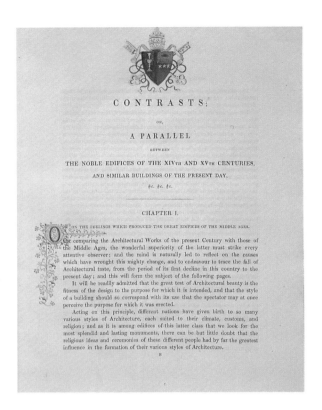

elsewhere. He even had some of his own copies bound in simplified versions, using silk-covered boards (plate 291). An edition of the Roman Breviary made for Pugin's church in Ramsgate in 1843 is in red morocco with gilded and gauffered edges;[7] on the cover is a design by Pugin which he called 'St Augustine's Mark'; the burial register of 1847 is in green morocco and has the same crest, which was also engraved by Hardman on the metalwork he made for St Augustine's.

Pugin employed his own 'mark' in a similar way: on the simple calf bindings of his sketch-books and scrap-books he used his monogram, AWNP, in a quatrefoil (plate 292). With that enthusiasm which often grips those who are not legally armigerous, he seems to have used his crest and monogram whenever possible – on furniture, wall-paper, metalwork, ceramics and books (plate 294).

In terms of innovation and influence however his 'trade bindings' are the most interesting. Pugin had served a long apprenticeship in publishing with his father, who was deeply immersed in the trade during the 1820s. The young Pugin helped to illustrate the books and would have met all the leading publishers of the day, including Taylor of Holborn, John Britton and Rudolph Ackermann, all of whom worked with his father. The leading lithographers and engravers – Harding, Le Keux and Hullmandel – turned the drawings of the Pugins and their pupils into illustrations. All of these were to be useful contacts when the young Pugin set up on his own. The elder Pugin seems however to have had no real interest in the outward appearance of his books and I have never seen a copy with a specially designed binding.

Pugin's first independent book was *Gothic Furniture of the 15th cent designed and etched by A.W.N. Pugin* printed for him by Ackermann, the son of his father's old friend (chapter 9) and the publisher of *Pugin's Gothic Furniture* of 1827 (plate 294). Pugin wished to produce it in a trade cloth

binding – a new departure in cheap mass-production. There is still debate about who pioneered the first use of cloth, but it seems likely to have been the Clerkenwell bookbinder, Archibald Leighton, in about 1823.[8] In 1832 Leighton perfected a technique for gold-blocking motifs on the cloth by machine; at first this was largely confined to the spines and perhaps a title on the front board. These advances were also applied to the embossing of leather bindings, which, until this time, had been a hand process.[9]

Having persuaded Ackermann to publish *Gothic Furniture* cheaply in cloth boards, Pugin naturally also wished to decorate the boards. He arranged for one of the new grained green cloths to be used, but would have been advised that extensive gold-blocking was not technically possible. He therefore took the unusual course of pasting a copy of the title page on the front board, so that only a frame of cloth showed. This, like the illustrations in the book, was first printed in black, then over-printed with the title and some other lettering in red, giving the effect of rubrication. On the title page (plate 294) and the board, the label at the bottom which reads 'London Ackermann & Co. Strand' is printed in red, but Pugin's four initials in the corners are actually coloured with watercolour, in some copies blue and in others green.

His intention of reaching a wide audience seems to have succeeded, for he wrote to Willson in January 1835 '. . . it will be published on 1st

February . . . I have a great many subscribers to it and I am paid a certain sum for each plate by Ackermann so that the work will pay me very well & as it is a useful cheap work I expect it will sell well.'[10]

For *Contrasts*, the next book, which he published himself, the same cloth was used, but without the title page being pasted on to it. Ackermann published the companions to the furniture volume – *Designs for Gold and Silversmiths* and *Designs for Iron and Brass Work*. Then early in 1837 – even though the title page says 1836 – his *Details of Antient Timber Houses* . . . (plate 295) came out. The bindings of these three exactly follow the pattern of *Gothic Furniture*. The copy of *Details* has the same cloth as the rest of this series and *Contrasts*: this has been described and illustrated as '. . . the first form of graining at all extensively used [which] was actually called, *and advertised as*, "morocco" cloth . . . so stamped as to suggest the patterned surface of actual embossed leathers.'[11] I have also seen the identical cloth on a copy of *Gothic Furniture*. I have never seen a copy of any of these with a binder's ticket, but in his diary for 22 February 1837 Pugin noted 'Paid Leighton'. *Details* was published on 20 February so Leighton is a real possibility as the binder of plate 295 and perhaps the others in the series. This attribution is strengthened by a note he made in 1839: 'Leighton

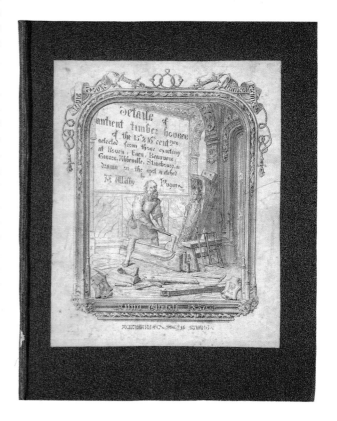

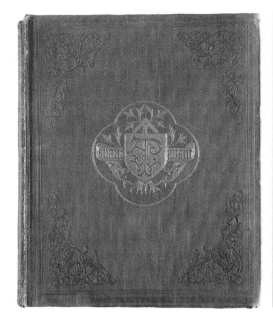

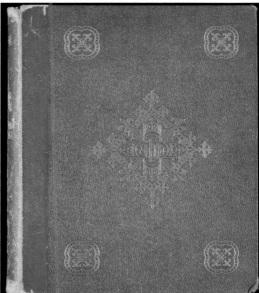

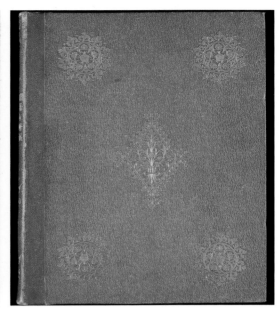

for binding £3.15.0'; he made a further payment in 1840. He would have been in good company, for, in 1841, Leighton bound *American Notes* for Dickens.[12] The same cloth was used on another of the key Gothic Revival books of this date, Willis's *Remarks on the Architecture of The Middle Ages*, published in 1835, where again there is no binder's ticket.

Here we see Pugin using the lastest binding technology, but this produced a fake morocco leather, the use of which ran completely counter to his 'True Principles' concerning marbling and graining to counterfeit expensive materials. Even after the publication of *True Principles* he continued this dishonesty: two of his later books (plates 297, 298) show fake red morocco cloth being used. Had he used an honest plain cloth or indeed a patterned one, that did not imitate leather, that would have been perfectly in line with his theories.

His next book actually was *True Principles of Pointed or Christian Architecture* of 1841 and this time the publisher was John Weale, the rising star of architectural publishing. By this date Pugin had decided that the new blocking technology had progressed sufficiently for him to exploit it. He designed a dramatic quatrefoil containing his motto and initials for the binding – this was blocked in gold, while the corners had blind stamped gothic foliage (plate 296). Unlike the books published in the 1830s, which were all cloth, this and his other 1840s books had leather spines, matching the colour of the boards, with the title tooled in gold on the spine. Here at least he followed his own principles and used a green cloth that did not mimic leather. He was again at the forefront of binding design and technology, for in the same year Owen Jones designed a blocked pattern to cover the whole binding for Lockhart's *Ancient Spanish Ballads*. This was 'the first instance of an historical style being consistently adopted (and not merely reproduced) for the modern requirement of book technology.'[13]

Pugin was in fact employing Owen Jones at this time as we shall see. Jones may seem to have been ahead of Pugin for he used a gold-blocked design over the whole board for *Ballads*.[14]

However, the fascinating correspondence with Weale concerning the production of *True Principles* reveals Pugin's intentions: 'I herewith send you the prospectus and the sketch of the title page & frontispiece. I fear the square pattern which is the right thing & copied from an old drawing will be too expensive. I have therefore sent you a monogram for the centre.'[15] It would seem that Pugin had originally planned to gold block the whole cover, but, in order to keep the price down for a mass readership, he opted for a cheaper option. His decision seems to have paid off for, by February 1843, he had sold 1200 copies[16] – a surprising number for a polemical architectural treatise. Again I have not seen a copy with a binder's label, but, by this date, several binders had the specialised new presses for blocking such bindings. He may have continued to use Leighton who died later in the year.

When his next book, *An Apology for the Revival of Christian Architecture*, was published by Weale in 1843 it had two alternative bindings. One is a feeble blind-stamped Rococo one, that has nothing to do with Pugin, and the other uses the same

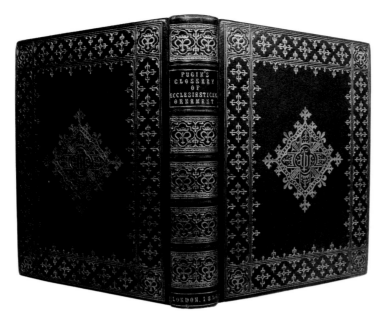

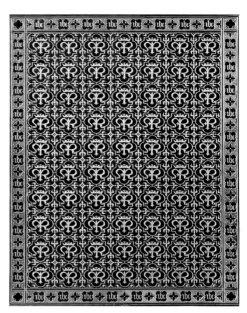

block as *True Principles*. A copy of the latter bears the binder's ticket of Runting & Jeffcoat of 7 East Harding Street, London EC4. Only one other book bound by them is known and they were not in business very long. They might also have bound *True Principles*, but the metal die for the cover would have been retained by the publisher – who in both cases was Weale – and lent to the binder. With both versions of this binding a plain green cloth was used.

It is likely that Hardman would have made steel or gunmetal dies for this and Pugin's later books – I have not searched their extensive records where details may survive. These dies needed to stand up to immense pressure and not wear out quickly. 1200 copies of *True Principles* had been blocked by 1843 and the bindings I have seen on the *Apology* from the same die are very crisp indeed. Also in 1843 Pugin's *The Present State of Ecclesiastical Architecture in England* was published by Charles Dolman; it has a ribbed brown cloth but a feeble Rococo binding, which I hope has no connection with Pugin.

In 1844, however, Pugin more than made up for this lapse, when he took the step he had wanted to take in 1841, and designed and published the glorious, fully gold-blocked binding of the *Glossary of Ecclesiastical Ornament* (plate 297), which is only marred by the fake red morocco cloth. The spine was actually leather and was broad enough to have a Gothic motif stamped on it as well as the title. The publisher in this case was Henry Bohn and the book sold well; a second edition was called for in 1846, and a third one as late as 1868, testifying to its continuing popularity with High Victorian architects and designers.

Matters architectural so occupied Pugin for the next year or two that it was not until 1849 that his next book *Floriated Ornament* appeared and this was also published by Bohn. Again there was a elaborate binding (plate 298), with the same red morocco cloth and, though close in character to *The Glossary*, it is an even more spare and powerful example of flat pattern, demonstrating Pugin's rapidly increasing mastery of this difficult aspect of design. Annoyingly there is no evidence of who bound *The Glossary*, I have never seen a copy with a binder's ticket. Of all the copies of *Floriated Ornament* that I have examined only one[17] has the binder's name stamped on it. He was John Wright, who had been at 14 & 15 Noel Street Soho since 1842 and was previously at number 21. Little is known about Wright but he was certainly involved with other Gothic Revival bindings for according to Redgrave's report on the 1851 Exhibition:

> . . . the best works being imitative of old German, French, or mediaeval bindings. 'The Illuminated Book of the Middle Ages' as bound by J. Wright (Class XVII, No 139), has much merit, although wanting a nice adaptation of the ornament to the corners. 'The Glossary of Ecclesiastical Ornament' is also good, although the whole surface is too generally covered, and the margins too narrow for the size of the diaper.[18]

This was a special leather-bound copy of *The Glossary* and Wright also worked for Owen Jones and Bohn himself:

> 'Pugin's Glossary' royal 4to, inlaid illuminated morocco, well and expensively executed; the design taken from the contents of the book, and

adapted to the decoration of the binding. The price of the binding, £10. Owen Jones and Humphrey's illuminated books of the middle ages imperial folio, dark brown morocco, blind tooled in imitation of an old monastic binding. 'Bohn's Classical Library' as a revival of the English style of binding of the period of 1760.[19]

Perhaps Wright was the binder of the 1844 edition and the subsequent ones? He obviously was involved with Bohn. It seems likely that the special Wright binding shown in 1851 is that from the Abbey Library now at the Center for British Art at Yale (plate 299). This is obviously not a Pugin design and Redgrave's criticism of the ornament covering the whole surface is immediately understandable. By 1851 Pugin was using Westley as his binder, so he is unlikely to have been designing for Wright that year. In 1846, however, an S. Wright stamped a binding of a copy of the second edition of the *Glossary* in full morocco (plate 300). The binding is, I suggest, a Pugin design which uses the same block with the IHC monogram as the cloth version (plate 296). A special tool must have been made for the quatrefoil and crown motifs and the floriated crosses. S. Wright does not exist in the 1840s Directories, so it could be a mistake for J. Wright. Certainly the binder had access to the Pugin IHC block. Until further evidence emerges I suggest that S. and/or J. Wright probably bound the cloth *Glossary*, as well as the full leather one. Then in 1851, using only the quatrefoil and floriated cross tools, J. Wright produced the sub-Pugin binding to show in the 1851 exhibition.

Early in 1851 Pugin's last book *A Treatise on Chancel Screens and Rood Lofts . . .* was published by Dolman. This had a strikingly ecclesiastical binding (plate 301) appropriate to its subject, but

[Embossing-Press.]

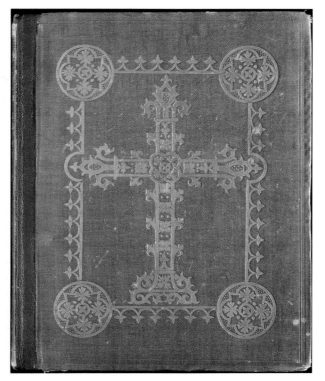

301. The binding of *A Treatise on Chancel Screens*, 1851.

302. The embossing press at Westley's, from *The Penny Magazine*, 1842.

perhaps less successful as a design than his previous two bindings. Here however he dispensed with morocco cloth and used instead an honest ribbed green cloth with a matching morocco leather spine of the same colour. He has used an all over blocked design, which is, I suspect, much like the 'square pattern' he wanted for *True Principles* in 1841. The advances in binding technology in the last decade had however made such an option much cheaper by 1851. The binder's ticket is that of 'Josiah Westley adjoining The Times office London', this was at Playhouse Yard, Blackfriars. Perhaps Pugin did not use Wright because of his involvement with Bohn, and Dolman may have had an agreement with Westley. Like Wright, Josiah Westley showed hand- and machine-made leather and cloth bindings at the 1851 Exhibition, but there is no detailed list to show if *Screens* was among them. Fortunately we have a splendid contemporary description of the process used by Westleys in 1842 to stamp their bindings:

The embossing-presses act on a different principle. The device is in this case engraved on a flat thick plate of steel or gun-metal, which is stamped down upon the leather or cloth. We have mentioned three embossing-presses as being situated in the basement of the factory (plate 302). These are of immense power; indeed one of them exerts a pressure of no less than *eighty tons*. The mode of use is simply thus: – The cover or the case for a book is laid flat on a tablet

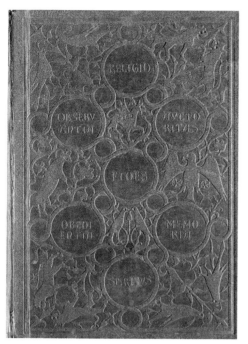

303. The binding of Ruskin's *The Seven Lamps of Architecture*, 1849.

304. The frontispiece of *True Principles*, 1841.

305. Frontispiece design of a scholar in his study, 1831 (RIBA Drawings Collection).

306. Coloured woodcuts in the text of *True Principles*.

or bed heated by gas from beneath or else on a counter-die similar to that by which it is to be impressed. The engraved plate (which is in 'intaglio' like a seal, but not so deep) is fixed to the press with its face downwards, and by manual labour, exerted on very powerful levers it is brought down upon the cover with such force as to impart its device to the leather or cloth.[20]

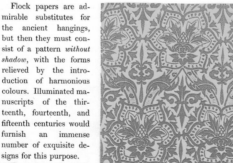

This description also tells us that:

If the book be a Bible, we have an emblematical device of a religious character if it be a Shakespeare, we have something pertaining to the great dramatist; if it be a lady's album or portfolio, we have a device of a graceful and ornamental character. This is an approach towards what may be termed a 'principle' in bookbinding, viz. that the subject of a book may be known from its cover; a principle which seems to have much to recommend it.

This could have come straight out of *True Principles* published just the year before. It throws up the interesting possibility that either the journalist who wrote this piece had himself read the book, or that Westley had realised that Pugin's ideas applied to his bindings and informed the journalist. In fact the use of appropriate motifs on book covers was long established by 1841, but the use of the term 'principle' in connection with this practice must derive from Pugin's book.

Ironically Pugin did not design a 'principled binding' for *True Principles* itself. By 1844 he had taken up the idea of a binding emblematic of the contents of the book it contained. Thus *The Glossary* has a prominent and entirely appropriate IHC, and *Floriated Ornament* has foliate motifs. Westley must have been delighted indeed to bind *Screens* where the Rood Cross is the crucial part of the design.

Pugin's pioneering bindings without doubt set a trend for the many Gothic Revival cloth bindings

of the 1850s and '60s. Ruskin's *Seven Lamps of Architecture* (plate 303) is an early and interesting example; published in 1849 and therefore inspired by *True Principles* and *The Glossary*, it is blind embossed without any gilding. The design is a remarkable and powerful one inspired by a very Ruskinian source – the mosaic floor of San Miniato in Florence – and, as one might expect, much more iconographically interesting than Pugin's bindings. It is indeed a principled binding for the seven lamps of the text are declared in the binding, though for some curious reason their Latin titles do not exactly match their English ones. Although the design is by W. Harry Rogers, Ruskin himself was responsible for the iconography. With his well known antipathy to Pugin, Ruskin would have denied any debt to him. Pugin's bindings are without doubt the inspiration for that of *Seven Lamps*, although it in no way copies a Pugin design. There is also the interesting possibility that, because Pugin drew and etched his own plates for his earlier books including *True Principles*, Ruskin himself was encouraged to do likewise, as he did for the first issue of the first edition of *Seven Lamps*. It was highly unusual for the author of a polemical architectural treatise to draw and etch the plates for it.

A copy of *Seven Lamps* bears the binder's ticket of 'Westley & Co. Friar Street'.[21] These premises were part of the same Blackfriars factory where *Screens* was bound and it is amusing to know that Ruskin's and Pugin's books were embossed on the same press.

The insides of Pugin's books are also pioneering examples of book making. As with the bindings he was always seeking to innovate and even in his relatively traditional books of 1835–7 the plates were printed in two colours. When designing the layout of *True Principles* he wrote to Weale:

> On looking over Dugdale's history of Warwickshire the other day I saw several etchings *among the text* & the same thing is remarked in all the old works. Now cannot we manage to print *some* of my etchings among the text the same as wood? I think it is a great advantage in some cases to have the illustrations before you as you were reading without turning to a plate. Now I will take any pains to do the thing well & would willingly engrave these separately if you could manage to print some of them among the text.[22]

Weale succeeded in accomplishing this complex exercise and in one case there are two coloured wood-cuts dropped into the text (plate 306), but it was Pugin who was suggesting the innovation to make the book easier to read, not the publisher himself.

Here we see Pugin creatively searching for precedents for the design of his books in early printed works like Dugdale's. With the actual subjects for the illustrations he was similarly inspired yet always adapting what he found to his particular purpose and making the final result his own. The frequently illustrated frontispiece of *True Principles* (plate 304) depicts an architect, perhaps Pugin himself, or perhaps his medieval *alter ego* in

307. The frontispiece of *Examples of Gothic Architecture*, 1836.

308. The frontispiece for Pugin's manuscript book 'St Marie's College', 1834. (Trustees of the Victoria & Albert Museum).

309. The medieval chronicler Monstrelet in his study, from N.X. Willemin, *Monuments Inédits*, 1827.

The Glossary of Ecclesiastical Ornament.

310. The frontispiece of
The Glossary.

311. A design for a border
from *The Glossary*.

his study. There are many medieval and Renaissance images similar to this in paintings and manuscripts and Pugin had drawn a version in 1831 (plate 305) and designed another in 1834 which was published in 1836 (plate 307). In 1834 he used the same form of a scholar at his desk in one of his manuscript books of designs (plate 308). All four and particularly the first are clearly based upon a portrait of the celebrated French chronicler Monstrelet in a manuscript in the Bibliothèque National in Paris. Pugin may have seen the original, but he could certainly have taken it (plate 309) from a book by Willemin[23] – who was a family friend – which was a source he frequently used for his designs (chapter 6). A similar exercise could be gone through for many of Pugins illustrations.

By the time he came to publish *The Glossary* the technology existed to illustrate it in glorious

colour (plates 310, 311). The new process of chromolithography had been pioneered by Owen Jones at his own press[24] with *Alhambra* in 1837–42 and *Ancient Spanish Ballads* in 1841. Pugin owned a copy of the *Alhambra* and certainly knew Jones at this time, for, in 1842, he recorded a payment in his diary, 'Owen Jones 18.5.0'. The reason for payment of this considerable sum is not known, but if Jones was doing some lithographic printing for him it does not survive. As well as Bohn's involvement in publishing *The Glossary*, he had published the first volume of Henry Gally Knight's *The Ecclesiastical Art of Italy* as early as 1842, with an elaborate chromolithographic title page and plates printed by Jones.

Others quickly began to challenge Jones: 'The printing of coloured Lithographs is now widely practised next to Mr Owen Jones most successfully perhaps by Messrs Hanhart from whose presses have issued some of the most perfect specimens of Lithographic printing.'[25] Jones mainly went into printing to produce his own books, but M. & N. Hanhart were not architectural publishers; they perfected their technique by printing thousands of coloured covers for popular sheet music,[26] with polychromatic Rococo ornaments. Pugin frequently changed publishers and binders in search of perfection and must have realised that Hanhart could make a marvellous job of the *Glossary* for him.

He may well have known Michael Hanhart already, for A.C. Pugin's *Ornaments* of 1831 was itself a pioneering lithographically printed architectural work. It was printed by Hullmandel, who had the year before just driven his main competitor, Engelmann, Graf, Coindet & Co., out of business.[27] In 1830 Hanhart set up his own business in Charlotte Street, a few hundred yards

from where the Pugins lived. Pugin might also have known another of Hanhart's old partners, Charles Graf at this time. Graf printed the elaborate chromolithographic title, probably to Pugin's design, of the fourth edition of Frederick Husenbeth's *Missal for the use of the laity* of 1843.[28] Then Graf printed in monochrome a new edition of A.C. Pugin's *Ornaments* which Bohn published in 1844.

Hanharts printed *The Glossary*, but the lithographer was the otherwise unknown Henry Maguire, who only appears in the trade directories in 1842 at 49 Great Queen Street, Lincoln's Inn Fields. Pugin however chose the right man, as the plates in *The Glossary* amply demonstrate, and the same team produced the even more remarkable plates in *Floriated Ornament* (plates 199, 312). These are a *tour de force* of chromolithography, but perhaps less original in design than some modern commentators have thought.

Pugin states in the text that he took the Latin plant names from '"Tabernae Montanus eicones Plantarum" printed in Francfort in 1590' and some reviewers took him to task for using such an ancient and obscure source. Pugin was obviously no Latin scholar, for Tabernae Montanus was the pseudonym of the herbalist Jacob Theodor of Bergzabern (1520–90). The book is *Eicones plantarum seu stirpium arborum nempe fructicum, herbarum, fructuum . . .* published in Frankfurt in 1590. These illustrations were rapidly plagiarised in 1597 by John Gerard for his famous *Herbal*. It is obvious when one looks at this remarkable and beautiful book that Pugin took more from it than the Latin names, for it includes, in more than 1000 pages, hundreds of black and white woodcuts of plants. I have not discovered a coloured copy, but one may exist.[29] While Pugin does not precisely copy these, his *Floriated Ornament* designs are quite closely based upon them, and they are likely to be the source of some of his naturalistic designs for textiles, wallpaper and marquetry. He seems not to have had a copy in his library, but he may well have seen the one in the British Museum Library which once belonged to Sir Joseph Banks.

Pugin strove to keep his books as cheap as possible and in this he succeeded to a considerable degree. The four 1830s books of furniture, metal-work and gables were only twelve shillings each; by comparison Shaw's *Specimens of Ancient Furniture* of 1836 cost two guineas. *True Principles* and *Screens* were only fifteen shillings, *An Apology* ten shillings and sixpence and *Present State* only nine shillings. The chromolithographic books were naturally more expensive and *The Glossary* sold at

312. Examples of medieval painted decoration from *Floriated Ornament*, 1849.

six guineas for the first edition and seven for the second, but considering that his father's monochrome *Antiquities of Normandy* had sold for that price in 1827 even this was not wildly expensive. *Floriated Ornament* had far fewer plates and was thus only three guineas.

Pugin's books as objects also exerted great influence on the design and manufacture of illustrations and bindings in High Victorian illustrated books. One obviously cannot separate the influence of the texts from that of the bindings and illustrations, for their buyers – many of whom were designers themselves – could be influenced by any or all parts of the books.

Had Pugin lived, he would not have supported

Morris and his followers, who pioneered the expensive hand-printed, private-press books produced in limited editions, which were to form a key part of the Arts and Crafts Movement. Pugin, by contrast, developed the use of the latest technologies to produce well designed and innovatory, fully illustrated books for the emerging mass market of art, architecture and design students, practising product designers and middle-class design enthusiasts throughout Europe and America. Some of his books were translated into French and German, for instance *Les Vrais Principes de l'Architecture Ogivale*, published in Bruges in 1850. Pugin's books represent an important, but somewhat neglected aspect of the history of publishing and the art of the book in this country.

CHAPTER TWELVE

Jewellery

SHIRLEY BURY

There is no evidence that after his early experience with Rundell, Bridge & Rundell, the Royal Goldsmiths (see chapters 2 and 13), Pugin went on working for the firm. He continued however to design jewellery and jewelled objects on his own account, gradually beginning to appreciate the necessity of studying medieval goldsmiths' work. Travel, antique shops, goldsmiths and brokers like Rundell's, who bought and sold old and modern artefacts, as well as publications such as A.C. Stothard's *Monumental Effigies*, 1817–32, were all grist to the mill. Tentative efforts at antiquarian reconstruction, ornate and oddly proportioned, are displayed in *The Chest* (plate 313), a volume of drawings of 1832 depicting the contents of an imaginary medieval coffer.[1] Several rings are included, one of which appears in a group of jewellery together with two brooches, the circular specimen being based on fourteenth-century wheel designs, an enamelled gold cross inspired by a late fifteenth-century German type, a chain with the pendant bearing the image of an ecclesiastic beneath a traceried canopy deriving from fourteenth- and fifteenth-century figurative examples,[2] a hunting knife and a dagger. Two morses, a rosary and a mitre, apparently jewelled, are drawn elsewhere in the volume.

Pugin also knew about Limoges enamels, to judge by a jewelled pectoral cross with a crucifix in another of his imaginary schemes, *The Shrine*, which followed hard on the heels of *The Chest* in 1832 and also contains a drawing of an episcopal ring. It is unfortunately impossible to chart Pugin's further progress from his *Designs for Gold and Silver Smiths*, begun in 1835 and published in etched form the following year, for it contains no jewellery.

Pugin's conversion to Catholicism in 1835

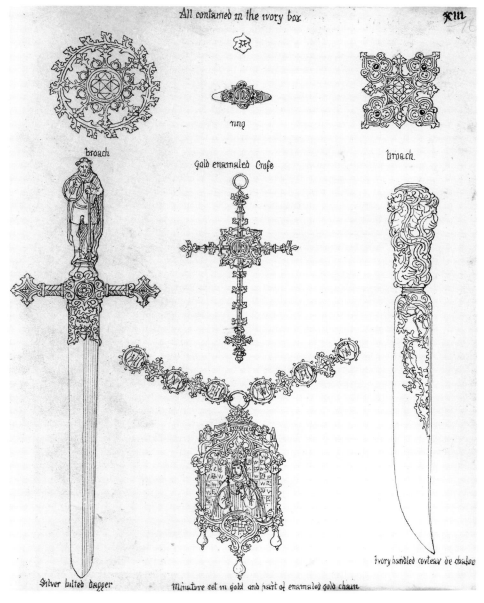

313.   Illustration from Pugin's manuscript book 'The Chest', 1832. (Trustees of the Victoria & Albert Museum).

focused his mind wonderfully, lending urgency to
his self-appointed mission to proselytize on behalf
of the Gothic as the only fit style for a Christian
country. He was now willing to cut corners, partly
to save time, evolving a visual form of shorthand
with a standard repertory of decorative Gothic
motifs later published in his *Glossary of Ecclesiastical Ornament*, 1844. His short-lived contact with
the Royal Goldsmiths inculcated in Pugin a lasting
respect for immaculate craftsmanship which later
erupted in moments of distress when confronted
with evidence of the shortcomings of the craftsmen working for his associate, John Hardman
the younger. Unless the pieces were intended
for Pugin himself, his heated protestations soon
ceased. He was enough of a realist to recognise
that the funds available from his patrons had to
be spread as far as possible and so reluctantly
acquiesced in some of Hardman's manufacturing
economies.

Commencing in 1838, Hardman transformed
himself with remarkable speed from a Birmingham button-maker into the head of an internation-
ally celebrated medieval metalworking firm. A
large part of Hardman's success was due to his
employment of outworkers in Birmingham and
elsewhere, though this was never openly acknowledged, as it would have undermined Pugin's
claims to have revived old techniques of enamelling and metalworking. After a trade depression
started in about 1840 Hardman had even less difficulty in recruiting leading local jewellers such as
Thomas Aston.[3] Skilled as they were in realising
modern designs, they often had difficulties in
working their way into Pugin's Gothic imagination, as did the enamellers in the jewellery trade,
some of whom must have practised their craft
on 'black ornaments' or mourning jewellery, for
which a knowledge of champlevé enamelling
was essential. William Burges, who realised that
Hardman used their services, found their enamels
somewhat strident,[4] but he was too young to remember the vogue for multi-coloured jewellery in
the 1820s and 1830s from which the craftsmen had
taken their cue.

Pugin was well aware of the foibles of his most
munificent patron, the Earl of Shrewsbury, one of
whose selective economies was a preference for
plated or gilt base metal, over gold and silver.[5] To
accompany his gift of a magnificent (and costly) set
of High Mass vestments at the consecration of St
Chad's Cathedral, Birmingham in 1841, Shrewsbury presented a gilt metal morse of quatrefoil
form enamelled with represensions of the Crucifixion, the Virgin Mary and St John.[6] The 'richly
enamelled' morse decorated with the Earl's arms
(plate 314) may perhaps be an alternative piece.
Shrewsbury was also a considerable benefactor to
Oscott College, but he had nothing to do with the
two silver crowns for a statue of the Virgin and
Child in the chapel (plate 315). Though supplied
in May 1852, nearly eight months after Pugin's
death, they are essentially his design.[7] The graceful progression of fleurs-de-lys on the crest of
the Virgin's crown echoes the lilies adorning a
crown in St Augustine's, Pugin's own church in
Ramsgate. These are works of Pugin's maturity,
their simple profile designed to tell from a distance, a device he learned from the stage jewellery
familiar from his youthful passion for the theatre.

Most of the great prelates of the Catholic
Church in England patronised Pugin and
Hardman both before and after the restoration of
the Hierarchy in 1850, with its consequent reor-
ganisation of districts or dioceses. Francis George

Mostyn, Vicar Apostolic of the old Northern District, died prematurely in 1847 but had some splendid ornaments, presumably supplied for his consecration as Bishop of Abydos on 21 December 1840, but not entered in the Hardman day book until 29 January 1841.[8] His episcopal ring, part of a comprehensive order including vestments which amounted to £140. 10s., was set with a topaz. Thomas Joseph Brown, Vicar Apostolic of the Welsh District, was translated as Bishop to Newport and Menevia in 1850, acquiring from Hardman's in the following year a 'gold episcopal Signet Ring set with Large Ruby in Centre' costing £4. 15s. and no fewer than three pectoral crosses, two of them gifts.[9]

Despite the sometimes repeated translations of several prelates, the plate and furnishings ordered for one or other of their cathedrals have often survived, together on occasion with gem-set mitres (plate 402)[10] and pastoral staves, both of which usually contained elements of jewellers' work. But the whereabouts of more personal items such as the episcopal rings and pectoral crosses, which they carried with them from diocese to diocese, have proved elusive. Among the exceptions is the episcopal ring belonging to Bishop Thomas Walsh (plate 318), a devoted supporter of Pugin who is known to have acquired an enamelled and gilt cross and a morse costing two guineas apiece from Hardman's in 1839.[11] Walsh, resplendent in his vestments, is shown wearing the ring in his portrait in Oscott. The piece in question, modestly set with cabochon emeralds and rubies arranged around a lozenge with minute trefoils, hardly announces itself as an example of Pugin's work, but

neither does one of the rings in Jane Knill's parure in plate 321.

The Pransorium at Oscott is hung with several fine portraits by J.R. Herbert. The future Cardinal Wiseman is depicted with an enamelled chain of about 1840 from which is suspended a pectoral cross (plate 317), perhaps the one he sent to Hardman's in 1848 to be fitted with a new front decorated with enamels and set with emeralds. Among others is Bishop Willson of Hobart, Tasmania, the younger brother of Pugin's friend and fellow architect E.J. Willson, clothed in Hardman vestments. His pectoral cross, costing £2. 10s., was entered in the firm's records of 17 November 1843.[12] Archbishop Polding of Sydney is similarly attired.

Minor clerics and members of the laity in both the Catholic and Anglican Church were usually content to wear 'Pugin's Crosses'[13] in silver or brass, with or without a Crucifix. The prices varied. Individual purchasers were usually charged between 3s. 3d. and 10s. for silver specimens, depending on size and ornament, or 6d. for the brass ones.[14] Discounts were usually offered to the firm's London agents, the first of whom was probably Pugin's publisher Charles Dolman. By 1848, the Catholic convert and bookseller James Burns had come to an agreement with the firm to act as their agent. He was sent '2 Silver Gothic Crosses' in June; they cost 7s. 6d. each, for they were not included in the discount. But the '24 Brass gothic crosses' despatched to him in 1850 cost him 4d. apiece, a reduction of a third of the retail price.[15]

Hardman's strung rosaries comparatively infre-

316. Detail of a portrait of Bishop Milner, who died in 1826, showing an earlier style of episcopal jewellery (St Mary's College, Oscott).

317. Detail of the portrait of Bishop Wiseman showing his pectoral cross (St Mary's College, Oscott). Bishop Willson is shown on p. 247.

318.† Bishop Walsh's episcopal ring (St Mary's College, Oscott).

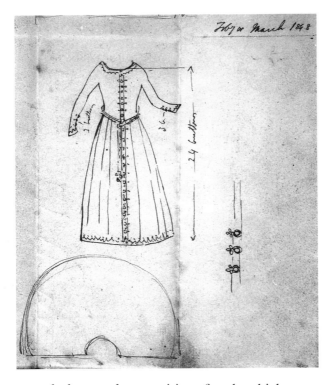

Feby or March 1848

and the model had to be replaced.[21] This is a rare documented instance of the firm undertaking the expense of introducing sculptural work into any of their 'toys' or small articles, including jewellery. A less ambitious sample 'card of Seals, Impressions in Mahogany Frames, with descriptions' was sent to Burns in March 1848 to show to customers.[22]

Pugin might have dreamed of a nation in Gothic costume in medieval architecture but in practice had to accept that it was only adopted on exceptional occasions even in his family (plate 319). Ideally he would also have had everyone wearing appropriate ornaments but in the event, aside from pieces intended for relatives and favoured patrons, Pugin designed little in the way of secular jewellery except for the mourning ornaments inseparable from a high mortality rate. Most of it has disappeared and very few items are entered in the ledgers in sufficient detail to suggest their appearance. A brooch acquired by Mr J. Gibson of Belmont Lodge, Tunbridge Wells late in 1848, is however described more fully. Gibson apparently furnished a miniature which was provided 'with Sterling gold Ornamented Setting & Engraved, with Fleur de Lys Border etc. etc.' at a cost of 16.15s.[23] The fleur-de-lys motif figures in Pugin's *Glossary* (see plate 311). A rich Anglican client, John Sutton, bought two jewels. The first, entered in the day book on 30 June 1848, was made of sterling gold set with a variety of precious stones and cost £42. 10s.; the second, a cross-shaped brooch in gold, engraved, enamelled and set with pearls and stones, was entered on 11 April 1849 and charged at £25.[24] Neither has been traced.

Some items bought from Hardman's seem too trifling for Pugin to have had anything to do with them: a small silver locket case with the enamelled initial M acquired by an army officer for £1. 2s. in 1848; an enamel and carbuncle brooch sold for £1. 17s. at about the same time; and a gold heart locket (a standard type of sentimental jewellery) costing £1. 10s. in January 1851.[25] But, (as with the locket case) they were probably all decorated with Pugin's standard Gothic ornament. Hardman was capable of abstracting appropriate motifs from one article and having them reproduced on another, while his nephew John Hardman Powell, who joined Pugin in his Ramsgate home as an apprentice-assistant in 1844, was soon able to translate the merest scribble of his master into a working drawing. Powell, of whom Pugin complained in January 1845 that 'he has not the first ideas of principles he has always worked from eye' (at Elkington's), survived his rigorous training to become a 'fine fellow',[26] married Pugin's eldest

quently but made quantities of seals which were popular with all types of purchaser. Miss Mostyn gave her relative the Bishop on his consecration an episcopal seal in steel engraved with the arms of St Cuthbert and Mostyn and priced at £4. 15s., together with a gold specimen set with an amethyst engraved with a mitre and armorials costing £3. 18s.[16] The first was probably a desk seal and the second might have been intended to be worn on a chain. Most of the seals produced by Hardmans to Pugin's design were made of steel, including 'A Gilt Steel Desk Seal cut with [the Bethune] Arms & Crest w[ith] Ebony Handle' costing £4. 15s., supplied on 28 May 1851. By way of variation, the architect William Butterfield bought 'A Brass Seal of Gothic Shape with Cross & Inscription engraved on seal parts' for £4 in 1851, choosing the pattern from several sketches made by Pugin.[17] Matthew Hadfield, ignoring the obsolescent vogue for wearing seals on the person, selected in 1853 'A Gold Signet Ring, cut with Shield of Arms' which cost him £5.[18] Augustus Wollaston Franks, later a distinguished antiquary, wrote to Hardman's in November 1845 concerning the two seals he wanted and asked for a preliminary design.[19] A complicated seal designed by Pugin for Lord Shrewsbury with a handle in the form of the Earl's crest (a talbot) was a near-disaster in 1843. Henry Weigall, a London sculptor and gem-engraver,[20] was commissioned to model the handle in wax preparatory to it being electrotyped. Unfortunately the process went wrong in the plating bath

daughter Anne in 1850 and succeeded his father-in-law as Hardman's chief designer.

The most important by far of the two parures of jewellery designed by Pugin is the one intended for his third bride, Helen Lumsdaine, to whom he attached himself in 1847 and whom he persuaded to convert to Catholicism, only to be parted from her at the insistence of her relatives in 1848.[27] Having expressed his grief and fury in a pamphlet recounting this perfidious behaviour which he distributed among his friends and supporters, Pugin soon met a Catholic girl, Jane Knill and married her on 10 August 1848. Jane received the jewellery and was painted in 1859 wearing some of the items, together with a memorial brooch with a central container for hair, probably the one supplied to E.W. Pugin in October 1852, a month after his father's death (plate 15), presumably as a gift to his stepmother. The society gossip Ralph Nevill recalled her as a very pretty woman, her every jewel mounted 'in a Gothic setting',[28] but the great parure would have been known only to her friends had it not been included in Pugin's Mediæval Court at the Great Exhibition of 1851,

where it was admired by Queen Victoria, according to Ferrey.[29]

Illustrated in a chromolithograph in Matthew Digby Wyatt's souvenir of the exhibition, *The Industrial Arts of the XIX Century*,[30] the jewellery (plate 320) includes an older piece in the form of the smaller of the two crosses and chains. This was made for Pugin's second wife Louisa Burton, who died suddenly in 1844. Though clearly recognisable in the sketch of Louisa in plate 10 it did not pass to her children but was given by two of Jane's descendants to the Victoria and Albert Museum in 1962, together with the quatrefoil brooch in the set (plate 321), while the headband shown with them was purchased from a sale in the same year.[31]

320.† Chromolithograph of the Pugin parure in M. Digby Wyatt, *The Industrial Arts of the XIX Century*, 1851–3.

321.† Group of jewellery, designed by Pugin, 1848, (Trustees of the Victoria & Albert Museum).

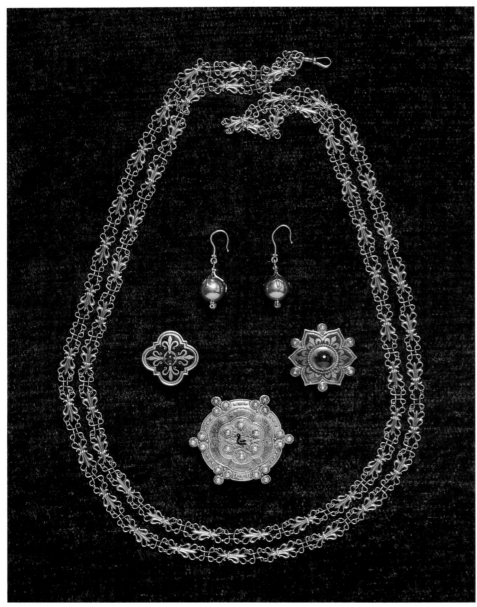

322.† Group of jewellery designed by Pugin (Private Collection).

323. Silver and enamel brooch set with cabouchon garnets (Private Collection).

alteration.'[34] Perhaps he was reluctant to admit that he had simply decided to incorporate it in the new parure. A fine piece of jewellery with a crisp and confident profile, its formalised interpretation of the Gothic represents Pugin's brilliant exploitation of the realities of Birmingham workshop production. Each unit in the chain was stamped out in two parts in the fly-press which were snapped together by means of a toothed flange.

All through the making of the new ornaments Pugin fretted about their cost, execution and appearance. As the crisis over his engagement to Helen Lumsdaine approached its climax early in 1848, his letters to John Hardman betray his anguish, not only about its ostensible subject, the quatrefoil brooch:

> The more I think the more I am distressed about the jewellry . . . the colour of the gold [brooch] is as bad as possible . . . I want gold like my old ring yellow gold rich looking gold precious looking gold like all the old work . . . I believe your jeweler is a humbug a real humbug . . . All the old examples shows the pearls etc. standing out fastened by gold wires if the earings I designed have the gold buried they will be perfectly beastly. I have been looking at all the authorities . . .[35]

Hardman took note and the pearls on the earrings were pinned. In another letter Pugin made a serious point about the execution of the brooch: it was too flat, he asserted, . . . 'all in a straight line whereas the 4 quatrefoils should have dropped from the center thus then we should have had light and shadow and the fleu (sic) de lis should have dropped in section to the point . . .'[36]

The new pieces, which Pugin accepted despite his strictures, were 'A pair of Sterling gold Bracelets richly Enameled & set with Stones' costing £72; 'A Sterling Gold letter M Brooch, set with Pearls & Stones' [after the so-called William of Wykeham piece at New College, Oxford] at £29. 17s.; 'A Sterling gold large Brooch, with Box at Back etc.' [the quatrefoil piece], £23. 4s.; 'A Sterling gold Large Cross & Solid gold Chain richly Enameled', £55. 11s.; 'A Sterling gold Small Cross set with Diamonds etc.', £9. 12s. 6d.; 'A Sterling gold head Ornament with Diamonds etc.', £28. 16s.; 'A Sterling gold pair of Earrings set with Pearls etc.', £14. 9s. and two rings, one set with four turquoises for £2. 7s. and the other plain at £1. 7s. A casket cost £3. 11s. He also designed a silver-gilt head band with applied rosettes, executed for £13. 18s., a double cloak clasp costing £7 and other ornaments, all presumably intended

Pugin's own account with Hardman's contains an entry of 21 December 1843 for 'A Gold enamel Chain & Cross' costing £47. 15s., eight months before Louisa's death.[32] Peeping through her loops of hair, a style also favoured by Queen Victoria, is a long tripartite earring, its lower two sections reminiscent of the form of the pair in the chromolithograph, but Louisa's earrings are of blue-enamelled gold, not gold and pearls. She might have been wearing 'A pair of Gold Earrings to drawing' costing £8. 15s. and charged to Pugin's account on 1 December 1842.[33]

Pugin, though very distressed by Louisa's death, apparently decided early in 1848 to 'dispose' of her necklace and chain, writing ambiguously to Hardman that 'it will require a little

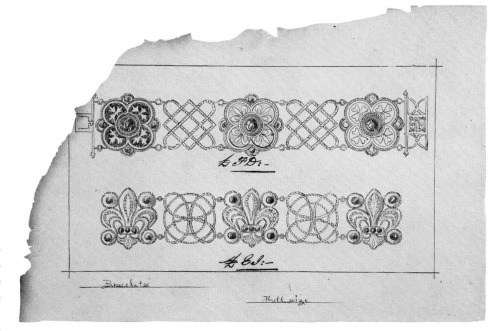

for the bride's costume at the wedding. Fortunately new monograms and armorials on the casket, and a re-cut silver seal, were virtually all the alterations necessary[37] when Pugin married Jane Knill.

The second parure, extremely modest by comparison, was made to the order of Stuart Knill in 1850 for his bride. It comprised a gold wedding ring with a cross on an enamelled shield, a gold rosary ring with enamel and turquoises, a gold headband, enamelled and set with turquoises and pearls, and a small gold brooch with enamelled M, costing only £15 in all, with a casket.[38]

Pugin designed a few more pieces for Jane, and, perhaps, a brooch for his daughter Anne.[39] He conceivably also gave her the slender gold earrings with a pearl drop in plate 13. Long earrings were fashionable from the late 1820s to the early 1840s, but not in 1850 when Anne married. However the vogue was revived in the late 1860s and lasted until well into the 1870s, which means that John Hardman Powell is most likely to have designed them for his wife or his daughter Mildred, for whom the firm made the elegant long chain.

J.H. Powell was a clever designer who never deviated far from Pugin's repertory (plate 324). He or Edward Pugin were responsible for a ring and two gold crosses commemorating the master which were sent to Ramsgate late in 1852.[40] Lack-

ing the proselytizing zeal of his master, Powell was then at liberty to create gentler, more diffuse variations on the Gothic theme, often taking one of Pugin's favourite motifs and building a complete design around it.

Burges admired the lightness and prettiness of two chains among the jewellery shown by Hardman's at the 1862 exhibition, and approved of 'a fair light blue' enamel decorating some pieces.[41] The colour does not appear in the bracelet designed by Powell for his wife in 1859 (plate 325, 326),[42] but remained in use by Hardman's for decades, during which time Powell and his associates continued to celebrate Pugin's genius.[43]

324.† Morse designed by John Hardman Powell, 1856 (St Mary's College, Oscott).

325. Design for a bracelet by John Hardman Powell for his wife, Anne (Birmingham Museum and Art Gallery).

326.† Bracelet made from the design in plate 325 (Private Collection).

CHAPTER THIRTEEN

Metalwork

ANN EATWELL and ANTHONY NORTH

327.† Monstrance, electroplated brass set with stones, by John Hardman & Co., Birmingham, *c.*1845 (St Giles's, Cheadle).

The transition from large-scale architecture to intricate works in metal is a difficult one for any designer. Few have been able to achieve as much success in this change of scale as A.W.N. Pugin. In many ways the Gothic style with its reliance on architectural forms is an ideal one for metalwork. The lecterns and interior fittings in metal which are some of the finest of the architect's designs are nearly all firmly based on Gothic architecture although the altar plate demonstrates a knowledge of the original objects. There are few secular wares in his *œuvre*, a fact explained by examining the sources to which the artist turned for inspiration when designing the various wares. The manuscripts and paintings which comprise some of his sources rarely depict secular metal wares, and only a few actual domestic wares had survived from medieval times for the artist to copy. Pugin did not 'invent' Gothic objects to fill this gap but concentrated on designing the kind of vessel or lighting that would fit naturally into what he considered to be a Gothic interior. The metalwork falls readily into two broad categories. First, there are what can be described as the architectural fittings. These are usually large objects designed to fill and enhance an architectural space. They include wrought-iron screens, large standing candlesticks, fire dogs and the various chandeliers and coronae. These large-scale items were invariably made in base metal as indeed were their original Gothic predecessors. Altar furnishings and plate naturally comprise the other substantial part of his output. The whole repertoire of Catholic ritual is represented: chalices, crucifixes, thuribles, ciboria, altar vases and dishes (plates 329–31).[1] In these smaller wares Pugin sometimes used precious metals and jewels, but he avoided the complicated facet cutting and settings of Victorian jewellery, preferring the simple rounded shapes of medieval times.

Pugin's introduction to metalwork design came early in his life. The goldsmith who found him copying Dürer in the British Museum, in 1826 or early 1827, was probably John Gawler Bridge, the nephew of one of the senior partners of Rundell, Bridge and Rundell, the Royal Goldsmiths. He was said to have been impressed by Pugin's skilful drawing and 'accosted him, and soon found that he possessed just the genius his firm was seeking.'[2] Surviving signed and dated but unexecuted designs in the Gothic style, by Pugin for Rundells, which were intended for St George's Chapel, Windsor, attest to his connection with the most important manufacturing and retailing goldsmiths of the period.[3] There is only one reference in Pugin's notes for an autobiography to confirm the relationship. On Monday 27 March 1827, he attended the first day of the sale of the Duke of York's collection with a Mr J. Bridge.[4] The Duke of York owned one of the largest collections of antique and historicist plate. Pugin's familiarity with it and his association with Rundells are clear indications of the antiquarianism that initially drove his passion for the medieval period.

In the early nineteenth century, Rundells were pioneers in the revival of historic styles, particularly the Rococo and work in a romanticised and imaginative Gothic mood. John Flaxman's design of 1819 for the National Cup, made by Rundells, was very much in this historicising medieval taste.[5] Pugin's designs, drawing on elements of medieval architecture and furniture for inspiration, create a feeling that is far from authentic. A gothic cup in the Royal Collection has been convincingly attributed to the fifteen-year-old Pugin, partly on the evidence of these designs (plate 328).[6] This richly

detailed, bejewelled and enamelled piece bears a stylistic affinity to the sideboard made for the dinning-room at Windsor Castle by Morel and Seddon (see chapter 2, plate 48). Despite Ferrey's claim that much beautiful plate was executed by Rundells to Pugin's design, only the Gothic cup has been positively identified.

For the next ten years, Pugin retained an interest in metalwork although it was apparently confined to sketches and illustrated books. Preliminary designs for metalwork are dated 1831[7] and the completed illustrated books, *Designs for*

328.† Standing Cup ('The Coronation Cup'), silver-gilt, enamelled and set with diamonds and precious stones, London hallmarks for 1826–7, mark of John Bridge (The Royal Collection, H.M. Queen Elizabeth II).

329.† Pyx, silver, parcel-gilt with enamel decoration, Birmingham hallmarks for 1851, mark of John Hardman & Co. (St George's, Southwark), given by John and Elizabeth Knill.

330.† Chalice, silver-gilt, 1837–8, mark of Tomlinson and Davis, overpunching another illegible mark (St Mary's College, Oscott). Ordered for the opening of the Oscott chapel, the chalice arrived in an unfinished state and Pugin himself scratched the crucifix on its foot.

331.† Cruet set, silver and silver-gilt, Birmingham hallmarks for 1843, mark of Hardman and Iliffe, made for Pugin's own use at Ramsgate (St Augustine's, Ramsgate).

Gold and Silversmiths and *Designs for Brass and Ironwork* were published in 1836 (plates 332 and 333). Metalwork formed a part of other design projects including *The Chest*, a group of pen and ink drawings dated 1832 (plate 62). While some of these images, for example the épergne, are impractical, fantastical and without precedent, many of the individual designs provided useful and workable models.

Converted to Catholicism in 1835, it was his

association with the seminary at St Mary's College, Oscott which provided the opportunity to produce metalwork again. To execute his designs, Pugin chose an obscure London silversmith, George Frederick Pinnel, about whom little is known, beyond the survival of teawares with his mark. The ewer and basin at Oscott (plate 334) are stylistically close to elements of Pugin's published designs. The impractical, angular handle of the ewer and the depressed lobes of the basin rim are characteristics found in the *Designs for Gold and Silversmiths*.

It was almost certainly at Oscott, in the spring of 1837,[8] that Pugin met John Hardman, junior (plate 336), who was a member of a prominent Roman Catholic manufacturing family in Birmingham. The two men became close friends, sharing a commitment to the revival of their religion and its practice. Their collaboration was responsible for bringing to fruition the bulk of Pugin's important designs for precious and base metals. Describing themselves as the first of the Medieval Metalworkers, Pugin and Hardman supplied church furnishings almost exclusively. The Pugin style, in its attempt to recreate the construction and detail of medieval metalwork, was a significant departure from the novelty Gothic of contemporary manufacturers. Under the influence of the Hardman products and Pugin's propaganda, new firms sprang up in Birmingham, London and Coventry to satisfy the growing demand of both Catholic and Anglican churches for more authentically medieval fitments.

The manufacture of the church furnishings necessary to accompany the rituals of Catholicism would have been a natural extension of Pugin's belief that Gothic was the only appropriate Christian style. Although already a partner in his father's button making firm, John Hardman developed a new enterprise to provide 'Ecclesiastical Ornaments', supplying the first items in June 1838.[9] The initial orders were for modest articles, china sprinklers, bells and book clasps but by the end of the year, silver-mounted cruets and ciboria were available. In 1839, Pugin advertised in Laity's *Directory*, offering a comprehensive list of church furnishings available from Hardman's.

In the early years of the scheme, Pugin provided all the designs, as and when required, either directly to the client, or on request, from Hardman. A letter sent by Hardman in late 1840 or early 1841, in response to an enquiry from George White of London, explained in detail the method of ordering work from the firm and the designer's role in that process.

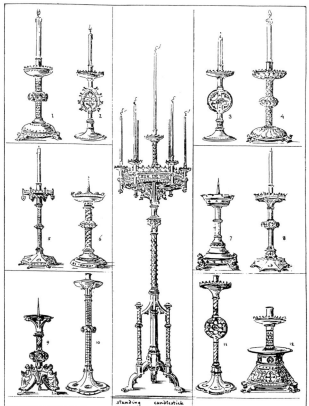

334.† Ewer and Basin, silver, London hallmarks for 1837–8, mark of George Frederick Pinnell (St Mary's College, Oscott).

335. Page from a catalogue illustrating a standing candelabrum and a range of candlesticks, signed with a monogram and dated 1846 (Minton Museum, Royal Doulton Ltd).

336.† Portrait of John Hardman junior, perhaps by J.R. Herbert, c.1843, shown in his study in his house in Handsworth, Birmingham with a view of the Convent of Mercy (Convent of Mercy, Handsworth).

My general method of working is this, either parties come and see the articles I have by me and purchase from *them* or otherwise they say what they want and how much they can afford to give and then trust Mr Pugin or me to send them as much as can possibly be done for the money – it is possible to make so much difference in all these articles by adding engraving and chasing or leaving it out as the case may be, adding or taking away other work, that it is almost impossible to give a correct list of prices.[10]

The highly specialised and individualised designs from Pugin and the more pragmatic requirements of the client's budget inevitably constrained the firm's output, particularly in precious metals. While the base metal candlesticks which formed a large proportion of production became codified into standardised designs that could be ordered by number (plate 335), tailoring the product to meet the customer's requirements was the more common approach, as Hardman's letter clearly states. This method of working often frustrated Pugin who wrote to recommend that Hardman make 'another of the same chalice for stock. I think it would be a good thing to make 3 or 4 of a sort when we have a good pattern.'[11] He advised this course to lower the cost of their products which appear to have been at the top end of the market. In a letter to Hardman of about 1845, Pugin mentions that a clergyman has 'told me the old story about your things being so dear and said he was going to Coventry where Dr Ullathorne had got his candle-

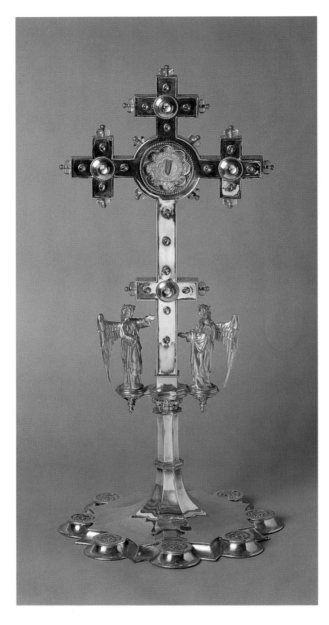

craft. Pugin complained in later years, no doubt with some exaggeration, that in order to start the Medieval Metalworking enterprise, he had been 'compelled, for the first altar lamp ever produced by us, to employ an old German workman, who understood beating up copper to the old forms.'[13]

An analysis of the structure of the business, based on the surviving ledgers and workbooks in the Birmingham Reference Library, reveals that Hardman's operated a system of in-house workshops and outworkers, typical of the silversmithing trade. If the button factory could not supply all the skills necessary, the vast pool of expertise in the Birmingham metalworking and jewellery trade could and did.

The complete object could be commissioned from an out-working firm using the designs supplied by Pugin. Alternatively, parts such as copper feet or enamelled medallions for chalices were bought in and then assembled in the Hardman workshops. It was equally common practice for work on particular stages in the manufacturing process including plating, gilding, engraving and sawpiercing to be sent out to specialist firms (plate 337). By 1845, when the ledgers detail industrial practices more fully, a silver workshop can be identified by its own account under Thomas Thomason. He was paid on a piecework basis but received £10 a year from 1847–49 for 'inspecting work in silversmiths shop'.[14] The workshop made, assembled and repaired items in precious and composite metals. Walter Evans, a general metalworker of base metal products, drew a weekly wage of £2.10. These were just two of the men who translated Pugin's designs into actuality. Hardman went into partnership with his nephew, William Powell, in 1845 and the activities of the manufactory, which had expanded into the making of stained glass and textiles, moved to Great Charles Street in separate premises from the button making firm. In the same year, Hardman and Powell entered their first mark at the Birmingham Assay Office. Previously, the business had used the newly acquired Hardman and Iliffe mark to validate items in precious metal. Before the registration of this mark in 1843, Hardman would have been effectively breaking the law by supplying unmarked silverwork. It was reported that the size of the entire workforce had reached over 200 at the time of the Great Exhibition.[15]

The medieval metalworking business expanded from a yearly turnover of just over £1000 in 1841 to more than £12,000 in 1848. The numerous and valuable orders for work to fit out the Palace of Westminster, the largest secular commission that

sticks at half price.'[12] The Coventry firm referred to here was probably that of Francis Skidmore & Sons.

By the late 1840s, the increasing demands, particularly from retailers in Birmingham and London, must have reinforced the need for greater standardisation and repetition of designs. James Burns of Portman Square, London, a Catholic book-seller, stationer and publisher, bought heavily from Hardman's in the late 1840s. Between October and December 1848, he ordered nearly £900 worth of goods. The button-making business which continued to thrive, winning a prize medal at the Great Exhibition in 1851, could not have possessed workmen to undertake manufacturing on this scale and of such complexity and

Hardman's undertook, would account for the unprecedented rise in business in the mid- to late-1840s. However, the ecclesiastical side of the firm's work continued to grow, for a time expanding into complete decorative schemes, often supervised on site by Pugin. His high public profile through influential contacts, publications and lectures, drew a steady flow of clients. For several years, he was paid a fee of 10% on the work generated by his agency. This amounted to £388 in 1848. From the unlikely formula of the strongest of religious, moral and artistic convictions, Pugin and Hardman had found a market for the products that they wanted to supply and had succeeded in making a profitable business from it. The church building boom of the mid-nineteenth century created a need for interior fittings. Similarly, the revival of interest, even among Anglicans, in the ritual of their church services, required the purchase of the necessary equipment.

The threat of a Catholic manufacturer supplying churches of all denominations, including the Anglican church, was taken very seriously and the Cambridge Camden Society, founded in 1839, set up a scheme to rival Hardman's production. In 1843 the architect and designer, William Butterfield (1814–1900), was appointed by the Anglican Society as their agent for the commissioning of church furnishings. The London silversmith, John Keith & Son worked with Butterfield to produce a prodigious quantity of church plate. It must have been reassuring for Hardman to receive a letter from a client in April 1843 stating 'I find your style of work so very much superior to the recent attempts at imitating ancient designs by the Cambridge Camden Society'.[16] Francis Skidmore and Sons, of Coventry, entered the medieval metalwork market in 1845 and by the early 1850s Hardman's had serious competitors in Birmingham. Messrs Evans, Thomason & Brown of St Paul's Square, Birmingham advertised in the 'English Churchman' of 1 May 1851 that they were recently established having 'for several years been under the superintendence of A W Pugin Esq, Architect'. Thomason who had supervised Hardman's silver workshop, continued to work in the Pugin style.[17]

However, Pugin's design had, by the mid 1840s, become synonymous with the Gothic taste. A London customer ordered 'a gilt tabernacle and candlesticks in Mr Pugin's or the Gothic style'.[18] For some clients nothing else would do.

Although Pugin's designs reflect a glorious past, it is interesting to note that he avoided all the obsessions of the later Arts and Crafts Movement

with manufacturing methods. The impression one forms from his huge correspondence with John Hardman about the actual execution of his designs is that he was much more interested in an impressive finished product than in using medieval methods of manufacture. Nearly all the base-metalwork is machine-made using the most sophisticated modern methods available to a mid-nineteenth-century Birmingham metal foundry. Objects are cast or die-stamped, bowls of chalices spun, where necessary large quantities of brass tubing are bought in for staffs and rails and full use is made of electroforming. In letters he declares his preference for 'plated German silver rather than Britannia metal' – both nineteenth-century alloys. The manufacture of items in precious metal did, however, place more emphasis on traditional silversmithing skills. Raising and chasing were widely used although often in conjunction with more industrial techniques.

The Hardman archives tell the story of a busy firm buying from the other suppliers ready-made elements which can be fitted to the required designs. The names of many of these firms are known and special praise should be given to J.S. Woolrich, 162 Great Charles Street, Birmingham, patentee of the Magneto-Process of plating and gilding, who from the many accounts that survive, seems to have been responsible for the superb gilding and silvering which is so much a feature of Hardman's base-metal wares. It is also noteworthy that some work was contracted out to Elkingtons.

The fine engraved work was almost certainly carried out by John Heath, 'Engraver and Printer' who had contracts for most of Hardman's engraved work throughout Pugin's association with the firm. Many of Pugin's larger designs incorporate figures; correspondence reveals that the wax models for these were made by John Powell. Pugin's usual working method seems to have been to send a design to Hardman, then with particularly complicated work to supervise its manufacture closely. Writing in 1845 to John Hardman he states:

I send you the pastoral staff for Scotland this must be done for about £40–45 – can you make the head of silver for that and the staff plated? Powell is modelling the Bishop of St Andrews and the foliage and crocket. Can you cast the head in two halves and solder it? Then put the crockets on.

Designs were modified during the manufacturing process. Writing about an altar cross in 1845 Pugin says 'respecting Lady Ann's arms it is quite

338. Lock-plates and door-handle, brass, made by John Hardman & Co., *c*.1849 (Eastnor Castle, Herefordshire).

339. Screen, brass, made by John Hardman & Co., Birmingham, *c*.1845 (St Giles's, Cheadle).

impossible to get them into the lozenge so we must introduce an "A" instead and have a large shield on the stem of the cross, by these means all the quarterings will come in.' The arms would almost certainly have been enamelled as Pugin made extensive use of champlevé enamels, in the medieval manner, to provide colour on his metalwork. These were usually heraldic with the emphasis on strong primary colours. Although enamelled work had long been used by jewellers, Pugin was the first designer for centuries to use it for large scale objects.

A neglected area of Pugin's architectural interiors is his work in wrought-iron. Iron was extensively used in medieval times for a variety of architectural elements and domestic wares. Pugin also grasped the fact that objects made of iron did not invariably have to be matt black – a popular misconception created by unskilled conservators in the early part of this century. Much of Pugin's ironwork is tinned or polychromatic, faithfully following medieval practice. He also carefully supervised the manufacture of individual items. In a letter to Hardman in 1847, Pugin specifically mentions that 'the hinges and handles in iron ought to be tinned.'

Pugin was fascinated with furniture mounts. Made in wrought iron and brass, their quality is quite exceptional. Mundane wares such as iron drawer-handles and brass hinges under Pugin's careful eye are given a lightness and variety which is especially pleasing. This also applies to his designs for door-furniture which seem both from his correspondence and the surviving examples to have been of particular interest to the architect (plate 338).

Pugin made use of the old wrought-ironwork in the museum at Oscott.[19] It is clear from the correspondence that Hardman's employed a number of blacksmiths to carry out Pugin's designs and in a letter in 1847 Pugin instructs John Hardman 'you should go at once to Oscott to borrow the different specimens of Ironwork from the museum and examine carefully the locks on the chests in the sacristy – if you can get one off so much the better – they will be most useful.' This particular letter also refers to a design for 'a pattern lock for the Palace of Westminster which will go with the hinges you made.' Included in the Great Exhibition were some very fine Gothic keys and in the Hardman correspondence there are several references to Gothic padlocks. The door furniture and the locks at the Palace of Westminster are especially fine and reflect credit on both locksmith and designer. Pugin also designed some very elegant wrought-iron screens; one from St Giles's, Cheadle (plate 339) is formed in a design of deceptively simple quatrefoils, surmounted by a delicate cresting composed of repeating fleurs de lys, the details highlighted with gilding.

A feature of Pugin's domestic architecture are the large open fire-places (plate 343). Pugin designed grates and fire-dogs to furnish these and where they survive, such as those at Eastnor (plate 342) and Bilton, they form splendid additions. They are of cast-iron and brass usually with a strong heraldic flavour (plate 341). An interesting

340.† Candelabrum, gilt brass and crystal, made by John Hardman & Co., Birmingham, *c*.1850 (Trustees of the Victoria & Albert Museum). Designed for the House of Lords, this was bought by the museum from the Great Exhibition of 1851.

341.† Pair of fire-dogs, wrought iron and engraved gilt brass, made for Adare House, *c*.1846 (Private Collection, Birkenhead).

342.† One of a pair of fire-dogs, cast and engraved brass, made by John Hardman & Co., Birmingham, *c*.1849 (Eastnor Castle, Herefordshire).

343. Fire-dogs and grate, cast iron, probably made by John Hardman & Co., Birmingham, *c*.1850 (Bilton Grange School).

pair of fire-dogs comes from the Bishop's Palace in Salisbury. Made entirely of cast-iron, the feet are formed as Gothic arches, with crenellated upper sections – a design known to have been used by Pugin. Attached by screws to the central bars are cast-iron escutcheons bearing the initials A.W.N.P. It has been plausibly suggested that these were originally intended for Pugin's own house in Salisbury, St Marie's Grange. The inspiration for their design is almost certainly two fire-dogs dating from 1500 illustrated in Shaw's *Ancient Furniture*.[20] These came from Godinton, Kent, and have the same arched feet and shield shaped escutcheons.

As a young man Pugin was already interested in lighting – among his earliest drawings are sconces and candlesticks, which seem to have been intended to be executed in brass.[21] His designs for lighting are specially successful and he was always interested in the effect sensitive illumination would have on his interiors. A letter to Hardman dated 1848 referring to some candlestick designs states 'the forms will take the light well and sparkle' and refers to the source of the design as an old candlestick at Oscott. His large scale candelabra (plates 340 and 345) such as those made for Erdington and the Palace of Westminster are particularly fine. Those at Erdington have very large bases, incorporating figures within niches. The altar candlesticks from Danesfield, now in the Church of the Sacred Heart, Henley, have similar

344.† Chandelier, gilt brass and crystal, made by John Hardman & Co., Birmingham, for Alton Towers (Palace of Westminster).

345.† Candlesticks and lectern, cast brass, made by John Hardman & Co., Birmingham, *c.*1849 (Jesus College, Cambridge).

figurative bases and the source for these are late Romanesque bronze candlesticks of the twelfth century.

The best chandeliers are those in the Palace of Westminster with their massive tiers of lights all of brass. Mention will be made elsewhere of the interior fittings for the Palace of Westminster (see chapter 18). Suffice it to say here that the quality of the brass rails, the large brass gates and other fittings is outstanding. An account of the Mediæval Court in the Great Exhibition of 1851 describes a chandelier of striking appearance and considerable dimensions decorated with heraldic shields. Of octagonal form, with pinnacles and pierced-work frames arranged around a central shaft, it was intended for the new dining hall at Alton Towers (plate 344).[22] Pugin used wrought-

iron extensively for lighting. In 1845 he is writing to Hardman about a corona and some sconces. 'I can make nothing simpler . . . a crocket of iron with some thin pierced work and seven standards with plain pans.' The coronae are made either of sheet iron pierced and painted or of pierced brass decorated with engraving and enamels.

At St Augustine's, Ramsgate, in the Lady Chapel is an iron candlestick with multiple sockets designed for tapers. This is formed of twisted iron bars and was shown at the Great Exhibition, where it was praised in the Juries' reports as 'a most elaborate piece of ironwork worthy of the ancient smiths – a striking proof that our operations when under proper directions are quite capable of representing the most beautiful works of medieval skill'.[23]

Many of the large-scale brass objects which Pugin designed are based upon so-called 'Dinanderie' – objects of brass and bronze produced by the metalworkers in the region of Dinand, in Belgium, in the late middle ages. The metalworkers of Dinand were justly celebrated for their large brass lecterns which were exported all over Europe.

A number of fine medieval lecterns had been preserved in churches and cathedrals – there was for example an important late medieval English lectern at Oscott College, which was formerly at St

Chad's, Birmingham.[24] Lecterns were an important product of the Pugin/Hardman partnership. Three were shown at the Great Exhibition, one being based on the example in the Cathedral at Courtrai. Particular notice was taken of a massive eagle lectern with two pricket candlesticks attached. The lower section consists of a large architectural base complete with pierced tracery, quatrefoils and figures and is supported on three lion's feet. The whole effect is one of Gothic splendour. In Jesus College, Cambridge, there is another of Pugin's brass lecterns with a large moulded column, twin candlesticks and three lion's feet (plate 345). Although less elaborate than that described above, it has a truly 'medieval' feel, and is flanked by two massive candlesticks also of Pugin's design.

The range of wares supplied for the altars of churches and chapels by Hardman's was wide. Although the finished products looked suitably splendid, to quote the late C.C. Oman 'all was not gold that glittered upon the altar'. It is noteworthy that even in his own church at Ramsgate, base metalwork predominates on the altar. The gemellions are silvered brass, the candlesticks are silvered copper and some of the chalices gilt copper. Even the beautiful monstrance shown at the Great Exhibition is of silvered brass. The quality of the gilding and silvering is very high and it is extremely difficult with many of Hardman's smaller objects to establish what is precious and what is base metal.

Surviving examples suggest that Pugin designed relatively few secular wares in base-metal. Best known are the gilt candlesticks he designed for his own house at Ramsgate (plate 349) and

there are some large dishes of plated brass which are based upon sixteenth-century Nuremberg dishes, as well as the silver-plate and enamel candlesticks made for Henry R. Bagshawe in 1842. In precious metal there is a flagon (plate 357). There are also some intriguing references in the Hardman archives to what are obviously domestic wares. For example in 1848 Pugin mentions a sconce for stock to be sold by Crace's and declares his intention of designing some dishes, a tankard-ewer and candlesticks for a side-board. It is possible that these exist but have until now been considered so outside Pugin's usual work that they remain as yet undiscovered.

The greater part of Hardman's production during Pugin's lifetime, as much as 95%, was in base metal (plate 347). Brass was abundantly used and

346. Corona, brass, made by John Hardman & Co., Birmingham, c.1845 (St Giles's, Cheadle).

347.† Processional Cross, electroplated brass with enamel and crystals, probably made by John Hardman & Co., Birmingham, c.1848 (Trustees of Ushaw College).

348.† Reliquary, electroplated brass and enamel, probably made by John Hardman & Co., Birmingham (St George's, Southwark).

349.† One of a pair of candlesticks, gilt brass, made by John Hardman & Co., Birmingham, c.1844, for The Grange, Ramsgate (Trustees of the Victoria & Albert Museum).

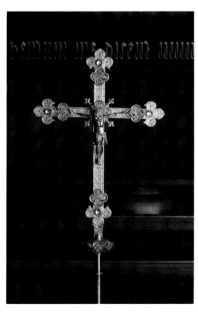

350. Page from a catalogue illustrating altar and processional crosses, signed with a monogram and dated 1846 (Minton Museum, Royal Doulton Ltd).

351.† Drawing of an altar and other church furnishings, inscribed 'Gallery Antwerpe', probably 1843 (Private Collection).

altar and processional crosses

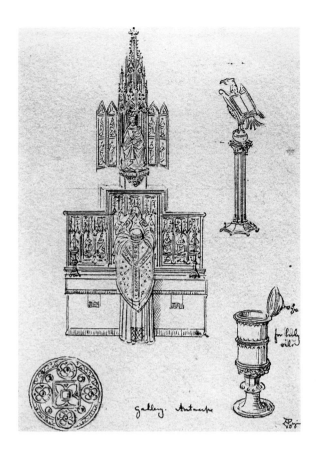

with copper, nickel or 'german silver' was often silver plated or gilt. The objects made entirely of precious metal formed a tiny if significant proportion of the manufactures. The illustration from Pugin's *Apology* (plate 333) gives some idea of the type and variety of products available in 1843, while those from Hardman's catalogue (plates 335 and 350) demonstrate the range and method of choice available to client. Of these, candlesticks, thuribles, ciboria, pyxes, chalices and patens, sanctuary lamps, sacring bells, altar crosses and monstrances could be made in precious metal. In practice this was rarely the case. Although, Pugin's proselytising texts appear to find base metal an anathema for items connected with the celebration of the mass, in reality, compromise, pragmatism and a willingness to meet clients' needs dictated the Hardman productions.

Pugin himself recommended adjustments to the materials used, to bring the price within the customer's budget. Composite objects – a pastoral staff, silver, partially made of plated metal, a plated monstrance with silver lunettes, a chalice with silver bowl and copper-gilt foot – were commonly ordered to cut costs while looking equally as glamorous as the real thing. Hardman's letter to George White listed the alternatives and their costs quite clearly. 'Ciborium, metal stand with

silver cup £13 10s, silver extra as weight.' and 'Monstrance – metal gilt silver gilt lunette £15 10s in silver extra according to weight'.[25] Even the grandest of Pugin's patrons, such as Lord Shrewsbury, preferred to buy composite objects.[26] Although Shrewsbury was not short of cash (it has been estimated that he spent more than £1400 on metal furnishings between 1845 and 1847[27]) many small Catholic parishes had no choice but to economise on the materials used to make their plate. Given that this trade was not unusual it is surprising that so few examples have yet come to light.[28] There were clergy for whom, perhaps following Pugin's strictures, such mixed objects were objectionable. The Rev. J.J. Murphy wrote to Hardman on 28 August 1845 rejecting a copper-foot chalice and requesting one in silver for £20. 'We all agree in hating copper. Others may not be so fastidious.'[29]

The Gothic style of Pugin's association with Hardman was distinctly archaeological. He dismissed random medieval detail applied superficially as 'patterns of Brumagem gothic'. His early antiquarian habits encouraged him to study surviving objects for models on which to base his designs. He recommended that Hardman do the same. On his frequent trips to the continent he studied and recorded objects in museums and cathedral treasuries wherever he travelled (plates 351 and 353). The forms of his pieces may resemble the structure of his sources but Pugin was no mere copyist. His work can be immediately distinguished by a preoccupation with certain elements of shape and a distinctive repertoire of ornament. A comparison of an Italian fifteenth-century chalice (plate 354) with a chalice designed by Pugin in the same style (plate 355), highlights the subtle differences of expression and emphasis between the original type and the nineteenth century re-interpretation. While the silver thurible from Erdington (plate 352) has a German source, not all of Pugin's designs were founded on medieval prototypes. The silver flagon from St Thomas's Church, Elson in Hampshire, is indicative of his fondness for Jacobean design which he had used previously in designs for furniture and plate.

The majority of the Hardman production to Pugin's design was for church furnishings but a few secular pieces in precious metal are known. Examples include the dish ordered by Pugin as a gift of thanks to Henry Benson for his unsuccessful intercession with the Lumsdaine family and the two salt cellars and spoons, made for Pugin's own use at home in Ramsgate (plate 355). These are rare survivals but the firm's business records do not make mention of many more items.

Towards the end of his life, Pugin's architectural practice diminished and it is from this period that his designs for Hardman surpass, in scale, ambition and finish, the work of the firm's competitors. The enormous orders from Barry for the Palace of Westminster which were entirely for base metal, the important commissions and the preparation for the exhibitions of 1849 and 1851 must have stretched the capacity of the business to

the limit. The elaborate service of plate ordered by W.W. Wardell, Pugin's friend and the architect of St Mary's, Clapham, illustrates the more spectacular aspects of the collaboration of designer and manufacturer (plate 356).[30] The silver monstrance was, at £125, the most magnificent and costly piece of its type. It is a variation of a shape familiar from many of his published works, including the *Apology* of 1843 and was shown at the Great Exhibition of 1851.

Hardman's display at the Birmingham Exhibition of 1849 secured the praise of Henry Cole in his influential *Journal of Design* and the firm's work for Pugin's Mediæval Court at the Great Exhibition won the highest accolade, a Council Medal. The exhibits covered an impressive 560 foot of floor area and 1360 foot of wall space and exemplified the judicious use of industrial

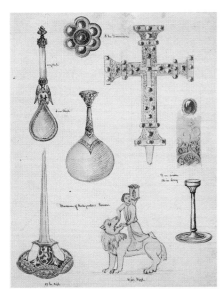

356. Ciborium, Monstrance and Chalice and Paten, silver, parcel-gilt and decorated with semi-precious stones and enamels, Birmingham hallmarks for 1850, mark of John Hardman & Co., 1850–51 (Trustees of the British Museum).

357.† Flagon, silver, made by John Hardman & Co., 1849 (Private Collection, Birkenhead).

358. Illustration of the products of John Hardman & Co., from *The Illustrated Catalogue of the Industrial Department of the International Exhibition of 1862.*

CLASS XXXI.—*Iron and General Hardware.*

HARDMAN, JOHN, & Co., 166 *Great Charles Street, Birmingham;* 13 *King William Street, Strand, London, W.C.;* 1 *Upper Camden Street, Dublin.*—Mediæval metal manufactures.

technique and traditional skills. These apparently incompatible methods of manufacture were combined to form magnificent items such as the Alton Towers chandelier (plate 344) or the chalice

(plate 355) bought for the Museum of Manufactures (now the Victoria and Albert Museum). Every aspect of church furnishings and fittings were shown with one glass case devoted to secular pieces and jewellery.[31]

By this period, John Hardman Powell, the nephew of John Hardman, junior, must have been taking some responsibility for elements of the designs if not for some of the designs themselves. Not long after the beginning of his apprenticeship with Pugin, he was advising his uncle of models that were from his hand. The sheer volume of work must have necessitated the need for more design input. This was certainly true of arrangements in the stained glass studio. No doubt Pugin's relentless energy allowed him to retain a supervisory control over the designs.

After Pugin's death, John Hardman Powell became Hardman's chief designer and continued to work in the style of his master. Some of his most interesting designs are for domestic wares in the gothic taste (plate 358). By the International Exhibition of 1862, the medieval style had reached its apogee, conquering the breakfast room and the parlour of respectable middle-class homes. Hardman's continued to supply church furnishings throughout the nineteenth century in a somewhat fossilised and repetitive Gothic. Pugin's influence can, however, be seen in the designs of his competitors, in those of his successors (such as William Burges) and in the continuing market for and belief in the truly Christian style, the Gothic.

pair of fire-dogs comes from the Bishop's Palace in Salisbury. Made entirely of cast-iron, the feet are formed as Gothic arches, with crenellated upper sections – a design known to have been used by Pugin. Attached by screws to the central bars are cast-iron escutcheons bearing the initials A.W.N.P. It has been plausibly suggested that these were originally intended for Pugin's own house in Salisbury, St Marie's Grange. The inspiration for their design is almost certainly two fire-dogs dating from 1500 illustrated in Shaw's *Ancient Furniture*.[20] These came from Godinton, Kent, and have the same arched feet and shield shaped escutcheons.

As a young man Pugin was already interested in lighting – among his earliest drawings are sconces and candlesticks, which seem to have been intended to be executed in brass.[21] His designs for lighting are specially successful and he was always interested in the effect sensitive illumination would have on his interiors. A letter to Hardman dated 1848 referring to some candlestick designs states 'the forms will take the light well and sparkle' and refers to the source of the design as an old candlestick at Oscott. His large scale candelabra (plates 340 and 345) such as those made for Erdington and the Palace of Westminster are particularly fine. Those at Erdington have very large bases, incorporating figures within niches. The altar candlesticks from Danesfield, now in the Church of the Sacred Heart, Henley, have similar

340.† Candelabrum, gilt brass and crystal, made by John Hardman & Co., Birmingham, *c*.1850 (Trustees of the Victoria & Albert Museum). Designed for the House of Lords, this was bought by the museum from the Great Exhibition of 1851.

341.† Pair of fire-dogs, wrought iron and engraved gilt brass, made for Adare House, *c*.1846 (Private Collection, Birkenhead).

342.† One of a pair of fire-dogs, cast and engraved brass, made by John Hardman & Co., Birmingham, *c*.1849 (Eastnor Castle, Herefordshire).

343. Fire-dogs and grate, cast iron, probably made by John Hardman & Co., Birmingham, *c*.1850 (Bilton Grange School).

344.† Chandelier, gilt brass and crystal, made by John Hardman & Co., Birmingham, for Alton Towers (Palace of Westminster).

345.† Candlesticks and lectern, cast brass, made by John Hardman & Co., Birmingham, c.1849 (Jesus College, Cambridge).

figurative bases and the source for these are late Romanesque bronze candlesticks of the twelfth century.

The best chandeliers are those in the Palace of Westminster with their massive tiers of lights all of brass. Mention will be made elsewhere of the interior fittings for the Palace of Westminster (see chapter 18). Suffice it to say here that the quality of the brass rails, the large brass gates and other fittings is outstanding. An account of the Mediæval Court in the Great Exhibition of 1851 describes a chandelier of striking appearance and considerable dimensions decorated with heraldic shields. Of octagonal form, with pinnacles and pierced-work frames arranged around a central shaft, it was intended for the new dining hall at Alton Towers (plate 344).[22] Pugin used wrought-

iron extensively for lighting. In 1845 he is writing to Hardman about a corona and some sconces. 'I can make nothing simpler . . . a crocket of iron with some thin pierced work and seven standards with plain pans.' The coronae are made either of sheet iron pierced and painted or of pierced brass decorated with engraving and enamels.

At St Augustine's, Ramsgate, in the Lady Chapel is an iron candlestick with multiple sockets designed for tapers. This is formed of twisted iron bars and was shown at the Great Exhibition, where it was praised in the Juries' reports as 'a most elaborate piece of ironwork worthy of the ancient smiths – a striking proof that our operations when under proper directions are quite capable of representing the most beautiful works of medieval skill'.[23]

Many of the large-scale brass objects which Pugin designed are based upon so-called 'Dinanderie' – objects of brass and bronze produced by the metalworkers in the region of Dinand, in Belgium, in the late middle ages. The metalworkers of Dinand were justly celebrated for their large brass lecterns which were exported all over Europe.

A number of fine medieval lecterns had been preserved in churches and cathedrals – there was for example an important late medieval English lectern at Oscott College, which was formerly at St

CHAPTER FOURTEEN

Monuments and Brasses

DAVID MEARA

Writing to his friend William Osmond (1791–1875), a stonemason of Salisbury,[1] in 1833, Pugin describes his tour of some of the Cathedrals and Abbeys of southern England. Among the treasures he describes are 'the tombs in the aisles round the choir' at Bristol, and the 'tombs, the Lady Chapel, the Vicars' Cloisters', at Hereford, 'of which you may be sure I took complete sketches'.[2]

Early in his artistic career Pugin was captivated not only by medieval architecture, but also by the funerary sculpture which he saw in abundance in the churches and cathedrals he visited. He was equally enthusiastic in his denunciation of the neo-classical style of Chantrey and Westmacott. Among the neo-classical sculptors only John Flaxman (1755–1826) escaped total censure. In his *Apology for the Revival of Christian Architecture* (1843) Pugin wrote:

> Had Flaxman lived a few years later, he would have been a great Christian artist; but in his day men never thought it possible to do anything fine in art that was not derived from paganism: hence his great powers were unhappily expended in illustrating fables of classic antiquity, instead of embodying edifying truths.

However, Pugin thoroughly approved of Flaxman's account of medieval sculpture and monuments, which he had given in his first lecture as Professor of Sculpture at the Royal Academy in 1811. Pugin found this lecture, which extolled the merits of late medieval English tomb sculpture and lamented the ravages of the Reformation, 'both heartfelt and eloquent'.[3] In his *Contrasts* of 1836 Pugin himself gave a brief history of the development of medieval monuments. Before the Reformation there were dignified recumbent effi-

359. Memorial brass to Mrs Anne Talbot (d. 1843), a relative by marriage of the Earl of Shrewsbury (St John's Hospital, Alton).

360. 'Contrasted Episcopal Monuments', from *Contrasts*, 2nd ed., 1841.

361.† Fragment of a monumental brass showing the head of a bishop or abbot, Flemish, *c.*1380 (Trustees of the British Museum).

gies with angelic supporters at the head, and brief but 'Catholic' inscriptions, while now there were pompous inscriptions, pagan allegories, pagan nudity, and cinerary urns.[4] He illustrated these comments with a plate entitled 'Contrasted Sepulchral monuments' which juxtaposes the monument by Francis Chantrey to the Earl of Malmesbury in Salisbury Cathedral (commissioned in 1822) with that to Gervase Alard, 1310, First Admiral of the Cinque Ports, in St Thomas's, Winchelsea, Sussex. In the second edition of *Contrasts* in 1841 Pugin added a plate 'Contrasted Episcopal Monuments', where the classical monument of a podgy Georgian Bishop is set beside the austere memorial brass of a medieval prelate under an elaborate canopy (plate 360).

Pugin's interest in medieval monuments and memorial brasses[5] is evident from his extensive library, which included *Illustrations of the Monumental Brasses of Great Britain*, published by the Cambridge Camden Society between 1840 and 1846, John Sell Cotman's *Engravings of the Brasses in Norfolk*, 1819, Edward Blore's *Monumental Remains*, 1826, and Richard Gough's *Sepulchral Monuments of Great Britain*, 1786–99. He also took rubbings of brasses[6] and, through his antiquarian expeditions across the Channel, collected at least one splendid fragment of a fourteenth-century Flemish brass to a bishop or abbot (plate 361), and two fourteenth-century incised slabs.[7]

In an article for the *London and Dublin Orthodox Journal*[8] entitled 'Monumental Brasses of the Fifteenth Century' Pugin briefly expounds the

history of brasses, revealing how important he believed them to be in the revival of 'true' Christian art. They are 'truly catholic' combining 'grace and simplicity', and are 'unobtrusive' yet 'appropriate' memorials for the dead.[9]

In his *Apology*, Pugin attacked modern sepulchral monuments as 'pagan abominations, which disfigure both the consecrated enclosure which surrounds the church and the interior of the sacred building itself.' He claimed that modern dress could be successfully adapted for monuments, and especially for brasses. He included three illustrations of its use, and set out in detail costume appropriate to the different classes of clergy and civilians. Pugin concluded that 'there is not the least practical difficulty in reviving at the present time consistent and Christian monuments for all classes of persons', illustrating his comments with examples of two brasses which he had recently designed – Lady Gertrude Fitzpatrick, 1842, Grafton Underwood, Northants, and Dame Margaretta Sarah Morris, 1842, All Saints, Great Marlow, Bucks.

Pugin had already set out in a footnote in *The Present State of Ecclesiastical Architecture*[10]

. . . the various sorts of monuments anciently employed, and the average cost of executing them at the present time: –
A high tomb under a canopied
   arch, crotched and pinnacled,
   with effigy of deceased vested
   of natural size, angels or

	£	£
weepers in niches round the high tomb, with scriptures, emblems, &c from	150	to 500
A high tomb with the effigy natural size, with weepers or tracery and shields round the sides	50	... 100
A plain arch in a chancel, with effigy natural size	50	... 100
Ditto, with a slab and monumental cross and inscription	25	... 50
A plain high tomb with inscription round edge and monumental cross on top	20	... 30
A whole length brass, under a canopy, with the evangelists in the corners, and inscription	100	... 200
A whole length brass without canopy or evangelists	50	... —
A half brass with inscription and	25	... 50
A ditto small	10	... 20
A quarter-size whole length effigy and inscription	10	... 20
A chalice with hand over in benediction, a very simple but ancient emblem of a priest's tomb	3	... 5
A brass of a cross fleury, with inscription on stem and effigy in the centre	25	... 50
A stone slab with a cross fleury, engraved in lines and inscription, shields, &c.	10	... 15
A ditto raised in Dos D'Ane, and cross fleury carved in relief on it; these are well calculated for external monuments in churchyards	10	... 15
Stone crosses with inscriptions, to set up at the heads and feet of graves	5	... 10
Plain oak crosses with painted inscriptions for the same purpose	1	... 3

Of course the exact cost of all these different monuments will vary in proportion to quantity of detail and enrichments about them, and the materials in which they are executed; alabaster will be more costly than stone, and Purbeck marble than Yorkshire slabs, and so on; but the above lists of monuments, which are strictly in accordance with Catholic traditions, has been drawn out to show that the pious memorials used by our forefathers may be revived at the present time by all classes.

Such a range of monumental designs was by then possible because in 1837 Pugin had made the acquaintance of John Hardman (1811–67). With Pugin's encouragement Hardman enlarged the family button-making business to include ecclesiastical metalwork and by the early part of 1838 he was turning out crosses, candlesticks, chalices and other items to Pugin's designs.[11]

Although an entry in Pugin's Diary for 1839 refers to memorial brasses for the Crypt of St Chad's, Birmingham, it was not until 1841 that we have the first record of a memorial brass. Through his association with Oscott College, Birmingham, he had the opportunity to design a memorial to Bishop John Milner. Pugin's original idea was to design a chantry chapel and tomb in the fourteenth-century style, modelled on that of John-de-Sheppey at Rochester Cathedral. An article in the *Orthodox Journal* describes the proposed monument to Dr Milner as

– one of the most correct and magnificent monuments in the pointed style erected in this or any country during the last 300 years . . . The author of the History of Winchester, or the Essay on Gothic Architecture, . . . certainly merits a tomb of this splendid character, and so eminently calculated to restore a taste for such beautiful ornaments to our old churches and cathedrals.[12]

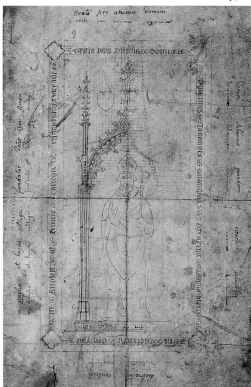

362. Memorial brass to Dr John Milner (Lady Chapel, St Mary's College, Oscott).

363. Drawing for the brass to Dr John Milner, partly squared-up ready for Hardman to engrave (on loan to Birmingham Museum and Art Gallery).

364. Tomb of the Revd George Augustus Montgomery (St John the Baptist, Bishopstone).

There are designs for this, dated 1839, in the Oscott College Archive. The chantry, however, was never built, and eventually Milner was commemorated by a brass, showing the Bishop in full pontificals under a single canopy with marginal inscription and evangelistic symbols. The design is based on the medieval brass to Bishop John Trilleck, 1360, Hereford Cathedral (plate 362).

A preliminary drawing shows how much care Pugin took over this first important attempt at a revived memorial brass (plate 363). The finished memorial, which cost £100, lies on the floor of the Lady Chapel at Oscott College, and is one of Pugin's most convincing brasses.

Pugin used John Hardman for the metalwork parts of the memorial, and he in turn subcontracted the engraving work to John Heath, of Great Charles Street, Birmingham, and the stonework to William Cook of New Hall Hill. But for his major masonry, stonecarving and building work Pugin turned to George Myers, a stonemason from Hull.

George Myers (1804–75) first met Pugin in 1827[13] when Myers built a scaffolding in Beverley Minster to assist Pugin who was sketching there. J.H. Powell gives a different account of their first meeting, in his *Memoir*, placing it in Holy Trinity Church, Hull.[14] His next encounter with Pugin may have been when he tendered to build Pugin's Church of St Marie at Derby. This is according to Ferrey, *Recollections of A Welby Pugin*, London 1861, pp. 185–6. However, Stanton says that Myers prepared the estimates for St Wilfred's, Hulme, Manchester, in October 1838, so their collaboration can certainly be dated from that year. George Gilbert Scott described Myers at the time as 'a strange rough mason from Hull',[15] and Pugin himself later described Myers as 'a rough diamond but a real diamond, for he is thoroughly acquainted with every branch of ancient construction and detail and a most honourable person in his transactions'.[16] In spite of, or perhaps because of this, the two men became good friends, and Myers became part of that select group of craftsmen-entrepreneurs who were so vital for Pugin's success. Myers was sympathetic to the Gothic cause, he was a competent businessman, and he was able to interpret Pugin's designs with understanding and sensitivity. He is said to have built thirty-six churches to Pugin's designs in addition to secular buildings such as The Grange, Ramsgate, his work for the Great Exhibition of 1851, and numerous pieces of woodwork, carving and sculpture. There is a fine reredos by Pugin and Myers at St Anne's R.C. Cathedral, Leeds, a

lovely Easter Sepulchre at St Giles, Cheadle, and altars in St Augustine's, Ramsgate. No doubt Pugin would have turned to Myers to build the proposed Milner Chantry at Oscott. He certainly used him for the stonework and carving of all his major church monuments.

The earliest of these is, surprisingly, to an Anglican clergyman, the Revd George Augustus Montgomery (1795–1842), Rector of Bishopstone, Wiltshire. In spite of Pugin's reputation as a Roman Catholic controversialist, a number of Anglican clergy and laity were not afraid to use his services.[17] Montgomery was a keen antiquary, and extensively restored Bishopstone church. He became a friend of Pugin, who, on his premature death, designed his tomb. Writing to the Revd J.R. Bloxam (1807–92) of Magdalen College, Oxford, Pugin says:

I was at Salisbury last week to inspect the progress of the tomb I am setting up at Bishopstone Church in memory of the Late Rector Montgomery. It will be a very good thing a brass in the tomb under the arch. I am also putting up some stained glass in a beautiful decorated window over it . . .[18]

The monument is in the form of a brass cross with evangelistic symbols and Agnus Dei, inlaid in a tomb-chest, surmounted by an elaborately

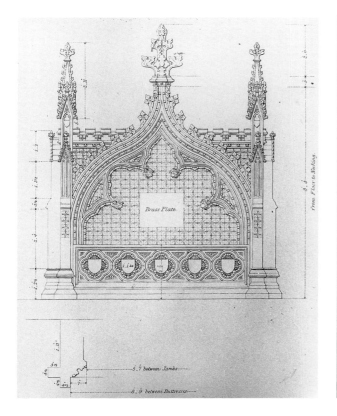

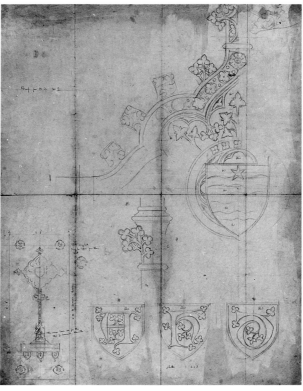

365. Measured drawing for the Montgomery tomb (plate 364), from *Weale's Quarterly Papers on Architecture*, 1845.

366. Working drawing for the brass to A.H. Drummond, St Peter and St Paul, Albury, dated 1843 (on loan to Birmingham Museum and Art Gallery).

crocketed canopy, and set against the south wall of the south transept of Bishopstone Church (plate 364). In Pugin's Diary for 1844 there is a series of financial calculations which may refer to this monument: –

Tomb and fixing	251- 6-2
Brass work for do	43-18-0
	295
Architects commission and journey	20-0-0
Stained glass window	48-0-0
	363-4-2
Received	100-0-0
Balance due	263-0-0

The monument is described by Owen Carter in *Weale's Quarterly Papers on Architecture 4* (1845) and is illustrated by a measured drawing of the tomb done by Pugin (plate 365). It is a convincing composition which fits well into the south transept.

The early 1840s were a particularly fertile period for Pugin's brass designs. They show considerable assurance, vigour and inventiveness, as well as a thorough knowledge of medieval precedent. The little figure of the Revd Edward Peach is barely distinguishable from medieval examples, while the brasses to Lady Gertrude Fitzpatrick (1842) and Mrs Anne Talbot (1843) show how Pugin could be inventive, while remaining true to the tradition. The use of colour on the Talbot brass is particularly effective (plate 359).

Pugin's architectural and design practice was by now extremely busy, and in December 1844 Pugin took on Hardman's nephew, John Hardman Powell, who came to live at The Grange, Ramsgate. He helped Pugin with his design work, and gradually earned Pugin's qualified approval: '. . . he (Powell) is of an excellent disposition and [I] really wish to do the best for him'.[19] Sometimes Powell drew out designs himself, as in the case of the brass to Bishop William Riddell (1807–47), the Coadjutor of the Northern District, who died of a fever.[20] In a letter to Hardman Pugin says, 'the brass for Dr Riddell goes off tonight and it is now a first rate job. Powell has drawn the effigy beautifully and it is a simple fine job.'[21]

Pugin's method of working was to send a rough sketch of the design to the client or to Hardman, drawing on previous designs or on his knowledge of medieval prototypes. When the order was placed he would send Hardman the finished design which would include the whole composition sketched in miniature, and the important details drawn out full-size, together with measurements, colours, heraldry, and details of the inscription (plate 366). His design repertoire was limited, and usually based on medieval precedent, although it is hard to find anything quite like the Challinor

367. Memorial brass to Reginald Phillipps, son of Ambrose Phillipps (Grace Dieu Manor Chapel). His pedigree is illustrated by the five heraldic shields.

368. Memorial brass to Mrs Catherine Chadwick, engraved 1847 (St Gregory's, Weld Bank, Chorley).

(1845), Phillipps (1846) (plate 367), or Stout (1846) brasses among medieval examples. Pugin was fond of heraldic detail, the floriated cross, and the kneeling figure. Other favourite design features included angels, and canopy-work with saints. Some of his designs are of excellent simplicity and directness. Good examples are the brasses to Mrs Catherine Chadwick (1847) (plate 368), Thomas Roddis (1847), and Joseph McFaul (1850) (plate 369).

Pugin enjoyed combining brass-work with stone carving, sculpture, and, when requested, a tomb-chest, as he had done at Albury, Surrey, where Henry Drummond had commissioned him in 1843 to design a chapel for his family in the south transept of the church of St Peter and St Paul. There brasses to the family lie on table tombs and the floor in a chantry chapel adorned with stained glass, painted decoration and wooden

screens, all by Pugin (plate 165). Myers, who worked on this commission, also worked with Pugin at St George's, Southwark. Many internal fittings at St George's were made in his workshops, and he was responsible for the beautiful Petre chantry. This commemorates the Hon. Edward Robert Petre (1794–1848), one of the main benefactors of the church, and consists of an enclosed chapel with table tomb and brass, altarpiece with Virgin and Child, and its own stone vault. Pugin's designs survive for the front panel of the altar and the Virgin and Child, annotated by Myers.[22] According to Bernard Bogan[23] the erection of a chantry must have been decided upon at an early date because in 1845 Pugin wrote to Myers:

– I don't think the sketch I sent you for the B. / Virgin for Mrs Petre altar was late enough in

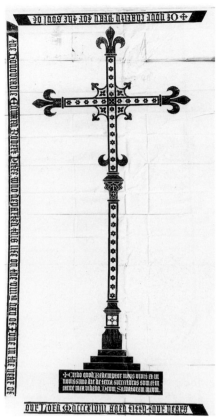

369. Memorial brass to Joseph McFaul, engraved 1850 (St Edmund's College, Ware).

370. Memorial brass to the Hon. Edward Robert Petre, engraved 1849 (St George's Cathedral, Southwark). Much of the original colour remains in this brass.

371. Tomb of the Hon. Edward Robert Petre (Petre Chantry, St George's Cathedral, Southwark). The stonework is by Myers and the brass by Hardman.

style / I now send you a better one. Of course the whole front / will be cut in bas relief. / The carving should be strictly of the same date as the chantry.

Because of fears of the anti-Catholic mob the family arranged that the chantry should be placed as remote as possible from the most public thoroughfare, St George's Road. The chantry was not completed until 1849, and the brass cross and fillet inscription were then sent up to Myers to be let into the slab (plate 370). From correspondence with Hardman Pugin appears to have had great trouble with the details of the inscription,[24] but it was eventually installed, and the result is delightful (plate 371).

In 1849 one of Pugin's great supporters died, Dr Thomas Walsh, (1779–1849), President of Oscott from 1818 to 1826, and at the time of his death Vicar Apostolic of the London District. His remains were deposited in the Crypt of St Chad's Cathedral, Birmingham, and Pugin, to whom Walsh often referred affectionately as 'Archbishop Pugens', designed his monument. It lies under the window in the north transept, and consists of a recumbent effigy of the Bishop in full pontificals, under a canopy made of Bath stone (plate 372). There is a brass inscription around the chamfered

edge of the tomb. Myers is said to have carved the effigy on the tomb with his own hands.[25]

One of Pugin's last monumental commissions was the fine tomb to John, Lord Rolle, owner of the Bicton Estate in Devon. He died in 1842, but it was not until 1850 that Louisa Lady Rolle decided to commemorate her husband with a mausoleum, created by Pugin from the south chancel chapel of the ruined medieval church of Holy Trinity. The ornate interior contains floor tiles by Minton, glass by Hardman, a painted roof, and on the north wall the elaborate Rolle monument carved by Myers.

Writing to the Earl of Shrewsbury in 1850 Pugin said:

> I found Lady Rolle a very cheerful happy sort of woman but with dreadful ideas on architecture. She actually suggested a sort of Turkish mosque with the light coming in from the top for a *mausoleum* however I managed so well that in half an hour she consented to call it a mortuary chapel, to have 2 painted glass windows, a proper ceiling with armorial bearings, a brass and tiles . . .[26]

The monument consists of a tomb-chest with ornate quatrefoil decoration, inlaid with a floriated brass cross, with angels and heraldic shields with supporters under ogee arches against the back wall (plate 373). The carving was again carried out by Myers who was by now operating from his premises at Ordnance Wharf, Belvedere Road, in Lambeth.

Of similar quality is the Sutton chantry at St Mary's, West Tofts, Norfolk, designed for the Sutton family of Lynford Hall. Pugin's work here began in 1846 with the design of a chantry chapel and the tomb of Mary Elizabeth Sutton (d. 1842). The chapel was probably attached to the Hall, according to references in Hardman's Painting Daybook for 1846, and when the Hall was demolished the tomb was moved to St Mary's, West Tofts.[27]

The stonework was executed by Myers, and drawings for it still exist, annotated in Pugin's hand (plate 374). Against the drawings of the bosses for the tomb Pugin has written, 'early vine leaf forms from Southwell', and next to the figures of the evangelists, 'early foliage from the Lincoln

372. Tomb of Bishop Thomas Walsh, brass inscription engraved 1851 (St Chad's Cathedral, Birmingham). The iron railings with sconces for funeral lights have since been removed.

373. Tomb of John, Lord Rolle, d. 1842, brass engraved 1852 (Rolle Chantry, Holy Trinity Church, Bicton).

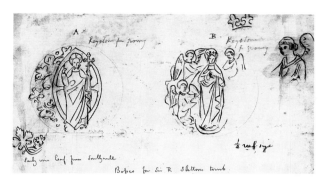

374. Detail of a sheet of sketches for the tomb of Mary Elizabeth Sutton (d. 1842), St Mary's, West Tofts (Private Collection).

375. Sheet of designs for tombs and grave slabs, some referring to an unidentified 'Hodges tomb' (Myers Family Trust).

376. Grave slab (St Osmund's, Salisbury).

377. Tomb of Mary Elizabeth Sutton (St Mary's, West Tofts), mother of John Sutton, Pugin's friend and patron.

casts.' We know that Myers had casts of medieval sculpture in his workshops which Pugin used for his own design work. Over the tomb-chest is an elaborate canopy with crocketed gables on trefoil arches, resting on marble pillars. A note in Pugin's hand on a drawing of the tomb in a private collection says, 'all the crockets & carving to be taken from Percy's tomb', a reference to the celebrated mid-fourteenth-century tomb in Beverley Minster. The Sutton tomb-chest is decorated with enamel shields on the sides, a floriated brass cross on the top, and surrounded by Minton tiles on the floor. This monument again shows Pugin's concern to follow ancient precedents and to work from correct 'authorities'. He once wrote in a letter to his friend, the Revd J.R. Bloxam: 'I seek antiquity not novelty. I strive to *revive* not *invent* . . .'[28] The tomb, set in the richly decorated Sutton Chantry, is one of Pugin's most elaborate pieces of tomb sculpture (plate 377).

These small but highly-detailed chantry chapels with their tombs and other decoration show us Pugin at his most inventive and assured. He was happiest when he had control of the whole decorative programme, and, assisted by his trusted craftsmen Hardman, Myers and Minton, able to integrate all the elements, improvising where necessary from his vast knowledge of medieval art.

In addition to these ambitious monuments[29] Pugin designed other more humble memorials (plate 376), as his list in *The Present State of Ecclesiastical Architecture* shows (see above). In a private collection of drawings belonging to a de-

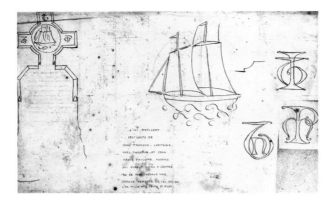

scendant of George Myers is a page of designs
for tomb-chests and grave-slabs (plate 375). In a
letter of March 1841 Pugin comments on such
monuments:

> . . . respecting the monuments the most catholic
> one would be a stone cross at the head of the
> grave with a simple inscription cut on it (illus-
> tration) This would cost much less than an altar
> tomb of this description (illustration) you may
> have what is called a Dos D'ane tomb which
> looks exceedingly severe & well & would not
> cost much more than the upright cross of course
> regular working drawings won't be required for
> either of these & they would cost 3 guineas for
> the ? tomb & 2 guineas for either of the others.
> (Ushaw OM/PU7)

Another drawing in the collection is of a grave-
stone to Captain Izan Thomaso, which stands in
the graveyard at St Augustine's, Ramsgate (plate
378). It consists of a chamfered slab with cross-
head within which is the outline of a ship under
sail. *The Tablet* for 31 October 1846 gave a description of the storm in which the Captain per-
ished. Pugin was ill in bed at the time, but on
seeing the disaster offered burial for the dead. The
bodies were carried from the harbour in coffins
covered with palls and given full Catholic rites by
Dr Weedall. Captain Thomaso's grave was against
the side of the East Cloister. Pugin designed other
similar memorials, for instance that to Henry and
Marie Magdalene Connelly, two children who
died in 1839 and 1840, commemorated by a joint
tombstone at Grand Coteau, Louisiana, U.S.A.[30]

Apart from his spectacular chantries, Pugin's
pièce de resistance was the brass he designed for the
Great Exhibition. He took great pains over this,
eventually designing a brass for a priest in mass
vestments under a canopy with triple super-
canopy and a border inscription (plate 379). The
figures of Saints Peter and Paul are undoubtedly
'borrowed' from the brass to John Strete, 1405,

Upper Hardres, Kent. Indeed Pugin admitted
in a letter to Hardman that the brass was, 'A
beautiful thing with capital authorities to work
from . . . these are such fine authorities such as we
cannot draw.'[31] The brass was eventually used to
commemorate Bishop John Milner in the Church
of St Peter and Paul (RC) Wolverhampton, where
Milner was buried. The brass was exhibited, together with two smaller ones, the Walsh tomb,
and numerous other pieces of Myers's carving,
in Pugin's final artistic triumph, the Mediaeval
Court of the Great Exhibition of 1851 at the
Crystal Palace.

In the field of monumental design his fruitful
partnerships with Myers and Hardman initiated a
revival of church memorial design which, over the
next hundred years, was to produce some fine examples of brasses, semi-relief slabs and recumbent
effigies in the Gothic style. Pugin, in spite of the
pessimism he felt at the end of his life, in this area
of design had not laboured in vain.

CHAPTER FIFTEEN

Stained Glass

STANLEY A. SHEPHERD

In his third lecture to his students at St Mary's College, Oscott[1] given probably in 1838, Pugin pointed to three reasons for the near demise, as he saw it, of good stained glass. One was the decline of pointed architecture, 'the only style calculated to exhibit this fascinating art to its full effect'; the others were the adoption in the sixteenth century of an entirely new principle of design by which the windows were rendered complete pictures, and the discovery at the beginning of the seventeenth century of a new process of enamelling, whereby a variety of colours could be produced on the same piece of glass. In explaining the shortcomings of the innovations, he in effect also laid down the fundamental elements of what he regarded as good design practice, to which he would adhere in the forthcoming years. The problem in his view with the new principle was that the pictures produced although, 'exquisitely beautiful . . . in design and colouring', were unconnected in form with the stonework and appeared to pass behind the mullions causing a total absence of union to occur between the framework and the glass, frequently producing: 'a most confused and irregular effect'.[2] The new process gave to the colours a 'want of brilliancy', and led to the subject matter being painted on to square panes of glass, making redundant the leads which had previously been used to hold together each separate piece of distinctly coloured glass. In consequence, the outline of the subject, previously defined by the leads, was now lost in a pattern of intersecting lines: 'as if a net-work were spread over it'. As an example of the deficiencies caused by the innovations he cited the west window of the Chapel of New College, Oxford, where eighteenth-century glass had replaced medieval, much to the window's detriment.

The revival of Gothic architecture brought about a new demand for stained glass with Pugin playing a leading role in both activities. Not surprisingly in the case of glass, he sought to recreate the styles of the Early, Decorated and Late periods, or broadly speaking those of the thirteenth, fourteenth and fifteenth centuries respectively. Initially he produced designs for windows to be made by William Warrington, Thomas Willement and William Wailes,[3] mostly for his own building projects, but from 1845 he became involved in all aspects of window making when he formed an association with John Hardman.

Pugin's efforts were directed not towards the reproduction of copies of medieval windows but the creation of original works on the basis of the old principles, thus having the aura of the old but also reflecting as he put it: 'the practical improvements of our times and our increased anatomical knowledge.'[4] The first of his designs was for the Sanctuary windows for the College Chapel at Oscott (plate 380). Made by Warrington they were in place by early 1838 and received high praise: 'one of the finest efforts of the art of staining on glass which has been seen in this or probably any other country for a very long period.'[5]

Pugin continued to use Warrington, and was highly satisfied with his work for the apse windows of St Chad's, Birmingham – finished probably in early 1841. He dispensed with his services later that year however, when it came to making the three light east window of the chapel of the Hospital of St John (plate 381) for Lord Shrewsbury at Alton, considering that 'he has become lately so conceited, [and has] got nearly as expensive as Willement.'[6] With the cost advantage over Willement no longer a factor, the latter was engaged in his place. Although Willement – unlike

380.   East end of the Chapel of St Mary's College, Oscott. The glass, showing the Virgin and Child with Saints, was made by William Warrington.

Warrington – was already well known as a glass maker and designer he nevertheless was required to work closely to Pugin's direction. This is made clear by Pugin's comments on the Alton window, which showed the image of the Virgin and Child flanked by St John the Baptist and St Nicholas: 'The figures too are very devotional and well drawn. I made full sized drawings of every detail.'[7] By late 1841, Willement had also been replaced – his prices were too high. For St Barnabas's, Nottingham, Pugin turned to Wailes and continued the association during the next four years. That they stayed comparatively so long together was perhaps indicative of their need for each other. Wailes was then only in the early years of establishing what was to become a considerable stained glass manufactory and benefited from some substantial contracts, which, in addition to Nottingham, included St Giles's, Cheadle and St George's, Southwark. Pugin on the other hand was able to obtain relatively cheap glass and so could cut his church building costs: 'In the article of stained glass alone, since I completed my arrangements with this northern man, a saving of 60 per cent over Willements prices has in many cases been effected'.[8]

Although the relationship with Wailes seems to have been perfectly equable, Pugin confided to John Hardman: 'I have some great schemes in my head which I will tell you by & by it does me good to scheme. I am scheming a stained glass shop but this is only between ourselves.'[9] This scheme presumably took shape in the workshop Hardman established in Birmingham in 1845 and for which Pugin supplied all the designs until his final illness in the early part of 1852.

The work was carried out at two distinct and geographically widely separated locations. Preliminary sketches and full-size cartoons including the leadwork design were drawn at Ramsgate and forwarded to Birmingham where the glass cutting, painting, firing and leading-up took place. Pugin's role was to produce all the designs in the form of preliminary sketches and oversee the preparation of the cartoons, marking in on the latter the colours of the glass that Hardman should use. The distance between the two operations made for considerable difficulties. There were of course the inevitable clerical and administrative muddles, which gave Pugin a good deal of heartache, but

381. East end of the Chapel of St John's Hospital, Alton. The glass, showing St John the Baptist, the Virgin and Child, and St Nicholas, is by Thomas Willement.

from Birmingham. The most important of these was Hardman's teenage nephew John Hardman Powell (1827–95), who was already there helping with metalwork designs at the time the glass workshop was established. Powell became the person upon whom Pugin depended not only to work on important cartoons, but also, in his absence, to look after matters at Ramsgate. As he wrote on one occasion: 'I do not think Powell can go away directly the whole study may as well be pulled down if he does . . . all the others will go wild quite wild.'[12] The 'others' were E. Hendren, F. Hill, T. Earley and Pugin's young son Edward (1834–75), of whom only the latter in Pugin's opinion came to approach Powell's competence in cartoon preparation.[13] E. Casolani, a pupil of the German painter J.F. Overbeck, was also taken on, but after an initial enthusiasm for his work, Pugin found him too slow and lazy.[14] When work was at its peak Pugin's wife Jane was called upon to help, doing 'a great deal of the Leading.'[15] Francis W. Oliphant (1818–59) was of considerable importance in producing cartoons for the workshop. Experienced in stained glass design, having previously worked for Wailes, he had set up as a self-employed artist operating from his home in London and from 1846 until the end of 1850 appears to have given a first option on his services to Hardman.[16] The cartoons he completed were sent to Ramsgate for approval, and on occasions he visited the Grange to work under supervision. Pugin was never really happy with him, largely because he was not directly under his eye and was inclined to draw in a 'modern academic fashion'. Nevertheless he was involved with many of the finest productions of the workshop and also earned Pugin's praise for the cartoons he did for the windows for St Paul's, Brighton; SS. Thomas and Edmund of Canterbury, Erdington; the Chapel of Magdalene College, Cambridge and elsewhere.[17] Pugin also acknowledged his value in handling the big windows, suggesting to Hardman: 'if we get any of the large windows with groups they must be done by Oliphant but for single figures I think Powell is far the best.'[18]

Given effective control over the workshop, Pugin looked to emulate medieval windows in all their qualities – glass, drawing and painting. At times he became depressed with the results but this only strengthened his resolve to overcome his inadequacies:

more important his absence from Birmingham meant that for the most part he was unable to influence the quality of a window as it was taking shape or prevent unsatisfactory work from leaving the shop. As he put it:

> Remember glass is the most difficult the most deceiving of all art & that I *ought to see everything before it goes* . . . I cannot see the effect in a cartoon not even a coloured one the transparent light changes the effect & deceives me altogether. It will be 20 years before I get sufficient experience to mark(?) the cartoons . . . what pains I took with that Mr Coleridges window[10] & if I had not seen it at Birmingham it would have been a total failure how often painters alter the colour of pictures & you laugh at me when I say I ought to watch the work you work splendidly *to* the cartoons but you cannot alter them as they require it & there is the difficulty.[11]

To assist Pugin at Ramsgate a number of young helpers were sent down at various times

> I am very miserable & dejected over our work. I am sure we don't advance. I am determined to go to Rouen, Evereux & c this month & have a good look at glass. I never troubled with that

Powell to go this year to study the foliage &c from old things *real size* with the *real strength of line* that the old men used,'[23] and 'I will go & make *full sized studies* myself because I know what has been done once can be repeated.'[24] Mastering the technique of the medieval painters, caused great frustration: 'I believe the true glass is unattainable unless we could raise one of the old painters to join us',[25] and Pugin having to work so far from the glass painters in Birmingham made matters worse: 'the old *artists* are the glass *painters* not the cartoon *makers* that is the secret . . . I shall light my furnace and see what I can do *on* the glass.'[26] The beneficial consequences of his total involvement with window making can be gauged by comparing some of the Hardman work with that of Wailes.

Due to his dependence on the use of deep colours, Wailes's windows tended to be too dark in appearance;[27] indeed, in the cases of St Barnabas's, Nottingham and St Giles's, Cheadle, the windows had to be altered by Hardman to allow more light to enter the buildings.[28] At the time though, at least as far as Nottingham was concerned, Pugin seemed satisfied: 'The effect is most solemn, some modern people complain it is too dark but it is just

383. South aisle, east window, University Church of St Mary the Virgin, Oxford, showing scenes from the life of St Thomas Apostle, by William Wailes, *c.*1844.

384. South aisle window, University Church of St Mary the Virgin, Oxford, showing scenes from the life of St Mary Magdalen, by John Hardman & Co., 1848.

view before. I saw glass & drew it but not with the idea of *making* it & I am sure there is a deal to learn.[19]

At Evreux he purchased a quantity of old glass, concluding:

I assure you we have hardly one of the old colours in our glass & I expect we shall have a deal of trouble to get them but at any rate we now have the patterns . . . I have learnt an immense deal this journey & I feel certain we must start de novo to get the true thing – but I feel certain that I now have the key to whole system (sic) & by keeping the glass of the different periods distinct we can make every window.[20]

He was being perhaps a little optimistic. James Hartley of Sunderland was asked to produce in quantity glass equivalent to that of Pugin's samples. He had mixed success[21] and there were constant calls for improvements in the colours, particularly the ruby.[22] Drawing and painting in the medieval manner posed as many problems as obtaining the colour of the glass. Making sketches of the overall designs (plate 382) was not enough, understanding the detail was essential: 'I want

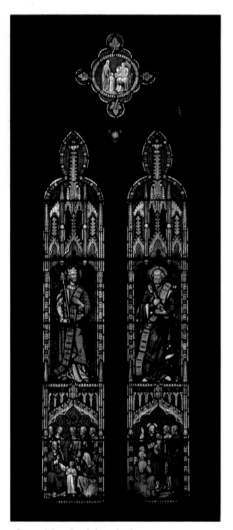

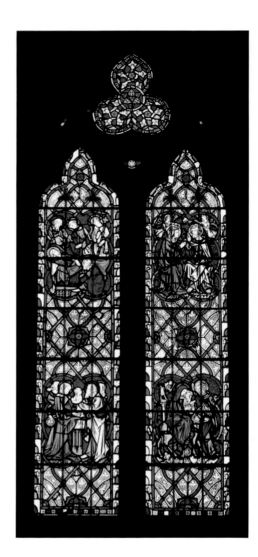

385. North aisle window, Holy Innocents, Highnam, Gloucestershire, *c.*1850, showing Solomon and St Peter, Hannah bringing Samuel to Eli, the Child placed in the midst, and Christ blessing the little children, by William Wailes.

386. South aisle window, Holy Innocents, Highnam, Gloucestershire, 1850, showing Isaiah and St John the Evangelist, the Birth of Isaac, the Annunciation and the Nativity, by John Hardman & Co.

387. South window of the Lady Chapel, St Augustine's, Ramsgate, tracery 1849, lights 1851, showing scenes from the life of the Virgin, by John Hardman & Co.

the thing they are not used to solemn building.'[29] Given his head with Hardman, this attitude appears to change and he looked for something much more vibrant: 'I am burning to produce something sparkling & brilliant, all our work is dead & heavy. We have not yet done a *brilliant* window.'[30] The two four-light windows at St Mary the Virgin, Oxford, identical in architectural style and commissioned by the same patron, George Bartley, as memorials to his son and daughter, are perhaps indicative of this change. The earlier Wailes window designed by Pugin *c.*1844[31] (plate 383) is very subdued in appearance, with large background areas of deep blues and reds as well as dark gold-brown canopy work, which prevent light from filtering through.[32] By contrast, in the Hardman window of 1848 (plate 384) the background colours are broken up into alternating patches of blue and red, which make patterns on the window plane with the canopy pinnacles that are formed largely of white glass, to give greater lightness and

brightness to the upper part of the window. The judicious use of white to produce this effect was well understood by Pugin.[33]

That Pugin advanced while Wailes seemingly stood still can be seen in the work the two men did in 1850 for Holy Innocents, Highnam, Gloucestershire (plates 385, 386), where two light windows, of figures under canopies with narrative scenes below, were made in the Decorated style. The north nave windows, designed and made by the Wailes manufactory, still appear dark and staid compared with those of Pugin and Hardman in the south. Again this is largely due to Pugin's use of white glass, combined with the yellow colouration of silver stain, his less sombre colours, the greater variety of pose, gesture and expression he gives to the figures and his livelier draperies. Also while Wailes restrains his narrative scenes under ogival arches and within columns, Pugin frames them in the expanding forms of quatrefoils which he allows to spread across the borders and up to the window's edges. In the following year he chose to use this form in the south windows of the Lady Chapel of his own church St Augustine's, Ramsgate (plate 387), rather than having canopied figures: 'they are far better than all images under canopies, they increase the size of the window . . . the groups fill the quatrefoils *perfectly*.'[34]

With growing experience, improvements were made even in the best of the Hardman windows, as Pugin acknowledged. He proudly proclaimed: 'the East window for Ushaw is nearly finished. The finest work of modern times & so you will say.'[35] Two years or so later, in respect of the east and west windows at SS. Thomas and Edmund of Canterbury, Erdington he wrote: 'we have had nothing like them before except the E Ushaw & that is nothing like so good.'[36] All three windows are large and colourful and each contains numerous figures in well organised groups. Those of saints in the east window at Erdington (plate 389) are not dissimilar in arrangement to the ones at Ushaw (plate 388), yet they seem more relaxed and fit more naturally into their allotted spaces, an indication perhaps of Pugin's and Hardman's increasing confidence in their ability to handle crowded compositions. In the west window at Erdington (plate 390) the events in the life of Christ are beautifully contained within geometrically shaped medallions, defined by thin stems of white glass that trace lines of flickering light across the window and must surely have satisfied Pugin's longing for something sparkling and brilliant.

In 1849 Pugin was anxiously working on the lancet windows for the east end of the Chapel of Jesus College, Cambridge[37] (plate 392). His desire to succeed in a style earlier than the Decorated was increased by competition from the French stained glass designer Henri Gerente.[38] Pugin made a special visit to Chartres to obtain 'not only accurate details but actually a lot of the real glass from a glazier and Mr Hardman is going to match the tints exactly.'[39] The galvanised iron framework, which Pugin considered an essential element, gives an authentic early look to the College windows, although the glass itself seems much lighter in appearance than that at Chartres. This point was noted at the time by Canon Sparke of Ely Cathedral, who remarked: 'it appears that there is too liberal a distribution of white in the Jesus College windows.'[40] Pugin's own assessment was that they were very disappointing: 'they don't look as if (sic) there was a powerful colour in them. Our ornament is too faintly painted we are afraid of black.'[41]

The use of black to strengthen the appearance was also advocated for the grisaille backgrounds which by 1850 were increasingly becoming a feature of Pugin/Hardman windows. Complaints had been received with regard to the four-light memorial window for the south choir aisle of

388. West window of the Chapel, St Cuthbert's College, Ushaw, 1847, showing the Church Triumphant, by John Hardman & Co.

389. East window, Erdington Abbey, Birmingham, 1850, showing the Heavenly Jerusalem, by John Hardman & Co.

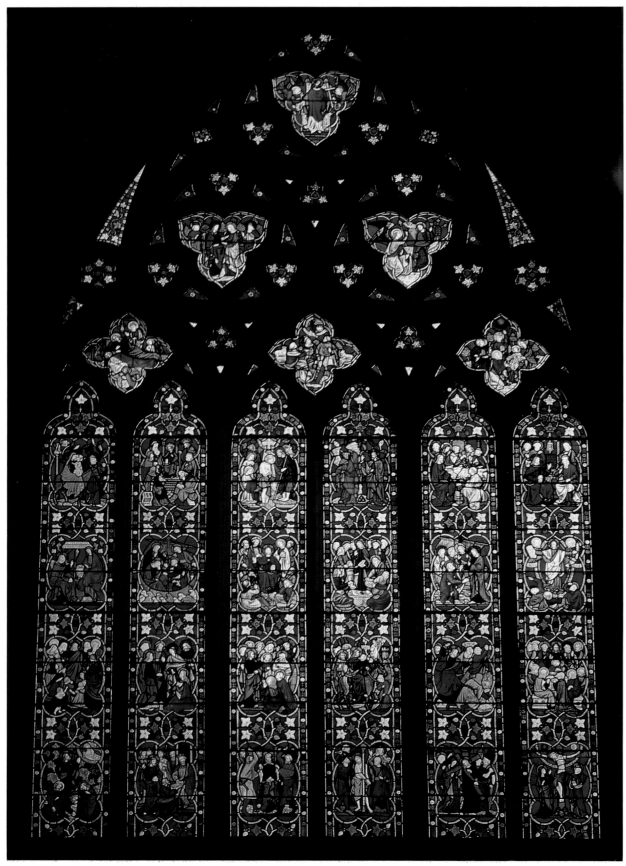

390.   West window, Erdington Abbey, 1850, showing scenes from the Life of Our Lord, by John Hardman & Co.

Chester Cathedral. The pictorial parts of the window were highly praised for excellent harmonies of colour and admirable execution but: 'the effect is much impaired by the dominance of white glass in the upper spaces. This gives a glaring effect to the whole which takes attention off the pictorial representations & kills them as we say', the window's proximity to 'the darkly coloured window Wailes executed'[42] emphasised the adverse effect. Pugin was extremely anxious to resolve the problem: 'a good deal will depend on the windows we do for *Cathedrals* they are seen by thousands. I would strain every nerve in such a job as this.'[43] He confirmed the existence of the problem and proposed the solution:

> I assure you my north window[44] looked like white glass *plain white* & if it does so then what must Chester be . . . *without loss* of time put on fine lines & hatch the ground get the darkest pieces of glass you can find & it will be a grand job.[45]

The alteration was duly carried out and Pugin, characteristically determined that the principles of strong grisaille should be properly understood, sent Powell to study the 'old things'.[46]

Although cathedral work was admitted to be extremely important, Pugin was prepared to argue strongly against making windows of inferior design, particularly if they failed to accord with the architectural surrounds. The aforementioned Canon Sparke, on behalf of some ladies at Ely, commissioned a four-light window for the south aisle of the Cathedral. It was to be part of a series and was required to be filled with groups illustrating eight biblical subjects. Pugin was appalled at the prospect of 'making a set of little(?) paltry subjects in such lights',[47] and recommended to Hardman:

> . . . on no condition to attempt it . . . it will go for nothing in that great church that window is only suitable for *4 saints under fine canopies* upon a grand scale . . . unless the design & parts of the glass are on a scale with the stone mullions & tracery the effect must be detestable . . . subjects in 1.5½ lights must be failures & I hope you will decline it.[48]

In the end he settled for four subjects under canopies, still protesting as he submitted the designs: 'The spaces are small but I will do my best.'[49] By the time it was completed he was already in the throes of his last illness and probably had no part in its execution.[50] His reservations however can be seen to have been justified, the subject matter

appearing unduly cramped within the narrow confines of the four lights.

Subjects under canopies preoccupied Pugin towards the end of 1850 and during 1851. Some of them were required to be in the Late style such as the east window at Magdalene College Chapel, Cambridge, and the chancel windows at St Andrew's, Farnham (plate 391). At this stage he lacked confidence in the firm's ability to handle such work. Predictably he suggested to Hardman looking at medieval examples for guidance:

> I should like to go to Fairford [St Mary's, Fairford, Glos] with you for that is a fine specimen of Later glass just what we want for Magdalene College Cambridge. I want to make a fine window of that but I don't *see my way yet* our late glass is not either drawn or painted like the old work.[51]

His designs for Farnham he thought were a fine job[52] but it was only with difficulty that he obtained satisfactory cartoons, and the glass painting exasperated him:

> It is not the least like the cartoons they have put powerful shadows where there are half tints and

391. East window, St Andrew's, Farnham, 1851, showing the Crucifixion and Ascension, by John Hardman & Co.

392. Centre lancet, Chapel of Jesus College, Cambridge, 1850, showing scenes from the Passion, by John Hardman & Co.

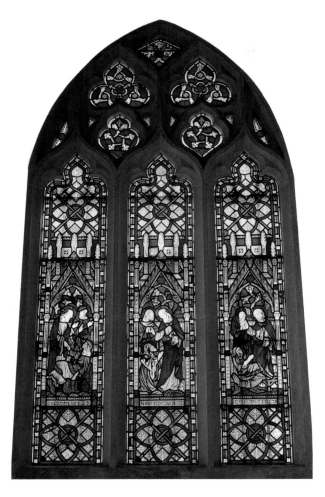

393. West window, Bicton Mausoleum, 1852, showing miraculous Raisings from the Dead, by John Hardman & Co.

half tints where there are strong shadows . . . nobody in the place has the remotest idea of Late work . . . the decorated is *perfect* but the Late is vile.[53]

The shadows of which Pugin complained were in the canopies, which unlike Decorated were three dimensional, creating space for the subject matter which for the greater part appeared in front of landscape background. The differences between the two styles can be seen by comparing the treatment of the Raising of Lazarus and Jairus's Daughter themes, in two windows designed by Pugin during the second half of 1851. In the Decorated windows at Bicton Mausoleum[54] (plate 393) the canopies are flat on grisaille backgrounds and the figures are compressed close to the window plane by screens which cut out all background views. At the church of Our Lady, Upton Pyne, near Exeter[55] where the north aisle window is in the Late style, the space beneath the canopies is such that the illusion of a three-windowed apse is created in the centre light, and open archways with landscape views beyond in the two side lights. Pugin was particularly pleased with this latter

window remarking: 'I think we have made a good job of S. Stafford Northcotes window . . . if well carried out it will be brilliant.'[56]

Pugin had reservations about taking the style further and embracing the pictorial tendencies of sixteenth-century glass. Even when considering windows of that period as accomplished as those of Kings College Chapel, Cambridge, he warned Hardman: 'I have just returned from Cambridge – don't talk about *beating* Kings yet. There is a long way to go but this late glass is in reallity (sic) a false system and the decline of the art.'[57]

By the time of the Great Exhibition of 1851, Pugin, in conjunction with Hardman, had produced high quality windows in all of the styles and saw the Exhibition as a good opportunity of acquainting the public of the fact – 'we ought to have something of each kind',[58] he wrote, but to avoid the additional expense of producing something new, he instructed, 'you will only show windows ordered & which will be paid for',[59] and put forward his suggestions.[60] These included for the Early style, the Hereford Cathedral east window,[61] ('it is a fine example of that style');[62] for the Decorated, the two light window from St Edmund's College, Ware,[63] ('because we can have it & it is an easy subject 2 Large Saints under canopies');[64] and for the Late, some of the lights from the Farnham windows. Also included were panels from the Lady Chapel windows at St Augustine, Ramsgate (plate 387) and to represent the firm's secular work, part of the Grand Talbot window from the dining room at Alton Towers.

With one exception secular work did not form a major part of the Pugin/Hardman output, although the firm was called upon from time to time to make stained glass windows for private residences. These were generally heraldic in nature, comprising a miscellany of initials, mottoes, shields of arms and the like. Examples are still in place at Chirk Castle, Clwyd; Bilton Grange, Warwickshire (plate 396); Burton Closes, Derbyshire; Lismore Castle, Ireland; Canford Manor, Dorset and the Grange, Ramsgate (plate 394).[65] The exception was the work for the Houses of Parliament, where, apart from the windows illustrating figures of Kings and Queens under canopies in the Lords' Chamber, made by Ballantine and Allan to Pugin's designs, all the stained glass, which was heraldic, was designed by Pugin and made by Hardman.[66] The work load was enormous and not only put Pugin under considerable strain, but also at times threatened to overwhelm the workshop. During 1850 and 1851 complaints from clients about delays in the progress of their windows

increased, sufficiently for Pugin to observe: 'I begin to be sorry that I persuaded you to do the glass for Westminster, it stops everything & I see clearly we shall disgust all the people.'[67] Part of the problem was the perfectionism of both Pugin and Barry which resulted in much reworking. The House of Commons cartoons for instance were drawn three times[68] and included a whole change in design from badges to arms,[69] and there were also many changes to the glass itself. But as Pugin pointed out there were compensations to the firm in terms of finance and the prestige to be derived from the scheme:

> It is no use moaning on the alterations in the Commons glass they will be paid for & I assure you *they are necessary to make a profit* . . . Mr Barry is quite right & in so great a work I think the expense is well laid out.[70]

Barry's further comment must have meant even more to Pugin, for it justified the whole aim of his artistic intent: 'a great deal of it leaves *nothing to be desired* & is as perfect as the old work & the finest of it.'[71]

1851 was a year in which Pugin not only publicly exhibited his artistry in stained glass, but also defended and explained the artistic principles on which his work was based. In doing so he also gave a reminder of the religious inspiration that lay behind the greater part of his output. The Bishop of Manchester had criticised a number of aspects concerning St John the Evangelist's, Broughton, as examples of 'symptoms' in the English Church,

'encouraging to Rome' including the fact that the Virgin Mary was crowned in the stained glass.[72] A report had appeared in the *Manchester Guardian*,[73] and, since the window concerned had been designed by Pugin, he wrote a lengthy response.[74] Insisting that 'the principles on which I objected to remove the crown . . . were *artistic* & not *religious*', that the church had no fixed rules for such matters and that he had excellent authority from many of the finest examples of medieval work. He continued:

> These representations do not profess to be accurate illustrations of costume . . . but rather devout & brilliant conceptions of Christian artists to suit the glorious fabric they were to decorate. Everything is glorified & shown in an ideal medium calculated to present to the people the majesty of the Godhead & the glories of the celestial kingdom surrounding our blessed redeemer . . . painted glass to be either beautiful or edifying or indeed suited to one of the most important objects the adornment of the temples of God must be treated after a conventional & symbolical manner . . . if the objection against the coroneted figure at Broughton was presented to its full effect we should not have a fragment of fine costume or a nimbus left.

Beautiful, edifying and appropriate were maxims that he had elaborated in the lecture to his students some fourteen years earlier and which he had followed in the years since. There were times however when as with Broughton he needed to resist clients' attempts to contradict them. Hence the suggestion that the crucifixion and the resurrection be used for the inner lights of the St George's, York east window brought the rejoinder: 'both the subjects . . . are central subjects, you cannot have the crucifixion as a pendant to anything.'[75] Again when J.D. Coleridge proposed that as a memorial for a brother who had died some years previously at the age of fifteen, the five-lancet east window of the north transept at Ottery St Mary, should include small figures of saints in medallions on either side of the Blessed Lord as a Child, he chided: 'the holy saints would be ridiculous for a Lad 15 years of age. I was a regular scamp long before that they are quite inappropriate (sic) after 2½ or 3 at outside.'[76] He thought it though perfectly reasonable to pick and choose among the Saints to achieve a better effect, as when he reproached Hardman:

> How could you select St Vincent of Paul for the East window of convent (sic) there is no colour about the costume & it will be invisible . . . pray see if you cannot take S. Vincent Deacon . . . do let us have some colour S. Vincent of Paul has nearly ruined our reputation in S. Georges.[77]

He would also change a composition in the face of good authority and sound principle, as occurred in the case of the St Oswald, Winwick chancel east window. Here he intended to illustrate the four greater prophets beneath the four evangelists, thus bringing together the Old and New Testaments, but then he observed:

> I find from a very learned treatise on the porches of Amiens and other authorities that all representations of prophets and personages of the Old Testament typical of the new should be confined to the western portion of churches, and *chancels* should be decorated with personages and subjects exclusively from the *New Testament*. This appears to me most beautiful in principle – particularly applicable to an east window.[78]

The prophets were duly substituted by four of the apostles.

Within a few months of the closure of the Great Exhibition, Pugin's declining health brought an end to his participation in the affairs of the glassworks. Replying to a client who had queried the cost of his window, Hardman wrote:

> I can only suppose that when Mr Pugin wrote the letter which you quote of January 16th (1852) he made a mistake . . . At that time he was very far from well, in fact the fatal malady which carried him off was growing rapidly upon him.[79]

Pugin's contribution to the revival of medieval forms of stained glass had been considerable. His early work for Warrington, Willement and Wailes meant that he made major glass makers aware of his ideas regarding the principles of good design, at a time when the revival was beginning to gain momentum.

With overall control in the Hardman enterprise, he became one of the first to look closely at the qualities of medieval glass itself and to attempt to reproduce their modern equivalents. His understanding of medieval techniques in drawing, leading and painting, combined with his own facilities as a draughtsman, designer and colourist ensured that the archaism was sound and the design of high quality in the windows that the firm produced. Gradually orders increased from outside the range of his own buildings and those of Roman Catholic persuasion and, from 1849 work was carried out for a growing number of architects, who, apart from Charles Barry, included William Butterfield, G.G. Scott, W.W. Wardell and numerous others. As with the earlier work his ideas and influence reached those who were engaged in the expansion of the Gothic Revival and were directed towards the production of stained glass according to the principles of the medieval masters.

CHAPTER SIXTEEN

Textiles

I: *Ecclesiastical Textiles*

Dom Bede Millard o.s.b.

The difference between John Carter's *Specimens of English Ecclesiastical Costume*[1] and the *Glossary of Ecclesiastical Ornament and Costume*[2] by Augustus Welby Pugin, a 'veritable encyclopaedia',[3] is the difference between Antiquarianism and Revival, curiosity and conviction. The former looks back, to record what had been; the latter, presents what had been as a valid, even vital, contribution to contemporary life. Looking at Carter's work, or any similar book, one remembers Newman's words, in his 'Second Spring'[4] sermon, preached at Oscott on 13 July 1852, 'The English Church was . . .'; and looking at Pugin's, one continues with Newman, 'the English Church is once again'. This shift in sensibility – 'a new archaeological atmosphere'[5] – is noticeable across the whole range of decorative arts under Pugin's influence.

As with his celebrated architectural principles, so also in terms of textile design and vestments Pugin sought out and vigorously promoted 'true ideas'[6] – chiefly:

> . . . appropriate design; each flower, each leaf, each device had a significant meaning with reference to the festival to which the vestment belonged. This principle is completely overlooked at present . . . hence the ecclesiastical costume of the day looks showy but not rich . . . On the contrary, the ancient vestments conveyed a symbolic meaning . . . (so) as to fill the beholder with reverence.[7]

Here he is speaking of embroidery, but the principle applies to textiles, and to vestment design particularly. Pugin concludes:

> The only hope of reviving the perfect style is by *strictly adhering to ancient authorities* . . .

397.† Cope with embroidered hood depicting St Thomas, one of three copes made of 'Gothic Tapestry' fabric for St Augustine's, Ramsgate (Trustees of the Victoria & Albert Museum).

398. Detail of the final plate of *The Glossary*, showing Pugin's misunderstanding of the form of a chasuble.

399. Chasuble of cloth of gold; orphreys decorated with velvet and raised embroidery, trimmed with gold braid, 1837 (St Mary's College, Oscott).

especially brasses . . . It is proper to observe that the heraldic law, of colour being always laid on metal, or metal on colour, should be strictly observed . . . and one of the five canonical colours should be selected as a field for the whole work. Velvet is the best material that can be used, after cloth of gold, for the ground.[8]

Pugin succinctly set out his ideas on the renewal of ecclesiastical textiles in an article he wrote in 1838 in the *Orthodox Journal*. Under the headings of Embroidery, Shape, and Colour and Material, he combines instruction with persuasion. His ideas on embroidery have been recounted above; on shape, he wrote:

The dignity of vestments depends principally on their form. Without flowing lines and grand easy folds no majestic appearance can be obtained. The old chasubles, unpinched in shape, fell gracefully from the shoulders and folded over the arms, pliant in material.[9]

Unfortunately, it is clear both from the pictures in the Glossary (plate 398) and from the many surviving Pugin chasubles (plate 399) that in fact he misunderstood the authentic form of its construction, as he invariably had them made with a seam along each shoulder, and cut at too shallow an angle, conceiving the garment as a front and back on which to mount the orphreys, whereas the ancient and medieval tradition was to have the chasuble made of two sides joined vertically, the orphreys covering the seams. However, it is prob-

able that no one knew this when Pugin was reviving shapes which were certainly nearer the authentic forms than any contemporary vestments.

Under the heading Colour and Material, he emphasises the need for flexibility in the garments (as opposed to the stiffness of contemporary work), appropriateness of design, i.e. correct symbolism rather than fanciful prettiness; and the use of the canonical colours, white or gold, red, green, purple and black, as a ground. He also mentions the need for dossals, frontals, hangings to match, and so on, all of which would need to be changed according to the feast or season; it is evident then that even a small parish church, fitted up in the manner Pugin convinced so many of his contemporaries as being correct and Catholic, would need a very large quantity of textiles and embroideries.

Almost every ecclesiastical vestment, from the surplice to the mitre, had in the course of centuries developed away from the medieval forms he advocated; since the Reformation, vestments had been illegal in Britain until Catholic Emancipation, and only a few medieval examples were 'yet preserved in Catholic families':[10] vestments in common use were imported from the Continent. The magnificent set Pugin designed for Oscott College (plate 399), which were worn at the dedication of the chapel in May 1838, were made from cloth of gold, woven at Spitalfields, London, 'at a less cost than it could have been imported from Lyons'.[11] Bishop Ullathorne wrote:

It was on that occasion that the old French style of vestment and surplice was changed for those of ampler form. Pugin, with his eyes flashing through his tears, was in raptures, declaring it the first great day for England since the Reformation.[12]

An article by Pugin, in the *Orthodox Journal* for 20 July 1839, provides a vivid description of his church at Uttoxeter, specifically mentioning the vestments which were:

> . . . in strict accordance with the style of the building; ample chasubles in graceful folds, with appropriate embroidery, appareled albs and amices (plate 400), narrow stoles and maniples, old English surplices,[13] etc.

It is hard for us to realise what a genuine revolution in taste is being masterminded here, and how novel and different Pugin's textiles were, compared with contemporary Continental design – 'the very focus of bad or paltry taste'.[14]

Pugin's insistence on an objective liturgical standard and an authentic tradition aroused opposition in some quarters. 'I do not like St Chad's or any of Pugin's work',[15] wrote Dr Bowden, the influential President of Sedgley Park College.

Bishop Baines of the Western District (i.e. the West of England) seems to have written to Propaganda (the Department of the Vatican responsible for England at the time) in Rome, to complain about the new vestments: Bishop Walsh in Birmingham was forbidden their use. 'The greater part of the vestments were filthy rags, and he (Dr Walsh) has replaced them with silk and gold. For this he has been censured!!!'[16] wrote Pugin to Ambrose Phillipps de Lisle. However, the matter was settled eventually[17] and the 'Gothic' vestments, having been seen in Rome to be perfectly 'Roman' in shape, were allowed; but 'in retrospect it seems extraordinary that (Pugin) succeeded so far in imposing (his) desires and convictions'.[18]

Pugin was not quite alone in his enthusiasm for and knowledge of the history and revival of ancient and seemly Catholic textile patterns and vestment forms, as the works of Dr Daniel Rock (1799–1871), especially *The Church of Our Fathers*, testify. Dr Rock records[19] how he lent the pattern he had devised from his study of brasses and paintings showing the full medieval surplice to Pugin, who then had it copied for Oscott College, St Chad's and his other churches. Similarly, Pugin borrowed a chasuble, apparels etc., copied by Dr Rock from fourteenth-century originals at Aachen

> . . . which he took with him to Birmingham. In a short time afterwards, the chasuble, in its graceful, true old form, and appareled albs and amices, were spread throughout the Midland District.[20]

402.† Mitre of red velvet with applied cloth of silver and cloth of gold; one of three mitres designed for St Chad's, (Birmingham Roman Catholic Diocese Trustees).

403. Altar frontal made for St Augustine's, Ramsgate (Trustees of the Victoria & Albert Museum).

404. Chalice Veil, made in Mrs Powell's workshop, Birmingham, 1847/8 for St Augustine's, Ramsgate (Trustees of the Victoria & Albert Museum).

To whom in Birmingham did Pugin take the vestments? Who made up all these textiles for him? It is known that Mrs Lucy Powell, mother of John Hardman Powell, Pugin's only pupil, and his son-in-law, made many of them. Mrs Powell, sister of John Hardman, and married to a partner of his, supervised the vestment making at the Hardman firm's premises from 1842. She died on 17 June 1863, aged seventy. Pugin's Diaries and various accounts, for example those for the Erection of St Augustine's Church, Ramsgate,[21] mention her frequently. He used her to mount medieval embroidered orphreys on to chasubles and copes (plate 401), as well as to create new vestments.

These same sources also mention the firm of Lonsdale & Tyler, 26 Bedford Street, Covent Garden, London, 'Gold and Silver Lacemen and Embroiderers to Her Majesty, Army Accoutrement Makers':[22] they made the magnificent cloth of gold vestments for St Chad's mentioned above (plate 402). So it seems Pugin called in a very professional firm when rich bullion work was needed and used Mrs Powell for more standard commissions. On Pugin's death in September 1852, advertisements in the Catholic press show that Mrs Powell took into partnership the Misses Lucy and Winifred Brown expressly to continue making vestments according to Pugin's designs: their advertisement claims they have 'for many years devoted themselves entirely to the production of Chasubles, Dalmatics, Copes, Albs, Surplices, etc . . . from the Designs by the late A.W.N. Pugin Esq.'[23]

Accounts for the funeral of the Earl of Shrewsbury in 1852 show that they made the pall, vestments and hangings for the chapel at Alton Towers and for the catafalque: the pall was the most expensive single item in the funeral.[24] The two sisters carried on after Mrs Powell's death and their advertisement appears regularly in the 1870s in wording almost identical to the one of 1853. In the 1870s they worked at 13 Easy Row, Birmingham; Pugin had noted their address in the front papers of his 1849 Diary as 3 Great Charles Street, Birmingham. Lucy Brown died on 18 February 1897, aged seventy-nine, and Winifred on 24 February 1900, aged seventy-five; both were buried in coffins with Hardman fittings on the south side of the crypt of St Chad's Cathedral.

As regards the weaving of materials, Dr Rock, at the end of the introduction to his descriptive Catalogue *Textile Fabrics* says:

. . . a loom at Manchester, which had been geared after his (Pugin's) idea, was throwing off textiles for church use, and orphreys, broad and narrow, were being wove (*sic*) in London.[27]

The identity of the firm at Manchester is unknown to the present writer.

Pugin's association with the firm of Crace, especially in relation to the Palace of Westminster and the Great Exhibition, is well documented. J.G. Crace (1809–89) often adapted Pugin's designs, and indeed had Pugin's blessing to do so: 'make any improvements you can, keeping to the principle',[28] wrote Pugin to Crace on 2 June 1846 regarding a carpet for Chirk Castle. Pugin wanted one design of theirs, Gothic Tapestry, used for vestments.[29] Textiles used for vestments at Pugin's church of St Augustine's, Ramsgate, were used by Crace as wall hangings and upholstery at Abney Hall, Lancashire, the Palace of Westminster and elsewhere (plate 212).[30] The extent to which Crace used other firms to weave the fabrics Pugin designed for him is rather uncertain, but at the Great Exhibition Daniel Keith & Co., 124 Wood Street, Cheapside, London exhibited Pugin pattern silks and J.W. Ward of Halifax a Damask.[31]

In 1851 the *Journal of Design and Manufactures*, reported:

> Aided by Mr. Crace, Mr. Minton, and a few other most intelligent manufacturers, Mr. Hardman comes before us as a perfect Briareus of production. In silk tissues, in hangings of silk fabrics, in embroidery etc. . . . Mr. Hardman seems to supply the 'hundred hands', Mr. Pugin the one dominant head.[32]

One can only regret that head and hands were severed after so few years of brilliant creativity, and only wonder at how much, and that of outstanding quality, had been achieved in those years.

II: *Domestic Textiles*

Linda Parry

In a letter to J.G. Crace dated 19 August 1850 Pugin refers to three patterns for 'common damask' which he had previously sent.

> They are ecclesiastical and simple and are badly wanted for altar curtains and I do not like using the same pattern for rooms and churches. There should be a distinction.[33]

As one of the first architect/designers to make use of fabrics and value them as an important part of his decorative schemes, it is not suprising that Pugin strongly believed that there should be a difference between religious and secular textiles. However, his words were not always heeded, as can be shown by comparing existing designs and textile samples with known commissions.

The patterns that Pugin referred to in his letter to Crace were dispersed floral sprig patterns inspired by late medieval *opus anglicanum* frontals in which applied embroidered motifs are 'powdered' across the surface of a plain, usually velvet, ground. Pugin cleverly adapted similar repeating designs, and in one case directly copied from historical fragments in his own collection.[34] These were all intended for woven textiles,[35] and many were made up in damasks of cotton and wool, both everyday and practical 'common' fibres. Clearly, this type of cloth proved highly successful as curtaining not only for the church but also for domestic use. Records of the Birmingham firm of John Hardman itemise examples ordered by churches throughout the 1840s,[36] but, at the same time, Pugin was suggesting similar patterns for specific domestic commissions. Four years before his advice to Crace he drew a repeating pattern of dispersed, crowned fleurs-de-lys for the decoration of the Dining Room of Henry Sharples's home, Oswald Croft in Bishop Eton, Liverpool.[37] Curtains for the house were, almost certainly, made up in woollen damask. The only known surviving example of the weaving is not in a domestic setting as originally intended, but in the collections of St Chad's Cathedral, Birmingham.[38] This pattern is also very similar to a curtain given by John D. Hardman to the V&A Museum in 1951, (plate 405) which, from its make-up, may well have been

405. Curtain, one of Pugin's 'common' damasks, jacquard woven wool and cotton, probably woven by J.W. Ward of Halifax, *c.*1847 (Trustees of the Victoria & Albert Museum).

used in the Hardman home. To emphasise further the dual nature of these patterns, J.W. Ward of Halifax, the most likely manufacturer of these textiles, recommended very similar items for domestic use at the 1851 Exhibition.[39]

Similar contradictions between Pugin's views and use of textiles are evident. The most popular of all his fabrics, a woven wool and silk fabric of traditional serpentine design, (referred to by Crace as 'Gothic tapestry'), was also used in a number of identifiable church and domestic commissions. In 1844, the year Pugin designed the fabric, he wrote to Crace:

> I am delighted with the stuff. I think it the best that has been done and I think I can get it extensively used for vestments. Now have you any objection to invest a little capital and keep about 50 to 100 yards?[40]

This textile formed part of the furnishings in a number of interiors associated with Pugin including Gawthorpe and Oxburgh Halls, the library at Longleat,[41] and it was used for the decoration of the Prince Consort's bedroom at Abney Hall, Cheadle in Cheshire.[42] It also proved popular for churches. Pugin recommended it for the chapel at Alton Towers, and it was used for a cope for St Chad's, and for no less than three for Pugin's own church, St Augustine's, at Ramsgate[43] (plate 397). One is tempted to deduce that Crace had the foresight to order a large quantity of the fabric in 1844, and that Pugin himself was the chief beneficiary.

Some of Pugin's more sumptuous silk and brocaded fabrics also had both secular and domestic

purposes. A repeating pattern of stylised pineapples and palmettes, brocaded in silver on cream, was one of a number of designs used to make vestments for St Augustine's. It also provided the emerald green silk wall coverings and upholstery for one of Crace's most striking interiors, the Drawing Room at Abney Hall in Cheadle and is visible in the background of Pugin's portrait (plate 16).[44]

Little criticism is intended by highlighting Pugin's opposing views on textiles. On the contrary, what is evident is a fertile and original mind constantly changing in an effort to balance his strong moral and aesthetic preferences with the practical uses of the items he designed and the circumstances of modern manufacture and trade. He was, above all, a very practical designer and, in his dealings with Hardman and Crace, displayed an entrepreneurial spirit which was to be copied and developed by many later textile designers from William Morris to C.F.A. Voysey. Pugin turned his mind to all aspects of decorative design, however unimportant these had seemed to most of the architects and designers of the past. No object was too small or menial to attract his attention, and textiles, fortunately, were no exception to this rule.

The Crace Archives at the V&A include designs for a wide range of domestic items. As well as woven and printed fabrics for windows, walls, doors and upholstery, Pugin turned his hand to hand-knotted and machine-woven carpets and a range of embroidered goods that included hangings,[45] monograms for chairbacks, lambrequin pelmets, polescreens, a christening mantle and a wedding veil.[46]

It is clear that Pugin had some knowledge of historical textiles and that, as in all his work, he turned to early decoration for inspiration. However, his designs rely almost entirely on the traditional repeating forms of the pomegranate, the artichoke and the palmette derived not from northern Gothic architectural decoration but from Renaissance silks and velvets woven in Lucca, Venice and other Italian centres from the fifteenth century. Existing drawings show a number of ideas collected from European churches,[47] whereas the majority of others are likely to have been drawn from printed sources. His interest in historic textiles must also have been encouraged by his friendship with the Rev. Daniel Rock,[48] and through him, the Swiss clergyman and collector Dr Bock, two men who were responsible for recommending and supplying some of the South Kensington Museum's finest early acquisitions.[49]

Whereas Pugin was aware of the tactile qualities

406. Furnishing textile, jacquard woven wool and cotton, probably woven by J.W. Ward of Halifax for Crace, *c.*1847 (Trustees of the Victoria & Albert Museum). Designed for curtains at Oswaldcroft, and used in green and yellow for a tester and bed curtains at The Grange.

407. Brocatelle, jacquard woven silk, woven by Keith & Co., for Crace, 1849 (Trustees of the Victoria & Albert Museum).

of certain cloths and differentiated between velvets, cloth of gold and figured silks when discussing textiles, his knowledge of the technique of weaving is questionable. On a design clearly meant for the loom he wrote:

> I send you also the stuff pattern very much improved, but everything depends on the *stitch* which I cannot show in the drawing . . . I think I have now got it into a good pattern if you carry it out well in respect of stitches.[50]

'Stitches' is a term applied to embroidery not weaving, although it is clear that here Pugin refers to the effect of yarns on the surface of the cloth. Despite this lack of technical knowledge and correct vocabulary Pugin was clear in knowing exactly what he did want, and in order to achieve this there could be no compromise. This is shown in his cruel criticism of well-meaning amateur embroideresses who 'transfer all their nicknackery of the workroom, the toilette-table, and the bazaar to the altar of God'. However, he also saw hope in such enthusiasm, concluding 'But why should not their efforts be turned into a good channel'.[51] While Lonsdale and Tyler, Lucy Powell and the Brown sisters supplied the level of expertise he demanded for his embroidery many other examples are likely to have been worked by talented amateurs, despite his words. However, for the commercial manufacture of Pugin's woven and printed textiles and carpets only the best British manufacturers were used. It is known that early experiments in weaving were carried out in Manchester,[52] and it is likely that some fabrics were supplied by Thomas Brown of 19A Kings Street.[53] Wool and cotton damasks were woven by J.C. Ward of Halifax (plates 405, 406), and high quality furnishing silks and cloths of gold were produced in Spitalfields[54] (plate 407). The archives of Warner Fabrics include two identifiable Pugin textiles almost certainly woven by their predecessor Daniel Keith and Co. The V&A owns designs for both of these as well as textiles of one of the patterns (plate 407).

Pugin designed few printed textiles and clearly reflected the mood of the times in either ignoring the technique completely or restricting its use to secondary areas in the home. Considering that he provided endless patterns for cheaper machine-woven carpets to be used in passages and service rooms, it is a great pity that only two examples of chintz have been discovered.[55] Crace employed the services of the Bannister Hall Printworks near Preston in Lancashire, one of the largest and busiest printers of the nineteenth century, for this work. One of Pugin's simplest yet most effective designs, showing repeating rose and crown motifs and printed in two colours only, was for window blinds for the House of Commons, the only known example of which is now in the V&A. This is unique in being the only traceable textile from the mountain of textile designs drawn by Pugin for Westminster.

At least one other printed textile was drawn by Pugin for Crace for which he levied a charge of £2.2.0d.[24] This was used in the furnishings of Gawthorpe Hall, near Burnley in Lancashire, carried out between 1849 and 1852, and is also likely to have been displayed in the Medieval Court of the 1851 Great Exhibition. Block-printed in startling blue, green, yellow and pink on a diagonally striped maroon and white ground, the pattern is one of Pugin's most original compositions (plate 408). The softly draping cotton ground provides a lightness of effect not seen before in Pugin's work and it is regretted that his early death prevented the development of what might have become a new freedom in the line and colour of his repeating patterns. Instead, for the true originality of form that naturally stems from a prodigious study of the antique, one has to look to the many British textile designers who followed. All of these men and women benefitted from Pugin's approach to textile design and manufacture, and he is now rightly recognised as one of the most intelligent and influential textile designers of his age.

408. Curtain, block printed and glazed cotton, manufactured at the Bannister Hall Printworks near Preston. This fabric was used at Gawthorpe Hall and possibly at the 1851 Exhibition (Trustees of the Victoria & Albert Museum).

III: *Woven Braids*

PAUL HARRISON

The English Roman Catholics . . . have introduced a kind of lace upon their church-furniture . . . which is perhaps cheaper than needlework, is woven of various widths, in different coloured silks on a ground of gold thread, and has . . . a very splendid appearance . . .[57]

This anonymous author is undoubtedly referring to vestments designed by Pugin.

On his tours of continental cathedrals Pugin had noted that priests depicted in monumental brasses and sculptures often wear narrow stoles and orphreys with repeating geometric patterns. He may also have seen medieval vestments with orphreys of woven braids instead of embroidery; these braids were produced at Cologne in the fifteenth and early sixteenth century and have patterns woven in silks on a gold ground.

Beside its striking visual effect, this revived technique had the great practical advantage over embroidery of ensuring a consistently high standard of design and execution. With a few small embroidered motifs such as Pugin designed for Mrs Powell's workshop (plate 409), complete sets of ornaments designed by Pugin could be supplied from stock.

The braids mentioned above are probably those on the vestments made by Lonsdale and Tyler of Covent Garden for St Chad's, Birmingham in 1841.[58] The design of the wider braid seems intended to match the quatrefoil motifs in the embroidery and the woven silk, making it the only braid that can be dated with any accuracy (plate 410). Lonsdale and Tyler are listed in Directories from the 1790s onwards as gold and silver lacemen,[59] and separate payments to them recorded in Pugin's papers between 1839 and 1851, some

409. Chasuble of cream and gold-coloured woven silk brocaded with gold thread, gold thread and silk braids, silk embroidery on velvet; 1847–8, made by Mrs Powell's workshop for Ramsgate (Trustees of the Victoria & Albert Museum).

410. Chasuble of cream and gold-coloured woven silk, gold thread and silk braids, 1847–8, made by Mrs Powell's workshop for Ramsgate (Trustees of the Victoria & Albert Museum). The wider braid was probably woven by Lonsdale and Tyler for vestments at St Chad's, 1841.

411. Stole and orphrey of woven braids in gold thread and silk, from the same set of vestments as plate 409 (Trustees of the Victoria & Albert Museum).

412. Design for a woven braid for Crace, watercolour and bodycolour (Trustees of the Victoria & Albert Museum).

413. Dalmatic of cream and gold-coloured woven silk, with silk braids probably woven by Thomas Brown & Son, Manchester, the dalmatic made by Mrs Powell's workshop for Ramsgate (Trustees of the Victoria & Albert Museum).

414. Dalmatic of green woven silk with silk braid. This braid was published in the *Glossary*, 1844, and was probably woven by Thomas Brown & Son, Manchester, the dalmatic was made by Mrs Powell's workshop for Ramsgate (Trustees of the Victoria & Albert Museum).

specifying 'for lace',[60] suggest that Pugin had an exclusive arrangement concerning these designs.

Pugin particularly recommended monumental brasses as a source of patterns for stoles and orphreys,[61] and in the plates of his *Glossary of Ornament* of 1844 he published his medieval models alongside his own designs developed from them. Among the braids on the vestments supplied by Mrs Powell for St Augustine's in 1847 and 1848, a few are based directly on these designs (plate 414);[62] others show a type of pattern related to several published examples with lozenge-shaped compartments containing various motifs, often with fleurs-de-lys filling the spaces between (plates 411, 413). A group of drawings among the Crace collection continues the development of this pattern without the compartments (plate 412).[63]

A later advertisement in *The Tablet*[64] boasts that Thomas Brown and Son of Manchester manufac-ture their own silks 'Orphreys, Laces, Fringes &c' for vestments; 'A Gothic Chasuble, of Silk, with Woven Silk Cross and Pillar' cost £3.2 s.6 d., and 'Crosses and Pillars, of Woven Silk Lace' cost 11s.6d per set. The appearance of the address of 'Mr T Brown, silk manufacturer, Manchester' in Pugin's diary for 1845[65] probably identifies Thomas Brown as the manufacturer of Pugin's silk braids.

In the Mediæval Court of the Great Exhibition, the woven orphreys on the vestments in Hardman's display drew special comment[66] and may have persuaded other manufacturers to adopt this type of ornament. Certainly by 1864 Gilbert French of Bolton was advertising 'BORDERS of Ecclesiastical Silk Lace . . . One inch wide, 2s.6d. per yard; one and a half inch, 3s. Borders embroidered . . . from 10s. to 25s. per yard', confirming the cost advantage of the woven braids.[67]

415. The Banqueting Hall, Lismore Castle, Ireland (Duke of Devonshire). This recently restored room is an example of the Pugin/Crace partnership at its most exuberant.

416.†   Lantern Clock, engraved brass with silvered dial, made by J. Hardman & Co., 1851 (Palace of Westminster).

CHAPTER SEVENTEEN

The New Palace of Westminster

ALEXANDRA WEDGWOOD

A large part of Pugin's working life was dominated by Britain's greatest architectural commission of the century, the rebuilding of the Houses of Parliament, usually referred to by contemporaries as the New Palace of Westminster. In spite of its importance it was never made clear during his lifetime what the nature of his involvement was and how he collaborated with the acknowledged architect, Charles Barry. After his death it became the subject of bitter controversy, when the sons of the two men quarrelled.[1] The project began with the fire on 16 October 1834, which completely gutted the inadequate facilities in the centre of the site. This was made up of a jumble of medieval buildings with later piecemeal additions and included both Chambers. Inevitably such an event drew a great crowd of spectators, among whom were, separately, the two men to be most involved in the rebuilding, Charles Barry and the young Pugin.

Pugin gave a vivid description of what he saw and his opinions on the probable results to E.J. Willson in a letter on 6 November 1834:[2]

417. The Houses of Parliament, view from the Clock Tower looking over the roof of the House of Commons towards the Central Tower and the Victoria Tower, 1897. (Sir Benjamin Stone MP, Birmingham Reference Library).

You have doubtless seen the accounts of the late great conflagration at Westminster which I was fortunate enough to witness from almost the beginning till the termination of all danger as the hall has been saved, (which is to me almost miraculous as it was surrounded with fire). There is nothing much to regret and a great deal to rejoice in. A vast amount of Soane's mixtures and Wyatt's heresies have been effectively consigned to oblivion. Oh it was a glorious sight to see his composition mullions and cement pinnacles and battlements flying and cracking, while his 2.6 turrets were smoking like so many manufacturing chimneys till the heat showered them into a thousand pieces. The old walls stood triumphantly amidst this scene of ruin while brick walls and framed sashes slate roofs &c fell faster than a pack of cards. In fact the spread of the fire was truly astonishing. From the time of the House of Commons first taking fire till the flames were rushing out of every aperture it could not have been more than five or 6 minutes and the effect of the fire behind the tracery &c was truly curious and awfully grand. What is most to be regretted is the Painted Chamber, the curious paintings of which I believe are totally destroyed. I am afraid that the rebuilding will be made a complete job as that

418, 419. The House of Lords and the House of Commons, competition designs by J. Gillespie, Graham, 1835, watercolours by A.W. Pugin (Private Collection). These designs, including the wooden frames, are typical of Pugin's early, heavy style.

execrable designer Smirke has already been *giving* his opinions which may be reasonable supposed to be a preamble to his *selling* his diabolical plans and detestable details. If so I can contain myself no longer but, boldly to the attack, I'll write a few remarks on his past works and if he do not writhe under the lash his feelings must be harder than his cement, as if I spare him I hope I may sink myself. His career has gone on too long, and this will be a capital opportunity to show up some of his infamous performances.

Sir Robert Smirke, one of the architects attached to the Board of Works, had been called in by the Prime Minister and the First Commissioner of Woods and Works.[3] He quickly provided efficient temporary arrangements for both Houses and in November had been directed to prepare plans for rebuilding on a 'moderate and suitable magnitude'. This high-handed treatment of a commission of such importance, which had so annoyed Pugin, in fact provoked a general groundswell of opposition and, after much lobbying, on 3 June 1835 the Lords and Commons Committees for rebuilding had announced that the architect should be chosen by a competition, to which anyone might submit an entry, as long as it was in either the Gothic or Elizabethan style. This condi-

tion about the style, which must have thrilled Pugin, prompted a defence of classicism by the architectural historian, A.W. Hakewill.[4] Finally Pugin had the opportunity he had been waiting for since his letter to Willson to make a passionate argument in favour of the Gothic in the first of his publications to contain a text.[5] This pamphlet, which he wrote in August 1835, also showed that his plans for *Contrasts*, which was to be published a year later, were already far advanced.

It seems probable that Pugin never considered entering the competition himself; he had as yet no real experience as a practising architect, and he was in any case already[6] working as a draughtsman for two competitors, Charles Barry and James Gillespie Graham. His first recorded meeting with Charles Barry was on 18 April 1835[7] and over the next few months he designed internal details, fittings and furniture in a Gothic style for Barry's new building, the King Edward VI Grammar School, New Street, Birmingham.[8] He had known James Gillespie Graham since 1829[9] and during 1835 he made drawings for him of the chapel of St Margaret's Convent, Whitehouse Loan, Edinburgh, and probably made designs of Balnagowan Castle, Rosshire, and the chapel of Heriot's Hospital, Edinburgh.[10] Both Barry and Gillespie Graham must have been deeply impressed by Pugin's superb draughtsmanship at this date, by his great fluency with Gothic detail and, most importantly, by the speed at which he could work. They both decided that his help with the competition drawings was vital. Pugin recorded his work for each of them from September in his diary, which gives clear documentation, but otherwise he seems to have kept this odd situation to himself. As the deadline, originally November, then extended to December, approached, he was immensely busy.

Sadly Barry's prize-winning entry does not survive,[11] though copies of some parts of it do.[12] Also the three perspectives which Pugin drew for Gillespie Graham exist, and can be studied for evidence of his involvement. The interior of the House of Lords (plate 418) with its heavy emphasis on wood, an impression reinforced by the frame, seems to reflect Pugin's preoccupations and indeed his recent work in Birmingham. The view of the River Front reveals a broken-up composition produced by an irregular plan which may well contain some of Pugin's ideas. It was the opposite of Barry's strongly unified design and there can be no doubt that Barry's plan was his own. Its essential elements included the integration of the surviving medieval buildings, a single range on the River Front which contained residences, libraries and committee rooms, and the location of all the principal rooms on one unified floor, with the House of Commons in the northern half and the House of Lords in the southern. All these features exist in the completed building, despite countless modifications. It seems clear that Pugin was both surprised and impressed by Barry's ideas, with their careful balance between symmetry and asymmetry. A friend, Talbot Bury, later remembered that Pugin described Barry's work as 'a very remarkable design, the plan being most ingenious and comprehensive, and the elevations treated in a very original and effective manner',[13] which he characterised as giving 'an Italian outline to Gothic details.' This is a similar view to Pugin's well known judgement on the River Front: 'All Grecian, Sir; Tudor details on classic body,'[14] and indicates a fundamental difference in their approach. Pugin's contribution to Barry's design was his splendid and convincing draughtsmanship which undoubtedly influenced the lay judges. Barry may indeed have used this skill of Pugin's unscrupulously, because, in the controversy over the winning design, it was alleged that Barry included extra drawings illustrating the ornament to be used, in contravention of the published instructions.[15] In the absence of the competition drawings themselves, this effect can best be judged today by looking at Pugin's ideal schemes of the preceding year (plate 58).

Pugin seems to have been unmoved by Barry's victory, which was announced at the end of January 1836; at least, he did not record it in his diary. He did, however, visit the exhibition of the designs of all the competitors which was held at the National Gallery in April. Barry had been asked to make various modifications to his plan, which was recommended to Parliament for adoption in May. He was also asked to prepare drawings so that a detailed estimate could be made of the projected cost of the building. As a result Barry again asked Pugin to help him and this second period of collaboration lasted between August 1836 and the end of January 1837, during which time it formed his major preoccupation. The details are again clearly documented in Pugin's diaries.[16] The drawings thus produced are known as the 'Estimate Drawings', and every one identified appears to be in Pugin's hand. They were not intended for execution, but to enable the quantity surveyors to fix a price, by judging the style and extent of the work. The character of Pugin's assistance was different this time. A letter of 23 September 1836 from Barry[17] makes it clear that Pugin is being sent plans from which he is to make his own designs for details of elevations and fittings throughout the building. It must have been work which he greatly enjoyed, and it reveals much about his style in his early and most imaginative phase. The results were certainly appreciated, as was his speed of production: Barry wrote to him on 22 October[18] '. . . the drawings of the House of Lords, King's Stair etc. which came safely to hand last night, and

420. The House of Lords, design for the throne and its surrounding canopy, pen and ink drawing 1836 (Royal Institute of British Architects Drawings Collection).

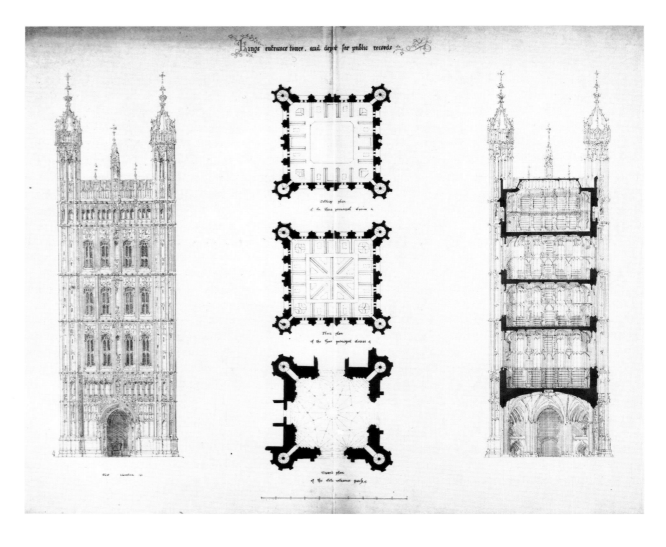

422. The King's Tower, design, pen and wash drawing, 1836 (Society of Antiquaries). This design was made by Pugin as part of a series on which the estimate for the building was based.

afforded me a rich treat. They will in all respects answer the purpose most admirably. I can easily imagine the great labour they must have cost you . . .' The original drawing for the throne and its canopy, a plan and elevation, survives (plate 420). The splendidly exuberant design, full of lively lions, has a wide ogee-arched centre with plenty of knobbly detail which has strong similarities with Pugin's nearly contemporary work at Scarisbrick Hall.[19] The richness of his vision for the exterior is demonstrated in another surviving drawing, his elevation for the King's Tower (later the Victoria Tower) (plate 422). He also produced a flamboyant design for the Clock Tower which includes metalwork canopies decorated with spiky stylised foliage motifs. Most of his designs survive in the many tracings[20] that were made of them by the appreciative young assistants working in Barry's office.

On 31 January 1837 Pugin wrote in his diary 'Finished at Mr. Barry's, drawings sent'. The estimate was then prepared from these drawings, and on 12 April a figure was finally agreed. Pugin's second period of collaboration on the project was at an end. There was indeed nothing for him to do, as a coffer-dam was first constructed, work on the river embankment and foundations followed, and much time was taken in selecting stone before even the first stone of superstructure was laid on 27 April 1840. Meanwhile 1837 proved an annus mirabilis for Pugin. In March he made his first visits to Scarisbrick Hall, Lancashire, and to St Mary's College, Oscott, near Birmingham.[21] He met John Hardman, the Birmingham metalwork manufacturer who was to become his closest friend and colleague in May. From October he enjoyed the patronage of John, 16th Earl of Shrewsbury. His career as an independent architect was launched; he had no need of Barry, as Barry had no need of him. Between August 1837 and September 1844 there is no documentary evidence in the diaries that the two men met. They remained friends, however, and, on the basis of a small collection of drawings with watermarks of 1841 which had remained until 1974 in the possession of the Barry family,[22] it is suggested here that during that period Pugin continued to offer Barry informal ideas and advice about suitable decorative details, especially for the main interiors. One of them is a preliminary design for the throne (plate 423). This version, which must have been made before the decision of the Royal Fine Arts Commission to place frescoes of history paintings at either end of the House of Lords, shows the throne and its canopy as a more sober version of the Estimate drawing, but with a projecting centre, making it a tripartite design. The drawing also shows the kind of stylised medieval wall paintings that Pugin, and probably Barry too, would have preferred to the history paintings.

This suggestion by Pugin, however, seems to have been an isolated one and Barry continued to work out the problems himself, as the building slowly developed west from the River Front. By the middle of 1844 he was struggling to complete his first main interior, the House of Lords, for the Peers were restive in their small temporary home. For all his ability to work out the essential elements of his design, he seldom drew rich Gothic details. He must also have feared that, unless he acted decisively, he would suffer further interference from the Royal Fine Arts Commission, who in 1843 had invited designs for decorative works, including the ornamental pavements, heraldic decorations, woodwork and stained glass for the New Palace. The entries had been exhibited in 1844 and, though they included Pugin's colleagues Minton and Crace, to judge from the illustrations of the work,[23] the vast majority were mediocre and ill-informed interpretations of Gothic forms. Barry was a perfectionist, who wanted to have control over all aspects of the interiors and their fixtures and fittings, and was determined to produce a great building. He turned to the one man who had the knowledge to help him.

It seems that Barry first approached Pugin again in June 1844.[24] Pugin was now a famous architect and writer, and he must have realised that at Westminster Barry would subject his work to alterations. The prestige of the project was, however, immense and it was at a moment when Pugin must have been depressed, less than a month after the death of his second wife, that Barry succeeded in persuading him. Barry's letter of invitation, written on 3 September 1844,[25] is known, andgives a most interesting picture of their relationship:

Dear Pugin, I am in a regular fix respecting the working drawings for the fittings and decora-

tions of the House of Lords, which it is of vital importance should now be finished with the utmost despatch. Although I have now made up my mind as to the principles, and, generally, as to the details of the designs for them, including a new design for the throne, which is at last perfectly satisfactory to me, I am unfortunately unable to get the general drawings into such a definite shape as is requisite for preparing the working details, owing to a lameness in one of my legs, which has laid me on my back . . . Now as I know of no one who can render me such valuable and efficient assistance, I am induced to write to you in the hope that you may be both able and willing to pass two or three days, or even a week, with me for the purpose of making out the drawings in question, and of enabling me to consult you generally, and enter into some permanent arrangement that will be satisfactory to you, as to occasional assistance for the future in the completion of the great work, as well as for the discharge of my obligations to you for what you have already done.

Pugin did go and visit him in Brighton between 12 and 16 September and Barry came to Ramsgate

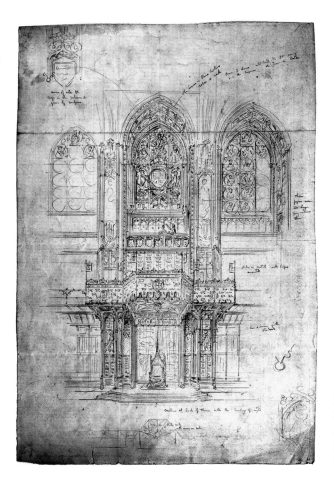

423. The House of Lords, preliminary design for the throne end, pencil drawing, c.1841 (Royal Institute of British Architects Drawings Collection).

424. Casts of medieval Perpendicular carvings from churches in King's Lynn, made *c*.1845 photograph *c*.1900 (House of Lords Library). The casts no longer exist.

between 7 and 10 November.[26] From then until his death, work at the New Palace of Westminster was to be one of Pugin's main concerns. They must have decided that Pugin should have some official standing and in December Barry completed arrangements with the Government for Pugin to be appointed to supervise the works of woodcarving at the New Palace, which were carried out at the Thames Bank Workshops.[27] Both men must have been aware of the potential hazards of the collaboration and the contents are known of an undated letter,[28] apparently of early 1845, in which Pugin sets out his conditions:

First, for the £200 a year, I agree to furnish drawings and instructions for all the carved ornaments in wood that may be required. Secondly, that all travelling expenses whatever in connection with the above work are to be paid extra to that sum. My residence being at Ramsgate, my journeys to London must be considered as travelling expenses, and paid accordingly, unless I am compelled to take the journey for other purposes not connected with the work. Thirdly, I am empowered to send persons to collect squeezes, etc., and all expenses connected with that object, or the purchase of original models, to be paid from time to time according to the accounts I will furnish you, and all journeys which I make for the purpose of finding out proper models. Fourthly, all drawings for glass, metal works and tiles, etc., will be paid for in the estimates for the same, according to the rates we agreed. Fifthly, you must include the expense of preparing these detail drawings in the estimate of the fittings and I will furnish you with the cost of them as you may require. Sixthly, I am only responsible to you in all matters connected with the work. I act as your agent entirely and have nothing to do with any other person.

There are many significant points in this statement. The emphasis on the woodcarvings indicates his primary responsibility, and the absence of any mention of stonecarvings clearly suggests that these were not his concern. The importance Pugin attached to the role of models of actual medieval work is most interesting. He wanted the carpenters to work surrounded by the best examples of the style he was aiming at. On 12 June 1845 he wrote to Barry, saying that he had sent a whole cart-load of casts to Westminster, and that he hoped when their present purpose was finished 'they may form the commencement of a great national gallery of Art.'[29] By March 1846 he had

built up in the Thames Bank Workshops a remarkable collection of more than 2000 casts[30] and a few actual wooden panels. Some of these wooden panels survive (plate 191) and some of the casts were photographed (plate 424). Much information about this collection exists in an inventory[31] made when the Thames Bank Workshops were closed. This helps to identify those areas of medieval Perpendicular carving that Pugin was looking at, with the majority of the casts coming from St Alban's cathedral and much from churches in Norfolk such as those at King's Lynn, Salle and Worstead, as well as, among others, a group from Amiens and another from Devon. Casts were taken of both stone and wood carving, with many of small details, like finials, crockets, cusp ends and pateras and some of larger items such as bench ends, carved panels and spandrels.

After the woodcarving, Pugin mentioned glass, metal works and tiles. It is obvious that Barry recognised the necessity for Pugin to work at Westminster, as he did on his own account, with that close group of colleagues, John Hardman, Herbert Minton and J.G. Crace, who understood his ways and who, most importantly, could interpret his rapid drawings. Anything else would have slowed the project immensely and Barry knew that he must prevent the Treasury sending schemes out to tender. Pugin's arrangements for payment suggest prudence, particularly given his small official salary, and his final stipulation was also eminently sensible, though it did perhaps lead to the true nature of his contribution being hidden. Barry, an efficient establishment figure, could protect Pugin from Parliamentary Committees and departmental enquiries of the Office of Woods and Works. This did not prevent, however, in 1845 the appearance of various articles questioning Pugin's

role in the architectural press[32] and cartoons in *Punch*.[33] To any practised eye Pugin's style was always distinctive.

The first priority, as Barry had stated, was the decoration of the House of Lords, with the design of the throne and of its canopy as its key feature (plate 425). This design is indeed a masterpiece, and has always been at the heart of the old quarrel about the respective contributions of Barry and Pugin. As such it has attracted much literary attention[34] and more is known about it than any other part of the building. It can to some extent therefore serve as an elaborate example of what generally took place in working out a design. As Barry had stated in his letter of 3 September 1844 to Pugin, he had finally decided on what he wanted: the canopy was to have a rectangular outline with a tripartite division and a raised central compartment. Pugin did not immediately accept this design and produced several alternatives.[35] His main scheme introduced a circular baldacchino with an elaborate superstructure over the throne (plate 426). This did not find favour with Barry. On 17 December 1844 he drew the chosen

elevations of the throne and the Strangers' Gallery at the other end of the Chamber on a contract drawing,[36] which no doubt incorporated ideas from both men, the result of their collaboration during the autumn, but Barry's views were paramount. Following this decision Pugin prepared the vivid and intricate detail drawings;[37] from these, contract drawings were made in Barry's office at Westminster, with some surviving ones dated 9 and 10 May 1845.[38] Barry, however, did not simply accept this magnificent design as it was. In his diary on 17 May 1845[39] Barry noted: 'HP at working drawings for Throne'. The same statement is made every day the following week and on 26 and 27 May, indicating the extent of his examination. There are indeed innumerable differences, mostly small but some significant, between the drawings and the executed work, such as replacing the angels carrying shields charged with the cross of St George, with statues of knights bearing the emblems of the five orders of chivalry.

Thus the design of the throne and its canopy was the result of Barry's outline, transformed by

quoted, Pugin went on to say: 'There will be upwards of 1000 detail drawings of ornaments for the carvings in the House of Lords alone . . . I have increased my shop at Ramsgate so that I shall be able to have all the figures and difficult parts modelled under my own eye.' Unfortunately none of these drawings seems to have survived and it also appears that most of the modelling for the carved wood was executed in London. John Birnie Philip (1824–75), the future sculptor, has left a good account[41] of what happened at Thames Bank:

> I was introduced by an eminent painter still living to the notice of Mr. Pugin, who engaged me to make models for the guidance of the numerous workmen engaged in executing the woodcarvings in the workshops at Thames Bank . . . The usual course was that Mr. Pugin visited the works, averaging certainly not oftener than once in a fortnight, leaving a great number of sketches executed during the few hours he was with us. Sir Charles Barry was in the habit of visiting the works two or three times in each weeks, or oftener; it continually happened on these visits that Sir Charles not only set aside and disapproved of Pugin's designs, but superseded them with designs made by himself.

In connection with this information it should be noted that it is impossible to learn when Pugin

426. The House of Lords, design for the throne and its canopy, pencil drawing by A.W. Pugin *c.*1844 (Royal Institute of British Architects Drawings Collection). Pugin's first ideas were quite different to Barry's.

427. The House of Lords, detail of the throne canopy showing the carved panelling behind the Prince of Wales's chair.

Pugin's marvellously fertile imagination, and then further refined by Barry's ideals of perfection. The quality of its execution was also outstanding (plates 201, 427), as was the carved woodwork on the ceiling and below the gallery in the Chamber. All in oak, either dark stained or gilded, it is in every way comparable to Pugin's fifteenth-century models. The organisation of the Thames Bank Workshops must have been excellent. The man in charge of the everyday work at Westminster, the 'Practical Superintendent', was Richard Bayne.[40] It seems that the carpenters selected for the carving were young men, perhaps because they would do what they were told. In whatever way it was done, an extraordinarily consistent style and high quality of work was produced. It can be observed that the less skilful carvers were used for the less prominent positions, such as the panelling in the gallery. In the undated letter of early 1845 already

with repeated inscription of 'Dieu et mon droit'. Each compartment contained four magnificent carved cartouches set in diamonds (plate 429). During the recent restoration of the ceiling it was discovered that several of these carvings had been signed by the craftsmen who had made them. They were clearly aware of the historical significance of their work.

As well as the wood fittings, Pugin designed the splendid furniture. He had been drawing thrones since 1835, most of them, like the executed version, closely based on the early fourteenth-century Coronation Chair in Westminster Abbey. He enlivened his design of it with strong linear carvings on the sides and, following indications on the original model, placed enamels decorated with heraldic lions on the back and crystals with trefoil patterns on the arms.[42] The upholstered x-frame consorts' chairs to either side had well known pro-

428. The House of Lords, one of the pair of brass candelabra beside the throne, by John Hardman. Pugin first designed them to be lit by gas, but this was altered to candles.

429. The House of Lords, the ceiling after its restoration in the early 1980s.

430. The House of Lords, the bench ends facing the throne, made in the Thames Bank Workshops.

visited Westminster, as he habitually made only the entry 'London' in his diary. The results, however, that they obtained were immensely impressive (plates 428 and 430). Particularly successful was the ceiling, which was divided into square compartments, surrounded by a pierced frieze

431.† The Prince's Chamber, an octagonal table. Two of these tables and sixteen x-frame chairs (plate 231) were designed by A.W. Pugin and made by John Webb. They were in place by April 1847.

432. The Peers' Lobby, looking towards the House of Lords. The great brass doors were made by John Hardman, and the encaustic tiles were made by Herbert Minton.

totypes in the sixteenth and seventeenth centuries. They and the throne were made by John Webb of Bond Street, who was both an antique dealer and a high-class cabinet maker, a contact of Pugin since at least 1837.[43] Webb also made the impressive Clerk's Table which stands in the centre of the Chamber (plate 250). It is almost square, with four legs to each side, a curious design whose symbolism was explained in the contemporary literature: 'They [the legs] are connected with each other by a deeply moulded bar, and bars stretch across from foot to foot having sunken panels between them, so as to convey in plan the general character of a portcullis – intended to represent the ancient arms of Westminster.'[44] The furniture in the Prince's Chamber was also part of this commission for Webb and consisted of two octagonal tables and sixteen chairs (plate 431), as well as two clock cases, all in oak.[45] Pugin had a particular love of octagonal tables and designed them throughout his life, always producing variations. The tables in the Prince's Chamber are among his most successful and important. The ogee braces to the legs show Pugin's deep understanding of timber framing, and the balance of the carved decoration is perfectly judged. The chairs (plate 231), with the x placed on the side and lion heads to either side at the back, are equally splendid.

After the woodwork the gorgeous examples of brasswork form the next most important surviving features of Pugin's fittings in the House of Lords,

though some have been removed and others altered. Brasswork had been a particular love of Pugin's ever since his first visit to Nuremberg, a medieval centre of the craft, in 1834. From 1838 he had persuaded John Hardman to manufacture metalwork, especially for ecclesiastical purposes, to his designs,[46] but the setting of the House of Lords, where the colour of brass was especially appropriate, gave him a whole range of new opportunities. The major items were the great pierced doors from the Peers' Lobby to the Chamber (plate 432), the massive candelabra by the throne (originally there were also candelabra on the bar, at the other end of the Chamber), and the railing to the gallery. Unlike the woodwork there were usually no close medieval precedents, but occasionally an example inspired him such as the early sixteenth-century bronze gates to Henry VII's Chapel in Westminster Abbey. These perform a similar function to the ones in the Peers' Lobby, and their design and motifs were also generally followed in the iron gates to the Victoria Tower. Usually the light fittings were designed to cope with the new technology of gas, but this caused no difficulties for Pugin, whose knowledge of medieval forms was so profound that he could always adapt them to new uses. He used quite a small repertoire of motifs and kept consistently to the 'True Principles' that he had declared in his book of 1841, placing his decorative detail so that it enriched, but never masked, the structure of the object. The impressive results of this policy can be seen in the rich and powerful design for the doors to the House of Lords. There were, however, many difficulties in the manufacture of the brasswork, particularly the railing, largely as a result of Barry's changes of mind, which are recorded in Pugin's constant letters to Hardman, where he could be very frank.[47] Early in 1845, probably on 26 February, for instance, he wrote:[48]

I now find that we shall have to begin quite afresh with the railing for last night Mr. Barry altered all the rose work at [the] bottom & we must start quite a new pattern. He is aware of the great loss of dies &c for I explained it to him & he says he can't be helped for he must have it perfection to his mind. I shall now have to send you an entirely fresh drawing. What vexes me most is the loss of time especially as the great gates of the House are to be made *entirely of brass* and these I am also at work at for you . . . You have no idea how I am harrassed (sic) just now. All this is a great charge in addition to other things especially as I have others to

433.† Stained glass window of William the Conqueror, a trial piece for the House of Lords.

please besides myself. The carvers have started & all that is in full swing. The moment the railing is quite to Mr. B[arry's] mind you may put as much strength as you like or can on it. Take care of all the old patterns as they will come very well for some Candlestics (sic) &c I have in my eye & you will get paid for them besides so it will not be lost time.

From this letter it appears that the gallery railing was the first piece of metalwork to be designed. Many of the problems were caused by uncertainty about the means of lighting to be used. At first the railing was designed so that it could accommodate gas fittings but these were abandoned by November 1846 for gas branches which sprang from the bases of the niches on the walls above the gallery. These branches, which no longer exist, followed the recommendations made by Michael Faraday and were not made by Hardman, and probably not designed by Pugin.[49] The final decision was that, though the gallery might be illuminated by gas, the floor of the Chamber was to be lit only by candles. This necessitated adding more branches to the candelabra and inevitably, and most unusually for Pugin, resulted in a cluttered appearance instead of clear flowing lines (plate 428). Later alterations have also resulted in the loss of the original subtle touches of colour on some of the brasswork. Enamel paint was used on the uprights to each compartment of the gallery railing to give a carefully organised sequence of coloured motifs, but the central one has now gone, destroying the overall pattern. Red enamel was also painted on the engraved brasses which were set as a border to the marble Tudor rose in the centre of the floor of the Peers' Lobby, but has been worn away.

Pugin and Barry saw stained glass as an important component in the decoration of their principal interiors, and the House of Lords received the most elaborate programme. The subject was chosen by the Royal Fine Arts Commission and consisted of standing figures under canopies of English and Scottish monarchs and their consorts between William I and Victoria.[50] The probable prototype for the scheme was the impressive sixteenth-century glass in the west window of St George's Chapel, Windsor. Sadly the glass in the Lords was destroyed during the Second World War and has been replaced with a different scheme. Pugin had always used stained glass as a decorative feature in his churches, but he had difficulties with various stained glass manufacturers, who were often unable to produce the results he wanted.[51] At the beginning of his involvement

with the decoration of the House of Lords Pugin was using for his stained glass William Wailes of Newcastle-upon-Tyne, but it was perhaps partly due to his lack of whole-hearted commitment to this firm that this was the one area where the Fine Arts Commission was responsible for giving the work in the summer of 1845 to the successful candidate from its 1843 competition. The unhappy results of this commission clearly revealed Barry's wisdom in keeping all the decorative work under his control and using only one designer, Pugin. The winners of the competition were Ballantine and Allan, an Edinburgh firm, and their sketch designs for the House of Lords windows survive.[52] The fussiness and weakness of the figures and the lack of understanding of the Gothic motifs filling the tracery shown in these drawings make it clear why Barry had no hesitation in rejecting their full-size cartoons during the early months of 1846. Barry's solution was to have the cartoons redrawn by a 'first rate artist' of his own choosing (Pugin), even though this involved an additional expense of £84 a window.[53] Ballantine and Allan were still to manufacture the glass, but in order to make doubly sure Barry got Hardman to make the first window, to serve as a model for them. Towards the middle of 1845 Pugin, who no doubt wanted to solve his own difficulties with glass as much as those at Westminster, had persuaded Hardman to add the making of stained glass to his business. This model window contained the figures of William the Conqueror, William Rufus, Henry I and Stephen with their respective consorts, and it was in place by April 1847, as were Hardman's windows with heraldic motifs in the Peers' Lobby and the Prince's Chamber[54] and figured quarries and inscriptions in the Division Lobbies. With the exception of the remainder of the windows in the House of Lords, which were not completed until September 1850, Hardman made all the stained glass in the Houses of Parliament. Recently a single specimen light, containing the figure of William the Conqueror, probably the work of Ballantine and Allan, has been discovered at Westminster (plate 433). This somewhat heavy and solemn design seems to be the sole surviving piece from which to judge the scheme, apart from partial views in some paintings (plate 434). The windows must have made a major contribution to the overall effect.

Apart from this glass, Barry and Pugin succeeded by April 1847 in completing the furniture and fittings of the House of Lords, together with those of the Peers' Lobby and the Prince's Chamber to either side, (plate 431) though there were still many gaps among the 'Fine Arts' items of fresco paintings and sculpture not under Barry's control. At the opening their achievement was received with universal praise. The building was seen to complement the balanced parliamentary regime which it housed and immediately became the source of great national pride. The descriptions given in the *Illustrated London News*[55] were repeated in the first guide books, where it was called 'without doubt the finest specimen of Gothic civil architecture in Europe: its proportions, arrangement and decoration, being perfect, and worthy of the great nation at whose cost it has been erected.' Hardman's work was mentioned with approval,[56] and so was that of John Webb, J.G. Crace and Herbert Minton.[57] Pugin's name is not mentioned in any account. 1846 had been an unhappy year for him and he had been very hard pressed to get the House of Lords open. His friends, especially Lord Shrewsbury and Ambrose Phillipps, urged him to go to Italy and on 26 March 1847 he set out on his longest continental tour.

Pugin had been in contact with Minton, the pottery manufacturer in Stoke-on-Trent, since at least 1840 and within a few years Minton's encaustic tiles were being used extensively in all Pugin's work, both ecclesiastical and domestic.[58] Pugin must quickly have persuaded Barry that these tiles would make the most suitable and hard-wearing surface for those main areas of the New Palace which were not to be carpeted. Together they visited Minton's factory on 2 October 1845.[59] The first pavement which was completed with his tiles was that for the Peers' Lobby (plate 432), where the main tiles are rather larger than usual. These designs emphasise Pugin's brilliance as a pattern maker using only two colours. The patterns are always balanced yet vivid, and the colours are rich and dark, blue, red-brown and chocolate-brown, all offset with a warm beige.

The final member of Pugin's team of colleagues at Westminster was J.G. Crace, the head of a well-known firm of decorators with premises at 14 Wigmore Street. It is not known exactly when the two men met, but Crace's relationship with Pugin is exceptionally well documented from 1844,[60] when he was in charge of the decorative work at Pugin's own house. The Grange, Ramsgate. His appointment at the Houses of Parliament in 1845, where he started work in the House of Lords on all the decorative painting, the ceiling panels, the reveals of the windows, the heraldic cove to the gallery, and the throne canopy, was made officially by Barry,[61] but must have been due to Pugin's recommendation. Pugin's correspondence again illustrates the way in which they worked together

on the project. In a letter of 1846 he writes:[62]

Things will be very active at the New Palace forthwith. I am preparing sketches which Mr. B. will forward to you for pounces for another ceiling and I have strongly urged the necessity of getting all the patterns ready for the cove in the House [of Lords]. They will be done a good deal like the rough sketch I leave but I will send you up a detail sketch and then I think you better do one *at once*. You will be obliged to draw out FS the various shields that are to be painted about the throne and the sooner these are done the better, it will all be so much ad-

434.† *The House of Lords, State Opening of Parliament 1851*, gouache painting by Joseph Nash (Palace of Westminster Collection).

435. *The House of Lords, the Home Rule debate of 1893*, oil painting by Dickinson and Foster (Palace of Westminster Collection). Above the gallery can be seen the original stained glass with the standing figures of monarchs.

436. The Peers' Lobby, the ceiling taken after its restoration in the early 1990s. The woodwork was painted by J.G. Crace.

fittings, including candlesticks, gas branches and gas pendants, mostly in brass, but also cast iron grates, and all made by John Hardman; and much excellent furniture, probably still made by John Webb. The textiles, carpets and curtains were supplied by Crace,[64] though it is not known who manufactured them. He had already, by 1847, supplied the dramatic carpet for the throne. In the Libraries and some of the Refreshment Rooms a number of designs for fabrics has survived. The harmonious effect that Barry wanted and Pugin could produce in these interiors, where every detail has been carefully considered, can still be appreciated.

As the decoration continued, the need for wallpapers arose. It seems that Pugin started to design wallpapers for J.G. Crace in 1847,[65] though his principles for such two-dimensional patterns had been powerfully stated and illustrated already in 1841.[66] Again it is not known who was responsible for the manufacture but Crace clearly handled all the technical side. One of Pugin's first wallpapers seems to have been always intended for Westminster and did indeed become widely used there.[67] Crace kept all the drawings that Pugin made for his use at the Houses of Parliament separate from the others and this, together with a surviving pattern book of wallpapers supplied there between 1851 and 1859,[68] provides a great deal of information about the original decoration of different rooms. Pugin's wallpapers were always designed with the scale of their locations in mind, and he worked in three sizes, small, medium and large. His smallest patterns, always stylised floral motifs, give diapered effect; indeed the best known of these is called the 'Crace diaper' (plate 217). Many of the medium and large patterns are based on fifteenth-century Italian textile designs incorporating pineapple or pine-cone motifs and a strong ogee stem which gives a firm structure to the pattern. As always Pugin could supply several variations on a theme, but in this respect it should be noted that he was always economical with his colours: a recurring note on his drawings is 'These patterns should be worked in 2 colour reds or 2 colour greens.'[69] Here, as in all other aspects of his work at Westminster, he produced many designs which were ultimately rejected by Barry. In this category fall a number of papers with 'historical' motifs connected with various medieval monarchs, which Pugin made early in 1851. Some of these designs were adapted, however, and one pattern including the Tudor rose, a portcullis and the initials 'VR' and another with the Tudor rose, a lion passant gardant and the initials 'VR' (plate 439)

vanced. The ceiling &c in the chamber next the House of Lords [either the Prince's Chamber or the Peers' Lobby] will be next done.

Crace's painted ceiling panels in the Peers' Lobby (plate 436) have recently been sensitively restored and give an excellent impression of the original work.

Pugin returned from his Italian tour in the middle of June 1847, but he remained very restless for the remainder of the year. The work at Westminster continued, of course, unabated. Apart from the two Chambers, it is difficult to know precisely when the various parts of the building were completed and in some cases it seems that rooms were used in an unfinished state.[63] The Libraries (plates 437, 438) and Refreshment Rooms on the River Front followed soon after the House of Lords. The elements of their decoration were much the same as before: splendid oak carvings made in the Thames Bank Workshops; stencilled ceiling panels painted by J.G. Crace; complex double hinges for swing doors, endless finger-plates and light

were widely used.[70] There was an overlap between wallpapers and textiles with some of the same patterns being used for each. He also designed carpets to the same principles, using similar scales and colours, with some particularly dense small patterns for corridors.[71]

It is remarkable how efficient Pugin's colleagues were in supplying high quality fittings. Minton's factory for example seems to have had no difficulty in providing the large number of encaustic tiles required, even those of unparalleled size and complexity in the Central Lobby which Pugin designed late in 1851,[72] where a surprising green colour makes an appearance. It seems that Pugin was delighted with his work; Ferrey quotes him[73] writing to Minton in January 1852: 'I declare your St Stephen's tiles the finest done in the tile way; vastly superior to any ancient work; in fact they are the best tiles in the world, and I think my patterns and your work go ahead of anything!' Hardman too provided substantial quantities of metalwork, and also had the difficult task of making satisfactory stained glass, which required numerous specimens and alterations. By the end of 1852 all the glass for the House of Commons and its lobbies was in place, also that for the Upper and Lower Waiting Halls, Members' staircase and adjacent rooms, Lords' corridors, the Upper and Lower Cloisters and many internal lights.[74] After the House of Lords, nearly all the major schemes were for heraldic glass, with figured quarries and borders and badges for the minor ones. An unusual range of motifs, however, appeared in the glass for the cloisters, which was destroyed in 1941, where Pugin drew attention to the pre-refor-

mation history of the place with some specifically Catholic symbols like the wounds of Christ. A more characteristic and well preserved example, actually made after Pugin's death, is that on the Public Staircase, where the iconography is devoted to the Black Prince (plate 440). The stained glass, however, was the one aspect of the decoration which proved to be unpopular from an early stage, with complaints from some Members about the lack of light.[75] In 1863 the coloured glass in the Lords and Commons corridors was taken out and sent back to Hardman, who repeated the design in

437. The Library of the House of Lords, Brougham Room, 1897.

438. The Library of the House of Commons, C Room, 1897. (Sir Benjamin Stone MP, Birmingham Reference Library).

439. The Prime Minister's Room *c.*1903, (Farmer Collection, House of Lords Records Office).

grisaille,[76] and there are indications that at about the same time alterations were made to the glass in the Royal Gallery.[77] Much more glass was destroyed in the Second World War, or removed or altered subsequently, but a surprising amount, including internal lights, still exists.

The large quantity of furniture needed led to several firms being used. In November 1850 Pugin drew a sketch in a letter to Crace of what became the standard chair throughout the building:[78]

> Mr. Barry wants a Pattern chair made for the commons lobbies. His idea is a light but strong chamfered chair like the above sketch covered in green leather & [sketch of a crowned portcullis] stamped on the back. Will you get one of them for Mr. Barry to see forthwith. Of course the nails must show [sketch of a large domeheaded nail in the shape of a cinquefoil flower].

Crace's involvement with furniture for Westminster was, however, probably a minor one. In the 1850s the two major cabinet making firms in the country, Gillow[79] and Holland and Son,[80] had large tenders for the Houses of Parliament accepted.

The House of Commons, which was destroyed in 1941, was of course the second most important interior, though always planned as slightly smaller and less glamorous than the House of Lords. It was ready to open in May 1850. Members, however, who were used to their comfortable temporary home, were immediately critical of their new facilities, particularly of the provision of seating, the lack of space in the division lobbies and the inadequate acoustics. After much inconclusive discussion Barry was forced to enlarge the galleries and the division lobbies, and to lower the ceiling of the Chamber, thus cutting the height of the windows in half.[81] These substantial alterations represented the main setback that Barry received to his plans for the building, and they were not completed until early 1852. The prevailing impression then (plates 441 and 442) must have been of dark carved wood, relieved only by the stained glass windows containing the arms of municipal boroughs,[82] and the painted ceiling panels. There was much less colour than in the House of Lords, with no frescoes or sculpture. Barry had originally proposed to decorate the cove to the gallery with the armorial bearings of the Speakers in colour on a gold ground, matching those of the Lord Chancellors in the House of Lords.[83] This scheme appears to have been abandoned in the general mood of annoyance at the expense and length of time that the rebuilding was taking.[84] The wider gallery resting on carved columns also contributed to the heavier effect. There were compensations for Barry, however, and on 11 February 1852, shortly after the state opening of Parliament, when both Houses were in use for the first time, he was knighted in recognition of his achievement at the New Palace.[85] At about the same date Pugin's final illness began and he was prevented from further work before his death.

So far discussion has centred on Pugin's interiors; his contribution to the exterior is harder to judge. Among specific details for which he was definitely responsible are the metal vanes and cresting to the roofs which Hardman was already manufacturing by April 1845.[86] It is much more difficult to be certain about his role in the design of the clock tower, the central tower and the Victoria Tower, which are crucial elements in punctuating the outline of the Houses of Parliament. It would seem that Barry habitually asked his advice about them. On 14 June 1851 he wrote[87] 'I enclose a rough tracing of the flying buttresses of the central tower and shall be glad of your advice and assistance respecting them at your earliest convenience.' He asked what to do about animal statues which decorated the architecture: 'Should they all hold bannerets, or labels, or shields, or what treatment of them would you advise?' Later on the same day Barry wrote again:[88] 'In my note of this morning I forgot to ask you your opinion of the mode of filling up the pannels (sic) flanking the open galleries between the windows of the Victoria Tower.' In the case of the clock tower it is known that Barry had great difficulty working out how to make the clock prominent,[89] and it is generally assumed that his solution, with a projecting clock storey surmounted by steeply sloping concave roofs, was taken from the prototype that Pugin had designed at Scarisbrick Hall in 1837.[90] It seems fair to claim that Pugin's ideas permeate the whole exterior of the building.

The ultimate proof of the key role that Pugin played as designer at the Houses of Parliament may be seen by what happened after his collapse early in 1852 and his death in September of that year. With the exception of the fitting up of the Speaker's House in the late 1850s, and those decorations and fittings designed by E.M. Barry in the 1860s, particularly the Crypt Chapel and the Robing Room, no new ideas were introduced in the interiors. In particular no new wallpapers appeared. The few textiles that Pugin had worked out were endlessly repeated. Ceilings were no longer stencilled, though this may have been the result of a general move to economy. Minton's work was more or less complete, and Hardman continued to work variations of both glass and metalwork from the drawings which Pugin had made for him over the years. It is, however, significant that he did not feel that he could produce an enormous chandelier for the Central Lobby without his friend's help, and in 1855 he put together a great corona instead,[91] surely an easier option. Much furniture was still needed, and bookcases, desks, tables and chairs were produced by Gillow

442. *The House of Commons, looking towards the Speaker's Chair*, 1858, gouache by Joseph Nash (Palace of Westminster Collection). This picture shows the House of Commons, finally opened in February 1852, at night.

and Holland, closely modelled on Pugin's designs. The only places where something different was produced were the residences, particularly the Speaker's House, which clearly called for a special effort. Though grand and sumptuous, the furniture and fittings there[92] lack Pugin's subtlety. Nowhere is this more obvious than in the heavy and lumpy woodwork for the State Bed.

The clarity of Pugin's work belied its originality and subtle individuality, which made it very hard to imitate. The perfect balance between structure and ornament had become instinctive to him and in an extraordinary way complemented Barry's careful proportions. It was a partnership of equals. Barry's requests and interventions seem to have inspired him, and given him unparalleled opportunities to work on a magnificent scale, far away from medieval precedent, combining grandeur with functionalism, in a range of objects from the throne in the House of Lords to umbrella stands, dispatch boxes and gas candelabra. The splendid results remain in the Palace of Westminster.

CHAPTER EIGHTEEN

The Mediæval Court

ALEXANDRA WEDGWOOD

All Pugin's working life was devoted to propaganda for his twin causes of the Gothic style and the Catholic faith. In the decorative arts he felt that, with the help of his colleagues John Hardman, Herbert Minton, J.G. Crace and George Myers, he could achieve much to improve design. It was inevitable that they should all look on the proposal for 'The Great Exhibition of the Works of Industry of All Nations' to be held in London in 1851 as a splendid opportunity to promote this cause – and their businesses.

Principally Hardman, but also Crace and Minton, had already collaborated with Pugin at the Birmingham Exhibition of Manufactures, which was held in September 1849 (plate 443), and most closely of all such British events in the early nineteenth century resembled the plan devised for the Great Exhibition. Henry Cole, who, together with Prince Albert, was one of the leading figures for the organisation of the London exhibition, praised their work at Birmingham in his *Journal of Design and Manufactures*,[1] and Pugin felt that the effort had been worthwhile. He wrote:[2] 'Our exposition at Birmingham was very creditable, has attracted a deal of attention, and done much good.'

In January 1850 a Royal Commission was established to organise the exhibition and all Pugin's group, this time also including Myers, were soon discussing what they should do. The decision for a group exhibit must have been made early on, though by doing so they combined several of the different classes into which the exhibition was organised. It looks as if they were making an unusual and difficult request: Pugin wrote to Crace on 4 March 1850:[3] 'I suppose they will publish a notice for the exhibitors to state what room they require – that seems to me the time for making the application and if they refuse it there is an end of the matter – I have no idea of begging and praying as if we [were] after a pension.' Again that month he wrote to him:[4] 'I send you up a plan and section of the sort of Room we want at the exposition and the adjoining space for your things. I am quite against sending any view of what we propose to do. If we should [get] space with [i.e. we] require it is quite sufficient – rely on it the quieter we keep about what we shall put into it the better, or there will be some vile *imitation* got up.'

Their exhibit eventually appeared under Class

(Altar Plate, manufactured by Hardman and Co.; Silk Hanging by Crace and Son London.)

443. Some of John Hardman's and J.G. Crace's exhibits at the Birmingham Exhibition of Manufactures, 1849, an engraving in *The Journal of Design and Manufactures*, II, 1849, p. 52.

XXVI which was classified as 'Decorative furniture and upholstery, paper hangings, papier maché and japanned goods.'[5] Minton's main exhibit, however, was in Class XXV, ceramics, and he also exhibited other encaustic tiles in Class XXVII, Manufactures in mineral substances for building or decorations. Hardman also exhibited in Class XXII, which was for general hardware including locks and grates, and Crace exhibited Italianate decorations elsewhere.[6] Myers was apparently only in the Mediæval Court, a good catchy name like the 'Crystal Palace', which was in use by March 1851. Pugin's colleagues were certainly prominent in the organisation of the exhibition as a whole; Minton and Hardman were both members of the Committee for Manufactures (Section III) and Crace was a juror for awarding prizes in Class XXVI, and Pugin was one for Class XXX (Sculpture, models and plastic art).[7] They were rewarded with one square bay, one of the main units of exhibition space, in an excellent location, just north of the central axis.[8]

During 1850 a major preoccupation for each member of the group was working on the items for their exhibit. On 1 January 1851 Pugin could inspect the Crystal Palace. He was not very impressed and wrote to Crace:[9] 'I went to the Vert Monstre today . . . The building appears to me a great failure, the great Length should have been *archd*. The transept is not half so important – it is a capital place for *plants*. What is it? A large greenhouse, very ingenious, a great credit to inventors, wonderful mechanism &&c but a beastly place to show off gothic work.' This view is interestingly close to that of Ruskin who wrote:[10] 'The quantity of thought it expresses is, I suppose, a single and admirable thought . . . – that it might be possible to build a greenhouse larger than ever greenhouse was built before.' By the end of January Pugin was planning where to place objects in their court[11] and by March he was discussing its decoration with Crace.[12]

From at least 1 March Hardman had one of his employees, Thomas Earley, installed in London to organise his part of the exhibit. The delightful letters[13] that he wrote to Hardman and to William Powell, Hardman's brother-in-law, give an excellent impression of the chaotic atmosphere in and around the building in the two months before the official opening on 1 May. On 1 March he wrote to Hardman:

> I met Mr Pugin at Mr Myers yard and after some trouble got admitted into the *Great Babel*. I found our Goods had come into the place but no one knew where to find them. Mr Pugin and I after an hours search discovered them stowed away among a multitude of other goods. Then came the difficulty how to get them into our departments as no one is admitted without [a pass] and only having one I could not employ men from outside. [This was solved by a small bribe to a soldier.] . . . Mr Pugin desires everything to [be] push'd along as quick as possible – Myers's people are fixing Dr Walsh's Tomb and a great quantity of stonework is ready for fixing on the spot.

On 31 March he wrote to Powell:

> There has a lot of cases arrived at Camden Town for us but I cannot state how many until they are delivered here which is a very tedious process for there are now outside the building more than a Mile of Waggons with Goods and each one has to wait his turn. Myers's man had to wait upwards of 5 hours before he could come in with a load of stone. Minton's flooring tiles are come and the tiles for the stoves will be here tomorrow afternoon.

There were, however, other difficulties and the deep controversy and antipathy often stirred up by Pugin's work is revealed in the following episode at the end of March. It seems that the evangelical Arthur Kinnaird saw the Great Rood from the screen at St Edmund's College, Ware, raised up high above the Mediæval Court and complained to Lord Ashley who passed on his fears to the Prime Minister, Lord John Russell, and Prince Albert. The background to this 'Protestant alarm' was the current acrimonious debate in Parliament on the Ecclesiastical Titles Bill which aimed to prevent the restoration of the Catholic hierarchy. Lord Granville, President of the Board of Trade, set out to calm things down and wrote to Lord Ashley with information to forward to Kinnaird on 20 March:[14]

> . . . a space was allotted to Pugin, Hardman, another whose name I forget, Minton and Crace which they have named a Mediæval Court. The only thing that has been brought into this court is a Cross, not a Crucifix, which was in the first instance placed as Arthur Kinnaird saw it. An intimation was sent to Mr Pugin that it could not remain there at a height which was inconsistent with the regulations. I have seen Mr Pugin this morning, who so far from objecting to this order, says that it was placed by a foreman who wished to save room, at an elevation where the wood carving would not have been well seen. It is now down and he proposes to put it in a corner . . . One side of this Court will be hung with Ecclesiastical ornaments, the other

three sides with Domestic furniture, and in the middle there will be a mixture of Fonts, stoves, flowerpots, armchairs, sofas tables &c &c, which I hope will give it a sufficiently secular character – the whole will be surrounded by a Frieze with the heraldic bearings of those who have bought largely Mediæval furniture.

Pugin's version of this incident also exists:[15]

We have just escaped a regular break up of our exhibition. If I had not been in London I don't know what would have happened. It appears that beast Lord Ashley went to the Exhibition & saw our great cross up and immediately sent to Lord J. Russell to say that a Popish chapel was being erected inside the exhibition. Lord J wrote to the executive committee & a regular row got up. Fortunately I saw them all this morning & Lord Granville of the Board of Trade who was exceedingly kind & said he was quite ashamed of the thing but the bigotry was so tremendous that they were anxious to keep as quiet as possible. I told them that if they objected to it *as a cross* I could not exhibit anything at all but they said by no means but only on exceeding the line in height. I have set [it] on the back of the Platform & it really is better seen as the great light all round obscured it before.

Henry Cole also felt that it was necessary to defend Pugin's position and he published a helpful plan in the *Journal of Design and Manufactures* and wrote:[16] 'On the south side of the Central Avenue will be the Mediæval Court, which will excite great notice . . . The accompanying diagram shews the arrangement of this court, and will remove the erroneous impression that Mr Pugin intended to erect a Roman Catholic chapel in the exhibition.' The Rood, however, does indeed seem to have been pushed into the background and is scarcely visible in most views. In the splendid lithograph which Myers commissioned (plate 444), he rearranged those exhibits executed by him, and it can be clearly seen, but without the figures of Christ and St John and St Mary intended for it. They must have been removed in deference to Protestant sensibilities. The unusual character of the Mediæval Court is emphasised by this story.

Preparations continued at a frantic pace during April, with many interruptions caused by the arrival of important visitors. On 16 April Earley wrote to Hardman: 'A very important event in my life occurr'd yesterday, no less, only think, a Dirty painter holding conversation with our Sovereign Lady the Queen for some five minutes or more.

444.† View of the objects in the Mediæval Court which were made by George Myers, lithograph of 1851, probably by L. Haghe (Myers Family Trust). Note the Great Rood from St Edmund's College, Ware, shown without the figures of Christ and St Mary and St John.

She was pleased to express her pleasure at the Beautiful things in our place, especially the tomb.' By the end of the month everything was in place. On 27 April Earley wrote to Powell: 'The Mediæval Court now begins to assume a very imposing appearance and has already become a great attraction as every person of note makes application at the Door to be admitted to *Pugin's Court* as it is called by them. Lord John Russell and Mr Pugin had a Conference in the court for 3/4 hour yesterday. The Premier expressed his delight at the Beautiful production of our manufactory.' After the opening Queen Victoria came again on 7 May. Crace wrote to Hardman:[17]

I had the pleasure this morning to receive the Queen and Prince &c in the Mediæval Court – quite unexpectedly – . . . she much admired all the things – especially the plate and the Corona for Wilton – she further asked if the large book-case with brass gates was sold – she asked who the Monumental Tomb was of – and asked who Dr Walsh was – The Prince admired the Papers and Carpets – I hope I did justice to Mr Pugin and yourself for I specially mentioned both names – Mr Minton was also in the Court having had a hint from the Duchess of Sutherland – and helped to talk to the Queen.

Each side of the Court was surmounted by a label identifying the four participants and their businesses. The general impression given by the

445. View of the Mediæval Court, engraving in *The illustrated London News*, XIX, 1851, p. 361.

446. The Mediæval Court, engraving in *The Illustrated Exhibitor*.

THE CRYSTAL PALACE.—THE MEDIÆVAL COURT.—(see next page)

The Illustrated Exhibitor.—No. V.

THE MEDIÆVAL COURT. DRAWN BY W. H. PRIOR.

Mediæval Court is well conveyed by contemporary illustrations (plates 445–7). They certainly confirm the crowded impression, 'the sensation of huddling together', which the *Illustrated London News* commented on.[18] Pugin in fact had considerable difficulty in keeping the peace among his colleagues as they all struggled to display their pieces to best advantage. He wrote to Crace in May:[19] 'Both myself and Hardman are greatly distressed at the annoyance you experience from Myers absurd conduct . . . Hardman says he will move his lectern to the other side and make room for the cabinet by the cross if that would be more satisfactory to Myers.' But there was encouraging news too: 'I hear on all sides the highest opinion of the Court.' Crace, however, seems to have continued to feel aggrieved at his treatment and Pugin wrote him another conciliatory letter:[20] 'I attach as much importance to the furniture as anything in the Place. In fact it is all one Concern.' He suggested moving the second stove to Minton's other stand in the Exhibition and this seems to have been done.

All the exhibitors were of course encouraged by the nature of the event to send in large and elaborate pieces and that seems to have been true also in the Mediæval Court. Myers's exhibits of the wooden Great Rood and Dr Walsh's tomb (plate 372) which was planned for St Chad's Cathedral, Birmingham, have already been mentioned. These two pieces exemplify, in wood and stone respectively, the stunning quality of the carving which Myers could achieve. For their exhibits, much clearly depended on the work that they had in hand and what they could persuade clients to lend. Thus Myers exhibited several pieces just made for the Roman Catholic church of St David at Pantasaph which had been commissioned by Lord Feilding. These consisted of the niche with the statue of the Virgin and Child, a copy of which is in the Pugin chantry at St Augustine's, Ramsgate, the High Altar, and the altar and reredos with the Annunciation from the Lady Chapel (plate 450). The enormous and elaborate font and tabernacle came from Pugin's own church, as well as part of the oak screen to the Pugin chantry. Myers also showed a portion of the staircase (plate 448) which had been designed by Pugin for Francis Barchard's house, Horsted Place, Sussex. The house was under construction at this date. It was designed by Samuel Dawkes and built by Myers. A large and elaborate fireplace (plate 449) destined for this house was also exhibited at the Mediæval Court. Francis Barchard, however, rejected it and,

448. The staircase at Horsted Place, Sussex, designed for Francis Barchard and made by George Myers.

449. The Fireplace in the Great Hall, Lismore Castle. It was made by George Myers for Francis Barchard, who rejected it.

450.† Reredos for the Lady Chapel and the High Altar, Roman Catholic church of St David, Pantasaph, lithograph in M. Digby Wyatt, *The Industrial Arts of the XIX Century, from the Great Exhibition of 1851*, 1853, pl.142. These pieces were both carved by George Myers.

with the emblems altered, it ended up in the Great Hall in Lismore Castle. Myers also contributed some pieces of furniture, including cabinets.

The chief supplier of furniture in Pugin's group was, however, J.G. Crace and no doubt there was some professional rivalry between Crace and Myers. Crace also supplied several massive pieces. One of these was the cabinet (plate 249), some-times also called a bookcase, which was purchased from the Exhibition by the Board of Trade for £154, and is now in the Victoria & Albert Museum. The shields in the top cresting bear Crace's initials and emblems and Pugin charmingly explained the iconography in a letter of April 1851:[21] 'The shields for the bookcase refer to you. 1. The 2 with initials. 2. The plummet which is an emblem of *uprightness* – the principle on which you conduct your business – the flourishing state of which is shown by the flowers. 3. The compass shows that you keep *within* estimates. The flourishing result of which is also exemplified by floriated work.' The Earl of Shrewsbury was obviously also a client who could be persuaded to lend items to the exhibition, and Crace showed the great sideboard which he had just made for the new dining room at Alton Towers. Another elaborate piece of furniture was the splendid walnut octagonal table with inlaid patterned top. This kind of work is unusual in Pugin's *œuvre* and he found it very difficult to design. He was working on it on 15 May 1850 when he wrote to Crace:[22] 'I worked as hard as possible, but this sort of inlay furniture takes as long as a church. Moreover I am not quite at home yet in these woods and I hope you will try the patterns in colour before you cut them to see if they may not be improved . . . I suppose the table will be walnut. I think it will look rich and something new in the old way.' He continued to work and eventually produced a design (plate 452). It is interesting to note that Crace repeated both the octagonal table and the Alton Towers sideboard for James Watts at Abney Hall in about 1853, after Pugin's death, and both these pieces survive. Crace's conscience may have been eased because the Earl had also died in 1852. Crace also exhibited other furniture, including tables, a priedieu with a triptych above which was lent by Pugin's client, Mr Scott-Murray, and also the case of a piano which was supplied by Messrs Burns & Lambert. His other important exhibits were textiles and wall-papers. It is difficult to identify the wall-papers with certainty, and there was apparently not much room for them, but contemporary accounts[23] refer to an 'old pine-apple gold pattern.' The design of one of his carpets is known (plate 451), and some of his other textiles were bought from the Exhibition by the Board of Trade, and one survives today in the Victoria & Albert Museum (plate 408).

Hardman undoubtedly provided the largest number of items, but by their nature many of them are hard to identify positively. Among the larger pieces the Earl of Shrewsbury lent the splendid brass chandelier from his new dining-room (plate 344), also a number of parcel-gilt ornamental dishes made for his sideboard and several coronas from the Talbot Gallery at Alton Towers. Another grand corona was intended for the newly built Anglican church at Wilton ('a church of Byzantine character,'[24]) which had been commissioned by Sidney Herbert. The church of St Thomas, Erdington, provided six tall brass pillars topped by angels who carried candles. Between the pillars were suspended silk curtains which enclosed a high altar. Hardman provided three examples of lecterns. The one described [25] as being from St George's cathedral, Southwark, is very similar to that now at St Cuthbert's College, Ushaw (plate 453). It has an eagle bookrest above a hexagonal column of open tracery-work, to which are attached three flying buttresses. The two buttresses to either side carry candlesticks. The base rests on three lions couchant. The second is described as being surmounted by a figure of St John the Evangelist and so can be identified as that made in 1848, commissioned by John Sutton for Jesus College,

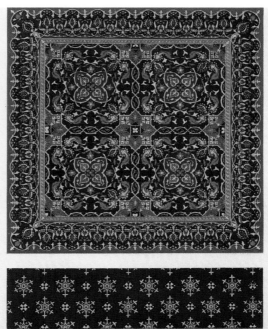

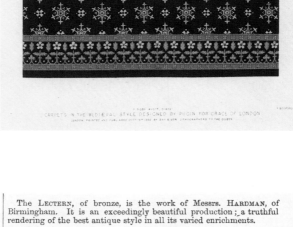

The LECTERN, of bronze, is the work of Messrs. HARDMAN, of Birmingham. It is an exceedingly beautiful production; a truthful rendering of the best antique style in all its varied enrichments.

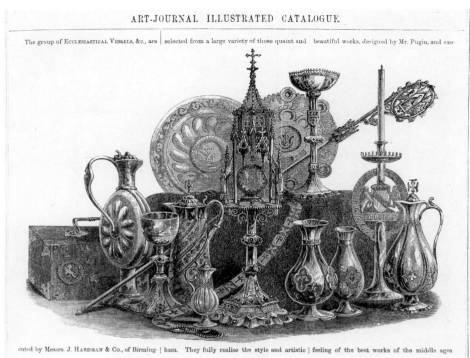

The group of ECCLESIASTICAL VESSELS, &c., are | selected from a large variety of those quaint and | beautiful works, designed by Mr. Pugin, and exe-

cuted by Messrs. J. HARDMAN & Co., of Birming- | ham. They fully realise the style and artistic | feeling of the best works of the middle ages

454. A group of exhibits made by Hardman, engraving in *The Art Journal Illustrated Catalogue*, 1851, p. 317.

Cambridge (plate 345). The third lectern had the un-Puginian device of two kneeling angels carrying the bookrest. Hardman placed the smaller things in two glass cases, one 'devoted to ecclesiastical ornaments, and the opposite one was filled with secular plate, jewels, etc.'[26] An engraving (plate 454) of a group of these objects enables some identifications to be made. Among the secular pieces were Pugin's own candlesticks and among the church plate was the splendid monstrance from St Mary's Church, Clapham. This, the most magnificent and costly of Pugin's monstrances, was part of a set with a ciborium and chalice and paten that were entered in Hardman's daybook on 22 April 1851 (plate 356).

Hardman also exhibited examples of his stained glass, which appears to have been set in the canvas on the north side of the Court (see plate 446). It seems clear from various comments that it was not seen to its advantage in this position. Among the windows displayed the Earl of Shrewsbury lent the figure of the Grand Talbot which formed the centre light in the south window of the new Alton Towers dining room. Two lights with figures of saints came from St Edmund's College, Ware, and three lights showing the life of St Andrew came from St Andrew's parish church, Farnham, which also provided lights of the Transfiguration and Crucifixion which were destined to form part of the large east window (plate 391). Pugin also lent several lights from his own church of St Augustine (plate 387). There were also two glass cases of

vestments (see plate 446), none of the contents of which have been identified. These were mentioned under Hardman's entry in the *Official Illustrated Catalogue* but were probably examples of work done in Birmingham by Mrs Powell, John Hardman's sister.[27]

Minton undoubtedly made the smallest contribution to the Mediæval Court; his energies were concentrated on his own display. His entry in the catalogue[27] states 'Ornamental tiles, porcelain and painted ware.' He certainly produced tiles for flowerpots and provided flooring tiles, no doubt encaustic ones, for the Court, but his biggest object was the stove (plate 455) which was surrounded by an ornamental grill made by Hardman. From the heraldry on the grill it may be presumed that this was another object lent by the Earl of Shrewsbury.

The Mediæval Court received general acclaim. Towards the end of the exhibition the *Illustrated London News* delivered the following judgement:[28]

> Amongst all the admirably arranged treasures of the Great Exhibition, the Mediæval Court, we may say, on mature reflection, presents the most unique and best harmonised display of art and skill – art in the artist and skill in the executant. The master-mind who suggested these forms and these colours has evidently supervised their development; each ornament and every detail bears the same evidence that the head which thought them directed the hands which wrought them. To Mr Pugin, then, who furnished the design for this gorgeous combination, is the highest honour due; and he has marvellously fulfilled his own intention of demonstrating the applicability of Mediæval art in all its richness and variety to the uses of the present day.

Pugin also received much praise in the perceptive 'Supplementary Report on Design'[29]

All Pugin's colleagues received medals for their exhibits, though none for Class XXVI under which the Mediæval Court was classified. Perhaps the fact that Crace was on the jury for this class had something to do with it. Minton received a Council Medal, the top award, for his exhibits in Classes XXV and XXVII.[30] Hardman also received a Council Medal for Class XXII:[31] 'The designs have been for the most part it is understood prepared by Mr A.W. Pugin and reflect great credit on that gentleman; but the Jury are more particularly impressed with the very perfect manner in which Messrs Hardman have developed the artist's conceptions.' He also received a Prize Medal, the next category, for Class XXIII,[32] for a rich collection of articles for church use. Crace received a Prize Medal in Class XIX[33] for specimens of Brussels and velvet-pile carpets and Myers received one in Class XXVII for works in Caen Stone:[34] 'The execution of the stonework is in all of them extremely good, different objects are perfectly correct in execution, and the distribution of the details is effectually and well combined with unity of design, showing clearly the artist's knowledge of his subject and his art.'

The promise of the Mediæval Court, however, was not to be fulfilled. Pugin certainly found the event wearying. He was accustomed to work in isolation, in his own world away from other influences. In 1851 he wrote to Crace:[35] 'Since I have had these fits I have been in a most dejected state – I am sure it was brought on by that detestable amount of Paganism & debasement in that exhibition.' In the same letter he also wrote: 'I deeply regret having anything to do with this doubly cursed jury business. I would much rather work in the N. sea with the Barking creek men than associate with the infernal Pagans.' Pugin was also appointed to the commission to choose works of ornamental design from the Exhibition, a collection which eventually formed the origin of the South Kensington Museum, later the Victoria & Albert Museum. His horror at the purchase of the shield made by Antoine Vechte, 'a positive revival of Pagan art', is recorded in his letter of 10

455.† 'Stove in the Mediæval Style', lithograph in M. Digby Wyatt. *op. cit.* fig.450, pl.106. The tiles were made by Minton and the metalwork by Hardman. The heraldry shows that it was destined for Alton Towers.

December 1851.[36] Shortly after this his final breakdown began. As the *Illustrated London News* had noted, he was the originator of all the ideas; without him there was no development.

CHAPTER NINETEEN

Pugin in Australia

BRIAN ANDREWS

In September 1848 the *Tablet* published a long letter from Pugin on the subject of Catholic church architecture.[1] Stung by criticism of his chancel screens in the newly founded liberal Catholic journal the *Rambler*, he penned an impassioned manifesto for the revival of Gothic architecture, noting with satisfaction that:

> England is, indeed, awakened to a sense of her ancient glory, and the reverence for things speedily passes on to the men and principles which produced them. But why do I say England, – Europe, Christendom is aroused; wherever I travel, I meet pious and learned ecclesiastics and laymen all breathing the same sentiments regarding mediaeval art, and more than one Bishop has departed across the ocean to the antipodes, carrying the seeds of Christian design to grow and flourish in the New World, and soon the solemn chancels and cross-crowned spires will arise, the last object which the mariner will behold on the shores of the Pacific till their venerable originals greet his glad view on England's shores.

Doubtless Pugin had in mind the Benedictine Archbishop John Bede Polding (1794–1877) of Sydney, founder of the Australian Roman Catholic hierarchy, and Robert William Willson (1794–1866), first Catholic bishop of Hobart Town, both of whom had used numbers of his church designs in Australia; designs in several instances specifically tailored to be within the means of very poor communities and to be realisable where building craft skills were minimal. In Willson's case, the relationship went well beyond mere business and was a close friendship which had arisen naturally from Willson's family situation and had developed further during his time in charge of the Catholic

mission in Nottingham. Moreover, there would have been a natural affinity between the two men. Both had a certain volatility of character, a spirit of religious tolerance in an age marked by sectarian bitterness[2] and a strong and practical social conscience.[3]

As for an immersion in architecture and art, Willson's father was a builder and his eldest brother was Edward James Willson, the architect who had written extensively on architectural antiquities for John Britton and had collaborated with A.C. Pugin and A.W.N. Pugin in providing descriptive text for *Specimens of Gothic Architecture*, 1821–3 and *Examples of Gothic Architecture*, Vols I and II, 1831–36.[4] He was close to the well known antiquarian and family friend Bishop John Milner, who ordained him to the priesthood in 1824 after his studies at Oscott College. Like Pugin, Willson had a taste for medieval art and owned a silver-gilt English chalice, *c*.1480 and a paten, *c*.1350, both of which he had acquired during a return visit to England from Hobart in either 1847 or 1853.[5]

Little wonder then that when Willson, a true 'chancel and screen' man, decided in 1841 to erect a new church dedicated to St Barnabas in Nottingham, his grand vision was realised through the generous benefaction of the Earl of Shrewsbury and with plans from his friend Pugin, resulting in a building which the *Orthodox Journal* described at its consecration as 'the largest [Catholic church] yet completed in this country since the Reformation'.[6] Willson himself acted as Clerk of Works for Myers, the builder.

In 1842 Robert William Willson reluctantly accepted appointment to the new see of Hobart Town. Since St Barnabas was not yet complete, Willson was consecrated in Pugin's Cathedral of

456.† Portrait of Robert William Willson, first bishop of Hobart Town (St Mary's College, Oscott).

457. Hardman plate acquired by Bishop Willson for Tasmania in the 1840s and early '50s.

458.† Episcopal ring, made for Bishop Willson by John Hardman & Co., *c*.1842, worn in plate 456.

St Chad, Birmingham on 28 October 1842, the consecrating prelate being Polding, assisted by Bishops Walsh and Wareing. Dr Wiseman preached the sermon. His episcopal regalia, including mitre, ring, pectoral cross[7] and pastoral staff, the latter a gift from the Earl of Shrewsbury, were all designed by Pugin. A portrait of Willson at Oscott College shows that the detail of the mitre was essentially the same as that on mitres illustrated in Plate v of Pugin's *True Principles* (plate 456).[8]

Some fifteen months were to pass before Willson would board the ship Bella Marina for the three and a half-month journey to his fledgling diocese. However, he had been given to understand that virtually nothing material could be obtained in Tasmania for the progress of religion[9] and so he busied himself raising funds and acquiring all things necessary, to be transported with him to Hobart. For this latter task he turned to his friend Pugin. In Willson's words:

I was called upon to come to a new land, where there was not a single thing for the use of a Bishop, and mark me, *where they could not be procured* – I procured – at the cheapest cost possible in Italy, France, Belgium and England through the zeal of my dear and valued friend Mr. Pugin one of everything requested for a Bishop, such as pastoral staff, mitre, Cappa Magna, pectoral Cross – knowing that I was coming, as I have observed before, to a *new country*, where Church furniture *could not be produced*, I determined upon making the greatest exertion and obtain whatever might be useful, or rather requisite for the service of AG. I therefore procured not less than 40 sets of vestments – linen of every description for several churches – such as albs, surplices, amices, Altar cloths, Chalice linen etc. common cloths – Crosses, Chalices, Ciboriums, Pixes (sic), holy oils stocks – a portable Altar for use of the Bp when travelling – and in order to introduce the proper church style in this distant land, I also procured a font rightly constructed and fitted which will serve as a model for all other churches, also stone picinas (sic), stone crosses, models of churches constructed on proper scales all by the great restorer of Church architecture and church furniture Mr. Pugin, together with a variety of things which I hope will tend & promote God's glory and your salvation.[10]

These, Willson stressed, were a result of 'the zeal talent and unpaid exertions of Mr. Pugin and other friends in England –'.[11]

Before he joined his ship at Plymouth, Willson spent a few days with Pugin at Ramsgate.

459. St Paul's, Oatlands, Tasmania, 1850, from the south-east.

460. St Paul's, Oatlands, looking east.

Pugin wrote enthusiastically to Shrewsbury:

> Bishop Willson has gone down to Plymouth to join his ship. He takes out a great deal with him 40 large chasubles!!! several tombs 2 altars compleat, fonts &c tiles & 3 models of small churches all to take to pieces with the roofs &c framed, simple buildings that can be easily constructed. It is quite delightful to start in the good style at the antipodes. It is quite an honour.[12]

Interestingly, in all this detailed catalogue, neither Pugin or Willson mentioned architectural drawings, presumably because of a conviction that there were not the skills in Tasmania to deal with them. But models were different; they could be studied and copied. These facts give the key to the character and quality of the Pugin churches built in Tasmania.

On 11 May 1844 Robert William Willson arrived in Hobart Town only to find that Polding's assurance that he would take over the new diocese free of debt was incorrect. He was saddled with repayment of a crippling sum which would take fourteen years to resolve, would sour his relationship with Polding and would severely constrain his ability to construct churches from Pugin's models.

The first of Willson's Pugin churches was that of St Paul in Oatlands, a town which had developed early as a staging post on the highway between Hobart and Launceston. The foundation stone was laid on 9 April 1850.[13] Willson chose as his architect Frederick Thomas, a clerk by trade and ex-convict, who was, at that stage, an unqualified draftsman in the Public Works Department.[14] The business relationship between the two men is clearly revealed in an 1852 letter in which Willson asks Thomas to state the terms on which he would undertake the carrying out of a Pugin design, in that instance for a cathedral.[15]

St Paul's is a small two-compartment church of ashlar sandstone (plate 459) in the St Marie's, Southport manner, with a 40 feet by 20 feet nave and a chancel 15 feet long by 12 feet wide. With the exception of a minor addition in the form of an enclosure around the west entrance it is in original condition. The nave and chancel are buttressed and a bellcote crowns the west gable as recommended in Pugin's *Present State*. The style of the church is Early English, but with a three-light Decorated east window containing reticulated tracery. This enrichment of the chancel, as at Southport, can be seen to be an expression of Pugin's theory of propriety, a concept well articulated by Ullathorne in 1846 when relating his influence on the design of Charles Hansom's church at Hanley Swan:

> I had also suggested the adoption of the transition from the plain lancet of the nave into the more floriated and lightsome, the passage from the secular to the more sacred and mystical portion of the building. It was thus I thought that the different styles might be combined with significative effect, now that we possess them all.[16]

There is a south porch and a small sacristy nestles against the chancel north wall. Generally Pugin gave his antipodean churches north porches, but this change may have been made from the model to suit the building's actual position, which is north-facing.

The detail elements on St Paul's are a dramatic vindication of Pugin and Willson's decision to employ models rather than drawings. The gable crosses, stoups and piscina are sophisticated in their modelling and archeologically correct; they came from England with Willson. The other details such as buttress set-offs, label terminations and corbels to the roof trusses are naïve and crude; they are the work of Thomas.

Originally, St Paul's had wooden sedilia. These have been removed leaving a niche in the chancel south wall. In recent times the plaster was stripped from the interior, revealing evidence that an Easter Sepulchre, 3 feet wide by 6 feet high with a pointed head, was intended for the north wall opposite the sedilia. This was crudely filled in with stone and plastered over during completion of the building. The church still possesses its chancel screen *in situ* (plate 460). It is a typical Pugin design with tracery echoing that in the east window and with the rood supported by a semi-circular brace, as for that shown in the illustration of St Marie's, Southport in the *Present State*.

Since Willson's arrival in Hobart he had been obliged to use as his pro-cathedral St Joseph's church, a Gothick building erected by Fr J.J. Therry and, somewhat irritatingly, a prime cause of his debts. Although a substantial episcopal seat remained beyond his means, Willson had decided by 1852 to erect an edifice more in harmony with his liturgical and architectural aspirations.

It would seem that his experience in Hobart had improved his perception of the local building craft capabilities and he had obtained from Pugin, probably in 1847, rough sketch plans for a medium-sized church.[17] These he would make the basis of his new cathedral. The plans were for an unbuttressed Decorated six-bay, triple-aisled church in the tradition of Southwark, Guernsey, Newcastle and Fulham. It was to have an overall interior length of 88 feet and a width over the aisles of 52 feet, with a plan very similar to that given for the proposed Islington Catholic chapel in Pugin's *Present State*, except that the tower would be over the south entrance, against the second bay, balanced by a porch in the corresponding position on the north wall. The nave and aisles had unbroken roof-lines from west to east. This troubled Frederick Thomas who had been engaged to draw up full working drawings and who felt that the long valley gutters so created would be a source of water damage to the fabric in the Hobart climate. He wrote to Willson suggesting the addition of a clerestory and the substitution of lean-to roofs for the aisles, following up with a reassurance:

> Your Lordship will observe, that in substituting the accompanying sketch embracing the proposed alterations (desiring to repeat my confidence that they are such as poor Mr. Pugin would under the circumstances have concurred with) I have strictly adhered to the truthfulness of that Gentleman's design as regards the Characteristics of a Catholic Church, namely substantial building and the fitness and correctness of its several details.[18]

The foundation stone of this building was laid on 2 February 1853, just prior to Willson's departure on a visit to Europe for health reasons. A Cathedral Building Committee was formed to raise funds for the project and, lacking a suitably inspiring image on which to base their campaign (Thomas had not yet produced detailed drawings), it seems that they made a strange borrowing. In the *Hobarton Advertiser* appeared an account of the laying of the foundation stone along with a description of the cathedral.[19] The description was a word for word copy of that for St Barnabas, Nottingham in Pugin's *Present State*, with the exception that blackwood, a Tasmanian timber, was substituted for oak in the text. All this was to no avail. Donations only trickled in and finally ceased in August 1854. Pugin's plans, modified by Thomas, were not proceeded with. Eventually in 1860, through a generous donation, Willson made a start on his cathedral, but this time the design was by William Wilkinson Wardell, who had recently migrated to the colony of Victoria for health reasons.[20]

The next church to be erected by Frederick Thomas from a Pugin model was St Patrick's at Colebrook, some twenty miles south of Oatlands. This remarkable building was chosen for the settlement of Jerusalem (later Colebrook) because it was expected to become an important centre. This never happened and Colebrook is a little out-of-the-way village, a factor which has doubtless contributed to St Patrick's, long a chapel-of-ease to Oatlands, surviving unaltered.

St Patrick's was opened on 21 January 1857. It is unlike any other Pugin design and is an extreme example of his efforts to produce the simplest, cheapest-possible, yet capacious church (plates

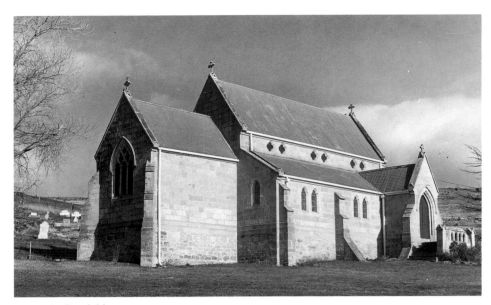

461. St Patrick's, Colebrook, Tasmania, 1855–6, from the north-east.

462. St Patrick's, Colebrook, looking east.

461, 462). It is an aisled clerestoried building in ashlar sandstone with an absolute minimum of detail and with the plainest chamfering to lights, arches, columns and doors (with the exception of the north porch), the only elaboration, for reasons of propriety, being a three-light reticulated tracery chancel east window. The three-bay nave is 44 feet long and 14 feet wide with 7 ft. 6 in. aisles. The aisle windows are paired cusped lights and the clerestory lights are paired quatrefoils. There is a single cusped light in the west front and a single lancet in the east wall of the north aisle. In a singular echo of St Marie's, Derby, the nave piers have no capitals and the arch chamfers run down to a stop about two feet above the floor. This is clearly

a Pugin economy measure, as any colonial architect of the period in striving to achieve a correct Gothic building would have inserted capitals and bases, however clumsy. Indeed Thomas's crude details are evident elsewhere, as in the corbels to the simple roof principals and in the stone railing for the porch stairs, needed because of the sloping site.

The 20 feet by 12 ft. 4 in. wide chancel with its unbraced roof still has its proper screen, piscina and sedilia. The piscina is one of Willson's stone imports and the sedilia are of wood. The wooden screen has tracery of similar design to that in Oatlands. Some years ago it was removed by Pugin's hated 'ambonoclasts' and placed at the west end of the nave, the rood being then suspended from the chancel roof. Later it was returned to its correct position, but minus the top beam and with the crocketted rood braces replaced upside down, leaving the rood still hanging from the roof.

At the same time as Colebrook was being constructed, the church of St Michael, Campbell Town (plate 463), was being erected to designs of Henry Hunter, brother of one of Willson's clergy. Willson made Hunter his protegé, starting him on a career which was to bring him the lion's share of Catholic commissions for over three decades, along with several important Anglican works, including supervision of the erection of G.F. Bodley's St David's cathedral, Hobart. For St Michael's, his first church, commenced in June 1856 and opened on 29 September 1857, Hunter turned for inspiration to the pages of Pugin's *Present State*, perhaps at Willson's suggestion and produced a building of form very much akin to the illustrations of St Marie's, Southport, but with no porch and with a triple lancet arrangement in the façade having the same staggered bases as shown in the illustration of Warwick Bridge.

With no prospect of a decent cathedral, Willson decided in mid-1856 to renovate St Joseph's. The building was closed for several weeks while work was carried out under Hunter's superintendence to give it a more ecclesiologically correct character. When re-opened on 6 August it boasted a number of improvements including two new sacristies, a rood screen, constructed of colonial wood and highly polished, a new altar and a reredos diapered in gold and blue, 'after a very elaborate medieval pattern'. The inscription on the rood brace, 'Per crucem tuam libera nos Domine', was the same as that on the brace in St Barnabas, Nottingham. Father Ryan preached an appropriate sermon, entitled 'The Rise and Progress of Church Architec-

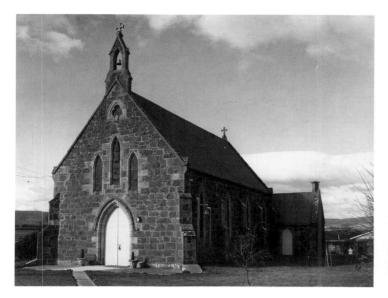

463. St Michael's, Campbell Town, Tasmania, by Henry Hunter, 1856–7, from the south-west.

464. Annunciation window, a gift from Pugin to Bishop Willson, St Joseph's, Hobart, Tasmania, 1847.

465. St John's, Richmond, Tasmania, stone piscina to Pugin's design brought out from England by Bishop Willson; wooden sedilia copied from detail on a church model.

466. St John's, Richmond, Tasmania, font; brought to Tasmania by Bishop Willson to 'serve as a model for other churches', though not in fact copied.

467. St John's, Richmond, Tasmania, 1836–7, with 1859 additions by Frederick Thomas derived from a model supplied to Bishop Willson by Pugin.

ture', to mark the event.[21] Doubtless for Willson, the most important change to St Joseph's on that occasion was the installation of a two-light Decorated window, a gift of Pugin's in 1847 (plate 464). The subject of the Hardman window was the Annunciation and it bore the very personal inscription, 'Orate pro bono statu Augusti Welby de Pugin'.[22] This window is still extant in St Joseph's although Willson's other improvements have long since been removed.

With regard to the third of Pugin's church models for Willson, the evidence seems to point to parts of it having been used by Thomas for alterations and additions in 1859 to the church of St John at Richmond, some sixteen miles north-east of Hobart.

In August 1835 Polding had visited Richmond and left plans for a small rectangular church by the Bath architect H.E. Goodridge.[23] This became the nave for Willson's more ecclesiologically appropriate scheme, to which were added an unbuttressed chancel with three-light Flowing Decorated east window, a sacristy and a west tower with broach spire (plate 467). The gables were crowned with Pugin stone crosses and the chancel (plate 465) contained a Pugin stone piscina along with wooden sedilia and screen (the latter now removed). This church also received Willson's model stone font by Pugin. As ever, Thomas's hand is visible, here in the Gothick four-pointed arches between nave and chancel and nave and tower.

Willson resigned from the see of Hobart in 1865 and died in England on 30 June 1866. He is buried in the crypt of his first Pugin church, now St Barnabas's Cathedral, Nottingham. His Tasmanian church building and furnishing activities everywhere bear the artistic imprint of his close

468. St Mary's, Sydney, the temporary bell tower, with Pugin's extensions to the 1833 cathedral in course of erection, 1850s (Mitchell Library, State Library of New South Wales).

friendship with Pugin. It was respected by his clergy and people[24] and the tradition was carried on by his protegé, Henry Hunter.[25]

In contrast, Polding's relationship with Pugin was purely professional. Nonetheless, it was to result in the erection of six churches, additions to a cathedral, a bell tower and an organ case to Pugin's designs.[26] Polding also ordered large quantities of church furnishings from Hardmans.[27] Pugin's first commission for Sydney came not from Polding directly, but from Bevington and Son, organ builders of London. It was to design the case for a large organ ordered by Polding in 1838.[28] The organ arrived in Sydney in late January 1841 and was installed in St Mary's cathedral in a gallery in the south transept, receiving in 1849 for niches in its case seven statues, about three feet high, carved by the sculptor monk Jean Gourbeillon, a member of the Benedictine monastic community of St Mary's.[29] No description of the St Mary's organ has survived and since Pugin designed a mere handful of cases it is all the more tragic that it was completely destroyed in the fire which consumed the cathedral on the night of 29 June 1865.

Polding probably requested plans to meet his various building needs from Pugin during his visit to England in 1841–2. On 20 June 1841 he was present at the dedication of St Chad's, Birmingham and was evidently impressed with its architect. Pugin's notebook recorded the delivery of drawings for Sydney to Polding's cousin and London agent, the Benedictine monk Thomas Paulinus Heptonstall in December 1842.[30]

The first drawing to be used related to improvements to his cathedral church of St Mary, a Gothick structure dating from 1833. He had the intention of extending the existing building to the west as the first stage in completely replacing it with a larger and more appropriate episcopal seat, almost certainly to Pugin's designs. In the meantime, pending the availability of funds for the extensions, he had a pressing need to house a peal of eight bells on order from England. Writing to his Vicar-General in Van Diemen's Land in May 1843 Polding spoke of the imminent arrival of a suitable tower design:

> The plan of the tower, which must be built with great skill by reason of the continued vibration of the bells, I shall receive very shortly from Mr. Pugin, the celebrated architect.[31]

The reason why the construction of this tower was so critical was because it was a temporary structure, with the upper section of wood (plate 468), as Polding revealed in a letter to Heptonstall in October of the same year:

> Our temporary tower is rising: it will be 16 feet square: walls 2 ft. 6 in. thick throughout: double thickness in buttresses. At twenty five having the Bells and rest of wood: altogether about 55 feet.[32]

Despite being temporary, the tower represented a dramatic advance in taste and style over the nearby cathedral, having archeologically correct details and composition, and it was capped with a pyramidal roof.

By 1851 there was a determination that the enlargement and completion of St Mary's should go ahead. The *Sydney Morning Herald* for 26 August 1851 noted that the main building was to be lengthened 51 feet. To this was to be added a chapel to the left of the entrance and a tower 18 feet square, capped by a broach spire some 200 feet high.[33] Work progressed fitfully over the ensuing decade only to be utterly destroyed in the 1865 conflagration. The stone shell was eventually demolished to make way for the completion of Wardell's great edifice. The extensions to old St Mary's may be ascribed to Pugin with a high degree of certainty. The plan form and details correspond with his work around the early 1840s and there was just no architect in Sydney at that time whom the Catholics would have employed possessing such a degree of stylistic sophistication and grasp of the Gothic vocabulary. The plan for the extensions was of the triple-aisled type with engaged south-west tower, having the gabled aisle roofs lower than that of the clerestoried nave. Overall, the style was Decorated, with some lancet lights, and the various elements related in many cases to details on Pugin's designs for Cheadle, Southwark, St Marie's, Liverpool and his illustration of Jesus chapel, near Pomfret, in the *Present State*. An enriched string course above the nave entrance was similar to that on the aisle west walls of St Marie's, Derby.

In designing an extension to the existing building Pugin was saddled with a nave some 40 feet wide, but with a wall height of just 47 feet. He achieved a satisfactory composition by making the gabled aisles about 22 feet wide and by creating a strong vertical emphasis to the façade through a massive gable coping, based on that of the east gable of Melrose Abbey, with the apex topped by a substantial niched pinnacle. Significantly, he had paid a visit to Melrose, recorded in his diary for 20 October 1842, just over seven weeks before he delivered Polding's plans to Heptonstall. Essentially, the additions added four 12 foot bays to the existing Gothick fabric and the tower was only carried up to just below the belfry stage.

In 1845 the foundation stone was laid of a triple-aisled church dedicated to St Benedict, on the Broadway south of Sydney's city centre. It was in plan form and composition a mirror-reversed version of Pugin's 'Proposed Islington Catholic Chapel', from *Present State*, but with a south porch on account of its corner site and with ten 12 foot bays to both nave and aisles. In respect of such triple-aisled designs, it is interesting to note that Pugin sent to Sydney at some stage tracings done in 1845 of his design for St Joseph's, St Peter Port, Guernsey.[34]

As for so many of his Australian designs, Pugin used the Early English style with its simple lancets for the nave and provided Decorated windows and statue niches for the chancel and adjacent side chapels for reasons of propriety (plate 469). The string course below the three large windows in the east wall was to be enriched with carved bosses as used on the aisle west walls at Derby. Here, as for the label terminations on St Benedict's, the roughly squared stone was never carved. The church, of ashlar sandstone, was completed in 1848 except for the top stages of the tower and spire which would eventually be added after 1856, apparently

to the designs of the Sydney architect William Munro.[35]

St Benedict's style was well regarded by an increasingly sophisticated clergy. Writing to a member of his former Downside Priory community in 1849 Henry Charles Davis, Polding's co-adjutor bishop, noted, 'We have in Sydney a very beautiful little church early English (and pretty correct) dedicated to St. Benedict'.[36] Davis, with a discerning eye for 'correctness', had acquired his episcopal regalia from Hardmans in 1848.[37] Alterations in 1942 significantly changed its appearance and proportions. It was shortened by 26 feet at its east end to accommodate the widening of Broadway and some 13 feet was added to the width of the nave, with two cusped lancets inserted in the nave east and west walls.[38] However the Puginian hand is still unmistakable, particularly when compared with the efforts of contemporary local architects used by the Catholic community.

John Bede Polding's next site for a Pugin church was nearly 650 miles north of Sydney, in Brisbane. This ashlar sandstone church, dedicated to St Stephen and built between 1847 and 1850, was a simple buttressed two-compartment design with a nave of five bays and a two bay chancel. It had a south porch and a bell-cote over the west gable. The style of the building was Early English, with simple lancets. The hood mouldings of these lights were tied together by a string course which ran around the north, east and south walls and the trinity of lancets in the chancel east wall was surmounted by an oculus similar to the arrangement in St Wilfrid's, Hulme. With its screen, sedilia and piscina and its collar beam roof with arched braces,

469. St Benedict's, Broadway, 1845–56, from the south-east (Mitchell Library, State Library of New South Wales).

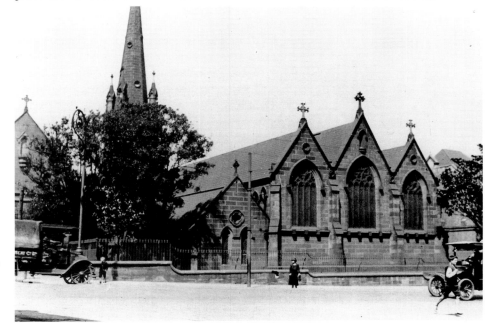

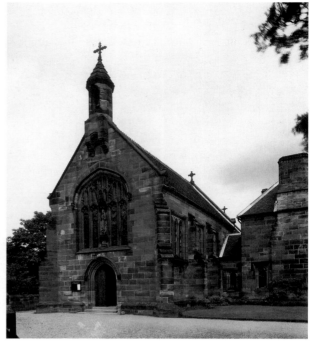

king post and raking queen posts,[39] St Stephen's shared many of the characteristics of Pugin's simplest small churches, with one exception. The west window was a large five-light Perpendicular design strongly reminiscent of that in the façade of the chapel of St John's Hospital, Alton, but with a diamond shape in the tracery of the centre light, as in the chancel east window of Melrose abbey (plate 470). Indeed, the whole façade composition of St Stephen's bore a marked similarity to that at Alton, designed some three years earlier.[40]

Another of Pugin's small church designs sent out to Polding in 1842 was used three times, at Balmain, a suburb of Sydney, at Queanbeyan, close to the present site of Canberra, and at Berrima, a village about 100 miles south-west of Sydney.[41] All were commenced during the years 1848 and 1849 and while St Augustine of Canterbury, Balmain, and St Gregory's, Queanbeyan, have been considerably altered over the years, St Francis Xavier's, Berrima, remains with its original fabric intact and with only the loss of its chancel screen from the interior. It provides an unrivalled example of a small early Pugin church design in the Southport mould, with the additional advantage over its Tasmanian cousin at Oatlands of having quite evidently been constructed by a competent builder, William Munro, from a complete set of working drawings including full-sized moulding profiles. It is a two compartment ashlar sandstone building with a four-bay nave 40 feet long by 22 feet and a two-bay chancel

20 feet long by 17 feet. The nave is lit by narrow lancets and has an antipodean north porch against the second bay. It is buttressed at the corners. The façade has two lancet windows and a cusped statue niche in the gable, above which is a bellcote with a single opening (plate 472). Unlike Pugin's other similar small churches of the period, it maintains its scholarly Early English throughout the chancel, which has diagonal buttressing, paired lancets in the north wall, a typical sacristy against the junction of the nave and south wall and a trinity of slender lancets in the east wall. Pugin's notions of propriety are nevertheless expressed here, but in a delicately subtle manner. The cross surmounting the eastern gable is slightly more elaborate than those on the nave and porch gables. Likewise the mouldings to the chancel north and east lancets have one more element than those on the nave, sacristy and porch.

Inside, the nave roof is of identical design to that of St Marie's, Southport and the chancel (plate 473) has a piscina, stone sedilia with cusped heads and, in the north wall, an Easter Sepulchre recess. St Francis Xavier's, Berrima is thus a near-perfect surviving exemplar of Pugin's concept for the revival of a small medieval country church. Only the label terminations and roof corbels still await a carver. By a singular coincidence, Berrima has another church directly indebted to Pugin, namely Holy Trinity Anglican church (plate 474). This 1847–9 building, by Edmund Thomas Blacket, the great architect of New South Wales'

nineteenth-century Anglican churches, was probably his first design and he copied details of Biddestone church, Wiltshire straight from the pages of Volume III of Pugin's *Examples*.[42] The bellcote was an exact copy, as were some of the windows and Berrima's proportions are the same as Biddestone's.

One more New South Wales building will be attributed to Pugin, the church of St Charles Borromeo at Ryde, a Sydney suburb. Although of 1857 vintage, at a time when Polding had been resorting to Charles Hansom designs for a decade,[43] this church is unlike Hansom's work, and is too sophisticated for local architects that Catholic patrons were then employing, but has Pugin's thumbprint all over it.

St Charles has been subsumed into a larger 1934 church, but all its detail elements have been incorporated in the later structure, albeit in different positions and the façade survives as a large south porch, thus enabling a good picture to be derived of the original church. It was an aisled ashlar sandstone Early English building with a western bellcote of two openings (plate 475) and a three-light reticulated tracery Decorated window in the chancel. Of the same genre as St Alphonsus', Barntown, whose design it predated and St Andrew's, Cambridge, it had a nave 17 feet wide, with 14 feet bays and lancet windows in the 6 ft. 6 in. aisles. Paired cusped lancets under a square head, inserted in the newer fabric most

probably came from the original sacristy.

All in all Pugin produced nine identifiable designs for Australian churches, not to mention his bell-tower, organ case, glass, plate and other creations, thus well meriting Ferrey's observation that he 'also designed many churches for Australia, and the other colonies'.

472. St Francis Xavier's, Berrima, from the north-west.

473. St Francis Xavier's, Berrima, looking east.

474. Holy Trinity, Berrima, by Edmund Thomas Blacket, 1847–9, from the north-west.

475. St Charles Borromeo's, Ryde, New South Wales, north-west elevation of the late 1850s building, which has been subsumed into a 1930s church, with the addition of a west porch.

476. St Francis Xavier's Cathedral, Adelaide, the 1881 Peter Paul Pugin west elevation, with matching 1920s spire by Walter Hervey Bagot.

477. St Dominic's, East Camberwell, Victoria; the 1952 tower by Tom Payne.

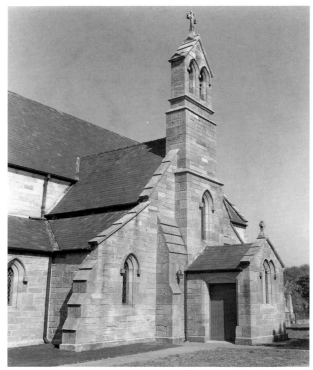

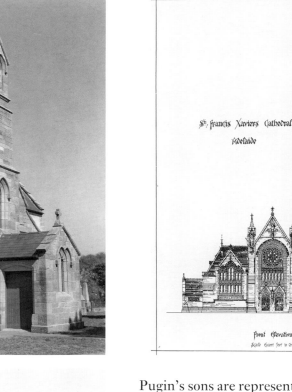

Pugin's sons are represented in Australia by just one work of Peter Paul Pugin, namely alterations and additions to St Francis Xavier's Roman Catholic cathedral in Adelaide, South Australia.

In 1881 Peter Paul Pugin was requested by Christopher Augustine Reynolds, Bishop of Adelaide, to enlarge an incomplete Charles Hansom cathedral, of somewhat parochial character and to imbue it with a dignity and grandeur more befitting an episcopal seat.[44] Pugin produced a design which consisted of a substantially widened north aisle, enlarged sacristies, altered details to the east end, completion of the nave and a splendidly fussy façade with south-west tower, all in his characteristic muscular Geometrical Decorated style (plate 476). For the sake of economy the widened aisle was designed to incorporate as much cut stone as possible from Hansom's existing Early English aisle. The proposed additions included large confessionals, typical of those in such later buildings as his church of Our Lady and St Edmund, Great Malvern and St Antony of Padua's, Forest Gate. This latter church's rose windows echo those in the east and west elevations of the Adelaide design. In its detail, the concept had much in common with his slightly earlier grand unexecuted plans for the virtual rebuilding of Belmont Abbey, Herefordshire. Indeed, initial schemes for the present tower of Belmont Abbey church were almost identical with that planned for St Francis Xavier's.[45]

478. St Patrick's, Melbourne, by William Wilkinson Wardell, 1858–1939, perspective c.1880, from the north-east (James Alipius Goold Museum).

479. St John the Baptist's, Clifton Hill, Victoria, by John Bun Denny, 1876–1907, from the west.

The chronically straitened circumstances of the Adelaide archdiocese resulted in just five bays of the widened aisle and the enlarged sacristies being built in the late 1880s to Pugin's plans. In the 1920s, local architect Walter Hervey Bagot produced a watered-down version of Pugin's façade and tower, again for financial reasons and this was erected, minus the top stages of the tower. Currently, there are plans to complete the tower to Peter Paul Pugin's original design.

Any consideration of Pugin's direct influence in Australia must include his contemporary, William Wilkinson Wardell and John Bun Denny, Lord Shrewsbury's resident master of works at Alton Towers. Wardell brought copies of his own English church designs to Australia in 1858 and used them as a quarry for plans, compositions and details.[46] His considerable corpus of works in Australia included a large number of churches, mostly in the Puginian archeologically correct mould as well as the two great cathedrals of St Patrick, Melbourne (1858–1939; plate 478) and St Mary, Sydney (1866–1928), larger than any attempted in Victorian England. Wardell had Denny appointed as supervisor of his church

works for Bishop Goold of Melbourne, thereby ensuring their meeting both the letter and the spirit of his designs. Denny designed a number of churches in his own right, including in them on occasion details from Pugin's St Giles, Cheadle. A fine example of his well-served apprenticeship under Pugin is the big clerestoried town church of St John the Baptist, Clifton Hill (plate 479).

More generally, Pugin's influence is evident in virtually every settlement in Australia, from massive cathedrals down to tiny Gothic boxes with perhaps a pair of pointed windows in each side and a pointed door. This influence was to last until the early 1950s, ending, not with a capitulation, but with a dramatic gesture. In 1952 the Melbourne architect Tom Payne added to the priory church of St Dominic, East Camberwell, a 132 foot central western tower (plate 477) which in its emphatic boldness makes most Australian Victorian towers seem trite and derivative by comparison. The diagonal buttressing rises sheer, without set-offs, to the powerful flame-like clustered pinnacles and the free-form tracery in the belfry stage is of concomitant strength. Astride its hilltop it is a defiant finale to the Gothic Revival in Australia.

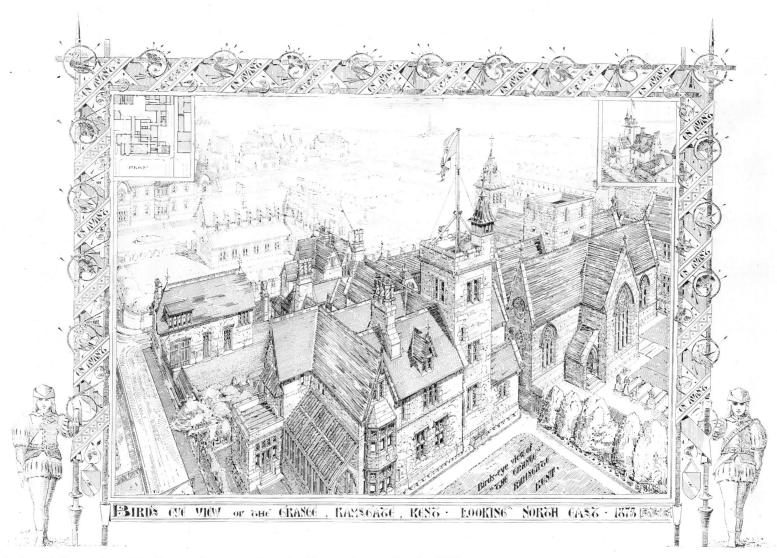

480.†   *Bird's-eye view of the Grange, Ramsgate, Kent. Looking north east. 1873*, by C.W.
Pugin, drawing shown at the Royal Academy in 1879 (Private Collection). E.W. Pugin
added the conservatory and garden porch to the Grange. St Augustine's Monastery
(1860) is visible in the distance.

CHAPTER TWENTY

The Later Pugins

RODERICK O'DONNELL

A.W. Pugin's death on 14 September 1852 in London left the eighteen-year-old Edward as his father's successor in practice. Edward was immediately involved with his father's elaborate funeral, attended by two bishops, at St Augustine's, Ramsgate.[1] He also designed Pugin's tomb, the first of his many works at Ramsgate. However, Jane Knill, who Pugin married as his third wife in 1848, was the only beneficiary of his will. In 1852 it was she, rather than the young Edward, who was head of the family (plate 481). They moved to Birmingham at the suggestion of John Hardman. Edward continued his own architectural education, later claiming that Sir Charles Barry refused him a pupilship.[2] Pugin described himself as helping his father from the age of seven. He was said to have been 'brought up in his father's office' and by the age of sixteen he had become 'quite his father's right hand man . . . (it was) mainly due to his exertions that his father's large family . . . widow and six or seven younger children were brought up . . .' Most of his father's patrons were prepared to take on the eighteen-year-old successor (plate 482).

Few of E.W. Pugin's private papers survive and the hagiography which surrounded his father did not attach itself to Edward. In his diary for 1856 E.W. Pugin emerges as an ambitious and precocious architect, closely dependent on his stepmother and large family, chaffing at the tutelage to the Hardman family and the stay in Birmingham. His highly finished drawing, perhaps intended for a fresco, showing the mourning Jane Pugin at her husband's tomb washed by the blood flowing from the crucified Christ is an example of the hot-house religious convictions of a mid-Victorian Catholic family and the diary shows Pugin following the religious disciplines of going to confession and

holy communion. There are reminders of his father's depressions and illness due to overwork and of his cultivation of sympathetic lay and clergy patrons. During 1856 Pugin met no fewer than five bishops to discuss commissions, as well as what was probably his first introduction to Cardinal Wiseman. He seemed happier with clerical company than was his father. He travelled to Ireland,

481. Louisa Pugin with her step-daughter, Anne, and her own children, Agnes and the baby Cuthbert Welby (The Grange, Ramsgate).

482. Edward Pugin as a boy (The Grange, Ramsgate).

483. The Granville Hotel, Ramsgate, by E.W. Pugin.

484.† The 'Granville' chair, a design of 1870 for the Granville Hotel, by E.W. Pugin (Private Collection, Birkenhead).

France and Belgium, where he was recognised as his father's successor with perhaps more ease than in England. He literally forced his way past protesting officials to inspect the Lille cathedral competition drawings on the strength of his father's name and had himself appointed to the jury. In London he met Sir Charles Barry and attended a meeting at the Architectural Museum where he met for the first time Scott and Burges; he inspected churches by his Catholic rivals such as J.J. McCarthy in Dublin and Wardell in London. There are negotiations over no fewer than four churches which ultimately slipped through his hands, as well as less justifiable resentment over the announcement of churches by Wardell and new Catholic convert Henry Clutton.[3] Overall, Pugin's energy and ambition shine through: the death of his patron the 17th Earl of Shrewsbury was countered by meetings with bishops and an introduction to the Duke of Norfolk at the funeral; church openings were recorded with comments such as 'the Bishop was exceedingly kind and promised to get me several church jobs'.[4] His success in the limited competition for the junior seminary at Ushaw College after much anxiety was greeted with the prayer 'please God this will give me much more standing in England.'[5]

In 1856 the Pugin family left Birmingham for London where they settled in Gordon Square, and in 1861 they returned to the Grange, Ramsgate (plate 480), where Edward made additions and kept an office as well as those at Liverpool and London, where he seems to have lived.[6] Like his father E.W. Pugin was a manic worker, and in-

veterate traveller. He was said to have inspected one of his churches only by night during elaborate railway journeys.[7] His powers of application were prodigious: he worked continuously over three days and nights on his successful competition design for the church of SS Peter and Paul, Cork. Such exertion was followed by the inevit-able illness and depressions lasting for days. The obituary in the *Builder* described Pugin: 'From early in the morning until late at night he worked without relaxation at his drawing board . . . he is said to have made £40,000 in five years'.[8] However in 1873 the failed Granville Hotel (plate 483) speculation in Ramsgate forced him to file for bankruptcy with liabilities of over £187,000, and to leave for the United States. Like his father he died of exhaustion aged 41, of 'syncope of the heart . . . partly through injudicious use of chloral hydrate'. Despite much ill-health noted in his diary, he died unexpectedly after a morning's work followed by an afternoon spent in the Grosvenor Turkish Bath, Buckingham Palace Road, which he had designed and built as a speculation. He was buried at Ramsgate on 10 June 1875. His funeral at St Augustine's was taken by the Bishop of Southwark, assisted by six priests. 'Most of the shops in the town were closed and the vessels in the harbour had their flags at half-mast.'[9] He is buried in the Pugin chantry, and is commemorated in a bust on the Victoria Terrace at Ramsgate, the scene of his business failure.

Pugin's life was in many ways tragic: aged 10 he lost his mother, aged 18 his father; although engaged two or three times, he never married.[10] He had stormy relationships with his early collaborators – his brothers-in-law G.C. Ashlin and J.H. Powell – with later pupils and with many patrons. Pugin's searing contest with the Barry family summed up in his pamphlet *Who was the art architect of the Houses of Parliament?* (1867),[11] found him in dispute not only with the Rev. E.M. Barry, but even with his father's friends – most notoriously with the painter J.R. Herbert, who even accused Edward of mental instability.[12]

Unaccountably, he did not authorise a biography of his father but he criticised the publication of Ferrey's *Recollections* in 1861.[13] Pugin is supposed to have said 'on my tomb I should like to have written "Here lies a man of many sorrows".'[14]

Unlike his father, Edward had many pupils and a number of professional partnerships. Some of Edward Pugin's most important mature churches are in Ireland, the fruit of his partnership (1859–69) with George Coppinger Ashlin;[15] SS Peter and Paul, Cork (1859–66) and SS Augustine and John, Dublin (1860–93), and finally St Colman's Cathedral, Cove (1868–1916) (plates 485, 486). There were shorter English collaborations with James Murray (1857–60), whose drawing skills were evidently responsible for many of the Pugin and Murray perspective drawings published at this time,[16] and with J.A. Hansom (1862–3), the break up of which led to disputes between them in the press.[17] Pugin and Hansom had first collaborated over Bishop Gillis's Leith church, where Edward handed over his father's drawings; the result is in the style of A.W. Pugin not J.A. Hansom.[18]

E.W. Pugin's major pupils later formed the backbone of Catholic church practice in the North West: Edmund Kirby in Liverpool, as well as the brothers James and Bernard Sinnott and Powell, and, in Yorkshire, Edward Simpson. Peter Paul Pugin (1851–1904) was Edward's most important pupil (see pp. 268–71); the older Cuthbert Welby Pugin seems only intermittently to have been involved.

A number of pupils or assistants were associated with particular Pugin offices and it was a final unnamed 'confidential assistant' who found Pugin dead in his bed. From the 1856 diary it is clear that clerks of works such as Stephen Eyre also played a vital role.[19] Occasionally he even employed priests, such as Dom Lawrence Shepherd OSB at Stanbrook Abbey. Unlike his father he allowed his churches to go out to competitive tender. He seldom employed Myers,[20] preferring local builders such as Haigh of Liverpool, for whom he also obtained the Ushaw, and later the Carlton Towers, contracts.[21] Disputes over estimates and tenders were frequent and Pugin wrote of one 'poor

485. St Colman's Cathedral, Cove, by E.W. Pugin and G.C. Ashlin, the west front.

486. St Colman's Cathedral, Cove, by E.W. Pugin and G.C. Ashlin, contract drawing, April 1869, pen and ink (Coleman Collection, Dublin).

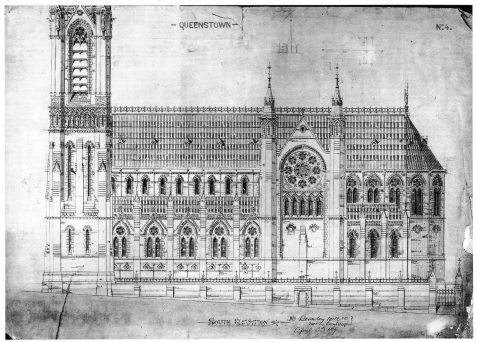

487. High Altar, originally at Danesfield House, by A.W. and E.W. Pugin, *c*.1852 (Church of the Sacred Heart, Henley).

488. High Altar, St Marie's, Derby, by E.W. Pugin, 1854–5.

Hevingham who built Longton for me is now in bankruptcy court and so it is with all my poor builders'.[22]

Again unlike his father, he was not chief designer for Hardmans: that was the role of John Hardman Powell, who produced E.W. Pugin's designs for stained glass, furniture, metalwork and vestments.[23] For architectural carving, after employing a number of different hands such as Lane and Lewis of Birmingham, and Farmer and Earp of London, he finally came to prefer R.L. Boulton of Cheltenham.[24] A fine example of his altar compositions of the 1850s which can be attributed to the sculptors Lane and Lewis of Birmingham is that from the private chapel at Danesfield, Berks (plate 487) a commission inherited from his father, whose style is evident in the two saints in niches.[25]

Pugin also set up in the 1860s the 'South East Furniture Company' at Ramsgate to manufacture his designs, possibly in partnership with Cuthbert Welby Pugin (plate 484). His secular furniture commissions included the complete furnishing including carpets for Croston Hall, Lancashire and the dining chairs for Ushaw.[26] Like his father he expected his designs to be reproduced exactly, and he criticised J.H. Powell and Boulton for not doing so.

Pugin was employed in almost every diocese and even claimed to be 'diocesan architect' for Shrewsbury.[27] In London he complained to Cardinal Wiseman that he was excluded because of the influence of 'Dr Manning and the Bayswater clique',[28] although later Pugin claimed to have designed a cathedral for Wiseman and did eventually design his tomb.[29] Pugin entertained Cardinal Wiseman at Ramsgate and when he moved to London in 1856 immediately attended his soirees.[30] At the opening of Shrewsbury Cathedral on 29 September 1856 by Cardinal Wiseman Pugin noted in his diary 'made a very complimentary speech which I should very much like to get printed.'[31] Pugin was made a knight of St Sylvester by Pope Pius IX, and invested by Cardinal Wiseman at the fiftieth anniversary in 1858 of Ushaw College.[32] He made cathedral designs for Shrewsbury and for Liverpool – the first, in 1854, and a second, more personal design, was begun in 1856 as a

Lady chapel for a larger scheme; another for Northampton (1861) was built to a slightly different scheme (1862–4), and most importantly Cove Cathedral, co. Cork (1869–1916). He also made additions and furnishings for many of his father's cathedrals, including Birmingham, Southwark[33] and Killarney.[34]

Like his father, Edward was primarily a church architect, receiving commissions from the parish clergy and religious orders, and the rich faithful. As his father's successor he frequently made additions or alterations to his father's churches such as St Marie's, Derby (plate 488) 1854–5,[35] Bishop Eton Liverpool (1857–8),[36] the extensions to St Marie's, Rugby (1864),[37] and St Augustine's, Ramsgate. He completed two of his father's Anglican church restorations, St Mary's, Beverley and West Tofts, Norfolk, where he added the chancel. He did much work at the seminaries where the elaborate style of his chantry and side chapel altars are indicative of clerical taste. At Oscott he added the Lady chapel or Weedall chantry (1861), and designed a hall, eventually built by P.P. Pugin. At St Edmund's, Ware, he re-arranged the Griffiths chantry (1856–7) (plate 489), and added the Lady altar (1861), and the Scholfield chantry (1862).[38] At Ushaw College he completed St Joseph's chapel with an altar after 1852, and added the sumptuous St Charles chapel (1857–9; plate 490) designed in 1856 as the St Aloysius chapel and the Gibson chantry (1856) executed as the chapel of St Michael (1858–9). He built the extensive junior seminary (plate 491) and replanned and furnished the Professors' dining room, one of his most im-

492.† Two chairs by E.W. Pugin, c.1856 (Trustees of Ushaw College).

493.† *Shrewsbury Cathedral*, by E. W. Pugin, watercolour, 1852 (Our Lady and St Peter of Alcantara, Shrewsbury).

portant surviving domestic interiors, with its distinctive x-frame chairs (plate 492).[39]

Among lay church-builders, Edward expected great things from the young Bertram Talbot, 17th Earl of Shrewsbury, who succeeded in 1852 with a promise to pay for the cathedral at Shrewsbury.[40] Since A.W. Pugin had drawn up plans before his death, the presentation watercolour signed 'E.W.

Pugin 1852' (plate 493) is probably a development of them. The young Earl's death four years later was a major blow.[41] Pugin also received large church commissions from Miss Monica Tempest for the Sacred Heart, Blackpool (1856–7), from H.R. Wegg-Prosser who paid for the monastery church at Belmont, Herefordshire, and from Sir Humphrey de Trafford at Barton.

E.W. Pugin built more than seventy substantial churches in England and Scotland in addition to many school, convent and presbytery commissions as well as having an Irish practice. It is difficult satisfactorily to categorise such a mass of work, but a number of stylistic themes can be distinguished. E.W. Pugin began to design in his father's revived fourteenth-century English Decorated style, but by the late 1850s he had turned to earlier thirteenth-century Geometric Gothic details. 1859–60 was a climacteric year which saw the building of the church of Our Lady of La Salette, Liverpool, the crucial example of what might be called his 'industrial' churches. Thereafter the Dadizeele Church (designed 1857, built 1859–92; plate 494) the Irish partnership with G.C. Ashlin from 1859, and, in his English practice, the 'rich' churches of the '60s such as Barton (1863–7) should be contrasted with the many 'industrial' churches built to house the large town congregations of the north of England.

E.W. Pugin's early drawings such as those for the unexecuted additions to the chapel at Ushaw, 1856 (plate 495), are indistinguishable from his father's. Other drawings for Ushaw of 1856, particularly the exquisite small sketches he exchanged with Dr Newsham for the transept shrine, could be confused with early designs of his father's. A number of his early churches are still in his father's rich English Decorated style.

The Shrewsbury Cathedral watercolour of 1852

with its marked attenuation of proportion show a distinctly different artistic personality in the making. Shrewsbury Cathedral (1853–6) is more personal to E.W. Pugin. It was to be a 'rich' church with a complex, additive plan, expressed in many gables and an off-axis tower and spire, as the *Builder* remarked, 'somewhat lofty and attenuated'.[42] The second design of 1855, with slightly reduced dimensions, is much tighter on plan, although still distinctly personal in its height. The elevations are simplified, with tower and spire replaced by a prominent bell-cote, an important feature of E.W. Pugin's churches. The tracery is still complex and the segmental clerestorey windows are unusual. The enormous seven-light sanctuary window, which 'occupies almost the entire east end',[43] is another characteristic feature. The internal elevation is more traditional, with octagonal Painswick stone piers and plastered arches, supporting a roof of alternate scissor and arched braced principals. The stone carving is elaborate, and rich furnishings were installed.[44] Originally estimated at £10,000 and to house 1000 people, the total cost of the reduced scheme was later quoted at the improbable figure of £3500.[45]

In contrast to Shrewsbury, Pugin's mature churches are quite unlike his father's. Our Lady of La Salette (1859–60) was built, not for an Earl, but for a large Liverpool dockside congregation of over 10,000, for the astonishingly low contract price of £4000, to house 1,800 people. The nave and apsed chancel were united under a roof of one pitch, and lit from a large plate tracery wheel window in the end gable, with closely set clerestory sexfoil windows. Internally the very wide span of the arcade provides uninterrupted views of the sanctuary. The piers are of banded sandstone, set on wide bases and crowned with large abstract scalloped capitals, characteristic of the mature E.W. Pugin. At La Salette we see for the first time the 'Pugin roof with double backed principals',[46] consisting of massive arched braced scissor trusses, with a louvre-type compartment above their apex, panelled in between.

It was at this church that, as contemporaries noticed, Edward Pugin successfully reconciled the Gothic Revival style with an essentially Counter-Reformation plan of an apsed basilica, instead of his father's subdivided plans and English square-ended chancels. The *Tablet* commented: 'In order that the high Altar may be visible to all the nave has been amplified, whilst the columns which divide it from the aisles are of sufficient width – viz twenty feet to each bay – to prevent any obstruction of view . . . the sort of church generally called

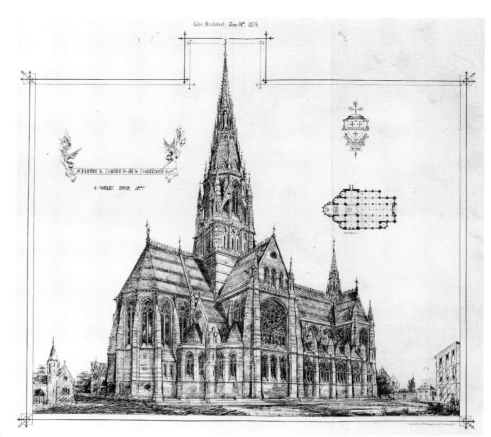

494.   Our Lady of Dadizeele, Belgium, designed by E.W. Pugin, drawn by James Murray for *The Architect*, 14 June 1873 (Charles Plante Fine Art).

495.   Drawing for a narthex addition to A.W. Pugin's Chapel, Ushaw College, by E.W. Pugin (Trustees of Ushaw College).

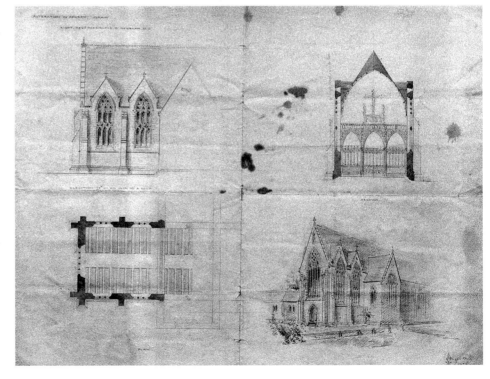

496. All Saints, Barton-upon-Irwell, Manchester, by E.W. Pugin, 1865–8; the east end, with the de Trafford Chantry bottom right.

497. All Saints, Barton-upon-Irwell, Manchester, the nave from the west end.

for amongst large congregations'.[47] The *Tablet* noted that Pugin's planning achieved 'a complete revolution in church-building.'[48]

There are many examples of Pugin's 'industrial' churches built for the manufacturing towns in the Midlands and North with their large Catholic populations. These churches were often cheaply built, some of the labour supplied by the congregation.[49] The façades were characterised by a gable rose window, set above an arcaded tympanum, with a central door. Massive bellcotes or set-off towers were typical. These churches follow the La Salette formula of wide nave and apses, tall attenuated arcades and steep roofs, restrained with metal ties, which often gave problems. The churches were well lit, in contrast to the 'dim religious light' of his father's interiors. The plan also followed a standard formula of west-end porches, supporting a west gallery, and often with a baptistry or mortuary chapel at the west end of the aisles. The naves were always pewed, with a central gangway division, and Pugin's characteristic deep plinths, squat shafts, and naturalistic capitals were designed to be seen above the benching. The arcades were wide – at St Bee's, Whitehaven over 20 ft across – so as to achieve the best sight lines. The aisles formed passages and gave access to confessionals, sometimes whole rooms forming an outer aisle, as at St Vincent de Paul's, Liverpool (1856–7), and Gorton. The east-end arrangement was tripartite with a shallow apsed sanctuary, flanked by side chapels usually dedicated to Our Lady or to the Sacred Heart, with other statues and particularly Stations of the Cross arranged in the aisles. Pulpits were arranged towards the east end of the nave outside the communion rails of stone, alabaster or metal which divided the chapels and sanctuary from the church. The massive high altars were made up of variegated stone, marble and metal and hanging from the roof was a wooden rood beam with figures and crucifix. The rood screens and sedilia for the officiating priest which A.W. Pugin had set such store by were dispensed with, replaced by the emphasis on the massive 'Benediction altar', with the pinnacled throne over the central tabernacle, and elaborate reredoses which sometimes continue round the sides of the apse. Separate sacristies for priests and altar-boys, usually with fireplaces, water closets and other services, were arranged behind the apse or side chapels.

All Saints', Barton-upon-Irwell, Manchester (1865–8), is Pugin's most lavish church (plate 496).[50] Contemporary commentators noted its visual richness and expense, whereas twentieth-century commentators, such as Pevsner, who called it 'Pugin's masterwork', found it 'rather fussy in its details. Fussiness was, of course, the curse of E.W. Pugin . . . yet it is undeniably splendid.'[51]

The church began with the building of the de Trafford chantry in 1863, a richly modelled, stone vaulted and cross gabled type like the chantries at Ushaw and at St Edmund's. It was the gift of Sir Humphrey de Trafford, who married in 1855 Lady Annette Talbot, niece of the Earl of Shrewsbury, whose coat of arms appears on the west front. All Saints is perhaps something of a rival to the 16th Earl's *ex voto* gift of Cheadle. The church (1865–8) was added to the chantry and the site and cost of over £25,000 were the gift of the de Traffords.

E.W. Pugin's 'Geometric English Gothic' is certainly fussy. The elevations are angular and attenuated. The characteristic bell-cote and *fleche* are flanked by two-over-life size angels crowning buttresses, which form the pinnacles of the tripartite west front. A massive recessed polychromatic arch, containing the rose window, is situated above an arcaded band with the recessed porch beneath and lean-to aisles. The chancel is separately roofed from the nave with a corona of windows under cross-gables. The materials were Stourton Freestone and Yorkshire Parpoint dressings with slate roofs and much prominent iron work of crosses, crestings and the like.

The interior (plate 497) is sumptuous, with a seven-bay arcade of banded Runcorn red and Painswick white sandstone columns set on raised bases, and having richly cut naturalistic capitals with carved saints' heads as label stops. Unlike in the 'industrial' churches, a chancel arch marks the distinction between nave and sanctuary. The polychromatic stonework continues in the reveal and chancel arch with its two orders, but, as the aisles are merely passages, the whole congregation would have seen the altar from the nave. The roof is another of Pugin's 'double-backed principal' types, with much iron-tieing in evidence. It is executed in the most expensive materials: English oak and Savannah pitch pine inlaid with coloured and gilded woods, originally intended for Alton Castle springing from wall posts supported on harp-playing angels, which can be attributed to Pugin's favourite sculptor Richard L. Boulton. Of the rich set of chancel two-light windows by Hardman only three survive re-assembled. The wall painting below (plate 498), showing the kneeling de Traffords with their children and Pugin himself with a plan of the church, is by J. Alphege Pippet of Hardman & Co.[52] The high altar is a fine

498. All Saints, Barton-upon-Irwell, Manchester, chancel, detail of a wall painting by Alphege Pippet, *c.*1868, showing E.W. Pugin, kneeling, with the plan of the church.

example of Pugin's design, executed by Boulton. The tripartite bas-relief of the Annunciation and the reredos with four scenes from the life of Christ flank the Hardman tabernacle surmounted by stone angels carrying a Hardman brass corona: these and much other metal work including the altar rails, were designed by Pugin. Finally the de Trafford chantry is screened from the chancel by an arcade of three stout columns on the chancel side, but thin shafts supporting the rib-vaulted stone chantry roof on the chapel side, the complex relationship between the two modelled on that between the chancel north arcade and its related outer aisle at St Mary, Beverley, which both Pugins had restored. The altar has a lifesize *Deposition of Christ* and a possibly later reredos, both attributable to Boulton.

Pugin inherited many of his father's domestic commissions, beginning with the furnishing and decoration of the chapel at Alton Towers for the lavish funeral of the 16th Earl of Shrewsbury, on 14 December 1852, for which he and John Hardman Powell made designs. The 17th Earl commissioned further work at Alton before his death in 1856, including the guildhall range at Alton Hospital (plate 499). Edward succeeded to a number of his father's commissions: for C. Scott-Murray at Danesfield, for Ambrose Phillipps de Lisle at Grace Dieu and Garendon.[53] His close collaboration with Lady Ann Scarisbrick at Scarisbrick Hall, is commemorated in a stained glass window showing the architect with a plan of the intended buildings. The enormous tower and spire and the east wing including alterations to the chapel and a kitchen, are his (plate 83). His enlargement of the great hall fireplace is, like the

499. The Guildhall Range, St John's Hospital, Alton, by E.W. Pugin, 1852–6.

500. Carlton Towers, Yorkshire, the porch, by E.W. Pugin, 1873–7.

altar at Danesfield, a text-book contrast between father and son.

Two large domestic commissions had nothing to do with his father. He built and furnished Croston Hall, Lancashire and the small church of Holy Cross for Rudolph de Trafford, the cousin of Sir Humphrey. For the 12th Lord Beaumont Pugin rebuilt Carlton Towers from 1872 (plate 500), part of a much larger scheme for a massive *donjon*, a baron's hall and a chapel. Edward Pugin was more of a speculative businessman than his father, with disastrous results in the ambitious Granville Hotel at Ramsgate.[54]

Pugin's career was not confined to Britain and Ireland. His most important foreign commission was for the enormous pilgrimage church of Our Lady, Dadizele, Belgium (1859–94), partly inspired by the Lille cathedral competition entries that he had seen in 1856. The church is entirely Pugin's design, the execution was handed over to the Belgian Gothic Revival architect Count Joseph Bethune. Pugin also designed the Château de Loppem for Count van Caloen and two other domestic commissions for the Bishop of Bruges, all executed by Bethune. There was an unexecuted design for the new chapel of the Venerable English College in Rome (1864);[55] and he made designs for houses in Denmark, Canada and the USA. When he travelled to America in 1873 he set up an office at Brevort House, 5th Avenue, New York, and, according to his obituary in the *Irish Builder* had orders for thirty churches in Washington, Chicago, which later involved P.P. Pugin.[56] He exhibited at the Royal Academy (1874) 'a chapel, bridge and lodge about to be erected over the Connecticut [River] USA'.[57] A church was designed for the Redemptorists at Brookline, Boston, with a central lantern forty feet square, with an octagon above, a high altar, sixteen altars and a monastery. He was also credited with a church and monastery in Cuba, and a commission for Hobart in Tasmania.[58]

*

Peter Paul Pugin (1851–1904) was Edward's partner before his unexpected death, and the younger man's influence can be detected in a number of Edward's later churches: St Mary's, Warrington, Lancashire (1875–7), Cleator (1869–72) and Workington, (1873–6), all for the Benedictines. The English Martyrs, London (1875–6) and St Anne's, Birkenhead (1875–7) also mark the transition.

Peter Paul Pugin's obituary[59] suggests none of the controversy associated with his father and brother. He died at Bournemouth attended by a Jesuit priest, and was buried at Ramsgate on 15 March 1892. In 1886 he had married the third daughter of the Catholic builder, John Bird, of Brook Green, Hammersmith and had had five children. He exhibited at the Royal Academy and elsewhere and was an accomplished watercolourist.

Almost exclusively a Catholic church architect, Peter Paul's most significant patron was Charles Eyre, Administrator and later Archbishop of Glasgow from 1869 to 1893. An Englishman from a Northumbrian gentry family, he had been parish priest at A.W. Pugin's church in Newcastle, for which he wrote a highly Puginesque guide, his

appointment was in anticipation of a formal restoration of the Scottish hierarchy in 1878. Unlike other bishops in this period he successfully established a central Finance Board.[60] The volume of church building was astonishing and Peter Paul was almost official architect to the diocese. The churches follow the formula used by Edward at La Salette, Liverpool – a single vessel church with a large apsed sanctuary under the same roof line as the nave. The proportions of the churches are, however, less attenuated than those of Edward, whose characteristic, but structurally troublesome, west-end bell-cotes were omitted. Among many churches, St Patrick's, Anderston (1897) is his most original.

Despite the bulk of his work in Glasgow, Pugin kept his offices in London and Liverpool. His richest and most important church is Princethorpe, built for Benedictine nuns, in red-brick (plate 501), with a magnificent altar and metal rood screen (plate 502). Cheaper versions of this red-brick style abound, particularly in Liverpool. The firm's strong connections in the north-west and Glasgow were continued after 1904 by Peter Paul's nephew, Sebastian Pugin Powell (b.1866), the son of Anne Pugin and John Hardman Powell, with Cuthbert Welby at Ramsgate as a sleeping partner.[61] P.P. Pugin built much for the Benedictines. At Stanbrook Abbey (1878) he added the small chapel of the Holy Thorn (1885) to Edward's church (1869–71).[62] His incomplete scheme for Fort Augustus Monastery in the Highlands, and a megalomaniac scheme to finish Edward's church at Belmont with three spires, show him to be in the line of Pugin visionaries.

Peter Paul Pugin's style is readily recognisable as a development of his brother's, and his churches quickly settled down to a formula, which can be defined as 'Second Generation Catholic High Victorianism'. It was apparently quite separate both from the highly intellectual constructional polychromy of contemporary Anglican church architecture, and certainly very different from the refinement of Bodley, who, ironically, revived the style and taste of A.W. Pugin at this time.

He took as much delight as his father and brother in designing altars and other fixed architectural furniture, and pleaded with the Glasgow Archdiocese Finance Board for higher percentages for this intricate work.[63] He had his favourite sculptors: R.L. Boulton, later Wall of Cheltenham, and Hardman for stained glass and metalwork. He was reprimanded by the Finance Board for including the names of these practitioners in his tender specifications.[64] Painted wooden statues, altars by Boulton and stencilling by Alphege Pippet are also associated with Peter Paul's interiors, for instance the high altar at St Peter Partick's, Glasgow, (1903) and the destroyed

501. Princethorpe, Warwickshire, the former Priory church.

502. Princethorpe, Warwickshire, the former Priory church, interior.

503.   High Altar, Ushaw College Chapel, by P.P. Pugin, 1900 (the metal grills in front are modern).

504.   St Mary's, Liverpool, as rebuilt by P.P. Pugin, 1884–5; 505.   Side chapel by A.W., E.W. and P.P. Pugin (photos: Downside Abbey).

high altar at Motherwell Cathedral (1902). If, to our eyes, Peter Paul Pugin seems to be stylistically quite different from his father, to Catholic contemporaries his work, like Edward's, was seen as the logical succession to A.W. Pugin's. Thus his enormous altar at Ushaw (plate 503) replaced that of his father in the new chapel by Dunn and Hansom (1882–4). Pugin is credited in his obituary with over 450 of these altars.[65]

The major example of the continuity of the Pugin and Pugin firm was the rebuilding for the Benedictines of St Mary's, Liverpool, when the original site was bought for the expansion of the Liverpool Exchange station. The unusual decision was taken to 'retain the actual building . . . to take the Church down and rebuild it . . . stone for stone'.[66] Internally the new church (1884–5) was a reproduction of the old, including A.W. Pugin's magnificent altar and canopied reredos, into which Peter Paul added one of his characteristic Benediction throne canopies (plate 504). The font, the Lady altar and the sedilia, as well as much stained glass by A.W. Pugin, were retained. The altar tomb of the priest founder, and an altar and reredos both by E.W. Pugin were re-installed in the Sacred Heart chapel (plate 505). Contemporary photographs show a heavily stencilled interior, which can be attributed to Alphege Pippet.

By contrast Peter Paul built almost no domestic architecture, and certainly no country houses. The change in patronage pattern is marked by the church of St Elizabeth at Scarisbrick (1887–90). It was paid for by the Marquis de Castega, who inherited from Edward's patron, Lady Anne Scarisbrick (1788–1872), herself the sister and heiress of A.W. Pugin's patron, Charles Scarisbrick (d. 1860?), both of whom had been content to allow the Catholic congregation to worship in a converted barn, while transforming Scarisbrick Hall. The contrast between the ethos and mood of the three patrons and architects could not be stronger.

In 1927 Kenneth Clark in *The Gothic Revival* wrote that 'today the elder Pugin is better remembered than his son', a somewhat Bloomsbury Group view obviously referring to A.C. Pugin,[67] but in 1933 Michael Trappes-Lomax's *Pugin*, written with the active co-operation of Sebastian Pugin Powell, who continued the practice with Charles Purcell, began to correct the balance.[68]

A.W. Pugin's last child, Cuthbert Welby Pugin, died in his eighty-eighth year; he was the last member of the family to be buried in the Pugin vault at Ramsgate on 28 March 1928. His death was noted, not with an obituary, but with a passing reference to his father's career, in the *Tablet*.[69] The Pugins were now history.

CHAPTER TWENTY-ONE

The Fate of Pugin's True Principles

ANDREW SAINT

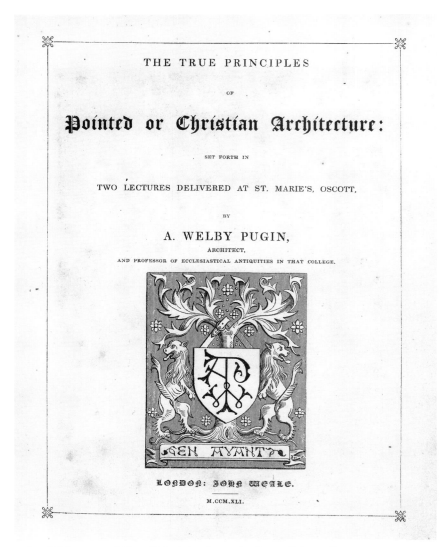

506. Title page of *True Principles*, from the first edition, 1841.

Architectural Htheories are judged not by their truth but by their force and influence. If it were otherwise, few of the canonical names from Vitruvius downwards would hold their place in the pantheon of western architectural thought. Pugin's, certainly, would not be among them. Pugin was a prophet, a moralist, a satirist, and a historian of a kind; but he was not a logician. His three best-known books, *Contrasts*, *The True Principles of Pointed or Christian Architecture*, and *An Apology for the Revival of Christian Architecture*, are not systematic aesthetic treatises (plate 506). They are, to use a later term, manifestoes – breathlessly written, haphazard in order, replete with rhetoric and feeling. In the terminology of Pugin's own time, they belong to the genre of religious tracts or pamphlets. The very titles of the two later tracts glory in their debt to the language and style of Christian apologetics. Proud professions of their author's Catholic faith, both culminate in the motto 'Laus Deo'. The incisiveness and seeming simplicity of *The True Principles*, above all, seize the imagination on a first reading. But as Pugin's modern biographers observe, it is the heart, not the head, that is appealed to. 'It is in a sense a muddle; but not the muddle of incompetence; rather, the turmoil of one who is fighting for what he values more than life itself,' remarks Michael Trappes-Lomax. The sentiment is echoed by Phoebe Stanton: 'as was Pugin's way he had plunged into the writing of his book without considering on what shore his reasoning would leave him.'[1]

To Pugin, it would have been unthinkable to divorce architectural principle from religious conviction. The overwhelming thrust of his argument was that a society which abandons religious truth is destined to produce a debased architecture. That message is dressed up with a young man's scorn and glee in the plates of *Contrasts*, then hammered home with graver zeal in the pages of the *Apology*. Pugin's prime value as a thinker depends upon the clarity with which his writings advance and develop this arresting, unpalatable and, in at least one critic's view,[2] pharisaical proposition. A better architecture without social and religious reform was impossible, he believed. It could not be 'imposed, so to speak, from without', as Kenneth Clark put it.[3] The most that better buildings or better-designed objects could do would be to help kick-start the wider process of reformation. And yet, *au fond*, it was architecture and design, not politics or theology, to which this seeming puritan was wedded, For someone of Pugin's temperament and abilities, art could never take a back seat. His vision of the past, of religion and of social reform alike, remained an aesthetic one.

That is the core of Pugin's theoretical legacy – the challenge and contradiction that lie at the heart of his writing. His many heirs and successors from Ruskin to Le Corbusier all likewise believed that there was some sort of two-way, chicken-and-egg link between architectural design and the state of society. Architecture mattered because it was the most eloquent of all witnesses to the moral and physical condition of a city or a nation. Improve it, and you have gone some way to improving the world; yet you cannot hope to improve architecture very much until you have first improved the world. Since few artists who hold this view have the patience or austerity to lay aside their art while they are improving the world, the world generally ends up with a queer and not very logical mixture of design, polemic and social action.

Pugin was not the first person to be aware of the paradox. It was implicit in the various holistic views of the world that took hold of European thought in the aftermath of the French Revolution; and it had been all but formulated in the early 1830s by the Saint-Simonians, who regarded architecture as the mere 'shell and visible embodiment of social institutions'.[4] Nevertheless, Pugin was the first to put the paradox clearly. After he wrote, buildings and their design became increasingly interpreted, not just by clients and users but also by architects, as more than ends in themselves. They became, in Robert Macleod's phrase, 'technical processes' towards a social product.[5]

In Pugin's formulation, the Catholic faith and the glory of the Gothic past were the key to solving this chicken-and-egg conundrum. His historical theory was, in a word, naive: at least in his moments of optimism and rhetoric, he believed that modern England could go back to better architecture and better society through the process of religious reform. Soon, however, the theological debate which was so compulsive a force in English life when Pugin wrote faded in fervour. At that point, his religious imperative became subsumed into a general social question. It was in secularized form, with its Gothic trappings discarded, that the paradox of style and society made its great impact upon the twentieth century. But anyone who looks into the psychology and the moral vanity of the Modern Movement at its high tide, with its insistence that we all needed a fresh start in architecture for our own future welfare, will find Pugin and his campaign for a 'Christian Architecture' at the bottom of things.

Over the past thirty years, there has been full reaction and revulsion against attempts to apply dominant moral certitudes like Pugin's to architecture. That, no doubt, is why the passage of his writings most often cited in architectural theory today is the one that seems, on the surface of things, to have least to do with social or religious questions. I refer to the clarion call with which Pugin opens *The True Principles*. Its authority and brevity excuse its citation anew:

> The object of the present Lecture is to set forth and explain the true principles of Pointed or Christian Architecture, by the knowledge of which you may be enabled to test architectural excellence. The two great rules for design are these: 1st, that there should be no features about a building which are not necessary for convenience, construction, or propriety; 2nd, that all ornament should consist of enrichment of the essential construction of the building. The neglect of these two rules is the cause of all the bad architecture of the present time.

In the lines which follow, Pugin glosses these rules with the riders that 'the smallest detail should have a meaning or serve a purpose', and that 'the construction itself should vary with the material employed.' 'Strange as it may appear at first sight,' he adds, 'it is in pointed architecture alone that these great principles have been carried out.'[6]

Here we have the bones of a theory which appears to have everything to do with design and nothing to do with religion. To this passage and its working-out in the later pages of *The True Principles*, its author owes his place in the history of architectural functionalism and rationalism. It represents another kind of link between Pugin and the Modern Movement – one seemingly far less imbued with discomforting connotations of 'positivism'. For it is one thing to impose a specific style of architecture upon society at large for its own good, but quite another to set out rules about how architects should go about designing a building and distinguishing between its parts. Because Pugin's 'rules of design' are about a relatively technical matter, they can be construed as relevant still to architecture.

In the original formulation, however, issues of morality lurk even here. Pugin lays down his two propositions in a lawlike way, and insists that 'bad architecture' follows from their neglect. Critics may argue, as many from Geoffrey Scott and Kenneth Clark onwards have done, that 'bad architecture' has everything to do with aesthetics and nothing to do with ethics. Pursuing this line of argument, we can (if we wish) wall off Pugin's rules of design from the rest of his ideas and enshrine them as the core of his 'true principles'. That is roughly what has happened in architectural theory. But as an interpretation of what Pugin intended, it is a travesty. The whole thrust and tone of his mature writings imply that obedience to his rules of design is a moral duty, not a technical nicety. To Pugin, every design and every detail have consequences for conduct beyond the confines of architectural or structural debate. This is difficult ground to hold. But few architects or writers on architecture ever wish to abandon it completely. For if the validity of an idea about style, structure or detail depends upon its acceptability to architects and critics alone; if, in other words, architecture just boils down to aesthetic fashion, how can it enjoy wider force or significance? In the final analysis, if architecture wishes to take itself seriously, it must respond to Pugin's challenge.

What, exactly, did Pugin mean by his rules of design, and how did they evolve? The genesis of *The True Principles* has been admirably set out by Phoebe Stanton.[7] She explains that the text derives from lectures which he gave at Oscott College, probably in 1838–9, and amended in 1840 for publication in the following year. After converting to Catholicism in 1835, Pugin had plunged himself into intense study of Gothic art; and the lectures, argues Mrs Stanton, consist in the main not of dogmas for a revivalist manifesto but of general principles of architecture he deduced from what he had found, as his boyhood facility for Gothic detail passed into mastery of Gothic construction. Two versions of a prospectus survive for *The True*

Principles. They show that Pugin attached much importance to the wording of his rules, but found it hard to give them the right mutual priority. The draft version consists of five 'important facts':

1. that all the ornaments of true pointed edifices were merely introduced as decoration to the essential construction of these buildings
2. that the construction of pointed architecture was varied to accord with the properties of the various materials employed shown by antient examples of stone, timber and metal construction
3. that no features were introduced in the antient pointed edifices which were not essential either for convenience or propriety
4. that pointed architecture is most consistent as it decorates the useful portions of buildings instead of concealing them
5. that the defects of modern architecture are principally owing to the departure from antient consistent principles.

In the published prospectus, two of these points were amended slightly, while Pugin slotted in an extra 'fact' on proportion: 'The true principles of architectural proportion are only found in Pointed Edifices'.

All these assertions are repeated, with more or less weight, in the final text. But we must, I think, take it that the two 'rules of design' with which *The True Principles* opens epitomize what Pugin felt he had discovered from his study of Gothic. They have always been taken to do so. The difficulty – and, perhaps, the continued currency of the rules – is due to the fact that neither is so unambiguous as it at first appears to be. The language is electrifying. Passages like these excited the young Gilbert Scott 'almost to frenzy', and 'morally awakened' him and many others.[8] Yet the full meaning of the rules is not so clear.

The former of Pugin's rules reads on first acquaintance as wholly reductive and negative: 'that there should be no features about a building which are not necessary for convenience, construction, or propriety'. Here to all appearances is presaged the killjoy austerity of much modern architecture: no room is left for invention, or craftsmanship, or serendipity. It is strange indeed (and psychologically significant) that the most talented English ornamentalist of his day could commit himself to so self-denying a sentence. To stress convenience, construction and propriety as the keys to a wise and reasonable way of building was nothing new. Such commonplaces can be found in Vitruvius, Alberti or almost any of their more down-to-earth successors. The novelty is Pugin's claim that these qualities are both necessary and sufficient for good architecture, with the implication that anything extra can only make a building worse, not better. That way, one may think, lies the road to vulgar functionalism in architecture, to a reductive philosophy of building in which purely economical means serve exclusively pragmatic ends. Can Pugin, the 'preterpluperfect Goth', really be the godfather of so cheerless a doctrine?

Almost no architectural writer has ever been a vulgar functionalist. Pugin is no exception to the rule. A functional misdemeanour – in other words, some shortcoming in 'convenience' or 'construction' – is the commonest of faults in architecture. It offers a weapon for anyone who wishes to undermine a designer or a style. The satirical plates of *Contrasts* and *The True Principles* do this as savagely as it has ever been done, with special gusto for the gimcrack Gothic of Pugin's father's friend Nash and others of his generation – what Summerson once called the 'Waverley' phase of the Gothic Revival, with its ludicrous, anomalous obsession with detail (plates 221, 507).[9] Functionally, Pugin felt, there was a vast amount to put right in modern architecture. Only the serious study of 'antient' (in other words, Gothic) example could do the trick. But though disciplined attention to convenience and construction might purify design, he did not suppose that such an exercise could ever dictate its forms. These would be guided by the third quality that he insisted upon in architecture: 'propriety'.

'Propriety' is Pugin's escape route from the path to vulgar functionalism. A term as old as art criticism itself, it is one very handy for any architectural theorist who is trying to avoid being pinned down by his own reductive logic. Sometimes propriety can mean something quite technical in Pugin, akin to 'character' – another fashionable term of the time. That is what he intends by the rule in *The True Principles* that 'designs should be adapted to the material in which they are executed' (a line already suggested in the 1830s both by Gottfried Semper and by the young John Ruskin[10]). But by propriety, Pugin generally means something broader. He implies by it the justification for almost everything that we today find dogmatic and distinctive in a Puginian building: why the separate parts of a church are to receive separate expression; why its ornament is to be most concentrated in the sanctuary; why a church should look different from a house, and a house different from a railway station; and so on. Any of these ideas may be rationally controverted;

507. St Katharine's Hospital, Regent's Park, London by Ambrose Poynter, 1826–8, showing the eastern end of the chapel built in a cheaper style than the show front at the west end – the kind of practice that Pugin execrated.

and, from the moment that Pugin set out his idiosyncratic value-system about what was 'proper' in architecture, many of them were so challenged. But the argument was never at heart about architecture. It was about theology, politics or social organisation. So, once again, 'propriety' in Pugin lifts us out of pure architectural debate and engages us in issues about what kinds of buildings a society requires or deserves. Without it, the functionalist void reopens.

Pugin's second rule of design is a far more positive and personal injunction. It states 'that all ornament should consist of enrichment of the essential construction of the building'. So we now hear about ornament, which the austerity of the first tenet had seemed to rule out; and priority is implicitly given to revealing, clarifying or otherwise expressing the structure, which ornament is to set off and to celebrate. Here is something definite which a designer can make something of and work with.

At the same time, Pugin craftily leaves this rule a little fuzzy. It is clear from the text of *The True Principles* and from Pugin's own habit of design that he wants ornament and structure to be visibly distinct. Ornament must inform the expression of structure, he believes; if it obscures construction, there is a danger of 'deceit', which he abhors. That is a practice which creeps in, as he acknowledges, in late Gothic buildings like the vault of King's College Chapel. Examples of the correct enrichment of construction are the stiff-leaf carving of a load-bearing capital; or the expression of the rib in a thirteenth-century vault; or, from Pugin's own

508. Floriated cross on the roof of St Augustine's, Ramsgate.

509. Angels from the, south transept Westminster Abbey. The decoration here plays counterpart to the structure, rather than belonging to it.

practice, the floriation of the limbs of a cross, or the chamfering of 'revealed construction' on a table or chair (plate 508). But the line between enriching and concealing structure is a fine one. What the Gothic builders often did, and what Pugin seems sometimes to endorse, is to ornament precisely the non-structural members in a building – in other words, to create enrichment *around* the essential construction, rather than enrichment of the construction itself (plate 509). Robert Willis had put the point at once more vaguely and more helpfully when he spoke in 1835 of the 'subservience of decoration to construction' in the best Gothic architecture.[11]

This apparently trivial point has had many ramifications. The question of where ornament should go and how it was to be treated became a *cause célèbre* of nineteenth-century design, from the arguments of the designers in the South Kensington circle in the 1850s through to architects like Sullivan and beyond. Often, Pugin's rule is loosely interpreted as meaning that there should be some sort of disciplined counterpoint between construction and ornament. What he actually said was that ornament should be 'of', in other words, attached to, construction, not separate from it. The plain frame and ornamental panel system of an architect like Perret is not really derived from Puginian principle at all. It seems to be so because it has medieval analogues and it stresses the value of 'revealed construction'. But revealed construction is not quite what Pugin endorses; it is 'enriched construction' which he approves – neither the rawness of plain structure, nor the deceit of concealed structure, but a happy medium of structure ornamented with propriety, which

he believed the Gothic builders in their heyday had achieved.

It is wrong, then, to say as J.M. Richards once did, that Pugin's 'particular contribution was to realise and expound the importance of structure as the basis of architecture'.[12] A precise kind of combination between structure and ornament is what is vital to his theory; the two reinforce and authenticate one another. More accurately, Roger Scruton has suggested that Pugin was interested in the idea of 'a valid detail'. But he trivialises Pugin's position when he adds that 'the valid detail is the detail that is structurally significant'.[13] These heresies have arisen because posterity, for its own ends, insisted on linking the puritanism of Pugin's first rule of design with a narrowly structural interpretation of his second rule. The idea of structural purity, or even of revealed construction, had only a limited role to play in his view of architecture. Detail, whether functional or ornamental, had for Pugin to transcend its structural role. One has only to turn to the wonderful ornamentalism and symbolism of his own designs, or read his almost Ruskinian enthusiasm for adapting and disposing the whole gamut of natural foliage in the preface to his late book, *Floriated Ornament* (1849), to grasp that a merely structural interpretation of Pugin's theory of design is a creative distortion of the truth.

Where did Pugin get his architectural ideas from, and how original was he as a thinker? This has never been quite satisfactorily resolved. Bound up with it is the question of his influence upon others, not least upon Ruskin. For when two writers have a common source, or when new ideas are generally in the air, as they were in English architectural circles during the 1830s and '40s, it is hard to say who said what first.

About the origins of Pugin's social and religious philosophy of art there is no mystery. At home, the tide of radicalism and reformism that had been gathering all through his youth came to a head in the 1830s. Mrs Stanton has shown how far *Contrasts* depends upon the holistic, backward-looking, Tory style of national commentary that had been flowing torrentially from the pens of Carlyle, Coleridge, Disraeli, Scott, Southey and Cobbett.[14] We should also perhaps remember the long and fearful sermons of national denunciation from Edward Irving, the fashionably emotional preacher to whom Pugin's blue-stocking mother had taken him in his youth.[15] His genius was to turn these jeremiads on the state of the nation into a concise, funny and compelling caricature of English architecture, past and present. After the crisis of his conversion to Catholicism, he also took in a good deal of foreign romantic thought. Above all there was 'Christian art', the emotional ideology which grew up during the reaction to the French Revolution among authors like Wackenroder and Schelling in Germany and Chateaubriand in France. The devotional principles of 'Christian' art-criticism were being systematized by Alexis-François Rio, who lived in London between 1837 and 1841 and cannot have failed to meet Pugin. Another Frenchman with good English contacts, the Comte de Montalembert, was exploring a Christian or Catholic interpretation of architecture on lines similar to Pugin's, though in the end Pugin seems to have had more effect on Montalembert than the other way round.[16]

All this is clear enough. But when one turns to Pugin's purely architectural ideas, in particular the austerity of *The True Principles*, it is not so easy to say where they come from. They have a fresh tang; yet the structural principles are half-familiar, and the phraseology of Pugin's first rule repeats terms well worn in architectural texts down the ages.

The obvious direction in which to look is towards France. Pugin's father was himself French; the son was at ease with the language, travelled often in France and Belgium from childhood onwards, and had French professional friends, notably among antiquarians and archaeologists. Moreover architectural theory, and in particular a rationalist attitude to structure, was more fully developed in France than elsewhere.

Augustus Pugin senior remains a mystery. Apart from the vivid sketch of him in Ferrey's life of his son, we know precious little about him. But he had nothing to do with architecture before he left France during the Revolution, so far as we know; and from what we can gather of his work for Nash and his later activities, he stuck to draughtsmanship in preference to the structural or practical side of an architect's life. So it is unlikely that Pugin junior absorbed any latent structural philosophy from his father, or for that matter from the architects whom he must first have met, like Nash or Wyatville. Nash, for instance, was a clever constructor, but not a very principled or rational one.[17] Had the boy Pugin moved in a different circle, say that of architect-constructors like Smirke or Laing or Fowler, he might have developed an earlier interest in structures instead of becoming so brilliant a delineator. As it was, *The True Principles* was a heartfelt reaction against the shameless picturesqueness of his own youth. When Pugin first set up in business in 1831, he had advertised 'to supply all the ornamental portions of buildings which could by possibility be executed apart from the structure and be fixed afterwards'.[18] That was the kind of sin which study of Gothic precedent and a true structural philosophy were now to atone for.

We know that Pugin senior had books by many of the great figures of French architectural literature in his library, some no doubt acquired on visits to Paris in the 1820s.[19] It would be unwise to make too much of them, as all the ones we know about were sold in 1833. They are likely to have been used by the Pugin drawing school for their plates, not their text. In any case, it is unnecessary and implausible to picture Pugin sitting down and reading rationalists like Laugier, Rondelet or Durand in preparation for *The True Principles*. For by the end of the 1830s, their ideas had slipped into the general currency and confusion of English architectural debate.

Three strands of French architectural theory, all bound up with one another, are relevant to *The True Principles*. One is the emergence of a structural way of thinking about architecture – a development which had much to do with the growth of an articulate engineering profession and traditions of teaching construction in France after 1750. The second is the re-evaluation of Gothic, not as a style for literal imitation or antiquarian study, but as a source of national pride and a point of reference in any discussion about architectural principle. The last is the methodological tendency, deep-rooted among French architects but perceptibly stronger after the Revolution, to split projects or buildings into clear, constituent, linked elements. Perronet and Rondelet are the key figures in the first strand; Frézier, Soufflot and Laugier in the second; and the pedantic Durand, teacher at the Polytechnique and systematiser of what others like Blondel had said or implied before him, in the third. To Durand's name should perhaps be added that of the great zoologist Georges Cuvier, whose way of analysing the structure of organisms in terms of the functions and relations of their constituent parts had vast influence in all walks of life.[20]

It is easy to see how all this relates to Pugin. A value-system in architecture which set a priority upon clarity and visibility of structure, which respected Gothic precedent in achieving this, and which called for a demarcation in design between different functional and structural and ornamental parts, was exactly his own. Yet there were reasons, too, why these ideas had to filter down to him second-hand. The French writers mentioned above were almost all rationalists and classicists. Architectural rationalism furnished Pugin with a disciplined way of thinking about structure; but the revolutionary and Napoleonic events had given it an irreligious savour. In so far as it seemed to imply a code of architectural values answering only man's material needs, it would have been anathema to Pugin. Classicism offered most French architects the values which prevented them from falling into that trap. But classical values had never been acceptable to him. It would have puzzled Pugin that someone like Soufflot could have admired Gothic structure and then tried to synthesise it with the classical tradition. If Gothic was both structurally superior and the national style, then surely the only logical answer was its full-hearted revival?

One signal of Pugin's debt, at one remove, to the French theorists is his stress upon 'truth' in architecture. It is there in the title of *The True Principles*, and in his intransigent opposition to deceit or subterfuge in design: 'the severity of Christian or Pointed architecture is utterly opposed to all deception', he thunders.[21] After Pugin, truth in architecture becomes one of Ruskin's celebrated lamps, a warcry of the Gothic Revival, and a cliché of architectural criticism. In an unpublished paper, Adrian Forty has shown that truth had been often applied to architecture as a term of admiration in the eighteenth century.[22] But so long as illusion, display and taste were the dominant values in design, its force was weak and diffuse. What the French rationalists did was to develop a structural and organisational set of criteria for judging truth in architecture. On this rationalising base, Pugin then set the ardent superstructure of

Christian art. So something that had started out as a way of analysing how buildings were put together acquired a whole baggage of implications for the life and conduct of those who designed, made and paid for them. This was a development which the enlightenment fathers of French architectural theory would hardly have recognised.

How did Pugin acquire his grasp of the traditions of French rationalism? There is no single answer to this. Though British writers had been slower to argue for the rationalism of Gothic structure than French ones, by the early nineteenth century they were doing so. The position was implicit by the 1830s in the scholarship of architects like Thomas Rickman, whose iron churches advance the case for a rationalised modern Gothic, and of antiquarians like the scientifically minded Robert Willis, whose analysis of Gothic vaults much influenced Viollet-le-Duc. Many authors had touched on the ideas that the constituent elements in architectural design should be defined, and that structure should be explicit and emphasised. The more intellectual English classicists of the 1820s, including Soane and Smirke, were familiar with and favourably inclined towards axioms of this kind.

Closest of all to Pugin on structural issues was Alfred Bartholomew, whose *Essay on the Decline of Excellence in the Structure of Modern English Buildings* (1840) argued trenchantly for the rationalism of Gothic and the corruption of modern British architecture, and even used the expression 'true principles'. But Bartholomew, like Willis or Georg Moller of Darmstadt, whose books on German Gothic were translated into English in the 1830s,[23] stood closer to the French theorists than Pugin in one vital respect. They analysed and admired the constructive science of Gothic. But they never deduced from their findings the moral or religious necessity for a nineteenth-century Gothic Revival. By the end of the 1830s, then, the concepts of structural truth and Gothic rationalism were *au courant*. It wanted only someone with Pugin's energy and genius for invective to kindle the fire.

The effects of that conflagration are well known. Whatever Pugin may have cribbed from this author or learnt from that architect, *Contrasts* and *The True Principles* are still the decisive instruments that transform the Gothic Revival and turn British architecture upside down. Pugin's preferred styles, his rules of design, and his intolerant tone of pamphleteering were immediately adopted by *The Ecclesiologist*; only his Catholic opinions were discarded. 'Second-Pointed' churches sprang

510. Centre of the garden front, Milton Ernest Hall, Bedfordshire, by William Butterfield, 1854–8. The arcading and variation of materials are arbitrary rather than truly structural, though in Puginian taste.

511. End tower on the front of the Natural History Museum, London, by Alfred Waterhouse, 1873–81. The terracotta cladding has no structural implications, but is like the marble cladding of Italian medieval buildings.

up all over the land, raised upon a wave of moral fervour and national conscience. The industry of scholarly church-restoration ground into action. Outside the compass of architecture, the whole debate of the 1840s and '50s within the Government School of Design and the infant South Kensington Museum about principles of ornament and pattern was governed by the moral urgency injected by Pugin into all questions of design and by the trenchant provocation of his rules. When Owen Jones set down his own ideas about decoration in 1856, he could proffer only Puginian numbered commandments – a formidable thirty-seven of them. It was almost thirty years after the publication of *The True Principles* before the Puginian tide began to ebb. Surely no architectural tract, not excluding *Vers une architecture*, ever had so dynamic a consequence.

Church-builders of the mature Gothic Revival had little difficulty in following Pugin's rules of design, for they had plenty of his drawings and buildings to guide them. But with secular buildings, things were less straightforward; and here the need that architects felt to interpret the fertile vagueness of *The True Principles* on the relation

between structure and ornament readily shows up. Take, for instance, the garden front of Milton Ernest Hall (plate 510) by William Butterfield, a loyal though by no means literal Puginian. Butterfield could well have designed this beautiful elevation far more simply and obeyed all the Puginian canons except for 'propriety': which is interpreted here as the due expression of a rich and respon-sible Victorian merchant's standing, achieved through dignified ornament. But it is rarely ornament of 'essential construction'. But-tresses are exaggerated, relieving arches are picked out in brick, and needless arcading is introduced for sheer delight of the thing. In the first phase of the Gothic Revival, details are thrown into designs regardless of function in order to create pictur-esqueness. Pugin's principles put a stop to all that; yet the picturesque urge remained. Instead, details became structurally plausible but practically redundant.

The same sort of thing occurs in a different way on another splendid building that would hardly have been built in the same way without *The True Principles*: Alfred Waterhouse's Natural History Museum (plate 511). No building of the English

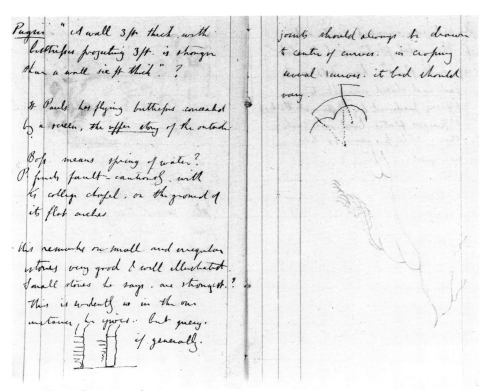

512. Notes from one of Ruskin's sketchbooks (Trustees of the Ruskin Museum, Coniston), showing that he had studied Pugin's *True Principles*.

Gothic Revival is more 'rational' in structural terms; and indeed the wonderful clarity of the relation between its parts may be indirectly due to Cuvier, since Sir Richard Owen, who drew up Waterhouse's brief and the programme of decoration for the museum, was a Cuvierist. Waterhouse conceived the museum in clear Puginian terms. The elevations reflect the plan, the structure is visibly articulated, and the beautiful ornament acts as a kind of commentary upon the structure. And yet there is a shadow of falseness about the whole thing. The terracotta facing blocks are hardly more than a cladding; their polychromy is just a pattern achieved by injecting some of the blocks with cobalt dye; and the ornamental panels are largely set off from the structural parts rather than attached to them. So once again, we find even in the most disciplined Gothic Revivalists like Waterhouse a decorative and exaggerated use of structural devices, rather than the strict enrichment of construction that Pugin had enjoined. This same tendency towards exaggerated stress on structural or quasi-structural members long outlives the Gothic Revival, and can be traced down to high-tech architecture. Pugin is not its only forefather – indeed the old Gothic builders had done it a great deal. But *The True Principles* had a lot to do with its revival.

It is easier to gauge the practical than the theoretical influence of Pugin's principles. The most contested case, that of Ruskin, has happily been sorted out now by Patrick Conner.[24] Ruskin, no doubt for religious reasons, once rather shrilly denied that he owed anything to Pugin, 'except two facts, one about buttresses and one about ironwork'.[25] The existence of a few sketch-notes based on *The True Principles* seems to prove Ruskin false, or at least forgetful (plate 512). But Mr Conner also shows that many of the ideas shared between the two were in common currency, while others – like the concept of truth to materials – had first been explored by Ruskin in *The Poetry of Architecture*, the precocious articles he contributed to the *Architectural Magazine* in 1837–8.

A different case is that of Viollet-le-Duc.[26] Such was the ideological climate in France, that Viollet could combine rationalism in architecture and secularism in politics with a passion for Gothic and a busy practice in cathedral restoration. That could not be squared with Puginism as it was practised in England; and indeed Viollet-le-Duc was never popular with *The Ecclesiologist*. Viollet owned Pugin's main writings in the eccentric French version of them put out by T.H. King of Bruges, but probably did not make much use of them. The rationalist case for Gothic he could find in the French originals, while for the Christian side of the argument he cannot have cared at all. Despite his French ancestry, his Catholicism and his antiquarian friends, Pugin's influence seems to have been slight in that country, so seldom open to British ways of thinking about architecture.

In Germany, his writings had wider success through the good offices of August Reichensperger (1808–95), equally indefatigable as a propagandist for a universal Gothic style and as a centre-party politician in the aftermath of 1848. Reichensperger had much to do with later phases of the com-pletion of Cologne Cathedral. An obsessive Anglophile, he knew Pugin, Scott, Beresford Hope and other leading figures of the Gothic Revival. His *Die christlich-germanische Baukunst* (1845) is a fairly literal attempt to translate Pugin's prin-ciples to Germany; later, in 1877, he wrote a long pamphlet on Pugin, *Augustus Welby Northmore Pugin, der Neubegründer der christlichen Kunst in England*.[27] In America, too, ecclesiology made much practical headway for a time among Episcopalians.[28] But his combination of moral crusade and of laying down the architectural law was too specific to the national mood for the whole package to get accepted elsewhere. It depended for its runaway success on a political and religious opportunity. Even in England, once that was gone, its irrationalism was manifest.

But Puginism did not die with the Gothic

Fig. 6. The interior of Notre Dame de Paris (1163–1250). The most characteristic and expressive elements of the ceiling of the large central nave are the projecting ribs which clearly show the intersection of the vaults which form the cross vaulting. These ribs are not statically essential, but they do follow the lines of maximum concentration of the internal stresses. That the ribs were brought out and continued to the large supporting columns shows the clarity and depth of the imagination of those magnificent builders.

Fig. 7. Bristol Cathedral (1298). The ribs of the vault become more elaborate. Although they lose the purity of those of Notre Dame, they still remain within the limits of static intuition.

Fig. 8. Exeter Cathedral (1307–1377). Here the ribs become even more elaborate, and begin to assume decorative characteristics.

Fig. 9. King's College Chapel, Cambridge (1441). From structuralism one has passed to pure decoration, although it is inspired by a refined static intuition.

16

Revival. The style of architecture he advocated may have become an embarrassment; the religious renewal he called for may have petered out. But his lines of argument, presentation and terminology have endured. They survive, for instance, in John Belcher's *Essentials in Architecture* (1907). This is a book without an ounce of Pugin's stylistic or moral purpose; yet Belcher automatically starts off with 'principles', of which the first and foremost is 'truth' and against which the cardinal sin is 'deception'. They survive too, though more from coincidence of temperament than conscious influence, in the manifestoes of Le Corbusier (plate 514), whose dashed-off sketches and hyperbolic prose so uncannily replicate the Puginian mood.

They persist still among those who believe there are structural lessons to be drawn from Gothic architecture. In 1966, for instance, the great engineer Pier Luigi Nervi published four lectures under the title *Aesthetics and Technology in Building* (plate 513). The burden of the first, which addresses the Gothic cathedrals, is wholly Puginian. Nervi traces 'the evolution of the structural elements from the first achievements of purely technical inspiration, to those of greater richness, and finally to forms almost exclusively decorative'; and he instances among the latter, as Pugin had done, the vault of King's College Chapel. In the central period of Gothic, Nervi finds an exemplification of 'correct building'. So the moral terminology is still in place. And he explains how, although the ribs in Gothic vaults are not statically essential, they follow the lines where the internal stresses are concentrated. 'That

18   VERS UNE ARCHITECTURE

Silos et élévateurs à blé aux États-Unis.

TROIS RAPPELS, LE VOLUME   19

tecture de prismes, cubes et cylindres, trièdres ou sphères : les Pyramides, le Temple de Louqsor, le Parthénon, le Colisée, la Villa Adriana.

L'architecture gothique n'est pas, dans son fondement, à base de sphères, cônes et cylindres. La nef seule exprime une forme simple, mais d'une géométrie complexe de second ordre (croisées d'ogives). C'est pour cela qu'une cathédrale n'est pas très belle et que nous y cherchons des compensations d'ordre subjectif, hors de la plastique. Une cathédrale nous intéresse comme l'ingénieuse solution d'un problème difficile, mais dont les données ont été mal posées parce qu'elles ne procèdent pas des grandes formes primaires. *La cathédrale n'est pas une œuvre plastique ; c'est un drame ; la lutte contre la pesanteur, sensation d'ordre sentimental.*

Les Pyramides, les Tours de Babylone, les Portes de Samarkand, le Parthénon, le Colisée, le Panthéon, le Pont du Gard, Sainte-Sophie de Constantinople, les mosquées de Stamboul, la Tour de Pise, les coupoles de Brunelleschi et de Michel-Ange, le Pont-Royal, les Invalides sont de l'architecture.

La Gare du quai d'Orsay, le Grand Palais, ne sont pas de l'architecture.

Les *architectes* de ce temps, perdus dans les « pochés » stériles de leurs plans, les rinceaux, les pilastres ou les faîtages de plomb,

the ribs were brought out and continued to the large supporting columns shows the clarity and depth of the imagination of those magnificent builders', he says; and he follows the development of the rib from Bristol to the more elaborated forms of Exeter and hence to the pure decoration of King's.[29] Here is Pugin's second rule of design discovered anew.

Did Nervi know his Pugin? It hardly matters. The point is that the same moral principles, structural instincts and historical curiosity animated both men. In an age of eclectic architecture, like

513. Double-page spread from Pier Luigi Nervi's *Aesthetics and Technology in Building*, 1966, showing a Puginian approach to the history of Gothic structure.

514. Grain silos from Le Corbusier's *Vers une architecture*, 1923. Pugin's emotional tone of manifesto-writing is renewed.

the one we are in now, or like the one to which the fervid Gothic Revival had in due course to give way a hundred and twenty years ago, *The True Principles* may seem to have died. Yet the book may still be lying in sly wait for a fresh call from the architectural conscience. What Pugin's biographer Michael Trappes-Lomax said about it in 1932 is pertinent still:

> Those who may wish to lay the foundations of some reasonable critical standard by which to judge the works both of the past and of the present time could do worse than turn to its yellowing pages. They need have no fear of being turned into 'preterpluperfect Goths': ferro-concrete and thousand-room hotels require a difference in application.[30]

So, one might now add, do business parks, air-rights developments, out-of-town shopping centres and the whole architectural paraphernalia of modern consumerism. Pugin would have known just how to sketch and just what to say about the way we build these things today. And he would certainly have relished lambasting the slack eclecticism of our age.

The Opening of the Pugin Burial Vault
St Augustine's Church, Ramsgate
29 October 1992

'Burial Vaults', says Julian Litten, in *The English Way of Death* (1991, p. 197), 'as dynastic burial chambers, were a short-lived phenomenon, popular between the first quarter of the seventeenth century and the second quarter of the eighteenth'. A vault is 'a subterranean chamber of stone or brick capable of housing a minimum of two coffins side by side and with an internal height of not less than 1.74 metres'. (Litten, p. 207)

Litten describes the various types of vault and their evolution from little more than a stone lined trough to such elaborately constructed vaults as that at Hinton St George, Somerset, designed by Sir Jeffrey Wyatville, and the Royal Mausoleum beneath the Albert Memorial Chapel at St George's Chapel, Windsor, created by George III in 1810.

The Pugin vault beneath the family chantry chapel in St Augustine's, Ramsgate, Kent, is a moderate-sized family vault with a brick-lined barrel roof and a single shelf. There are no stairs, so access is by ladder, and coffins would have been lowered into the vault on ropes.

Pugin died at Ramsgate on 14 September 1852, and his funeral took place on Tuesday, 21 September at St Augustine's, Ramsgate. On the preceding evening, according to the account in *The Tablet* of 25 September, Dr Wareing, Bishop of Northampton, had presided at the chanting of Matins and Lauds for the Dead. On the Tuesday a Solemn High Mass of Requiem was sung by Dr Doyle, Provost of Southwark. Dr Grant, Bishop of Southwark gave the oration, and Dr Moore of Oscott, Messrs Herbert, Hardman and Crace, Sir Charles Barry and C.R. Scott-Murray were among those present. 'The mortal remains of the great Catholic architect . . . were [then] consigned to the vault prepared by himself for that purpose . . .'

The church architect thought that structural movement in the south wall of the chantry might have been due to subsidence in the vault, and the decision was taken to inspect it. On 29 October 1992 it was opened for the first time since 1928 when Cuthbert Pugin, A.W.N.'s youngest son, was interred. On that occasion a plan of the vault was made by the undertakers and a copy is held by the V&A Museum. No other record of the internal arrangement of the vault seems to exist.

Within the vault lie thirteen lead-lined coffins belonging to the Pugin family and others associated with St Augustine's Church. Opposite the entrance, in the bottom right-hand corner, lies the coffin of A.W.N. Pugin, still retaining most of its brass fittings made by Hardmans, including a fine brass floriated cross running along the top ridge. Because the wooden case has rotted at the head end, it is possible to measure the lead case. It measures 25″ across by 18″ at the highest point of the gable, and is 66″ in length. The approximate length of the effigy on the tomb in the chantry is 65″, and the width at the shoulders is 17″, so the effigy would fit the coffin neatly, suggesting that it was closely modelled on Pugin's actual body size.

It was a solemn moment when the workmen pulled on the chains to raise the massive stone slab. Only moments before, during a short service conducted by the Abbot, the grave was sprinkled with water from the holy water bucket designed by A.W.N. Pugin that had been used at the funerals of all those buried in the vault. Sharing in this impressive piece of historical continuity were experts from the V&A, English Heritage, and the Kent Archaeological Society. Also present was Mr Robert Arnold-Pugin, reputedly one of the last surviving relatives to bear the Pugin name. It was good to think that 140 years after his death there were still many who revered Pugin's memory and held him in genuine affection.

DAVID MEARA

The End.

Notes

ABBREVIATIONS
BPRL   Birmingham Public Reference Library
HLRO   House of Lords Record Office
NRO   Northumberland Record Office
PRO   Public Record Office
RIBA   Royal Institute of British Architects
SRO   Scottish Record Office
The following books are cited in the notes in abbreviated form; for a complete list of Pugin's publications see Belcher, 1987.

BELCHER, M. *A.W.N. Pugin, An annotated critical bibliography*, London and New York 1987

FERREY, B. *Recollections of A.N. Welby Pugin, and his Father, Augustus Pugin*, London 1861

PUGIN, A.W.N. *The True Principles of Pointed or Christian Architecture*, London 1841

PUGIN, A.W.N. *The Present State of Ecclesiastical Architecture in England*, London 1843

PUGIN, A.W.N. *An Apology for the Revival of Christian Architecture in England*, London 1843

PUGIN, A.W.N. *The Glossary of Ecclesiastical Ornament and Costume*, London 1844

WEDGWOOD, A. *Catalogue of the Drawings Collection of the Royal Institute of British Architects, The Pugin Family*, Farnborough 1977

WEDGWOOD, A. *Catalogue of Drawings in the Victoria & Albert Museum, A.W.N. Pugin and the Pugin Family*, London 1985

Chapter 2, The Early Years

1. B. Ferrey, *Recollections of A.W.N. Pugin and his father, Augustus Pugin*, London 1861, p.30.
2. He registered at the Royal Academy School on 27 March 1792.
3. Ferrey, p.6.
4. Ferrey, p.42 and letters in Rare Books Department, Yale Center for British Art, New Haven.
5. Volume of MS notes for an uncompleted autobiography, Victoria & Albert Museum, L5204-1969, , transcribed with notes by A. Wedgwood, *Catalogue of Architectural Drawings in the Victoria & Albert Museum, A.W.N. Pugin and the Pugin Family*, London 1985, pp.24-31.
6. Ferrey, p.33.
7. Wedgwood, 1985, p.24.
8. Wedgwood, 1985, p.24.
9. Victoria & Albert Museum E132-1982; Wedgwood, 1985, pp.122-3.
10. Wedgwood, 1985, p.24.
11. Ferrey, pp.33-4.
12. *Pugin's Gothic Furniture*, n.d., plate 11.
13. Ferrey, p.53.
14. Wedgwood, 1985, p.27.
15. G. de Bellaigue and P. Kirkham, 'George IV and the furnishings of Windsor Castle', *Furniture History*, VIII, 1972, pp.1-34. The Morel and Seddon account book for the Windsor commission has come to light since the publication of this article (Royal Collection, Stable Yard House). This detailed document, which it is hoped to publish in full in due course, clarifies certain previously unresolved points relating to numbers of items supplied, alterations and original locations. (Information from Hugh Roberts)
16. Information from Hugh Roberts.
17. Ferrey, pp.51-2.
18. S. Bury, A. Wedgwood and M. Snodin, 'The Antiquarian Plate of George IV: a Gloss on E.A. Jones', *Burlington Magazine*, CXXI, pp.343-50.
19. For a more detailed consideration of Pugin's designs for the stage see Chapter 3.
20. Wedgwood, 1985, pp.24-8.
21. Ferrey, p.14.
22. I. Guest, *The Romantic Ballet in England*, 1954, pp.50-2.
23. Wedgwood, 1985, p.27.
24. Wedgwood, 1985, p.28.
25. J. Macaulay, *The Gothic Revival 1745-1845*, Glasgow, 1975, pp.247-9.
26. Cash book for New Mansion House at Murthly, Scottish Record Office GD 121/68.
27. J. Macaulay, 'The Architectural Collaboration between J. Gillespie Graham and A.W. Pugin', *Architectural History*, XXVII, 1984, p.408.
28. See Chapter 4, Domestic Architecture, and Chapter 17, The Palace of Westminster.
29. Ferrey, pp.62-3.
30. Ferrey, p.63.
31. Wedgwood, 1985, p.28.
32. Victoria & Albert Museum E56-87-1955; Wedgwood, 1985, pp.182-5.
33. *The Builder*, X, 1852, p.606.
34. Wedgwood, 1985, p.28.
35. B. Ferrey, 'Ferrey's Recollection of Pugin', *Ecclesiologist*, XXII, 1861, pp.367-9.
36. Ferrey, pp.43-5.
37. A. Wedgwood, *Catalogue of the Drawings Collection of the Royal Institute of British Architects, The Pugin Family*, Farnborough 1977, p.46.
38. Victoria & Albert Museum E133-1982; Wedgwood, 1985, pp.123-7.
39. Victoria & Albert Museum E648-E673-19; Wedgwood, 1985, pp.129-32.
40. Victoria & Albert Museum L5179-1969; Wedgwood, 1985, pp.132-6.
41. Public Library, St Louis, Missouri.
42. Public Library, St Louis, Missouri.
43. Present whereabouts unknown; see P. Stanton, 'Pugin at Twenty-one', *Architectural Review*, CX, 1951, pp.187-90.
44. Victoria & Albert Museum L5178-1969; Wedgwood, 1985, pp.140-4.
45. Victoria & Albert Museum L5176-1969; Wedgwood, 1985, pp.136-40.
46. Victoria & Albert Museum L5175-1969; Wedgwood, 1985, pp.147-52.
47. Public Library, St Louis, Missouri.
48. Letter in private possession.
49. The drawings for the Deanery and Bishop's Palace, Wells, were published after A.C. Pugin's death in *Examples of Gothic Architecture*, II, 1836, and the Vicars' Close in III, part 1, 1837.
50. Ferrey, p.68.
51. Ferrey, p.68; letters from Adlard Welby to Selina Welby, Yale Center for British Art, MS Pugin 93 and 95.
52. Letter to E.J. Willson, 17 September 1834, Johns Hopkins University, Baltimore.
53. Letter to E.J. Willson, 26 February 1833, Johns Hopkins University, Baltimore.
54. Letter to E.J. Willson, 31 March 1834, Johns Hopkins University, Baltimore.
55. Letter in a private collection.
56. Letter to E.J. Willson, 17 September 1834, Johns Hopkins University, Baltimore.
57. Letter to E.J. Willson, 22 August 1834, Johns Hopkins University, Baltimore.
58. Victoria & Albert Museum E2588-2600-1910; Wedgwood, 1985, pp.152-4.
59. Scottish Record Office GD121/Box66/401.

60. Wedgwood, 1977, note 37, p.49.

61. Victoria & Albert Museum L5177-1969; Wedgwood, 1985, pp.156-8.

62. Victoria & Albert Museum L5156-1969; Wedgwood, 1985, p.32.

63. Royal Institute of British Architects Drawings Collection and King Edward VI School, Edgbaston, archive.

64. Wedgwood, 1985, note 37, pp.49-51.

65. See chapter 17, Palace of Westminster.

66. See chapter 4, Domestic Architecture.

67. Letter to E.J. Willson, 16 August 1835, Johns Hopkins University.

68. The drawings for *Iron and Brass Work* are in the Public Library, St Louis, Missouri and those for *Gold & Silversmiths* are in the Victoria & Albert Museum E1198-1983; Wedgwood, 1985, pp.160-2.

69. Advertisement in A.W. Pugin, *Contrasts . . .* , Salisbury, 1836.

70. Letter to E.J. Willson, 6 May 1836, Johns Hopkins University, Baltimore.

71. See also chapter 7, Pugin Writing.

72. Letter to Nicholas Wiseman, 1 June 1838, Wiseman correspondence, Ushaw College.

73. Ferrey, pp.122-4.

74. Pugin's diary for 1836, Victoria & Albert Museum L1517-1969; Wedgwood, 1985, p.36.

75. See chapter 4, Domestic Architecture.

76. See chapter 5, Church Architecture.

77. See chapter 17, The New Palace of Westminster.

78. See chapter 4, Domestic Architecture.

Chapter 3, Pugin and the Theatre

1. A.W.N. Pugin *Remarks on the Rambler*, 1850, p.7.

2. Benjamin Ferrey *Recollections of A. Welby Pugin* (1978 edition), p.44.

3. Ferrey p.45.

4. H. and A. Gernsheim, *L.J.M. Daguerre: The History of the Diorama and the Daguerrotype*, London, 1956, p.178.

5. *Westminster Diocesan Archives* [MS SEC 21/4:2], as quoted in Margaret Belcher *A.W.N. Pugin: An annotated critical bibliography* London and New York, 1987, p.89.

6. Ferrey, p.61.

7. A.W.N. Pugin, *Autobiography*, published in A. Wedgwood, *A.W.N. Pugin and the Pugin Family* V&A, 1985, p.28.

8. Wedgwood, 1985, p.28.

9. Wedgwood, 1985, p.28.

10. Wedgwood, 1985, p.28.

11. Wedgwood, 1985, p.28.

12. Wedgwood, 1985, p.28.

13. E.W. Pugin, *Who was the architect of the Houses of Parliament?* 1867, p. 3.

14. In a letter to E.J. Willson dated 26 February 1833, as quoted in Belcher, p.159.

15. *Salisbury and Wiltshire Herald*, 8 October 1836.

16. R. Simpson, 'Recollections of Pugin', in *The Rambler* (3rd series) September 1861, p.400.

17. J. Fergusson, *History of the Modern Styles of Architecture*, London, 1862, p.318n.

Chapter 4, Domestic Architecture

1. Entries in Pugin's diaries and references in his letters are the most important sources. The diaries are transcribed in A. Wedgwood, *Catalogue of Architectural Drawings in the Victoria & Albert Museum, A.W.N. Pugin and the Pugin Family*, London, 1985. The forthcoming edition of Pugin's letters by Margaret Belcher will provide invaluable source material.

2. I. Nairn and N. Pevsner, *The Buildings of England, Surrey*, Harmondsworth, 1982, p.93. Pugin certainly added a verandah, and probably made minor internal alterations, but it is wrong to attribute the Gothic red-brick exterior to him. It seems that major work was done there by George Myers, *c.*1847-56 (P. Spencer-Silver, *Pugin's Builder*, 1993, p.35).

3. Letter in Johns Hopkins University, Baltimore.

4. I am indebted to Mr and Mrs Peter Higgins for much help and kindness.

5. The engraving reproduced in Ferrey, p.72, misleadingly shows an unexecuted scheme.

6. Letter in Johns Hopkins University, Baltimore.

7. Letter of 5 January 1836 in Johns Hopkins University, Baltimore.

8. P. Stanton, *Pugin*, London, 1971, p.18.

9. See Chapter 2, The Early Years.

10. For the argument see Wedgwood, 1977, pp.74-5.

11. R. Hasted, *Guide to Scarisbrick Hall*, 1987, pp.9-11.

12. For Hull's connection with Pugin see Chapter 2, The Early Years.

13. Diary for 1837 Victoria & Albert Museum Library L5158-1969.

14. They are now in the RIBA Drawings Collection, see Wedgwood, 1977, pp.74-84.

15. See P. Stanton, 'Pugin at 21', *Architectural Review*, CX, 1951, pp.187-90.

16. M. Girouard, *The Victorian Country House*, New Haven and London, 1979, p.116.

17. Bills in Lancashire Record Office, DDSC 78/4(15), are quoted in R. Hasted, op.cit. note 11, pp.34, 47.

18. Girouard, op.cit. note 16, p.115.

19. Two letters in Lancashire Record Office DDSC 78/4(8), are quoted in Hasted, op.cit. note 11, pp.20-1, where they are incorrectly dated.

20. I am indebted to Dr James Macaulay for help in identifying the joint work of Gillespie Graham and Pugin.

21. Letter in the Scottish Record Office (SRO) GD/112/20/5 quoted in J. Macaulay, *The Gothic Revival 1745-1845*, Glasgow, 1975, p.249.

22. Letter in the SRO GD/121/Box 101/vol.XXI/87.

23. Sir Thomas Dick Lauder, *Memorial of the Royal Progress in Scotland*, Edinburgh, 1843, pp.285-6.

24. Ian Gow, *The Scottish Interior*, Edinburgh, 1992, p.56.

25. SRO GD/112/20/1/3/33. I am indebted to Ian Gow for much help with elucidating the relationship between Gillespie Graham, Trotter and Pugin, and for these references in the Scottish Record office. See also I. Gow, 'New Light on Late Trotter', *Country Life*, 11 August 1988, pp.100-3.

26. T.F. Dibdin, *Tour in the North Counties of England and Scotland*, 1838, p.505.

27. Trotter Albums, vol.I, f.105, National Monuments Record of Scotland.

28. Trotter Albums, vol.I, ff.66,68,70, vol.II, ff.34,50, loc.cit.

29. See Chapter 2, Early Years.

30. Scottish Record Office GD 112/20/5/28.

31. Pugin's letters to J.G. Crace are in the RIBA Library and his drawings for him are in the Victoria & Albert Museum, Department of Prints and Drawings.

32. SRO GD/112/20/1/46.

33. There are designs in the Birmingham Archdiocesan Archive.

34. Letter to John Hardman, 10 June 1837, in the Birmingham Archdiocesan Archive, B.465. I am indebted to David Hemsoll for drawing my attention to this letter and to Margaret Belcher for providing me with a transcript.

35. A.W. Pugin, *The Present State of Ecclesiastical Architecture*, London 1843, p.104.

36. A.W. Pugin, *The True Principles of Pointed or Christian Architecture*, London 1841, p.52.

37. *True Principles* (note 36), p.60.

38. *True Principles* (note 36), p.61.

39. D. Verey, *The Buildings of England, Gloucestershire: The Vale and Forest of Dean*, Harmondsworth, 1980, pp.162-3.

40. A.W. Pugin, *An Apology for the Revival of Christian Architecture*, London 1843, p.38.

41. *An Apology* (note 40), p.39.

42. '"Gothic House", Cheyne Walk, Chelsea', *Building News*, LII, 1887, pp.352, [371].

43. *An Apology* (note 40), p.15.

44. Letter to Lord Shrewsbury, V&A L525-1965 No.37, transcribed in Wedgwood, 1985, p.108.

45. Royal Institute of British Architects, Crace correspondence PUG13/6.

46. Stanton, op.cit. note 8, p.176. This judgement no doubt comes from references in Pugin's letters to Hardman.

47. *Illustrated London News*, 27 January 1855, p.93.

48. Pugin mentions it in a letter of *c*.1847 to Lord Shrewsbury in a private collection (HLRO, Hist. Coll. 339/52).

49. W. Adam, *The Gem of the Peak*, London, 3rd edition, 1843, p.256.

50. Op.cit. note 49, p.257.

51. Op.cit. note 49, p.274.

52. See for example the list of work he made in his diary in 1838; transcribed in Wedgwood, 1985, p.43.

53. Op.cit. note 49, p.259, and letters to Lord Shrewsbury, V&A L525-1965 Nos.22 and 24.

54. Op.cit. note 49, pp.267-8.

55. Op.cit. note 49, pp.259, 267.

56. Op.cit. note 49, pp.277, 278, 280.

57. Op.cit. note 49, pp.280-1.

58. Op.cit. note 49, p.271.

59. Letter to Lord Shrewsbury, V&A L525-1965 No.52, transcribed in Wedgwood, 1985, p.111.

60. Letter to Lord Shrewsbury, V&A L525/56-1965 No.95, transcribed in Wedgwood, 1985, p.120.

61. Letter to Lord Shrewsbury in a private collection (HLRO Hist. Coll. 339/31).

62. In the census of 1861 the castle is referred to as 'a large pile of new buildings incomplete' (RG9/1950), and in the census of 1871 a priest and teachers are listed as the occupants (RG10/2886).

63. Letter to Lord Shrewsbury in a private collection (HLRO Hist. Coll. 339/46).

64. Letter to Lord Shrewsbury, V&A L525-1965 No.52, transcribed in Wedgwood, 1985, p.111.

65. Designs for Dartington Hall are in Exeter City Library and for Hornby Castle are at the Yorkshire Archaeological Society, Leeds.

66. Designs of 1841 for Garendon, Leicestershire, are in the RIBA Drawings Collection.

67. See chapter 8, Wallpaper.

68. See chapter 9, Furniture.

69. Furniture originally designed for the Grange, and now at the Palace of Westminster is discussed in chapter 17.

Chapter 5, Pugin as a Church Architect

1. A.W. Pugin, *Diary* 6 June 1835, A. Wedgwood, *A.W.N. Pugin and the Pugin family*, 1985 pp.33, 75.

2. *Tablet*, 1854 pp.597, 612, obituary of E.J.Willson 1778-1854.

3. Pugin to E.J. Willson, January 1834 in Ferrey, pp.83-9.

4. *Dublin Review* (1839) pp.240-71, quotation p.244.

5. John Henry Newman, *The letters and diaries of John Henry Newman*, (ed. C.S. Dessain) 1961-77, XIV, pp.212-14.

6. Pugin, *Some Remarks*, pp.17-18.

7. *Some Remarks*, pp.18-19.

8. Ferrey, p.88.

9. R. Currie *et al.*, *Churches and Churchgoers: Patterns of Church growth in the British Isles since 1700*, 1977, pp.27, 23-9.

10. A. Welby Pugin, *An Address to the inhabitants of Ramsgate*, London, 1850.

11. R. O'Donnell, 'Pugin's church in Cambridge', forthcoming.

12. Pugin to W. Dunn, 9 July 1844 Northumberland Record Office, Dunn Family papers NRO 2988/AWP/1-63, AWP/24.

13. *Some Remarks*, p.18.

14. Pugin to Phillipps, 1 December 1839, E.S. Purcell, *Life and Letters of Ambrose Phillipps de Lisle*, 2 vols, London 1900, II pp.222-4.

15. *Some Remarks*, p.18.

16. *Some Remarks*, p.18.

17. *Some Remarks*, p.12.

18. *London and Dublin Orthodox Journal*, IX, 1839, pp.33-6, and pp.129-32. Pugin's early journalism is investigated in Belcher.

19. Pugin to Dunn, 'Vigil of the Ascension' 1842, NRO 2988/AWP/5. For Pugin's letter on the report in the *Kent Argus*, *Tablet*, 1846, p.5.

20. Pugin to Rev.J.R. Bloxam, no date *c*.1845, Bloxam Collection, Magdalen College, Oxford, no.32.

21. Pugin to Phillipps, n.d., *c*.1841, Purcell, *Phillipps*, II, pp.213-5.

22. Pugin to Dunn, NRO 2988/AWP/13.

23. Pugin to Dunn, NRO 2988/AWP/24.

24. Pugin's church of 1841-2 was widened and lengthened in 1851-2 by G.R. Blount, architect; E. Meaton, *The church of St Augustine of England*, *c*.1990.

25. The altar is now at Bromsgrove Catholic church.

26. Purcell, *Phillipps*, II, pp.288-93.

27. H.-R. Hitchcock, *Early Victorian Architecture*, 2 vols, 1954, p.74.

28. The church was largely paid for by Pugin's friend and collaborator in the book on plainchant John (later Sir John) Lambert. Similar nave-and-aisle-with-tower plans were used at Marlow (1845-8), and at the Handsworth convent church (1846-7) (see note 108 below).

29. Pugin to Dunn, 30 April 1842 and 'vigil of the Ascension' 1842, NRO 2988/AWP/4,5. Pugin to Riddell, 1842 NRO 2988/AWP/8. Pugin also recommended this type in *Present State*, pp.109-10.

30. Pugin to Riddell, 26 June 1841, NRO 2988/AWP/1.

31. Pugin's unexecuted design for the screen is at the V&A (Wedgwood, 1985, p.231), and for choir stalls is at the RIBA (Wedgwood, 1977, p.71 (54)).

32. Pugin to Dunn, NRO 2988/AWP/5.

33. Pugin to Riddell, St Mary Magdalene 1842, NRO 2988/AWP/8, 25 July 1842, AWP/9.

34. Pugin to the Benedictine missioner at Liverpool, September [1845], Downside Abbey Archives, Liverpool, St Mary box file.

35. *Tablet*, 1853, pp.410, 412.

36. W.A. Wickham, *Transactions of the Antiquarian and Historical Society of Lancashire and Cheshire*, 59, n.s.23 (1907), pp.132-60.

37. *A History and Description of the Restored Parish Church of St Mary, Wymeswold, Leicestershire*, 1846.

38. *Ecclesiologist* NS 5, January 1846, pp.10-16.

39. *Catholic Magazine and Review*, Birmingham, IV, 1833, p.lxxiv.

40. For Pugin's relations with the 'Committee for the erection of the Catholic church', Newcastle, and its secretary, William Dunn, and the priest [from 1844 Bishop] William Riddell see NRO Dunn family papers, NRO 2988/AWP 1-63.

41. Wedgwood, 1977, (3) 1-5, p.55; Pugin, *Diary*, 5 March 1839, Wedgwood, 1985, pp.42, 82.

42. *The Orthodox Journal*, XI, 1840, p.140.

43. Wedgwood, 1985, Pugin, *Diary* 16 December 1839, end paper between pp.8-9; cat.237, pl.39, pp.180-1; Wedgwood, 1977, no.8, p.55.

44. *Civil Engineer and Architects Journal*, II, December 1839, p.477, extract from the *Midland Counties Herald*.

45. A general description is given in the *Tablet*, 19 June 1841, pp.397-8. See also *Tablet*, 26 June 1841, pp.413-5; *Orthodox Journal* XII, 26 June 1841, pp.399-410; Wedgwood, 1985, pp.49, 86.

46. *Present State*, 1843, no.1, no.3, pp.63, 73, 79.

47. Pugin to Shrewsbury, March 1842, HLRO 339/38. See also Pugin to Shrewsbury, 24 December 1840, no.21; 5 January 1841, no.22; 29 September 1841, no.23, Wedgwood, 1985, pp.102-5.

48. *Present State*, p.34.

49. HLRO Historical collection, Shrewsbury to Pugin, no.339.

50. De Montalembert, although invited, did not attend (*Annales Archeologiques*, Paris, V, 1846, p.304). For Pugin's description of the opening see *Morning Post*, 3 September 1846, pp.5-6; *Tablet* pp.568-9; *Builder*, 1846 pp.447-8.

51. Newman, *Diaries*, (op. cit., note 5) II, p.210; see note 69 below.

52. H.-R. Hitchcock, *Early Victorian Architecture*, p.83.

53. *Present State*, pl.I, XIII, XVI, *Some Remarks* pp.9-10.

54. Wedgwood, 1977, (4), p.57.

55. Pugin to Shrewsbury, March 1842, HRLO 339/38. *Present State* pl.IV, VI.

56. Pugin to Shrewsbury, 25 April 1844, Wedgwood, 1985, no.38, p.108.

57. *Annales Archeologiques*, Paris, vol.I, 1844, pp.57–9.

58. Pugin to Shrewsbury, 30 May 1844, Wedgwood, 1985, no.39, p.108.

59. Wedgwood, 1985, p.187.

60. HLRO Historical Collection, Shrewsbury to Pugin, no.339.

61. Newman, *Letters and Diaries*, XI, p.210.

62. *Illustrated London News*, 9 January 1847, pp.28–30.

63. A.N. Didron, 'Promenade en Angleterre', *Annales Archeologiques*, Paris, V 1846, pp.284–308.

64. *Some Remarks*, pp.11–13.

65. Pugin to Bloxam, 24 December 1850, Magdalen College, Oxford, Archives, no.153.

66. A. Wedgwood, ' "Pugin in his home" a memoir by J.H. Powell', *Architectural History*, vol.33, 1988, pp.171–205; Pugin's manuscript 'Expenses for the erection etc of St Augustine's Church Ramsgate' is in the V&A: Wedgwood, 1985, p.121. See also Pugin to Shrewsbury, ?1846, no.51; 16 August 1847, no.53; 14 July 1848, no.58, and 26 December 1848, no.63, ibidem pp.110–3.

67. Wedgwood, 'Pugin in his home', (note 74) p.194.

68. J. Summerson, 'Pugin at Ramsgate', *Architectural Review* 103, 1948, pp.163–6. Pugin to Shrewsbury, 1846?, no.51; Wedgwood, 1985, p.110.

69. *Some Remarks*, p.11.

70. Hardman daybook, 1849–54, p.64, 14 December 1849.

71. Wedgwood, 'Pugin in his home', op. cit. note 74, p.194.

72. R. O'Donnell, 'Pugin at Oscott', in J.F. Champ (ed), *Oscott College 1838–1988*, Birmingham 1988, pp.45–66.

73. Although Potter's unsigned and undated contract drawings at Oscott show a straight-ended plan, there were many alterations during execution, as the print 'St Mary's College Oscott' by W. Radclyff and 'St Mary's College [late Oscott], north-east view' show.

74. Pugin's etching 'Chapel of the new college of St Marie's Oscott' has the date 1837 with an '8' superimposed. The original drawing is at Westminster Cathedral.

75. *The Autobiography of Archbishop Ullathorne with selections from his letters*, 2 vols, 1891–2, p.142.

76. Shrewsbury to Phillipps, 16 April 1839, Purcell, *Phillipps* I, pp.105–6.

77. Pugin to E.J. Willson, 10 June 1839, Johns Hopkins University Collection.

78. Oscott Archives, Pugin's 1838 furnishing bill.

79. Ibid, box 1839, no.1202, 'Thomas Morley in account with A.W. Pugin for carpentry and metalwork . . . 18 May 1839'.

80. Pugin to Dunn, 28 August 1842, NRO 2988/AWP/13.

81. Oscott Archives, Box 1840, undated bill in Pugin's hand.

82. Pugin advertised from Hull's address in the *Catholic Directory*, 1839.

83. W. Greaney, *The Buildings, Museum, Pictures and Library at St Mary's College Oscott*, Birmingham, 1899.

84. D. Milburn, *A History of Ushaw College Durham*, 1964, pp.176–9. A similar book of sketches was made by Pugin for Balliol College, Oxford.

85. The *Liber Vitae* is kept in the sacristy at Ushaw.

86. Pugin's drawings for the Relic and the St Joseph's Chapels (1852) are in the uncatalogued collection of architectural drawings at Ushaw College.

87. For comments on the 'popish chapel' at the Mediæval Court, 1851, see pp.228–9.

88. A.W. Pugin, *A Treatise on chancel Screens*, 1851, p.117; B. Ward, *St Edmund's College Chapel*, 1903, and *History of St Edmund's College Chapel*, 1903.

89. B. Ward, *St Edmund's College Chapel: an account, historical, and descriptive, written on the occasion of the fifteenth anniversary of the opening*, London, 1903, p.265. The high altar (the gift of the clergy of Westminster and Southwark) was paid for by 1848 (pp. 37–8, 85), and it appears in sketches of 1848 (pp. 189–90), but no designs survive for it. The stone gradines were added later (p. 85). All the above drawings are in the collection of St Edmund's College. Like the Ushaw high altar, the tabernacle and throne are prominent; the tripartite stone altar table was probably installed by 1851.

90. *Tablet*, 1851, p.565; for the opening, ibid. 1853, pp.275, 341–2.

91. *Catholic Directory*, 1839, pp.108–11.

92. Sister M. Angela Bolster (ed.), *The Correspondence of Catherine McAuley 1827–1841*, Cork, 1989, letter to Bishop Walsh, 4 February 1840, pp.120–1.

93. John Hardman (1767–1844) gave the site, the buildings and furnishings at a cost of £5535; the Earl of Shrewsbury gave £2000. Mother Mary Juliana Hardman (1813–84) was a nun here.

94. *Present State*, pp.108–10, pl.XII. There was in addition a later three story 'house of mercy or refuge for unemployed servant girls' and a further cloister. There are frequent references to the furnishing and decoration of the convent and church in the Hardman Daybook 1845–50, (e.g. '13 inscriptions over the cell doors', p.7 at £11).

95. Bolster, pp.147–8, to Bishop Walsh, 5 August 1840.

96. Pugin, *Contrasts*, 1841, pl.20 shows the 'antient poorhouse' based on St Cross Winchester.

97. *Orthodox Journal*, X, 1840, p.192; *Tablet*, 1848, p.452; 1852, p.756.

98. *Present State*, 1843, pp.92–6, pl.V.

99. Op. cit., pl.VI. The south, or Guildhall, range is by E.W. Pugin.

100. A. Phillipps de Lisle, *An Appeal to the Catholics of England on behalf of the Abbey Church of St Bernard Charnwood Forest Leicestershire*, 1842. Pugin to Shrewsbury, 13 April 1843, Wedgwood, 1985, p.106, no.27.

101. *A Concise History of the Cistercian Order by a Cistercian monk* [Dom Bernard Palmer], 1852, pp.280–2. For Shrewsbury's views, see Purcell, *Phillipps* I, pp.66–90. Pugin to Shrewsbury, 1840, Wedgwood, 1985, pp.101–3, [19] [20].

102. *Present State*, pp.96–101, pl.VII–VIII.

103. Phillipps, *An Appeal*, p.13. Palmer (op. cit., note 116), pp.287–92.

104. Palmer (op. cit., note 116), p.292. Llewellyn Jewitt, *Guide to the Abbey of Mount St Bernard, Charnwood Forest with some account of the monks who live there*, Leicester, n.d., c.1882, p.16. The later chapter house was by E.W. Pugin.

105. *Orthodox Journal*, XIX, 1844, p.141; *Tablet*, 24 August 1844, p.532 quoting *The Times* and referring to the three-arch stone jubé occupying one bay of the nave.

106. Phillipps, *An Appeal*, p.13.

107. Purcell *Phillipps*, op. cit., I, pp.80–1.

108. R. O'Donnell, 'Pugin designs for Downside Abbey', *Burlington Magazine*, CXXXIII, April 1987, pp.231–2.

109. *True Principles*, 1843, pp.46–9.

110. *True Principles*, pp.43–6.

111. Pugin's bird's-eye perspective is at the RIBA (Wedgwood 1977, p.71 [53] and is illustrated in *The Maynooth Commission Report*, Dublin, 1855, between parts I and II; I, pp.65–6; II, pp.259–64; Bishop John Healey, *Maynooth Chapel: its centenary history*, Dublin, 1895.

112. The phrase attributed to Dr Walsh by Dr Bowden, President of Sedgley Park school, Canon E. Buscott, *History of Cotton College*, 1940, pp.143–4.

113. Pugin to Phillipps, 18 December 1840; Purcell, *Phillipps*, II, pp.213–15; W.G. Ward, *Life of Wiseman*, I, p.358.

114. Purcell, *Phillipps*, II, p.288.

115. A full screen was described at the foundation of St Chad's in November 1839 and is noted in Pugin's *Diary* 1839, list including 'Great screen and rood', at £350, between pp.8–9 opposite p.28, Wedgwood, 1985, pp.43–4, 83. Exterior and interior appeal sheets for St Chad's were sold at 6s the pair and the screen is prominent; *Tablet*, 1841, p.39, p.41. It is discussed and illustrated in *Present State*, 1843, pp.74–9, pl.no.4.

116. Pugin to Phillipps, 18 December 1840; Purcell, *Phillipps*, II, pp.213–15.

117. Pugin to Dr Rock, 2 February 1841, quoted in Belcher, *Bibliography*, p.194.

118. *Present State*, p.78. The dado was

removed in 1854 when the screen was re-erected to enlarge the sanctuary. It was finally demolished in 1967.

119. A.W. Pugin, *A Treatise on chancel screens and rood lofts, their antiquity use and symbolic signification*, London, 1851.

120. *Present State*, pp.32–3, pl.XII; Belcher, *Bibliography*, cites a Pugin letter at St George's Cathedral of 23 May 1847 pleading for the screen, p.97. It was removed to the rear of the church in 1889.

121. *Rambler*, 8 July 1848, pp.227–8; Pugin's reply, *Tablet*, 1848, p.563. The 'Controversy' continued for some years in the Catholic press.

122. *Tablet*, 1 July 1848, p.419 on the demolition of the screen at Fulham.

123. Ferrey, pp.127–8. See also Pugin to Phillipps, Purcell, *Phillipps*, II, p.218.

124. Although the chancel of 1855 is by E.W. Pugin, the screen can be attributed to A.W. Pugin.

125. Pugin to Riddell, 4 July 1843 NRO 2988/AWP/16.

126. B. Ward, *A History of St Edmund's College*, p.265.

127. *Present State*, 1843, pp.16–17, 38.

128. Op. cit., pp.17, 38–9. For Easter sepulchres in the medieval Sarum rite, see E. Duffy, *The stripping of the altars: the attack on traditional religion in England*, 1992, pp.29–37, 109.

129. *Present State*, pp.94, 101–2, pl.no.5–6, no.9–10.

130. Wedgwood, 1977, p.77 (46). The '4 confessionals' listed at the low cost of £80 among estimates for designs for St Chad's in 1839 suggest very simple *prie-dieu*-like benches (Wedgwood, 1985, pp.43, 83). Three-seater confessionals are marked on the plan of St Marie's, Manchester (Wedgwood, 1977, p.71 (51), no. 2).

131. Pugin to Dunn, 28 August 1842 NRO 2988/AWP/13. The draft building specification, including seating to Pugin's design, AWP/28 [no date] and for the fittings names the pulpit, sedilia and sacraria, font and cupboards, high altar and reredos, sacristy furniture but no confessionals AWP/29 [no date].

132. *Present State*, p.38.

133. Pugin to Phillipps, 1 December 1839/1840, Purcell, *Phillipps*, II, pp.222–4.

134. *Present State*, p.27.

135. *Present State*, pp.66–73.

136. *Present State*, pp.39–46.

137. *Present State*, pp.13, 45.

138. *Present State*, p.35, pl.no.3, pp.63–4.

139. The 'altar for a country church' was shown (with the unrelated reredos suitable for a Lady Altar) at the Mediæval Court, and published as 'altar and reredos designed by the late A.W. Pugin . . .' in Matthew Digby Wyatt, *Industrial Arts of the XIXth Century*, 3 vols, 1851–3, vol.2, pl.cxlii. It is described as 'a mensa, supported on marble columns with an elaborate sub-reredos under it', *Ecclesiologist*, n.s. vol.XII, June 1851, p.180. Both subsequently installed at St David's, Pantasaph (plate 450). Wedgwood, 1977, p.72 (57).

140. *Present State*, p.37.

141. Pugin to Dunn NRO 2988/AWP/24.

142. Pugin to 'My Lord Bishop' NRO 2988/AWP/22.

143. C. Hadfield, *A History of St Marie's church and Mission, Norfolk Row, Sheffield*, Sheffield, 1889, pp.98–9. Pugin letters to M.E. Hadfield are at the British Architectural Library, BAL.Pug.12/2/1–7. Drawings in the Myers Collection are slightly different from the altar as executed.

144. *Tablet*, 1841, p.398.

145. *Orthodox Journal*, IX, 1839, pp.33–6. *Present State*, pp.40–2.

146. *Present State*, p.42.

147. *Tablet*, 1841, p.398. For the Guild's role in John Hardman Senior's funeral *Tablet*, 1844, p.533.

148. A.W.N. Pugin and B. Smith, *Glossary of Ecclesiastical Ornament and Costume*, 1844, pl.73, 'the End' (plate 515).

149. Wedgwood, 1985, pp.56, 90; *Tablet*, 14 September 1844, p.580, death of Louisa Pugin.

150. The original chantry was later incorporated into the rebuilding of the church (1849–56) completed by E.W. Pugin.

151. E.W. Pugin to Hardman, 19 November 1852, Hardman Collection.

152. *Builder*, 1843, pp.98–100.

Chapter 6, The Antiquary and Collector

1. Yale University Library Y. 747. I am indebted to Rosemary Hill who kindly pointed this letter out to me and also for sharing her many new ideas concerning Pugin with me.

2. F. Arquie-Bruley, 'Les Monuments inédits (1806–1839) de N.X. Willemin et la decouverte des antiquités nationales', *RACAR*, X, 2, 1983, p.155 lists the dateable plates. I would like to thank Marian Campbell for giving me a copy of this article.

3. E.J. Willson letters, The Milton Eisenhower Library, Johns Hopkins University, Baltimore. These letters are not individually numbered but are filed by date, I am indebted to Alexandra Wedgwood for giving me this 1834 reference and to Rosemary Hill for pointing out a number of other interesting passages in the letters.

4. I would like to thank the late Dom Bede Millard for information about the cottage and chapel.

5. E.W. Brayley, *Delineations of the Isle of Thanet*, I, London, 1817, p.116, also illustrated.

6. Willson, ibid. (note 3).

7. Willson, ibid. (note 3).

8. Ferrey, p.93.

9. Willson, ibid. (note 3). The book mentioned is R. Vestigan's *Theatrum Crudelitatum Haereticorum Nostri Temporis*, Antwerp, 1588.

10. Ferrey, p.63.

11. A. Wedgwood, '"Pugin in his home" A memoir by J.H. Powell', *Architectural History* XXXI, 1988, p.187.

12. Wedgwood, op.cit. (note 11), p.175.

13. Willson, ibid. (note 3).

14. For Hull, Swaby, Isaacs and Webb and a discussion of the London brokers at this date see C. Wainwright, *The Romantic Interior: The British Collector at Home 1750–1850*, New Haven and London, 1989, pp.42–5.

15. I am indebted to Dr Lorne Campbell for drawing my attention to Pugin's purchases at this sale and to the following unpublished quotation from Crabb Robinson's Diary. For Aders see also M.K. Joseph, 'Charles Aders A biographical note with some unpublished letters . . .', *Auckland University College Bulletin* No.43, *English Series*, No.6, Auckland, 1953, 1–44.

16. Ed. D. Hudson, *The Diary of Henry Crabb Robinson an abridgement*, London, 1967, pp.197–8. For a contemporary description of the Aders Collection see M. Passavant, *Tour of a German Artist in England*, London, 1836, pp.201–19.

17. Wedgwood, 1985, p.42.

18. I would like to thank John Hardy for giving me access to this catalogue and for his encouragement of my work on Pugin since 1967. The 1839 Christies catalogue does not in fact include measurements but these pictures had been put up for auction by Fosters in 1835 – largely bought-in for Aders – and the measurements were given in that catalogue.

19. I am grateful to Mr L. Libsom of the Leger Galleries for obtaining a photograph of the painting for me.

20. I would like to thank Richard Kingzett of Agnew's for providing me with a photograph of this picture.

21. Wainwright, op.cit. (note 14), pp.46–53.

22. Willson, ibid. (note 3).

23. P. Stanton, 'Sources of Pugin's Contrasts', *Concerning Architecture . . .*, ed. J. Summerson, London, 1968, p.129.

24. A.E. Popham and P. Pouncey, *Italian Drawings in the Department of Prints and Drawings in the British Museum*, London, 1950, p.197. I would like to thank Anthony Griffiths and Michael Snodin for bringing this to my attention.

25. 'Sepulchral Brasses', *Gentleman's Magazine*, CLXXXIV, ii, 1848, p.601. *A*

Manual for the Study of Monumental Brasses, with a Descriptive Catalogue of the Four Hundred and Fifty Rubbings in the possession of the Oxford Architectural Society 1848. C. Boutell, *Monumental Brasses and Slabs . . .* , 1847. I would like to thank John Cherry for all the help he has given me with the Pugin objects in the collection of the British Museum.

26. I am indebted to my colleague Anthony North, who, when shown the Willemin plate, with that talent for which he is celebrated, immediately recognized the coffer as being in the store with other ironwork.

27. *A Catalogue of the Museum of Ornamental Art at Marlborough House Pall Mall Fifth Edition* London, 1853, p.39.

28. J.C. Robinson, *The Treasury of Ornamental Art Illustrations of objects of Art and Vertu . . .* , 1857, p.69. The knocker is also illustrated in colour with Pugin's key.

29. I would like to thank Anthony North for his opinion on this piece.

30. Wedgwood, 1985.

31. *Gentleman's Magazine*, CXCIII, I, 1853, 281.

32. M. Longhurst, *Victoria & Albert Museum Catalogue of Carvings in Ivory*, London, 1929, II, p.22.

33. O.M. Dalton, *Catalogue of the Ivory Carvings of the Christian Era . . . of the British Museum*, London, 1909, pp.79–80. I would like to thank Paul Williamson for also bringing to my attention the reference to this object in J. Beckwith, *Ivory Carvings in Early Mediaeval England*, London, 1972, p.153.

34. I would like to thank Paul Williamson for suggesting that these may have been in Pugin's collection.

35. Op.cit. (note 31).

36. This is illustrated and discussed by Timothy Wilson in 'The origins of the Maiolica Collections of the British Museum and the Victoria & Albert Museum 1851–55', *Bollettino del Museo Internazionale delle Ceramiche di Faenza*, LXXI, 1985, p.71, pl.XXI. I would like to thank Timothy Wilson for identifying this object in the British Museum collection for me.

37. A.C. Pugin, *Gothic Ornaments Selected From Various Ancient Buildings In England And France . . .* , London, 1831, pls.24, 53, 75.

38. *The Treasury of St Marco Venice*, ed. D. Buckton *et al.*, exh. cat., British Museum, London, 1984, pp.237–43.

39. P. Williamson, 'Roof bosses from Utrecht and Jan van Schayck, Beeldensnijder', *Oud Holland*, 1991, p.140.

40. *Catalogue of Arms and Armour . . . including late Gothic wood Sculpture, a 13th Century Limoges Champleve Enamel Cross, bygones and Ivory carvings The Property of the late Sebastian Pugin Powell Esq . . .* Sotheby & Co., 22 December 1960. I am indebted to the late Dom Bede Millard for showing me this catalogue.

41. I would like to thank Giles Ellwood for his kindness in obtaining for me photographs of several of the objects sold by Sothebys.

42. Wedgwood, (note 11), p.191.

43. Wainwright, op.cit. (note 14), p.44.

44. H. Shaw, *Specimens of Ancient Furniture*, 1836, pl.XLV. This was issued in batches of plates from 1833–6 and, while many are dated, the lectern plate is not.

45. J. Crab, 'The Great Copper Pelican in the Choir: The Lectern from the Church of St Peter in Louvain', *The Metropolitan Museum of Art Bulletin*, XXVI, No.10, 401.

46. A. Farrell, 'Pugin and Oscott', *The Oscottian* V, no.3, 1905, p.108. I would like to thank Richard Barton for bringing this article to my attention and for all the help he has given me with the collection at Oscott.

47. R. O'Donnell, 'Pugin at Oscott', *Oscott College 1838–1988 A volume of commemorative essays*, ed. J.F. Champ, Birmingham, 1988, p.52.

48. W. Greaney, *A Catalogue of Pictures Wood-Carvings Manuscripts and other works of Art and Antiquity in St Mary's College Oscott Birmingham*, 1880, p.21.

49. Greaney, op.cit. (note 48), p.38.

50. I would like to thank Alexandra Wedgwood for showing me the documentation of this gift that she has discovered in the House of Lords Record Office.

51. This letter in the Hardman Archives in Birmingham and though undated is likely to date from 1847–52. I would like to thank Ann Eatwell for bringing it to my attention.

52. RIBA Crace letters PUG 6/11.

53. *Sale Catalogues of Libraries of Eminent Persons Volume 4 Architects*, ed. A.N.L. Munby and D.J. Watkin, London, 1972.

54. I had intended to discuss this question here, but space precluded it. I will publish my research on this interesting aspect of Pugin at a later date.

55. Wainwright, op.cit. (note 14), chapter 9.

56. This important collection has recently been investigated by Janet Myles in her Ph.D. thesis, 'L.N. Cottingham, 1787–1847, Architect: his place in the Gothic Revival', Leicester Polytechnic 1989.

Chapter 7, Pugin Writing

1. When this contribution was written, the author had no knowledge of what items would be displayed in the Pugin exhibition in 1994; the essay is therefore directed at general considerations, not at specific objects.

2. Pugin's publications are listed in M. Belcher, *A.W.N. Pugin: an annotated critical bibliography*, 1987.

3. Ushaw College MS Wiseman correspondence 823.

4. Quoted in Belcher, p.11.

5. Quotations from reviews are taken from the *Athenæum*, 14 January 1837, *Fraser's magazine*, March 1837, *Gentleman's magazine*, March 1837, *Dublin review*, October 1837, *Civil engineer and architect's journal*, January 1838 and September 1839 and *British critic, and quarterly theological review*, April 1839 and from Matthew Habershon, *The ancient half-timbered houses of England*, 1836 and 'An Architect', *Reply to 'Contrasts,' by A. Welby Pugin*, 1837.

6. All extracts from Pugin's letters to Hardman are taken from unpublished correspondence in a private collection; permission to quote is gratefully acknowledged. On the microfilm of this correspondence in the House of Lords Record Office, Historical Collection 304, the quoted letters, all except one undated, are numbered 6, 116, 150 (22 December 1850), 153, 444, 452, 453, 460, 461, 467, 471, 472, 473, 476, 477, 484, 489, 492, 497, 499, 558, 568, 748, 752, 757, 789, 938 and 1008.

7. *Apologia pro vita sua*, New York 1968, p.84.

8. The question of possible 'sources' for *Contrasts*, not touched on here, is one needing more sophisticated treatment than it has yet received.

9. Book IV, chapter 3.

10. 17 June 1837, p.440.

11. p.61.

12. The writer is indebted to Alexandra Wedgwood for pointing out Powell's contribution to *Floriated ornament*.

13. An undated, unpublished letter in the collection of David Franklin. On the microfilm of this set in the House of Lords Record Office, Historical Collection 339, this letter has the number 116. Permission to quote is gratefully acknowledged.

14. pp.98–9.

15. 28 December 1850, p.3. The writer is grateful to the late Dom Bede Millard for drawing Pugin's contributions to this journal to her attention.

16. *Catholic standard*, 22 February 1851, p.6.

17. *Catholic standard*, 15 March 1851, p.5.

18. 29 March 1851, p.12.

19. *Catholic standard*, 15 March 1851, p.5.

20. p.13.

21. pp.2–4, 11, 12 and 14.

22. HLRO Hist. Coll. 339/30, postmarked 13 May 1847.

23. *Some remarks on the articles which have recently appeared in the 'Rambler,' relative to ecclesiastical architecture and decoration*, 1850, p.11.

24. *Catholic standard*, 15 March 1851, p.5.
25. HLRO Hist. Coll. 304/477, n.d. The quotation with which Phoebe Stanton concludes *Pugin* (1971) begins with this sentence but no more of her quotation is taken from this letter.

Chapter 8, Wallpaper

1. C.L. Eastlake, *Hints on Household Taste*, London 1867, p.117.
2. A.V. Sugden and J.L. Edmondson, *A History of English Wallpaper, 1509–1914*, London 1926, p.142.
3. *Catalogue of the Select Specimens of British Manufacturers and Decorative Art*, London 1847, p.4.
4. R. Redgrave, *Report on Design*, London 1852, p.25.
5. A.W.N. Pugin, *The True Principles of Pointed Architecture*, London 1973, p.29.
6. Quoted in M. Archer, 'Gothic Wallpapers – An Aspect of the Gothic Revival', *Apollo*, 78, 1963, pp.109–16.
7. *True Principles* (note 5) p.29.
8. Jeffrey & Co. Pattern Book 1837–44 in the Prints & Drawings Department of the Victoria & Albert Museum E.431–1943.
9. *True Principles* (note 5) p.29.
10. Royal Institute of British Architects Library (RIBA), Crace Mss. Box 1, PUG 8/55.
11. RIBA, PUG 1/2.
12. M. Aldrich ed., *The Craces: Royal Decorators 1768–1899*, Brighton 1990, p.138.
13. For example, Public Records Office BT.43/79/14919.
14. *English Wallpaper* (note 2) p.206.
15. Public Records Office BT.44/9.
16. Cited in A.V. Sugden and E.A. Entwisle, *Potters of Darwen. A Century of Wallpaper Printing by Machinery*, Manchester 1939, p.112.
17. For example, *The Illustrated Catalogue of the Exhibition of 1862*, 2, London 1962, p.54, and 'Materials for Wall Decoration', *The House Furnisher*, 1, 1871, p.74.
18. RIBA, PUG 7/24.
19. A.W.N. Pugin, *Floriated Ornament*, London 1849, pl.28.
20. RIBA, PUG 1/30.
21. RIBA, PUG 4/11.
22. RIBA, PUG 4/26.
23. *Report on Design* (note 4), p.26.
24. *The Builder*, IX, 1851, p.473.
25. *Report on Design* (note 4), p.26.
26. *The Illustrated Catalogue of the 1862 Exhibition*, 2, London 1862, p.52, and p.58.
27. *Household Taste* (note 1), p.123.

Chapter 9, Furniture

1. I have discussed several aspects of his furniture in print before. 'A.W.N. Pugin's Early Furniture', *Connoisseur*, CXCI, pp.3–11. 'Furniture', *The Houses of Parliament*, ed. M.H. Port, New Haven and London, 1976, pp.282–98.
2. Ferrey, p.18.
3. A.W.N. Pugin, *The True principles of Pointed or Christian Architecture*, London, 1841, pp.40–1.
4. Ferrey, pp.64–5.
5. *Illustrations Landscape Historical and Antiquarian to The Poetical Works of Sir Walter Scott*, London, 1834. The pages are not numbered, the furniture chapter was written by Thomas Moule.
6. C. Wainwright, 'Only the True Black Blood', *Furniture History* XXI, 1985, pp.250–5.
7. S. Jervis, *Printed Furniture Designs Before 1650*, London 1974, p.41, pl.301. I would like to thank Simon Jervis for the many interesting discussions we have had on Pugin and his works since 1968.
8. N.X. Willemin, *Monuments Inédits . . .* Paris, 1806–39
9. C. Wainwright, *The Romantic Interior: The British Collector at Home 1750–1850*, New Haven and London, 1989, p.97.
10. A.W.N. Pugin, *The Present State of Ecclesiastical Architecture in England*, London, 1843, pp.102–3.
11. Pugin, *True Principles*, London, 1841, pp.37–8.
12. *True Principles* (note 11), p.34.
13. *True Principles* (note 11), p.1.
14. The best analysis of the this complex subject is S. Williams, 'The Birth of functionalism. Pugin's furniture designs for St Mary's College, Oscott', Dissertation submitted for History of Art Tripos, Cambridge, May 1991. I am very grateful to Simon Williams for sharing his discoveries at Oscott with me.
15. I would like to thank Michael Whiteway for this fascinating observation and for sharing his other ideas concerning Pugin's furniture.
16. *Present State* (note 10), p.104.
17. *Present State* (note 10), p.99.
18. Wedgwood, 1977, pls. 55 & 56.
19. J. Glancey and C. Wainwright, 'Pugin Reunion', *The Architectural Review*, CLXXVI, 1984, pp.58–63.
20. *Furniture in the House of Lords A report by The Victoria & Albert Museum*, London, 1974.
21. C. Wainwright, 'Furniture' *The Houses of Parliament*, ed. M.H. Port, New Haven and London, 1976, pp.282–97. 'Furnishing the New Palace: Pugin's furniture and fittings', *Apollo*, CXXXV, 1992, pp.303–7.
22. C. Wainwright, 'Eastnor Castle II', *Country Life* 20 May 1993, pp.90–93.
23. M. Aldrich, 'Abney Hall', *The V&A Album* V, London, 1986, pp.76–84.

Chapter 10, Ceramics

1. I am grateful to Clive Wainwright for bringing this to my attention.
2. Joan Jones, *Minton: The First Two Hundred Years of Design and Production*, Swan Hill Press, 1993, p.159.
3. Llewellyn Jewitt, *The Ceramic Art of Great Britain*, London, 1878.
4. Ferrey, p.251.
5. Ferrey, p.254.
6. Tile plans are among a large collection of Pugin drawings held by the Myers Family Trust.
7. John Sandon, *The Dictionary of Worcester Porcelain*, Vol. I, 1751–1851, Woodbridge, 1993, p.337.
8. For help with the identification of this and other patterns from documents held in the Minton Archive I am grateful to Joan Jones, the curator of the Minton Museum, Stoke-on-Trent.
9. I am grateful to Richard Dennis for bringing this to my attention.
10. This information was given to me by Joan Jones, the curator of the Minton Museum, Stoke-on-Trent.
11. I am grateful to Michael Whiteway for bringing these comments, possibly from *The Journal of Design* to my attention.
12. I am grateful to John Scott for bringing this to my attention.

Chapter 11, Book Design and Production

1. Belcher, 1987.
2. P.B. Stanton, 'The Sources of Pugin's Contrasts', *Concerning Architecture Essays on Architectural Writers and Writing presented to Nikolaus Pevsner*, ed. J. Summerson, London, 1968.
3. I.G. Brown, ' "With an uncommon splendour" The bindings of Robert Adam's *Ruins at Spalatro*', *Apollo*, January 1993, pp.6–11.
4. P.B. Stanton, *Pugin*, London, 1971, p.104.
5. Wedgwood, 1977, p.102. pl.103.
6. J. Bryson, 'The Balliol that might have been: Pugin's rejected designs', *Country Life*, CXXXIII, p.1561.
7. I would like to thank the late Dom Bede Millard for bringing this binding to my attention and for sharing his vast knowledge of Pugin and Ramsgate with me over the last twenty years.
8. D. Ball, *Victorian Publishers' Bindings*, London, 1985, pp.11–15. I would like to thank Robin de Beaumont for his advice on nineteenth-century cloth bindings.
9. E. Jamieson, *English Embossed Bindings*, Cambridge, 1972.
10. Belcher, 1987, p.3.
11. Sadleir, *The Evolution of Publishers' Binding Stules 1770–1900*, London, 1930, p.46, pl.4a.
12. Ball, op.cit. (note 8), p.180.

13. G. Dry, 'John Leighton and bookbinding design in England', Unpublished thesis, Munich Institute for the History of Art, pp.11–13. Quoted by Ball, op.cit. (note 8), p.46.

14. R. McLean, *Victorian Book Design*, 1963, p.154.

15. Belcher, 1987, p.59. These letters are in the Metropolitan Museum of Art in New York.

16. Belcher, 1987, p.64.

17. This was the copy which belonged to the Earl of Arundel and Surrey, who knew Pugin well. It is still in the library at Arundel Castle. I would like to thank Sara Rodger for showing this to me.

18. R. Redgrave, *Report on Design prepared as a Supplement to the Report of the Jury of Class XXX of the Exhibition of 1851*, London, 1852, p.78. I would like to thank Lady Wedgwood for bringing this reference to my attention. I am also endebted to Elizabeth Fairman for her help with the binding in plate 299, which she has allowed me to illustrate.

19. *Exhibition of the Works of Industry of All Nations 1851 Reports of the Juries*, London 1852, Class XVII, p.424. I would like to thank Robin de Beaumont for bringing the binding in plate 300 to my attention and allowing me to illustrate it. He also informs me that the Jones/Humphrey 'Old Monastic' binding still survives.

20. 'A Day at the Bookbinders', *The Penny Magazine Supplement*, 1842, p.383.

21. I would like to thank Christopher Firmstone for telling me about this surviving ticket.

22. Belcher, 1987, p.61.

23. N.X. Willemin, *Monuments Français Inédits Pour Servir à L'Histoire des Arts . . .*, Paris, 1806–39, pl.182. This came out in parts and plate 182 was published in 1827.

24. McLean, op.cit. (note 15), pp.53–9.

25. W.S. Williams, 'On Lithography read to the meeting on 22 December 1847', *Transactions of the Society for the Encouragement of Arts Manufactures and Commerce*, Supplementary Volume, 1852, p.242.

26. A Hyatt King, 'Some Victorian Music Titles', *The Penrose Annual*, XLVI, 1952, pp.43–7.

27. McLean, op.cit. (note 15), p.54.

28. Belcher, 1987, p.138.

29. There is an uncoloured copy in the Botany Library of the Natural History Museum and I would like to thank Malcolm Besley, the Librarian, for his help.

Chapter 12, Jewellery

1. Wedgwood, 1985, pp.129–30, cat.108.

2. Id., pl.7, ff.9, 14, 21; cf. J. Evans, *A History of Jewellery 1100–1870*, London, 2nd ed., 1970, pl.17b, 26b–d; R.W. Lightbown, *Mediaeval Jewellery*, London, 1992, figs. 82, 77–8, 106.

3. S. Bury, *Jewellery 1889–1910*, Woodbridge, 1991, I, pp.300, 302; Birmingham Public Reference Library (BPRL), Hardman letters; T. Aston to Hardman, letter dated 20 December 1845.

4. W. Burges, 'The International Exhibition', *Gentleman's Magazine*, CCXII, 1862, pp.674–5, stating his (largely adverse) views on the enamels of all the medieval metalworkers exhibiting at the International Exhibition of 1862.

5. BPRL, Hardman letters; Pugin to Hardman, 4 January 1845.

6. Leith, 1849+, I, p.226; perhaps entered in Shrewsbury's account on 24 August 1840 as '1 Morse Richly Gilt & enameled', £7. 15s.

7. BPRL, Hardman Daybook, 1845–9, 3 May 1853, St Marie's College Oscott. The Virgin's Crown, set with rock crystal (quartz), cost £9. 10s.; the Child's, set with four garnets, £6. Both crowns were sawpierced.

8. BPRL, Daybook, 1838–44, 29 January 1841.

9. BPRL, Daybook, 1849–54, 25 July, 16 October, 22 December 1851. The crosses cost respectively £3, £8, £8. 8s.

10. Victoria & Albert Museum, Victorian Church Art, exh.cat.1971, cat.B7.

11. BPRL, Daybook, 1838–44, 29 June/? July 1839.

12. Id., 17 November 1843.

13. BPRL, Hardman letters; Charles Dolman to Hardman, 3 November 1845.

14. BPRL, Daybook, 1845–9; 23 September 1848, Seton Rooke, 'Small Silver Engraved Cross', 3s. 3d.; Daybook, 1849–54; 24 May 1852, Miss Warren, 'A Silver Cross with Figure . . .', 10s.; Daybook, 1845–9; 15 September 1843, [Cardinal] Wiseman, '2 Brass Gothic Crosses', 1s.

15. BPRL, Daybook, 1849–54, 20 June 1848, James Burns; 26 April 1850, Burns & Lambert [later the publishers Burns & Oates].

16. BPRL, Daybook, 1838–44, 29 January 1841, Miss Mostyn.

17. Bethune seal, BPRL, Daybook. 1849–54, 28 May 1851; Butterfield seal, BPRL, Hardman letters, Pugin to William Powell, annotated August 1851; Daybook, 1849–54, 26 November 1851, William Butterfield.

18. BPRL, Daybook, 1849–54, 6 May 1853, Matthew Hadfield.

19. BPRL, Hardman letters; A.W. Franks to Hardman (from Trinity College, Cambridge), November 1845.

20. Henry Weigall; see L. Forrer, *Biographical Dictionary of Medallists*, London, VI, 1916, pp.422–3; Weigall worked on another seal (for William Leigh) for Hardman's.

21. Wedgwood, 1985, p.106, cat.28, Pugin-Shrewsbury letter, 5 June 1843 (an earlier letter in a private collection also refers to the seal).

22. BPRL, Daybook, 1845–9; 25 March 1848, James Burns.

23. Id.; 26 December 1848, J. Gibson Esq. Was Gibson related to the Rev. J. Gibson, Dean of Jesus College, Cambridge who with the Rev. Oswald Fisher and John (later Sir John) Sutton commissioned Pugin's restoration of the College chapel from Pugin, 1846–9? (see Wedgwood, 1985, cat.247). C.H. Davidson, *Sir John Sutton: A Study in True Principles*, 1992.

24. John Sutton (1820–73), fellow commoner of Jesus College (see 23 above). On inheriting the baronetcy from his father in the mid-1850s he left for Bruges and as a Catholic convert established a seminary there (see I. and G. Morgan, *The Stones and Story of Jesus Chapel Cambridge*, Cambridge, 1914/1919, pp.294–5, 300–2, 315).

25. BPRL Daybook, 1845–9, 20 October 1848, Lieut. Robins (locket case), 1 September 1848, T.J. Burton (enamel brooch); Daybook, 1849–54, 2 February 1851, Viscount Fielding (gold heart locket). Rudolph Basil Feilding (1823–92), a Catholic convert, succeeded as 8th Earl of Denbigh, 1865.

26. BPRL, Hardman letters; Pugin to Hardman, 4 January, 9 October, 10/11 October 1845.

27. Helen Lumsdaine's identity, indicated by Pugin in his pamphlet, *A Statement of Facts*, was protected by Ferrey, who substituted an initial for her surname (Ferrey, 1861, pp.193–222). See S. Bury, 'Pugin's Marriage Jewellery', *V&A Year Book*, I, 5 1969, pp.85–96; Wedgwood, 1985, p.95, note 27 passim.

28. BPRL, Day-book. 1849–54, 22 October 1852; see sketch in House of Lords Record Office, Hardman designs, no.21. For a somewhat similar commemorative brooch, see City Museum and Art Gallery, Birmingham, Birmingham Gold and Silver, 1773–1973, 1973. exh.cat.C52; see also Ralph Nevill, *The Gay Victorians*, 1930. p.117.

29. Ferrey, 1861, p.221.

30. Matthew Digby Wyatt, *The Industrial Arts of the XIX Century*, 2 vols., 1851–3, II, pl.LXXXII.

31. Bury, op.cit., note 27, p.85.

32. BPRL, Daybook, 1845–9, 21 December 1843. I am much indebted to Paul Atterbury for bringing the sketch of Louisa to my attention.

33. The earrings were probably repaired by Hardman's in 1843; BPRL, Hardman letters; Pugin to Hardman (letter

postmarked 22 November 1843), complaining of neglect: 'if you knew what I suffer [for] want of the Earrings – you would not serve me so . . .'

34. Pugin-Hardman letter, ? January 1848, transcribed by Professor Phoebe Stanton and kindly communicated to me: 'I have disposed of the large necklace you made for me sometime ago and it will require a little alteration.'

35. Pugin-Hardman letter transcribed as above, undated but probably written before 23 February 1848.

36. Pugin-Hardman letter transcribed as above, undated but probably written towards the end of February 1848.

37. BPRL, Day-book, 1845–9, 18 April, 8 August, 1 September 1848.

38. BPRL, Daybook, 1849–54, 16 January 1850; Stuart (later Sir Stuart) Knill (1824–96), wharfinger of the City of London and, like his father, a generous benefactor to St George's Cathedral, Southwark. Both father and son became Lord Mayor of London.

39. BPRL, Daybook, 1849–54, 12 June 1850, Pugin.

40. Edward Pugin (1834–75) certainly had an enamelled mourning brooch set with pearls and hair from Hardman's; BPRL, Daybook, 1849–54, 22 October 1852, E.W. Pugin.

41. Burges op.cit. note 4, p.675.

42. C. Gere and G.C. Munn, *Artists' Jewellery*, Woodbridge 1989, Colour Plates 37, 38.

43. Id., Colour Plate 40; City Museum and Art Gallery, Birmingham, *Birmingham Gold and Silver* 1773–1973, 1973, exh.cat.C54.

Chapter 13, Metalwork

1. A.W.N. Pugin, *An Apology for the Revival of Christian Architecture*, London 1843, pl.x, 'Church Furniture revived at Birmingham.

2. B. Ferrey, *Recollections of A.W.N. Pugin and His Father Augustus Pugin*, London 1861, pp.51–2. See also chapter 2, The Early Years.

3. Designs on five sheets, unexecuted, for a set of altar plate, signed 'A. Pugin junr, 1827' (except E755–1925) and countersigned by John Gawler Bridge. V&A Museum. E 751–1925. Published in A. Wedgwood, *A.W.N. Pugin and the Pugin Family*, London 1985.

4. Op.cit. (note 3) p.26.

5. *Carlton House, The Past Glories of George IV's Palace*, London, 1991–2, cat.no.322, p.413.

6. S. Bury, A. Wedgwood and M. Snodin, 'The Antiquarian Plate of George 4th: a gloss on E.A. Jones', *Burlington Magazine*,

vol.CXXXI, June 1979, pp.343–53 and *Metropole London*, Essen 1992, cat.no.322, p.413.

7. A. Wedgwood, op.cit. (note 3) cat.no.117, p.156.

8. Pugin's diary for 1837 recorded, 'May 29th. Dined at Mr Hardman's.' Reproduced in A. Wedgwood, op.cit. (note 3) p.37.

9. Birmingham Public Reference Library (BPRL). Metalwork Daybook, 1838–44, 76/1. The authors are most grateful to the staff of the Birmingham Reference Library for their assistance with the Hardman Archive Material.

10. BPRL, clients letter box, 1839–44, undated letter.

11. BPRL, Pugin to Hardman, undated letter, 1845–6 letter bundle.

12. BPRL, Pugin to Hardman, undated letter, 1845–6 letter bundle.

13. From 'Some Remarks on the Articles which have recently appeared in the "Rambler" relative to Ecclesiastical Architecture and Decoration', quoted in S. Timmins, *The Resources, Products and Industrial History of Birmingham and the Midland Hardware District: A Series of Reports, Collected by the Local Industries Committee of the British Association of Birmingham in 1865.*, London 1866.

14. BPRL, Ledger 2, 1847–9, 13/1, p.31.

15. W.C. Aitken *et al*, *The Official Descriptive and Illustrated Catalogue*, Great Exhibition, 1851, Supplement p.1510.

16. BPRL, E.G. Estcourt, Cirencester, to Hardman, 24 April 1845, clients letter bundle.

17. Kenneth Crisp Jones *et al*, *The Silversmiths of Birmingham*, Norfolk 1981, p.257, plate 30.

18. BPRL, clients letter bundle, dated 8 March 1845.

19. *Domestic Architecture*, nos 2 and 3 'Iron handle and lock from the author's collection'. Plate published January 1830 by Aug. Pugin.

20. H. Shaw, *Specimens of Ancient Furniture*, London 1843, pl.54.

21. A. Welby Pugin, *Designs for Gold and Silversmiths Drawn and Etched*, V&A E 1198–1983, nos 11, 13.

22. Shaw, op.cit. (note 20), p.232.

23. *The Great Exhibition of the World's Industry*, 'The Mediaeval Court', Church Ornaments, Metalwork etc., p.231.

24. Now in the Cloisters, Metropolitan Museum, New York.

25. BPRL, clients letter box, 1839–44, undated letter.

26. BPRL, Pugin letter bundle, 1845–6, undated letter of about 1846.

27. S. Bury, 'In Search of Pugin's Church Plate', *The Connoisseur*, CLXV no.663, 1967, p.34.

28. For an example of a pastoral staff in

precious and base metal, see City Museum and Art Gallery, Birmingham, *Birmingham Gold and Silver, 1773–1973*, 1973, cat.no. C 9.

29. BPRL, clients letter bundle, J.J. Murphy to Hardman, St Joseph's, 28 August 1845.

30. S. Bury, 'Pugin and the Tractarians', *Connoisseur*, January 1972, p.19.

31. *Tallis's History and Description of the Crystal Palace and the Exhibition of the World's Industry in 1851*, London and New York, 1852, p.231.

Chapter 14, Monuments and Brasses

1. Osmond was from 1818 mason to Salisbury Cathedral and executed a number of monuments there. According to Edward Pugin, A.W.N. Pugin lived at Osmond's house before moving into St Marie's Grange, just outside Salisbury.

2. B. Ferrey, *Recollections of A.N. Welby Pugin*, London 1861, pp.78 and 80.

3. *Apology for the Revival of Christian Architecture in England*, London 1843, p.42.

4. *Contrasts*, London 1836, pp.11ff.

5. For a full account of Pugin's revival of memorial brasses, see D. Meara, *A.W.N. Pugin and the Revival of Memorial Brasses*, London 1991.

6. Op.cit (note 5) pp.29–30.

7. Op.cit (note 5) pp.12–13.

8. 12 May 1838.

9. Op.cit (note 5) text reproduced pp.30–3.

10. *Dublin Review*, February 1842, reprinted in book form in 1843, p.54.

11. The total number of brasses made by Hardmans during Pugin's lifetime has been catalogued by Meara (op.cit. pp.82–99). Of the 240 brasses produced, Pugin took an active part in the design of at least two-thirds. Fortunately the Hardman Archive in Birmingham Central Library and Museum gives an almost complete picture of Hardman's collaboration with Pugin.

12. *Orthodox Journal*, vol. VII, 29 June 1839, p.403, almost certainly written by Pugin himself.

13. According to a writer in *The Builder*, 25 September 1852, pp.605–6. For a full account of Pugin's working relationship with Myers, see P. Spencer-Silver, *Pugin's Builder, The Life and Work of George Myers*, Hull, 1993, especially chapters 1–5.

14. *Pugin in His Home*, p.28, ed. A. Wedgwood, 1988.

15. Scott, *Recollections Personal and Professional*, 1879, pp.88–9.

16. Letter to J.R. Bloxam, Magdalen College Archive 528/59.

17. Shirley Bury, in *The Connoisseur*, 1967, pp.29–35, and 1972, pp.15–20, gives an

interesting account of Pugin's relations with Anglican clergy.

18. Letter to J.R. Bloxam, Magdalen College Archive, 528/20.

19. HLRO, Pugin/Hardman correspondence, no.434.

20. HLRO, Pugin/Hardman correspondence, no.381.

21. HLRO, Pugin/Hardman correspondence, no.360.

22. Wedgwood, 1977, p.60.

23. *The Great Link*, London, 1948, p.138.

24. Op.cit. (note 5) pp.166–7.

25. Personal information, T. McCann. (Quoted in Patricia Spencer-Silver, 'George Myers, Pugin's Builder', *Recusant History*, vol.20 no.2, October 1990).

26. Quoted in Phoebe Stanton 'Welby Pugin and the Gothic Revival', unpublished PhD. Thesis, University of London, 1950.

27. *Sir John Sutton, A Study in True Principles*, C.H. Davidson, Oxford 1992, Chapter 3.

28. Letter to J.R. Bloxam, Magdalen College Archive, 528/9.

29. Other tombs by Pugin and Myers are: –
    i) Bishop Thomas Griffiths (1791–1847), tomb-chest and recumbent effigy at St Edmunds College, Ware, Herts.
    ii) Henry Howard of Corby Castle, d. 1842, founder's tomb, Our Lady & St Wilfred, Warwick Bridge, Cumbria (plate 163).
    iii) John Ryland, (d. 1814, engraved 1845). Tomb with brasses in Ryland chapel. All Saints, Sherbourne, Warks.

30. For further information about the Connelly family, see *Pugin's Builder* (note 13), p.195, note 29.

31. HLRO Pugin/Hardman Correspondence, no.155.

Chapter 15, Stained Glass

1. Published in the *Catholic Magazine*, 1839, pp.19–34 & 89–98.

2. Pugin repeats the criticism in 'The Present State of Ecclesiastical Architecture in England', *Dublin Review*, vol.XII, February 1842. p.109, adding a line against modern glass painters' use of light and shadow in their windows.

3. William Warrington (1786–1869) was based in London. He wrote *The History of Stained Glass*, London, 1848, in which he states (note p.33) that he was at one time in Willement's establishment. Thomas Willement (1786–1871) was based in London. He was an antiquary, writer on heraldry, and decorative painter as well as glass painter. William Wailes (1808–81) was based in Newcastle upon Tyne. His involvement with stained glass

manufacture seems to have commenced c.1838.

4. *The Builder*, 1845, p.367.

5. *The London & Dublin Weekly Orthodox Journal*, 1838, pp.90–1, reproduced from the *Birmingham Journal*, 16 January 1838.

6. P. Stanton, 'Welby Pugin and the Gothic Revival', Appendix VIII unpublished Ph.D. Thesis, University of London, 1950, letter to Lord Shrewsbury, 28 August 1841.

7. Stanton, *Welby Pugin* (note 6), letter to Lord Shrewsbury, 24 December 1841.

8. Stanton, *Welby Pugin* (note 6), Appendix VII, letter to Lord Shrewsbury, 1 December 1841.

9. Hardman Archives, Birmingham Central Reference Library, letter undated, marked 1845 box.

10. Presumably one of those at St Mary's, Ottery St Mary, Devon.

11. HLRO, Historical Collection no.304, letters from Pugin to Hardman, undated letter no.109 (c.1849).

12. HLRO, no.576, undated (c.July 1851).

13. HLRO, no.784, undated (c.mid-1851).

14. HLRO, no.543, undated (c.1847), 467 (c.end 1850 – beginning 1851), 416, 821 (c.March 1850). A letter from Pugin introducing Casolani to Hardman, marked 1847 Box, is held in the Hardman Archives, Birmingham.

15. HLRO, no.1038, undated (c.February 1849).

16. T. Fordyce, *Local Records, Newcastle upon Tyne*, 1867, p.200, 'Oliphant left Wailes for London in late 1845', this item was kindly brought to my attention by Mr Neil Moat. Hardman Archives, ledger and Oliphant's correspondence with Hardman.

17. HLRO, undated letters, nos.54 (c.July 1849), 837 (c.June 1849), 930 (c.December 1849), 693 (c.May 1850).

18. HLRO undated letter, no.819 (c.February 1850).

19. HLRO undated letter, no.406, seems to refer to the trip of 24 August to 5 September 1849 noted in Pugin's Diary (Wedgwood, 1985, p.67).

20. HLRO undated letter, no.982.

21. Hardman archives, Birmingham, letters from James Hartley to John Hardman.

22. HLRO, undated letters, nos.692 (c.July 1850), 696 (c.July 1850), 743 (c.end 1850), 744, 957 (c.end 1849), 969 (c.end 1849), 975, 986 (c.end 1849).

23. HLRO, undated letter no.693 (c.May 1850).

24. HLRO, undated letter no.696 (c.July 1850).

25. HLRO, undated letter no.692 (c.July 1850).

26. HLRO, undated letter no.686 (c.1850). This is interesting, and not altogether surprising, evidence of Pugin trying his hand at glass painting.

27. Something commented on by the

Ecclesiologist, July 1846, pp.37, 38.

28. Hardman archives, Birmingham; re St Giles's, Cheadle, letter from Pugin to Hardman postmarked JU 20 1846; re St Barnabas's, Nottingham, letters from Rev. F. Cheadle to Hardman, and entries in Daybook, October 1848 and April 1849.

29. Stanton, *Welby Pugin*, (note 6), Appendix VII, letter to Lord Shrewsbury, February 1844.

30. HLRO, letter no.985 undated (c.May 1848).

31. Hardman archives, Birmingham, a letter to John Hardman from George Bartley, dated 6 April 1848, notes that, 'Mr Wailes of Newcastle', executed the first window. Ferrey (1978 ed., p.188), recalls Pugin sketching out its design.

32. *Ecclesiologist* July 1846 p.38: 'the whole effect is dingy'.

33. HLRO, undated letter no.187. According to his diary (Wedgwood, 1985, p.64), Pugin visited Oxford on 23 August 1848. The architect G.E. Street noted the use of white to give a brilliant effect in Hardman's windows, *Ecclesiologist*, 1852, p.245 – a point made by M. Harrison, *Victorian Stained Glass*, London, 1980, p.29.

34. HLRO, undated letter no.640 (c.first half 1851).

35. HLRO, undated letter no.394 (c.March 1847). This is now the west window of the present chapel. An undated letter from J. Hardman Powell to J. Hardman, in the 1847 box of the Hardman archives, links Oliphant with the cartoons for the window.

36. HLRO, undated letter, no.908 (c.second half 1849).

37. Hardman archive, Birmingham, the entry for the windows in the First Glass Day Book is dated 12 February 1850.

38. HLRO, undated letter, no.144 (c.March 1849). Gerente died on 6 August 1849, having returned to France from England a few weeks before, *Ecclesiologist* n.s.XXXVIII, no.LXXIV, October 1849, p.100.

39. Jesus College Archives, letter undated, addressed to 'My dear Sir'. R. Willis, *The Architectural History of the University of Cambridge* 4 vols, Cambridge, 1886, ed. J.W. Clarke, vol.2, p.152, says this is a letter to Mr Sutton (the window was commissioned by the Rev. John Sutton).

40. Hardman archive, Birmingham, letter to Hardman dated 22 February 1851.

41. HLRO, undated letter, no.686 (c.1850). According to his diary (Wedgwood, 1985, p.68), Pugin visited Cambridge on 4 April 1850.

42. Hardman archive, Birmingham, letter to Hardman from G.B. Blomfield, Canon of Chester Cathedral, dated 10 May 1850.

43. HLRO, undated letter, no.898 (c.May 1850).

44. North window in choir of St Augustine's, Ramsgate. Hardman archive, Birmingham, entered in First Glass Day Book, 9 May 1850.

45. HLRO, undated letter, no.713 (c.May 1850).

46. HLRO, undated letter, no.693 (c.May 1850). Hardman archive, Birmingham – the First Glass Day Book has an entry for 18 May 1850 regarding alterations to the window.

47. HLRO, undated letter, no.460 (c.February 1851).

48. HLRO, undated letter, no.504 (c.March 1851).

49. HLRO, undated letter, no.508 (c.September 1851).

50. Hardman archive, Birmingham – the entry for the window in the First Glass Day Book is dated 22 March 1852. It was ordered on 7 March 1851.

51. HLRO, undated letter, no.688 (c.1850). According to his diary (Wedgwood, 1985, p.68), Pugin visited Fairford from Birmingham on 29 July 1850.

52. HLRO, undated letter, no.700 (c.May 1850).

53. HLRO, undated letter, no.466 (c.March 1851).

54. Hardman archive, Birmingham, entered Day Book 6 April 1852, ordered 27 October 1851.

55. Hardman archive, Birmingham, entered Day Book 8 September 1851.

56. HLRO, undated letter, no.118 (c.June 1851).

57. HLRO, letter, no.665 postmarked B'ham NO. 20 1851. The comparison with King's was made by Sutton in respect of two three-light windows – replaced c.1914 – on the south side of the choir of Jesus College Chapel, Cambridge. The windows were entered in the First Glass Day Book (Hardman archive) 24 October 1851, having been ordered 26 March 1850. The windows are described in the *Ecclesiologist*, XCVIII, n.s.LXII, October 1853, p.370. According to his diary (Wedgwood, 1985, p.72), Pugin visited Cambridge on 20 November 1851.

58. HLRO, undated letter, no.159 (c.February 1851).

59. HLRO, undated letter, no.693.

60. HLRO, undated letter, no.456 (c.February 1851).

61. Hardman archive, Birmingham, letter from N.J. Cottingham to Hardman, 17 February 1851, notes that permission to include the window in the exhibition was refused, on the grounds that the committee required it to be placed in the Cathedral without delay. The window was replaced by Hardman's in 1871, F.C. Morgan, *Hereford Cathedral Church Glass*, 3rd ed. revised by P.E. Morgan, 1974, p.23.

62. HLRO, undated letter, no.456.

63. Window destroyed by bombing in the Second World War.

64. HLRO, undated letter, no.456.

65. Bilton Grange and Canford Manor are now schools, Burton Closes is a retirement home and the Grange is a private residence.

66. J. Christian, 'Stained Glass', *The Houses of Parliament*, ed. M.H. Port, New Haven and London, 1976, pp.245–57. See also chapter 17, The Palace of Westminster.

67. HLRO, undated letter, no.236.

68. HLRO, undated letter, no.228.

69. HLRO, undated letter, no.966 (c.October 1849).

70. HLRO, undated letter, no.459 (c.March 1851).

71. HLRO, undated letter, no.462.

72. *Ecclesiologist* LXXXII, n.s.XLVI, February 1851, p.46.

73. Hardman archive, Birmingham, letter to Hardman from I. Nidd, Rochdale, dated 3 February 1851, refers to a semiofficial report in the *Manchester Guardian* of Saturday.

74. HLRO, undated letter, no.418, apparently a copy, not in Pugin's hand.

75. HLRO, undated letter, no.578 (c.June 1851).

76. HLRO, letter, no.972, postmarked SP 29 1849. Hardman archive, Birmingham, Coleridge made the proposal to Hardman in a letter dated 25 September 1849.

77. HLRO, undated letter, no.996 (c.1848). The Convent may have been at Birmingham. St George's was presumably the Cathedral at Southwark.

78. W.A. Wickham, 'Pugin and the re-building of Winwick Chancel', *Transactions of the Historic Society of Lancashire and Cheshire*, 1907, 59, n.s.23, p.152.

79. Hardman archive, Birmingham, Hardman Letter Book, letter to Revd R. Wilson, Staplefield Crawley, 27 May 1853. The subject of the letter – the lancet east windows of Staplefield Crawley Church – was replaced c.1914. Hardman had written previously on 12 March 1852 to say that the cartoons had been sent by Mr Pugin and were beautiful in design.

Chapter 16, Textiles

1. J. Carter, *Specimens of English Ecclesiastical Costume*, London 1817.

2. A.W. Pugin, *Glossary of Ecclesiastical Ornament and Costume*, London 1844.

3. P.F. Anson, *Fashions in Church Furnishings 1840–1940*, London 1965, p.31.

4. J.H. Cardinal Newman, *Sermons on Various Occasions*, London 1908, p.169.

5. T.S.R. Boase, 'The Decoration of the New Palace of Westminster 1841–1863', *The Journal of the Warburg and Courtauld Institutes* XVII, 1954, p.338.

6. A.W.N. Pugin, 'The Present State of Ecclesiastical Architecture in England', *The Dublin Review* XXIII, February 1842, p.104.

7. Ibid., p.106.

8. Ibid., p.108.

9. A.W.N. Pugin, 'Chasuble of Cloth of Gold, Embroidered', *The London and Dublin Orthodox Journal of Useful Knowledge* VI, no.146, Saturday 14 April 1838, p.227.

10. A.W.N. Pugin, 'The Present State etc.' p.106 (footnote).

11. Ibid., p.108 (footnote).

12. D. Gwynn, *Lord Shrewsbury, Pugin and the Gothic Revival*, London 1946, p.57.

13. A.W.N. Pugin, 'Chancel of St Maries, Uttoxeter', *The London and Dublin Orthodox Journal of Useful Knowledge* IX, no.212, Saturday 20 July 1839, p.35.

14. A.W.N. Pugin, 'Chasuble of Cloth of Gold', p.226.

15. D. Gwynn, op. cit. p.74.

16. E.S. Purcell, *Life and Letters of Ambrose Phillipps de Lisle*, London 1900, vol.2, p.222.

17. E. Lester, S.J., 'The Gothic Revival', *The Tablet*, vol.143, No.4381, 26 April 1924, p.565.

18. D. Gwynn. op. cit, p.75.

19. D. Rock, *The Church of Our Fathers*, London 1903, p.285ff.

20. Ibid., p.287.

21. A.W.N. Pugin, 'Expenses for the Erection etc. of St Augustine's Church, Ramsgate', V&A MS.L.50/3–1982.

22. *Birmingham Gold and Silver 1773–1973*, exh. cat., City Museum and Art Gallery, Birmingham 1973, n.p. entry C 12.

23. *The Catholic Directory and Ecclesiastical Register for the Year 1853*, London, n.p.

24. J. Morley, *Death, Heaven and the Victorians*, London 1971, pp.114–17.

25. A.W.N. Pugin, *Diary, 1849.* V&A MS.L.5168–1969.

26. Cathedral Clergy: *A History of St Chad's Cathedral, Birmingham*, Birmingham 1904, p.149.

27. D. Rock, *Textile Fabrics*, London 1870, p.clx.

28. A. Wedgwood: 'Crace and Pugin', in M. Aldrich (ed.), *The Craces: Royal Decorators 1768–1899*, Brighton 1990, p.138.

29. Ibid., p.143.

30. M. Hall, 'Crace in Favour', *Country Life*, 11 October 1990, pp.74–77.

31. *Journal of Design and Manufactures*, no.7. May 1851, p.74 and p.78.

32. Ibid., no.7, September 1849, vol.11, p.55.

33. RIBA Library Crace MSS PUG 7/49 quoted in Wedgwood, 1985, cat.818.

34. A cope hood was made for use at St Augustine's, Ramsgate sewn from

fragments of late medieval ecclesiastical orphreys and strips of a powdered altar frontal containing the same crowned fleur-de-lys motif used by Pugin in a number of his designs. The hood is now in the V&A.

35. Sandra Wedgwood refers to three of Pugin's designs of this type from the Crace Archive at the V&A. (op. cit., note 1, cat.816–18).

36. Hardman Archives, Birmingham Public Reference Library. I would like to thank Ann Eatwell and Tony North for references.

37. V&A D.887–1908 (Wedgwood, 1985, 356). See also note 2.

38. This is a long strip (possibly used as superfrontal or curtain valance) the pattern picked out in gold on a dark red ground.

39. Ward exhibited in Classes XII and XV of the Exhibition as manufacturers of jacquard woven cotton and worsted damask and makers of worsted damask for draperies. A cotton and wool sample showing a Puginesque design of this type is illustrated in the *Journal of Design*, no.27, May 1851, p.74.

40. Letter dated 24 December 1844, RIBA Library MSS PUGI/43. Quoted in A. Wedgwood, 'J.G. Crace and A.W.N. Pugin', *The Craces: Royal Decorators*, ed. M. Aldrich, 1990.

41. Examples of these three schemes survive either in the houses or in private collections.

42. See bed hangings and upholstery on the day-bed in a 1912 photograph illustrated in *The Craces: Royal Decorators*, op. cit., note 8, p.93.

43. These form part of the collection of vestments from Ramsgate now in the V&A.

44. There is some confusion as to whether wallpaper or textiles were used on the walls. A design inscribed (not in Pugin's hand) 'Drawing Room paper/Watts . . .' is in the V&A. D.902–1908 (Wedgwood op. cit., note 1, cat.259) whereas silk is suggested by Megan Aldrich in 'The Victorian Craces', Aldrich, op. cit., note 8, pp.86, 87.

45. One design for hangings, intended for The Grange, shows Pugin's motto and emblems of repeating birds. D.1102 – 1908 (Wedgwood, 1985, 580).

46. V&A Collection: for monogram see D.942–1908, (Wedgwood, 1985, 673); lambrequin, E.1655–1912 (808); polescreen for Chirk, D.1121–1908 (272); christening mantle for Mr S. Murray, D.1119, 1129–1908 (284, 285); wedding veil for Helen Lumsdaine, D.1104–1908 (1048).

47. See drawings taken from late medieval and sixteenth-century patterns in St Mary's, Lübeck, E.77(42, 40, 43)–1970

(Wedgwood, 1985, 964–6). Alexandra Wedgwood also notes that a series of strong patterns follow Pugin's only visit to Italy in 1847.

48. See part I, Pugin's ecclesiastical textiles by Dom Bede Millard.

49. J.H. Pollen, 'Textile fabrics in South Kensington', from *The Month*, vol.I, January–June 1870, p.227. I am indebted to the late Dom Bede Millard for this and many other references.

50. Letter RIBA Library Crace MSS PUG 7/4. Alexandra Wedgwood associates this with a design in the V&A–D.766-1908, Wedgwood, 1985, 821.

51. A.W.N. Pugin, 'On the Present State of Ecclesiastical Architecture in England', *Dublin Review*, 1841.

52. See Dom Bede Millard, part I.

53. T. Brown is mentioned in Pugin's diary for 1845 (V&A Library 86 MM 63). This is transcribed by Sandra Wedgwood as 'J' Brown.

54. A.W.N. Pugin, 1841, op. cit., note 19.

55. Chintz refers to a glazed printed cotton, the most fashionable form until the 1870s when the unglazed 'cretonne' became fashionable.

56. RIBA Library Crace MSS PUG 13/8.

57. C.E.M., *Hints on Ornamental needlework as applied to Ecclesiastical Purposes*, London, 1843, p.42.

58. *Victorian Church Art*, exh. cat., London, 1971, p.11.

59. Information from Kay Staniland, Museum of London.

60. Pugin's diary, 9 April 1839 (V&A 86.MM.70); notebook, 1 February 1851 (V&A VI.RC.Box 13, p.46).

61. *On the Present State of Ecclesiastical Architecture in England*, London, 1843, p.108; this passage first published *Dublin Review*, February 1842, pp.80–183. *Glossary of Ecclesiastical Ornament and Costume, compiled and illustrated from antient authorities and examples*, London 1844, p.70.

62. *Glossary*, op. cit. n.5, pattern of alternating trefoils on a priest's stole on a brass in plate 5 and in a design for a altar frontal plate 8, used as a braid on a dalmatic (V&A, T.293.C-1989, plate 4); pattern of circles enclosing quatrefoils in plate 42 (right) used as a braid on an altar frontal (V&A, T.284–1989), and a pair of dalmatics (V&A, T.387&A-1989, plate 5).

63. V&A, D.811-1908, D.808-1908 (plate 5), E.1668-1912, D.927-1908. In 1908 J.D. Crace identified D.811-1908 and D.808-1908 as designs for the Houses of Parliament; on the basis of his comments, Alexandra Wedgwood catalogued these four drawings as carpet borders (*A.W.N. Pugin and the Pugin Family*, London 1985, cat.502, 503, 849, 866). It is now proposed in view of their similarities with braids on

Pugin's vestments and the scale of the patterns that they are designs for woven braids.

64. *The Tablet*, Saturday, 14 January 1871.

65. See part II, note 53.

66. *Tallis's History and Description of the Crystal Palace and the Exhibition of the World's Industry in 1851 . . .*, London and New York 1852, p.233.

67. *Descriptive Catalogue of Articles of Church Decoration Designed and Manufactured Exclusively by Gilbert J. French, Bolton, Lancashire*, 31st edition, Manchester 1864, p.18.

Chapter 17, The New Palace of Westminster

1. E.W. Pugin, *Who was the Art-Architect of the Houses of Parliament?*, 1867, and A. Barry, *The Architect of the New Palace of Westminster. A Reply to a Pamphlet by E.W. Pugin Esq.*, 1868.

2. Letter in the Fowler Collection, Johns Hopkins University, Baltimore. The punctuation and spelling have been standardised in this transcript.

3. See M.H. Port ed., *The Houses of Parliament*, New Haven and London 1976, pp.20–1. This book provides the best account of the rebuilding.

4. A.W. Hakewill, *Thoughts upon the style of architecture to be adopted in rebuilding the Houses of Parliament*, London, 1835.

5. A.W. Pugin, *A Letter to A.W. Hakewill, architect, in answer to his reflections on the style for rebuilding the Houses of Parliament*, Salisbury, 1835.

6. See chapter 2, The Early Years, for details of Pugin's relationship with Charles Barry and James Gillespie Graham up till 1835.

7. Pugin's diary for 1835, Victoria & Albert Museum, L5156-1969.

8. A. Wedgwood, *RIBA Drawings Collection Catalogue, The Pugin Family*, Farnborough, 1977, pp.49–51.

9. Pugin's Autobiography, Victoria & Albert Museum, L5204–1969.

10. These identifications of entries in Pugin's diary for 1835 have been made by Dr James Macaulay.

11. It should be in the Public Record Office along with the other prize-winning entries. It is known that Barry borrowed it and in 1845 its return was asked for (PRO Works 1/28 p.281). Barry replied that he would like some time in which to make copies, and the file contains nothing more. The general assumption is that it was destroyed at some date by a member of Barry's family to remove evidence of Pugin's involvement in the project.

12. PRO Works 29/3204.

13. A. Barry, op. cit. note 1, p.7.

14. Ferrey, p.248.

15. T. Hopper, *A Letter to the Rt. Hon. Lord Viscount Duncannon*, London, 1837, p.7.

16. Pugin's diaries for 1836 and 1837, Victoria & Albert Museum, L5157-1969, L5158-1969.
17. E.W. Pugin, op. cit. note 1, pp.23–4.
18. Ferrey, p.245.
19. See chapter 4, Domestic Architecture.
20. For example at the Victoria & Albert Museum E67-1912, E68-1912, E69-1912 and at the Public Record Office, Works 29/555, 642, 2107 and 3251.
21. See chapter 5, Church Architecture.
22. Wedgwood, 1977, pp.62–64.
23. F. Knight Hunt, *The Book of Art*, 1846, pp.148–67.
24. Barry, op. cit. note 1, p.53.
25. Barry, op. cit. note 1, p.39.
26. Pugin's diary for 1844, Victoria & Albert Museum, L5164-1969.
27. PRO Works 1/27 p.318.
28. Barry, op. cit. note 1, pp.55–6.
29. Barry, op. cit. note 1, pp.57–8.
30. PRO Works 11/9/4 f.33.
31. PRO Works 11/28/16 f.19 et seq.
32. 'Charles Barry and His Right-Hand Man', *The Artizan*, n.s.1 1845, p.137; *The Builder*, III, 1845, pp.250; 416; 426; 460.
33. *Punch*, IX, 1845, p.150, p.186 and p.238.
34. E.W. Pugin, op. cit. note 1; Barry, op. cit. note 1; Port ed., op. cit. note 3; A. Wedgwood, 'The throne in the House of Lords and its setting', *Architectural History*, 27, 1984, pp.59–68.
35. Wedgwood, 1977, p.63.
36. RIBA Drawings Collection, C. Barry Ran 2/H/4.
37. Two copies of this set of drawings are known; one is now in the House of Lords Library.
38. PRO Works 29/200, 202, 203 and HLRO Moulton-Barrett volume ff.230–4, 236–9 and 242.
39. RIBA Drawings Collection, C. Barry diary no.22.
40. Port ed., op. cit. note 3, pp.131, 137, 217.
41. Barry, op. cit. note 1, p.89.
42. Port ed., op. cit. note 3, pp.263, 285–6.
43. Pugin's diary for 1837, V&A L5158–1969.
44. *Illustrated London News*, X, 1847, p.260.
45. Op. cit., note 44, p.281–2.
46. See chapter 13, Metalwork.
47. Pugin's letters to Hardman are in a private collection (microfilm HLRO Historical Collection 304) and in Birmingham Central Library (photocopies in HLRO).
48. Birmingham Central Library (HLRO no: 65).
49. Port ed., op. cit. note 3, p.262.
50. *Parliamentary Papers* 1846 [685] XXIV, Fifth Report of the Commissioners on the Fine Arts, pp.9–10.
51. Chapter 15, Stained Glass.
52. HLRO Historical Collection 176.
53. PRO Works 11/9/4 ff.42–3.
54. *The Palace of Westminster with a descriptive account of the House of Lords*, W.

55. Op. cit. note 44, pp.245–7.
56. Op. cit. note 44, p.247.
57. Op. cit. note 44, pp.247, 260; Minton's name is given in the guide-book op. cit., note 54, p.10.
58. See chapter 10, Ceramics.
59. Pugin's diary for 1845, V&A L5165-1969.
60. Pugin's letters to J.G. Crace are in the RIBA Library, and most of the drawings he made for him are in the Department of Prints and Drawings in the V&A.
61. V&A, Mostyn-Crace bequest, JGC-20; *Builder*, III, 1845, p.426.
62. RIBA Library MSS PUG 3/11.
63. PRO Works 11/9/7, ff.1–69, the architect's progress reports.
64. Wedgwood, 1985, pp.218–20, 227–8.
65. Wedgwood, 1985, p.278.
66. A.W. Pugin, *The True Principles of Pointed or Christian Architecture*, London, 1841, p.26.
67. Wedgwood, 1985, p.221.
68. V&A E137-1939.
69. Wedgwood, 1985, p.225.
70. Wedgwood, 1985 pp.225–7.
71. Wedgwood, 1985 pp.218–20.
72. Pugin's diary for 1851, V&A, L5170-1969.
73. Ferrey, pp.251–2.
74. J. Hardman, First Glass Day Book 1845–53 (Birmingham Central Library). I am indebted to the researches of Stanley Shepherd.
75. *Parliamentary Debates*, 3rd series, 1853, CXXIX, 1316–8.
76. PRO Works 11/7/9, ff.8–16.
77. PRO Works 11/22/1, ff.9, 11; see also note 82 below.
78. Wedgwood, 1985 pp.216–8.
79. The Gillow records are held at Westminster Public Library.
80. The Holland records are held in the Design Archive, V&A.
81. Parliamentary Papers 1850, (650-I) and 650-II, XV.
82. *The Houses of Parliament*, H.G. Clarke and Co, 1860, p.56. It seems probable that this glass was removed to the Central Lobby during the 1860s and replaced with the simpler emblems of the United Kingdom which may be seen in photographs of 1897.
83. *The New Palace of Westminster*, Warrington & Co., 1855, p.53.
84. *Parliamentary Debates*, Third Series, 1851, 302–4.
85. *Builder*, X 1852, p.97.
86. Barry's letters to Hardman, Birmingham Central Reference Library.
87. E.W. Pugin, op. cit. note 1, p.48.
88. E.W. Pugin, op. cit. note 1, p.48.
89. A. Barry, *The Life and Works of Sir Charles Barry*, 1867, pp.255–6.
90. See chapter 4, Domestic Architecture, and plate 82.
91. Op. cit. note 44, XXVI, 1855, p.252; see

also Port ed., op. cit. note 3, p.266.
92. PRO Works 29/2560–92.

Chapter 18, The Mediæval Court

1. *Journal of Design and Manufactures*, II, 1849, p.52.
2. Letter in Jesus College Cambridge archive, quoted in M. Belcher, *A.W.N. Pugin: An annotated critical bibliography*, London, 1987, p.263.
3. Letter to J.G. Crace, 4 March 1850, RIBA Crace MSS PUG 7/14.
4. Letter to J.G. Crace, March 1850, RIBA Crace MSS PUG 7/19.
5. *Official Illustrated Guide*, 1851, p.761.
6. Plate 141 in M. Digby Wyatt, *The Industrial Arts of the XIX Century, from the Great Exhibition of 1851*, London, 1853, shows 'Painted Arabesque with decoration in composition by J.G. Crace and Jackson & Sons of London.'
7. *Reports of the Juries*, I, 1851.
8. Ground plan of the Crystal Palace, inserted at the front of *Journal of Design and Manufactures*, V, 1851.
9. Letter to J.G. Crace, 1 January 1851, RIBA Crace MSS PUG 8/1.
10. E.J. Cook and A. Wedderburn, *The Works of John Ruskin*, 1903-12, IX, p.450.
11. Letter to J.G. Crace, 27 January 1851, RIBA Crace MSS PUG 8/13.
12. Letter to J.G. Crace, March 1851, RIBA Crace MSS PUG 8/25.
13. Letters from Thomas Earley, 1851, Hardman Archive, Birmingham Central Library. I am indebted to Mrs Spencer-Silver for drawing these letters to my attention.
14. Copy of a letter to Lord Ashley. Royal Commission for the Exhibition of 1851: Windor Archives – on permanent loan to the Royal Commission for the Exhibition of 1851 from the Royal Archives at Windsor Castle and housed with Imperial College Archives at Imperial College of Science, Technology and Medicine, vol.VI/36. I am indebted to John Physick for drawing this letter to my attention.
15. Letter to John Hardman 20 March 1851 in a private collection (HLRO Historical Collection 304/487). I am indebted to Margaret Belcher for drawing this letter to my attention.
16. *Journal of Design and Manufactures*, V, 1851, p.37.
17. Letter from J.G. Crace, 1851, Hardman Archive, Birmingham Central Library. I am indebted to Mrs Spencer-Silver for drawing this letter to my attention.
18. *Illustrated London News*, XVIII, 1851, p.397.
19. Letter to J.G. Crace May 1851, RIBA Crace MSS PUG 8/35.
20. Letter to J.G. Crace May 1851, RIBA Crace MSS PUG 8/37.
21. Letter to J.G. Crace April 1851, RIBA

Crace MSS PUG 8/27.

22. Letter to J.G. Crace 15 May 1850, RIBA Crace MSS PUG 7/31.

23. *Illustrated London News*, XIX, 1851, pp.362–3 gives a long description and identifies many exhibits.

24. Op.cit. note 23.

25. Op.cit. note 23. Earley's letters also identify the lectern as coming from Southwark.

26. Op.cit. note 23. See also Chapter 12, Jewellery.

27. See Chapter 16, Textiles.

28. *Official Illustrated Catalogue*, 1851, p.761.

29. Op.cit. note 23.

30. *Reports of the Juries*, 1852, pp.708–49.

31. Op.cit. note 30, p.540.

32. Op.cit. note 30, p.502.

33. Op.cit. note 30, p.516.

34. Op.cit. note 30, p.475.

35. Op.cit. note 30, p.557.

36. Letter to J.G. Crace, 1851, RIBA MSS PUG 8/8.

37. Quoted in Ferrey, pp.140–1.

Chapter 19, Pugin in Australia

1. A.W.N. Pugin, 'Catholic Church Architecture', Letter to the Editor, *Tablet*, IX, 435, 2 September 1848, p.563.

2. The high esteem in which Willson was held by Protestant and Catholic alike was consistently attested to through resolutions, declarations and testimonials during his years in Nottingham and in Hobart, particularly as a result of his disinterested labours for the most disadvantaged members of society. See T. Kelsh, *Personal Recollections of the Right Reverend Robert William Willson, D.D. (First Bishop of Hobart Town), with a Portrait of His Lordship, and an Introduction to the State of Religion in Tasmania, prior to the year 1844*, Hobart, 1882.

3. Willson continued his work for the amelioration of conditions in lunatic asylums, which he had commenced in Nottingham, during his Australian years and was consulted by the colonial governments of New South Wales, Victoria and Van Diemen's Land (Tasmania). He also played a major role in achieving the improvement of conditions for convicts and the cessation of transportation to Norfolk Island.

4. See also 'Diocese of Nottingham. Sudden Death of Alderman Willson, of Lincoln', *Tablet*, XV, 755' 30 September 1854, p.613.

5. For a history of these items see E.H. Willson, 'Our Pre-Reformation Chalices', *Ampleforth Journal*, XXXIII, 3, 1927.

6. 'Consecration of the Catholic Cathedral, Nottingham', *Orthodox Journal*, 19, 31 August 1844, pp.143–4, quoted in

Belcher, 1987, p.225.

7. In fact, the pectoral cross was not acquired from Hardmans until November 1843. See Hardman Day Book (Hdb) for 1838–44, entry of 17 Nov. 1843, 'A Pectoral cross 2-10-0'.

8. Specifically item IX and that on the reliquary bust, item III. See also the mitre in the Plate, 'Church furniture revived at Birmingham', in Pugin's *Apology*.

9. Almost certainly Polding and his friend, the Benedictine William Bernard Ullathorne, who had spent some years on the Australian mission.

10. Draft of a speech by Willson on 'the state of church temporalities' to a meeting of the clergy, Hobart, 23 October 1844. Archdiocese of Hobart Archives (AHA), Willson Papers, CA.6/WIL.12. Hdb for 1838–44 records the furnishing of the plate mentioned by Willson under entries for 18 October, 17 November and 27 December 1843 and 20 January 1844.

11. AHA, Willson Papers, CA.6/WIL.12.

12. Pugin to Shrewsbury, 30 January 1844. Wedgwood, 1985.

13. The *Hobarton Guardian*, 10 April 1850, p.3.

14. E.G. Robertson, *Early Buildings of Southern Tasmania*, Melbourne, 1970, I, p.19.

15. Willson to Thomas, 22 December 1852. AHA, Willson papers, CA.6/WIL.536.

16. W.B. Ullathorne, *From Cabin-boy to Archbishop – The Autobiography of Archbishop Ullathorne*, Shane Leslie ed., London, 1941, p.211.

17. The plans were probably obtained during Willson's visit to England from January 1847 to January 1848. On a single sheet, they are now in the RIBA library.

18. Thomas to Willson, 14 January 1853. AHA, Willson papers, CA.6/WIL.536.

19. 'Foreign Catholic Affairs'. 'New Catholic Church at Hobarton (From the *Hobarton Advertiser*.)', *Tablet*, XIV, 691, 9 July 1853, pp.436–7.

20. The design was based on Wardell's church at Poplar. Transepts, chancel and tower were opened in 1860, after Willson's death. Grave structural problems, the fault of the builder, led to the demolition of the main part and re-erection to a modified reduced design without tower by the Hobart architect, Henry Hunter.

21. E.C. Marum, 'Ecclesiastical Memoranda of the Diocese of Hobarton', AHA, Willson papers, CA.6/WIL.521.

22. Hardman's first glass day book, 1845–53, records against Hobart Town, 1847–21, 'Bishop Willson Dec 13 A window for church of 2 lights with figures 3 small tracery pieces'. The only price recorded is 5/- for case and packing. Pugin also gave Willson at that time two brass

processional lanterns engraved, 'Ex dono Augusti Welby Pugin', (Hdb 1845–49, p.261, 6 December 1847).

23. This building is here attributed to Goodridge. Polding was a monk at Downside Priory in 1823 when Goodridge's complex of school, monastery and chapel were being erected there. Richmond church had a strong stylistic affinity with Downside's chapel.

24. It seemed for a time that the standard gift for clergy was a fine piece of Hardman plate. Examples include an inscribed 1850 siver-gilt chalice for William Hall and an inscribed silver-gilt 1854 chalice and paten for Willson. Indeed, it says much about Willson's taste in such matters that he had a standard Roman chalice and paten given to him in the spring of 1847 by Pius IX melted down and remade by Hardman, with more silver added, to a Pugin design (Hdb 1845–49, 2 Dec 1847 refers). These items are still in the Archdiocese of Hobart, along with many others from Hardman, ranging from brass crucifixes and alms basins to monstrances, processional crosses and oils stocks, as well as Willson's ring, pastoral staff, ewer and bugia.

25. For example, as a memorial to Willson's Vicar General, William Hall, who died in 1866, Hunter ordered a memorial brass from Hardman, now in St Mary's cathedral, Hobart, which is almost identical with that illustrated in the lower right-hand corner of Plate X, 'Church Furniture Revived at Birmingham', of Pugin's *Apology*.

26. The material on Pugin's New South Wales churches is based heavily on Professor Joan Kerr's studies, principally E.J. Kerr (EJK), 'Designing a Colonial Church: Church Building in New South Wales 1788–1888', unpublished D.Phil. thesis, University of York, 1977. Regarding Pugin's work for Polding, there is a possibility that he also provided designs for St Mary's Benedictine monastery, Sydney, but this needs further investigation.

27. Not uncritically. Regarding a tabernacle, part of a large order for St Patrick's church, Sydney (Hdb 1845–49, p.343, 20 July 1848), Polding remarked to a colleague, 'The tabernacle has a je ne sais quoi petty appearance about it', (Polding to Heptonstall, 31 January 1849, Downside Abbey Archives (DAA), M.136).

28. P. O'Farrell (ed.), *St Mary's Cathedral Sydney, 1821–1971*, Sydney, 1971, p.160.

29. R.F. Kean, 'The Cathedral, Choir and Chapter Room at Old St Mary's', *Tjurunga*, 40, May 1991, pp.63–83.

30. EJK, op. cit. (note 26), II, p.42.

31. Polding to Therry, 4 May 1843, quoted in

H.N. Birt, *Benedictine Pioneers in Australia*, London, 1911, II, p.59.

32. Polding to Heptonstall, 23 October 1843. Quoted in Birt, II, p.67.
33. O'Farrell, op. cit. (note 28), p.14.
34. The tracings are signed 'A W Pugin 1845'. EJK, op. cit. (note 26), 1, p.232; 2, p.43.
35. EJK, op. cit. (note 26), 1, p.234.
36. Davis to Sweeney, 28 February 1850. DAA, M.246.
37. Hdb 1845–49, p.282, 20 February 1848; p.284; p.288, 11 March 1848 and p.327, 15 June 1848.
38. EJK, op. cit. (note 26), 1, p.235.
39. EJK, op. cit. (note 26), 1, pp.241–2.
40. Time has not been kind to St Stephen's. The sandstone of which it was constructed was of the worst, most friable kind and most of the detail has either disintegrated or been removed. For a time it served as a pro-cathedral, but it has long been de-consecrated.
41. Clearly the builder of Queanbeyan, a crude, primitively detailed church, had access to the Pugin plans, as the overall morphology is the same and certain key dimensions are identical. Beyond that, there is no similarity to Pugin's work.
42. J. Kerr, *Our Great Victorian Architect, Edmund Thomas Blacket (1817–1883)*, Sydney, 1983, p.16.
43. B. Andrews, 'The English Benedictine Connection – The Works of Charles Hansom in Australia', *Fabrications*, 1, December 1989, pp.33–55.
44. Reynolds had a reputation for taste and erudition in architecture, art and antiques and was known to Pugin's widow. In correspondence with Reynolds, Peter Paul Pugin mentions that, 'my mother wishes to be remembered to you', (Pugin to Reynolds, 21 October 1881, Archives of the Catholic Archdiocese of Adelaide). See also B. Andrews, *Gothic in South Australian Churches*, Adelaide, 1984, pp.16–21.
45. Uncatalogued drawings held in the archives of St Michael's Abbey, Belmont, Herefordshire.
46. B. Andrews, invited response to U.M. de Jong, 'Some Ramifications of Wardell's English Work on his Australian Practice. St Patrick's and St Mary's Reconsidered'. *Proc. Soc. Architectural Historians, Australia and New Zealand*, 5th Annual Conf., Sydney, May 1988.

Chapter 20, The Later Pugins

1. *Builder*, 1852, pp.605–6. *Illustrated London News*, 1852, p.243. The two bishops were Dr Wareing of Northampton, and Dr Grant of Southwark. Bishop Brown of Shrewsbury and Bishop Gillis from Edinburgh had visited the dying man.
2. E.W. Pugin, *Who was the art architect of the Houses of Parliament. A statement of facts, founded on the letters of Sir Charles Barry and the diaries of Augustus Welby Pugin*, London, 1867, p.viii. For Pugin's other personal papers see Wedgwood, 1985, pp.312–14.
3. *Tablet*, 1875, p.760.
4. HLRO, Historical Collection, E.W. Pugin Diary, 7 December 1856; see below note 18.
5. E.W. Pugin Diary, 14 March 1856; see below note 28.
6. E.W. Pugin Diary, 12–13 September, 2 November and 7 December 1856. E.W. Pugin practised from the Grange, and later 21 Savile Row, 91 Victoria St, London and from Liverpool. P.P. Pugin practised from the Grange, and from 159 Kensington Church St, London, and 51 North John St, Liverpool.
7. St Austin Stafford, (1861–2). *Builder*, 1861, p.275; 1862, pp.553–4; *Building News*, 1862, p.75. *Irish Builder*, 15 June 1875. The same story is told of Belmont.
8. *Builder*, 1875, pp.522–3.
9. Wedgwood, 1977, p.792. For other obituaries see *Building News*, 11 June 1875, p.432; *Illustrated London News*, LXVI, 1875, p.571; *Irish Builder*, 5 June and 15 June 1875, p.372, *Dictionary of National Biography*, XLVII, 1890, p.10; J. Gillow, *A literary and biographical history or bibliographical dictionary of the English Catholics*, 5 vols, London, 1885–1902, 5, p.381.
10. E.W. Pugin Diary, 16 April 1856, where the marriage of Jane Joyes, 'an old flame' is noted.
11. Pugin, *Who was the art architect* (note 7). For the dispute see, Belcher, *Pugin Bibliography*, D499–D522, D573–8.
12. Pugin designed a house in Kilburn for Herbert about which there were disputes, *Tablet*, XLIII, p.727; *Catholic Opinion*, XVI, 675.
13. For Pugin's reaction to Ferrey, see Belcher, D518, p.338.
14. *Builder*, 1875, pp.522–3.
15. George Coppinger Ashlin (1837–1921), b. co. Cork, educated at Oscott, pupil *c*.1856–9 and partner 1859–69 of E.W. Pugin in Ireland, and of P.P. and C.W. Pugin in England 1875–80; and of Coleman in Ireland *c*.1902–21. The practice continued into the 1960s, and its drawings are now deposited at the Irish Architectural Archive. Ashlin married Mary Pugin, E.W. Pugin's sister.
16. James Murray was an Irishman, who joined Pugin in partnership, 1857–60; *Tablet*, 1863, p.729. A number of photographs of drawings were presented to the RIBA from Murray's collection (Wedgwood, 1977); these seem to represent his main contribution to the partnership.
17. *Tablet*, 1864, p.763; p.779. The partnership lasted from 1862 to 1863. St Wilfred, Ripon, (1860–2) built during the partnership is evidently to Hansom's design – or even that of his pupil, Benjamin Bucknall – but the altar is by Pugin. *Tablet*, 1862, p.272, quoting the *Hull Advertiser*, distinguishes the two hands. *Builder*, 17 May 1862.
18. Leith, St Mary Star of the Sea (1852–4), for which A.W. Pugin had made drawings, and E.W. applied successfully to Bishop Gillis to be allowed to continue the work. An aisle was added in 1901, and the church re-oriented with an apse, added by Pugin and Pugin 1912. The large presbytery (1860), is by E.W. Pugin, *Builder*, 3 March 1860, p.114. Drawings for the 1911–2 works survive at the Oblate Presbytery, Leith.
19. E.W. Pugin, Diary, 1–5 February 1856. He is recorded at Ushaw, and at St Vincent de Paul Liverpool. He was described as 'surveyor' of Pugin's school at Birkenhead; *Building News*, 1856, p.328. He was at the Liverpool office in 1859. *Tablet*, 1863, p.700.
20. Pugin met Myers about the Knill chantry at Southwark and he dealt with the difficult foundations contract for Shrewsbury Cathedral.
21. Haigh was the builder at St Vincent de Paul, Liverpool, who was also appointed at Ushaw (E.W. Pugin, Diary, 19 June 1856, 26 July 1856).
22. E.W. Pugin to Dom Laurence Shepherd OSB, 23 February 1870, Stanbrook Abbey Archives.
23. John Hardman Powell appears frequently in the diary in 1856, including the critical reference 'found great opposition ? in Jno Powell he sadly wants energy', 23 July 1856.
24. For Boulton see the *Tablet*, 1863, pp.746–7 And the *Builder*, 1863, p.902; Lane and Lewis executed the high altar at Shrewsbury Cathedral; Farmer, the Scholefield chantry; and Earp, the statue of Our Lady at St Edmund's College.
25. Danesfield Chapel, although built by A.W. Pugin (*The Illustrated London News* obituary described it as his last work), was continued by E.W. Pugin, who claimed the St Charles chapel as his in the *Catholic Directory*, 1856. The altar, saved from demolition in 1908, was re-erected in 1939, in the church of the Sacred Heart, Henley.
26. Priced furniture sketches are among unidentified designs in Wedgwood, 1977, p.117 [26]. They were probably commissioned by Canon Huddlestone,

whose name appears frequently in E.W. Pugin's diary for 1856.

27. *Tablet*, 1866, p.549.

28. Archdiocese of Westminster, Wiseman papers W3/52/55, Pugin to Wiseman, 26 February 1862.

29. *Dublin Builder* (later *Irish Builder*), 1865, p.96, 'a cathedral in memory of Dr Wiseman. Pugin to be the architect'. E.W. Pugin repeated this claim, *Tablet*, 1868, p.667. Wiseman's tomb, announced in November 1865, was built at Kensal Green Catholic Cemetery (*Tablet*, 1867, p.20), and removed to St Peter's Crypt at Westminster Cathedral in 1907.

30. E.W. Pugin Diary, 15 December 1856; *Tablet*, 1857, p.132.

31. E.W. Pugin Diary, 29 September 1856.

32. The papal knighthood was in recognition not of English work, but of Dadizeele church, Belgium (*Irish Builder*, 1875, p.378). Peter Paul Pugin was made a knight of St Sylvester by Leo XIII, *c*.1888.

33. Pugin added the Knill chantry in 1856 and the Talbot chantry was begun in 1854 but not completed by him. There were also unexecuted designs for a St Joseph chapel.

34. E.W. Pugin designed the high altar in 1854 but the church was only completed in the twentieth century, by Ashlin and Coleman. All the furnishings are now removed.

35. E.W. Pugin replaced his father's wooden altar in Caen stone, lengthened the aisles, and erected the metal rood screen. The Pietà altar is by P.P. Pugin.

36. E.W. Pugin extended his father's chapel of 1845–6, E.W. Pugin Diary, 17 September 1856. *Builder*, 1858, p.508. George F. Drew, *Bishop Eaton and its shrine 1851–1951*.

37. E.W. Pugin incorporated his father's church as the south aisle of his new church, 1864. *Builder*, 1864, p.502. D. and L. Thackray, *A brief history of St Marie's Church 1844 to 1986*, Rugby, 1987.

38. B. Ward, *The History of St Edmund's*, pp.278–9; ibid, *St Edmund's College Chapel*, 1903, pp.56–7, 115–23, 193. Pugin also made what must have been a unique classical design for the relic of St Edmund of Canterbury exhibited on the Papal stand at the 1862 Exhibition; Ward, *Chapel*, pp.123, 175–6.

39. Drawings for all these (except the parlour re-arrangement) survive at St Cuthbert's College.

40. E.W. Pugin sent drawings received in Naples by the 17th Earl of Shrewsbury, who acknowledged them on 28 November 1852, promised to pay for them, but apologised for not being able to proceed until he came of age in December 1855. See 17th Earl of Shewsbury to E.W. Pugin, HLRO Historical Collection,

no.339, letter no.114. The 16th Earl had corresponded with A.W. Pugin (but no drawings were yet available), letter 1 March 1852, ibid, no.112. E.W. Pugin Diary, 16 August 1856.

41. Pugin noted that while he expected to continue work at Alton, but the projected 'Birkenhead Cathedral' would lapse. Diary, 16 August 1856.

42. *Builder*, 1854, p.249, J. Hall, *Shrewsbury Cathedral: a sacrament in stone*, Stoke on Trent, 1984, pp.22–3.

43. *Builder*, 1855, p.544.

44. The high altar was by the sculptors Lane and Lewis, an east window by Hardman & Co, with the kneeling Earl as donor, and a west end baptistry, encaustic tiled floors to the chancel and benches designed by Pugin. The high altar was truncated, the baptistry dismantled and the benches disposed of in 1984.

45. *Builder*, 1853, p.772. *Builder*, 1855, p.544. The site and some fittings were the gift of Canon Cholmondeley, which may have reduced the estimate. There were two different specifications, and two contracts, one with George Myers for the difficult foundations.

46. Pugin's phrase in a dispute as to authorship of this type with the architect S.J. Nicholl (*Tablet*, 1867, pp.267, 283, 298).

47. *Tablet*, 1859, p.54.

48. *Tablet*, 1859, p.629. Although deprived of its furniture, Pugin's intentions at La Salette can still be followed at St Mary's, Warwick (1859–60), a smaller church to the same plan, where the altar and reredos follow the curve of the windowless apse, and the aisles are reduced to passages. This church was evidently the model for the larger La Salette.

49. For example as St Francis's, Gorton (1866–78), St Bee's, Whitehaven (1863–8) and St Mary's, Leadgate, co. Durham (1868–9).

50. All Saints, Barton-upon-Irwell, Trafford, Manchester (1863–8). *Catholic Directory* (Ireland), 1866, p.357; *Builder* 1865, p.107; *Tablet*, 1867, p.374. Fr Edmund O'Gorman OFM Conv., *The History of All Saints Church Barton upon Irwell. From the Earliest Times to the Present Church*, Manchester, 1988. Fr Brendan Blundell OFM Conv., *All Saints Church Barton-upon-Irwell. Restoration 1985–1991*, Sleaford, 1991.

51. Pevsner, *Buildings of England. South Lancashire*, pp.74–5.

52. J. Alphege Pippet (died 1904), was one of the chief draughtsmen and decorators at Hardmans in succession to J.H. Powell. Two other later wall paintings are evidently by Hardmans. Designs for the glass survive at the Birmingham City

Museum and Art Gallery, Hardman collection.

53. *Builder*, 14 May 1864, p.362. Purcell, *Life of Ambrose Phillipps*, II, p.286 (Garendon), p.314 for estate buildings at Grace Dieu. E.W. Pugin also continued his father's work for Henry Drummond at Albury Park, Surrey (*Builder*, 1857, p.437), where he also built almshouses; at Chirk Castle, Denbighshire, where he also built a school; at Burton Closes Manor, Staffordshire (*Builder*, 4 April 1857, p.183); and in Ireland for Lord Dunraven at Adare, co. Limerick. He also completed his father's convents at Birr and Waterford.

54. Other commercial commissions included Seel's Buildings, 4 Church Street, Liverpool; Hudson's flour mills (1865), and the Granville Hotel at Ramsgate. (*Architect*, 7 May 1870, p.230); and in London a project for flats in Victoria Street (1871) and the Grosvenor Turkish Bath Company, 119 Buckingham Palace Road. He built complete new houses for the painter J.R. Herbert at Kilburn (1875); for T. Stewart Kennedy at The Towers, Meanwood, Leeds (1867); for Major Molyneaux Seel at Harrington House, Leamington.

55. *Builder*, 30 December 1865, p.919; M.E. Williams, *English College Rome*, illustration pp.116–17, 120, 203. The commission went instead to Count Vespignani.

56. *Irish Builder*, 15 March 1865, p.84.

57. *Builder*, 1874, p.387, Royal Academy 1874.

58. *Irish Builder*, 15 June 1875, quoting the *Kent Argus*.

59. *Tablet*, 19 March 1904, p.457, p.464.

60. Archives of the Archdiocese of Glasgow, Finance Board Minute Books.

61. Cuthbert Welby Pugin and Peter Paul were in practice (1875–80) when Cutbert Welby 'retired 1880 to Ramsgate to run the workshop of his father A.W. Pugin', *Builder*, 30 March 1928, p.524, although technically he came back into partnership with Sebastian Pugin Powell from 1904. Peter Paul practised on his own from 1880 to 1884, as 'Pugin & Pugin'.

62. Earlier drawings for E.W. Pugin's church, and for the chapel of the Holy Thorn (1885), are in the uncatalogued collection of architectural drawings at Stanbrook Abbey. E.W. Pugin's high altar and reredos (*Builder*, 6 April 1878) was demolished in 1971. R. O'Donnell, 'Bendictine Building in the Nineteenth century', *English Benedictine Congregation History Symposium* (1983) III, pp.38–48.

63. Archives of the Archbishop of Glasgow, Finance Board Minute book vol.7, January 1892–15 December 1893, Pugin

attended the meeting on 4 March 1892 to plead 'that for churches and altars on account of the amount of labour he expends on details in his plans he would ask the Board not to reduce the rate of his fees from 5%.'

64. Pugin was told to remove the name of Hardman and Powell and the Lion Foundary from the specification for the church of the Holy Redeeemer, Clydebank (1903). Loc.cit., 15 November 1901.

65. *Builder*, vol.86, 19 March 1904. Pugin 'designed over 450 altars in all parts of England and Scotland'.

66. Archives of Downside Abbey: St Mary Liverpool box file circular 12 October 1883, 'St Mary's Edmund Street, Liquidation of debt'.

67. K. Clarke, *The Gothic Revival; an essay in the history of taste*, London, 1928, p.140.

68. M. Trappes-Lomax, *Pugin: a mediaeval Victorian*, London, 1932, p.155. Archives of the Archbishop of Glasgow, Finance Board Minute book FR/4, 12 January 1904–18 December 1906, 22 March 1904 'in view of Mr Pugin's death it was agreed to wait until definite information arrived as to the continuance and constitution of the firm of Messers Pugin and Pugin'; 19 April 1904, a circular was received 'that the firm is to be continued by Mr Cuthbert Welby Pugin and Mr Sebastian Pugin Powell'. The firm actually continued in the hands of S. Pugin Powell (1866–1949) and his cousin Charles Henry Cuthbert Purcell (1874–1958) until the latter's death.

69. *Tablet*, 31 March 1928.

Chapter 21, The Fate of Pugin's True Principles

1. M. Trappes-Lomax, *Pugin, A Mediaeval Victorian*, 1932, p.65; P. Stanton, *Pugin*, 1971, p.84.

2. Paul Frankl, *The Gothic*, 1960, p.563, argues that the line of 'moralizing aesthetics' applied in Britain to the interpretation of Gothic by Pugin and his successors 'should not be called neo-Romanticism, for with its pharisaism it is a completely isolated English phenomenon and very characteristic of the England of that time. It was a cul-de-sac.'

3. K. Clark, *The Gothic Revival*, 1928 edn., p.176.

4. Léonce Reynaud, quoted by David Van Zanten, *Designing Paris*, 1987, p.47; for the Saint-Simonians and architecture, ibid., pp.46–61.

5. Robert Macleod, *Style and Society*, 1971, p.10.

6. A.W.N. Pugin, *The True Principles of Pointed or Christian Architecture*, 1841, p.1.

7. Stanton, op.cit. (note 1), pp.79–85.

8. George Gilbert Scott, *Personal and Professional Recollections*, 1879, p.88. Scott's manuscript (in the RIBA Library) reads 'frenzy'; the printed version reads 'fury'.

9. John Summerson, *Architecture in Britain 1530–1830*, 1970 edn., p.512.

10. Gottfried Semper, *The Four Elements of Architecture*, tr. Mallgrave and Herrmann, 1989, p.48; John Ruskin, *The Poetry of Architecture*, 1839, esp. Chapters 7 & 12.

11. Robert Willis, *Remarks on the Architecture of the Middle Ages*, 1835, Ch.2.

12. J.M. Richards, *An Introduction to Modern Architecture*, 1970 edn., p.62.

13. Roger Scruton, *The Aesthetics of Architecture*, 1979, p.174.

14. Phoebe Stanton in *Concerning Architecture, Essays Presented to Nikolaus Pevsner*, ed. J. Summerson, 1968, pp.120–39.

15. Benjamin Ferrey, *Recollections of A.W.N. Pugin*, 1861, pp.43–4.

16. For Rio, see M.C. Bowe, *François Rio, sa place dans le renouveau catholique en Europe*, 1938. For Montalembert: Mrs Oliphant, *Memoir of Count de Montalembert*, 1872.

17. On Nash as a constructor, see some interesting remarks of 1829 in P.F.L.

Fontaine, *Journal 1799–1853*, vol.2, 1987, pp.798–9.

18. Ferrey, op.cit. (note 15), p.65.

19. Sale catalogue of Augustus Pugin's library, 1833, kindly communicated by Clive Wainwright.

20. For Cuvier, see W. Coleman, *Georges Cuvier Zoologist*, 1964. He was quickly translated into English and had a considerable following in England.

21. Pugin, *True Principles*, p.27.

22. I am grateful to Adrian Forty for showing me his paper on 'truth' – part of a larger lexicographical endeavour on 'key words' in architecture that he is undertaking.

23. Bartholomew relies much on Rondelet for structural ideas. For an old article about him, see G.G. Pace in *Architectural Review*, 92, 1942, p.99. Georg Moller's more important book appeared in English as *Memorials of German-Gothic Architecture*, with additions by W.H. Leeds, 1836. Moller wrote extensively about Gothic but never built in the style; 'we may admire and imitate these works, but we cannot produce the like,' he says, op.cit., pp.30–1.

24. Patrick Conner, 'Pugin and Ruskin', *Journal of the Warburg and Courtauld Institutes*, 41, 1978, pp.344–50.

25. *The Works of John Ruskin*, ed. Cook and Wedderburn, vol.5, p.429.

26. See R. Middleton, 'Viollet-le-Duc's Influence in Nineteenth-Century England', *Art History*, June 1981, pp.203–19.

27. A copy of this rare pamphlet is in the RIBA Library. Further on Reichensperger, see Georg Germann, *Gothic Revival in Europe and Britain: Sources, Influences and Ideas*, 1972, pp.99–101, 151–63.

28. Phoebe B. Stanton, *The Gothic Revival and American Church Architecture*, 1968.

29. Pier Luigi Nervi, *Aesthetics and Technology in Building*, 1966, esp. pp.6–16.

30. Trappes-Lomax, op.cit., p.167.

Glossary of Ecclesiastical Terms

NOTE TO THE GLOSSARY

The Second Vatican Council (December 1961 to December 1965) has had a profound influence on the ordering of churches and the manner of worship. Perhaps the most obvious changes relate to the celebration of the Mass. This glossary is concerned with the Church of Pugin's time; such a style of art and worship still exists - especially in the Church of England - but you need to search for it. Many things remain the same; a chalice is a chalice, 'yesterday, today and for ever'.

Fr Anthony D. Couchman
Parish Priest
St Barnabas', Walthamstow

ABBOT   The senior or superior monk of a large religious house (monastery). The insignia of office are the same as those of a bishop, namely, mitre, pastoral staff, pectoral cross and ring.

ALB   A white linen garment, reaching from the neck to the feet, worn by the priest and other sacred ministers at the Mass.

ALB APPARELS   Strips of embroidery, or woven panels, sometimes used to adorn the alb at the hem and on the cuffs.

ALMS DISH   A large dish, of metal or wood, used to collect the offerings of the people. They appear to originate from the 'decent bason' used to collect the Alms for the poor during the Holy Communion service of the 1662 Prayer Book of the Church of England.

ALTAR / HOLY TABLE / TABLE   The most important item of furniture in a church since on it is offered the Holy Mass. On the surface of the altar are incised five crosses - centrally, and at each corner - representing the Wounds of Christ. In the Church of England the altar is sometimes referred to as the Holy Table.

ALTAR CROSS   The most important of the altar furnishings. A symbol of Christ's Resurrection from the dead, the altar cross is usually ornamental in character and design.

ALTAR CANDLESTICKS   The principal or high altar would be furnished with six candlesticks - three on each side of the cross - usually standing, with the cross, on a Gradine or shelf. In chapels or side altars two or four candlesticks are considered sufficient. An important chapel, e.g. of the Virgin Mary, would have four.

AMBRY or AUMBRY   A small wall cupboard close to the altar for the safekeeping of the sacred vessels, reliquaries, monstrances, etc. Often used in the Church of England for the reserved Sacrament.

AMICE   A neckcloth of white linen worn under the alb, sometimes with an apparel (embroidered or woven panel) forming a collar.

ANNUNCIATION   The term used to describe the message given to the Blessed Virgin Mary by the angel Gabriel that she was to be the Mother of Christ.

ASPERGES BUCKET   Container for Holy Water sprinkled on the people before Mass. The name derives from Psalm 51 which is chanted during the ceremony, 'Asperges me, Domine, hyssopo . . .'.

ASPERGILLUM   The sprinkler used in the Asperges ceremony.

BEADLE'S STAFF   The symbol of office carried by the Beadle, whose duties included keeping order in church and heading processions, especially when the Bishop was present.

BIER   A stand on which a coffin is placed. Often wheeled for transporting the body to the grave.

BISHOP   The most senior member of the orders of the Sacred Ministry, thus Bishops, Priests and Deacons.

BRASS   A form of monument on which the figure of the deceased was engraved on a brass panel.

BRASS RUBBING   Copy of a brass made on paper by the use of heelball.

BURSE and CHALICE VEIL   The burse is used to hold the corporal, a square of white linen on which are placed the chalice and paten at the celebration of the Mass. It consists of two square cards covered and hinged with material matching the vestments. The chalice veil, also in matching material, is used to cover - veil - the chalice when not in use. They are often embroidered with the Sacred Monogram.

CALVARY   A representation of the Crucifixion of Christ, often set up in church grounds and sometimes as wayside shrines. Calvary was the place of the Crucifixion.

CATAFALQUE   The platform or staging, sometimes elaborately draped and occasionally canopied, on which the encoffined body rests prior to and during the funeral service.

CATHEDRA   The bishop's chair or throne in his cathedral church, hence the phrase 'ex cathedra' - 'from the throne'.

CATHEDRAL   The church which contains the bishop's chair or throne.

CENSER or THURIBLE   Metal container, sometimes ornate, hung from chains. It contains the hot charcoal on which is burnt the incense; used ceremonially, at Sung Mass and other services, e.g. Benediction.

CHALICE and PATEN   The chalice (cup) and paten (small plate) of precious metal used to contain the elements of wine and bread consecrated at the Mass. These sacred vessels are usually of matching design and sometimes jewelled.

CHANTRY CHAPEL   A chapel specially set aside for the saying of Mass for the souls of the faithful departed. They were often established, maintained and endowed by guilds as well as individuals.

CHASUBLE   The outermost garment worn by the priest in celebrating Mass. They are found in two main styles, 'Gothic' (tent-like) and 'Roman' (with the sides cut away).

CHRISMATORY   A small box, often casket-shaped, used to contain the three Holy Oils consecrated by the bishop at the Chrism Mass of Maundy Thursday, vis. oil of the catechumens, oil of the sick and the chrism oil.

CIBORIUM   Similar to a chalice but with the addition of a lid, used to contain the wafer breads (hosts) of the Mass, especially when there are many communicants.

COMMUNION PLATE   The collective name for the precious metal vessels used in celebrating the Mass.

CONFESSIONAL   The place at which a penitent kneels to confess sins to the priest; sometimes just a kneeling desk with a simple screen to afford privacy, but very elaborate confessionals are also to be found.

CONVENT   Commonly used to describe the buildings in which the members of a religious community live. Today the term tends to be restricted to the houses of nuns.

COPE   A semi-circular cloak, often or elaborate design, used in ceremonial processions and on other occasions.

COPE HOOD   Embroidered panel, or actual hood, hanging from the neck at the back of the cope.

CORONA LUCIS   A crown of tiered candles. A 'crown of light' used to illuminate the sanctuary of a church, or to add to the splendour of a shrine.

CROWN   Placed on the head of some images of the Virgin Mary to signify that she is Queen of Heaven and/or on the head of the infant Jesus to show that He is King of kings.

CRUCIFIX   A cross carrying the figure of the crucified Body (corpus) of Our Lord.

CRUETS   Jug-shaped vessels used to contain the unconsecrated wine and the water that is to be used in the Mass.

DALMATIC   The outer vestment of the deacon at the Mass; of square shape and with cut-away sides.

EPISCOPAL GLOVES   Worn by bishops at Mass, but only until the Offertory (the preparation of the bread and wine).

EPISCOPAL RING   Worn by a bishop to symbolise his betrothal to the Church.

FLAGON   A vessel of precious metal used to contain the wine to be consecrated at the Mass. Most commonly found in cathedrals and greater parish churches.

FONT   Freestanding integral stone basin and pedestal for baptismal water. The font is usually covered by a plain or ornate wooden lid when not in use.

INCENSE SPOON   Used to transfer incense from its container, the incense boat, to the hot charcoal of the thurible.

JUBÉ SCREEN   Another name for the Rood Screen which spread across the chancel arch. Of great antiquity, they had many uses but chiefly as a loft from which cantors and choirs could sing.

LECTERN   Reading desk for Bible or Gospel Book, often in the form of an eagle.

MANIPLE   A band of material, matching the vestments, joined to form a loop and worn at the left cuff of the alb by both priest and deacon. Said to originate in the towel carried by deacons (servers) in the Early Church.

MASS   The name most commonly given to the Church's celebration of the 'Last Supper', in which the priest consecrates the bread and wine to be the Body and Blood of Christ. Also known as the Eucharist and the Holy Communion.

MISSAL   The name given to the book containing all the readings, prayers and instructions necessary for the celebration of the Mass throughout the year.

MITRE   A two-horned cap worn by a bishop. From the back hang two bands, or lappets; these appear to have originated as bands to tie under the chin.

MONSTRANCE   An ornate vessel, often of precious metal and sometimes jewelled, used to expose the consecrated Host (the bread of the Eucharist) for veneration.

MORSE   The metal clasp, sometimes jewelled, used to fasten the cope across the chest.

ORPHREY   The strips of rich embroidery or material used to decorate the vestments of the Sacred Ministers at Mass, i.e. the chasuble of the priest, the dalmatic of the deacon and the tunicle of the sub-deacon.

PALL   A cloth, often of black, purple or white velvet, used to cover the coffin at funerals.

PASCHAL CANDLESTICK   The large candlestick used to hold the Easter or Paschal Candle, which signifies the light of the Risen Christ.

PASTORAL STAFF   A crook-shaped staff of office carried by bishops and abbots; also known as a crosier. They may be of elaborate or simple material and design.

PECTORAL CROSS   A cross of precious metal, sometimes jewelled, suspended from a chain and worn by bishops, abbots and some other high-ranking clergy.

PISCINA   A small sink set into the wall near the altar to carry away to earth the water used to cleanse the vessels at Mass.

POOR BOX   A traditional wooden strong-box used to receive the charitable giving of worshippers. The Church of England Prayer Books of 1549 and 1552 make special mention of the 'poor men's box'.

PORTABLE FONT   As the name implies, a small font that can be moved or carried about in order to provide for special pastoral needs, e.g. the baptism of an infant in danger of death.

PRESBYTERY   The house of the parish priest.

PRIE-DIEU   (Fr., 'pray God') A small prayer-desk, usually of wood.

PROCESSIONAL CANDLESTICKS   Candlesticks carried in procession by servers (assistants to the priest) at Mass.

PROCESSIONAL CROSS   A cross or crucifix mounted on a stave and carried at the head, or towards the head, of processions.

PULPIT   The raised edifice from which the sermon is preached. It may be a simple platform or an elaborate architectural masterpiece towering over the congregation.

PYX   A container for the reserved Host (the consecrated bread of the Mass). It is especially used of the small, flat, precious metal box used for carrying the Sacrament to the sick and dying.

RELIQUARY   A receptacle for relics of the Saints or other items of devotion, e.g. fragment of the True Cross. They may be seen in a multitude of forms and sizes depending upon the relic contained, from simple boxes to elaborate caskets representing human limbs, arms, legs, head etc.

REREDOS   A screen of stone or wood placed behind the altar, often carved or painted with scenes from the Crucifixion or the lives of the saints.

ROOD SCREEN   The screen, simple or ornate, spanning the chancel arch and which carries a large cross or crucifix often flanked by figures of Our Lady and St John.

SACRING BELL   A bell in turret, steeple or bellcote rung at the elevation of each of the consecrated elements at Mass to alert the faithful and solicit their devotions.

SANCTUARY BELL   A small bell, or set of bells under a single domed cover, used to draw the attention of the faithful to the most important moments in the Mass, e.g. the Sanctus (just prior to the Consecration) and the Elevation (the raising of the Host and chalice for the adoration of the faithful).

SANCTUARY LAMP   A hanging lamp, usually ornate, suspended in the sanctuary. A lamp showing a clear white light signifies that the Blessed Sacrament is reserved in the tabernacle.

SEDILIA   The seats of the Sacred Ministers at the Mass (priest, deacon and sub-deacon). They are usually to be found on the south side of the sanctuary.

SEMINARY   A college for the training of male students aspiring to the priesthood.

STATIONS OF THE CROSS   The fourteen episodes (stations) which particularly mark the incidents from when Pilate condemned Jesus to death to the time His Body was laid in the sepulchre. In churches they are marked by fourteen crosses set up on the walls, sometimes accompanied by plaques or paintings depicting the scenes. The faithful are encouraged to make the devotions known as Stations of the Cross by chronologically following the route of these episodes.

STOLE   A narrow strip of material to match the vestments, often embroidered, draped from the neck of the alb and hanging to the knees of a bishop or priest. The stole of the deacon is worn over the left shoulder and is tied or fastened on the right side.

SURPLICE   A loose-fitting white linen garment worn over the cassock by the clergy, servers and members of church choirs. It is especially popular with clergy of the Church of England.

TABERNACLE   A small safe, often with an ornate door, fixed centrally at the altar, and used to hold the Blessed Sacrament reserved for the communion of the sick and dying.

TUNICLE   A slightly simpler version of the dalmatic, worn by the sub-deacon at the Mass.

VESTMENTS   The collective name for any garments worn by the priest at Mass.

Index

Pages including illustrations are shown in *italic*. A.W.N. Pugin's relations are indicated simply as 'aunt', 'cousin' etc. Churches and urban buildings are listed under their place-names, e.g. 'Hobart', 'London', 'Upton Pyne'.

Photographic Acknowledgements

Photographic material has been supplied by Graham Miller, photographer to the Pugin exhibition, the photographic department of the Victoria & Albert Museum, or the owners, by whose courtesy it is reproduced, unless otherwise indicated below.

Arthur Sanderson & Sons Ltd Archive 212
Bartlett, Michael 472, 473, 474, 475
Beaver Photography 20, 100, 248, 271, 444
Bell's *New Guide to Westminster Abbey* 509
Birmingham Catholic Diocese Trustees 314, 337, 402
Birmingham Museum and Art Gallery 325, 362, 363, 365, 366, 367, 368, 369, 371, 375, 378, 379
Birmingham Public Reference Library 64, 238, 417, 425, 437, 438
Butler, Geremy 429, 430
Cambridge, Syndics of the University Library 195
Christie's Education 511
Donnelly, Peter 459, 460, 461, 462, 463, 464, 465, 466, 467
Douai Abbey Library 200
Downside Abbey 504, 505
Edwards, Barry 79, 104, 106, 141a
Fine Art Society, London 23
Garbutt, George 15, 16, 201, 344, 416, 432

Hammersmith and Fulham Archives and Local History Centre 103
Irish Architectural Archive 485, 486
John Perry (Wallpapers) Ltd. 211
Kersting, A.F. 84, 85, 500
Kingsbury, Lucilla 323
National Monuments Record, Scotland (Magnus Jackson collection) 53
National Monuments Record, Scotland 65, 86, 87, 418, 419
National Monuments Record 83, 88, 98, 102, 112, 114, 116, 118, 122, 125, 130, 131, 137, 141, 142, 143, 153, 155, 160, 236, 372, 433, 440, 483
Oxford, President and Fellows of Magdalen College 194
Private Collection 147, 148
Royal Collection, H.M. Queen Elizabeth II 49, 234, 328
Saunders, Martin 478, 479
Stringer, Richard 470
Wartski, London 326
Whiteway, Michael 220, 241, 285, 357, 484